Fashion Buying & Merchandising

Fashion Buying & Merchandising

Second Edition

Sidney Packard
Professor and Former Chairperson
Textile and Apparel Marketing Department
Fashion Institute of Technology

Dr. Arthur A. Winters
Professor and Chairperson
Advertising and Communications Department
Fashion Institute of Technology

Nathan Axelrod
Professor and Former Chairperson
Fashion Buying and Merchandising Department
Fashion Institute of Technology

Fairchild Publications
New York

Book Design by Catherine Gallagher
Illustrations by Barbara Scholey
Cover Illustrations by Alicia Tapp

First Edition, Copyright © 1976 by Fairchild Publications, Inc.
Second Printing 1978
Third Printing 1979
Fourth Printing 1980

Second Edition, Copyright © 1983 by Fairchild Publications
Division of Capital Cities Media, Inc.
Second Printing 1985

Standard Book Number: 87005-445-7

Library of Congress Catalog Card Number: 82-083881

Printed in the United States of America

Preface

An increasing number of college students view fashion buying and merchandising as a rewarding and prestigious career. In response to this trend, colleges have broadened their fashion merchandising curricula, and hundreds of institutions now offer either two- or four-year programs in this specialization.

Fashion merchandising as a college major is essentially the outgrowth of programs in retailing. Although retailing is the broadest aspect of the marketing of consumer goods and the largest component of our Gross National Product, many students prefer to concentrate on the more specific subjects of planning, buying, and selling of apparel which prepare them for a career in fashion merchandising. (Retailing principles and practices are included in this text as they relate to the buying and merchandising functions.)

Retailers in the past believed that fashion buying did not require special training; a buyer of any type of goods was able to perform in any merchandise sector. And to some extent, this philosophy was valid. At first, buying techniques were limited to when and how merchandise was presented. However, as fashion merchandising became of prime importance to numerous retailers, executives realized that fashion specialization was required to cope with unique characteristics, such as the need of a relatively fast stock turnover; the conditions that necessitate high markdowns; the constancy of the obsolescence factor; the nature of fashion's intrinsic value to the consumer; and the difficulty of evaluating and predicting consumer merchandise preferences.

The overriding considerations of the second edition of *Fashion Buying & Merchandising* remain the same as for the first edition—to present the following subjects in a realistic and "jargon-free" manner.

- Current fashion buying and merchandising practices
- Information about the responsibilities of fashion buying and merchandising, to aid orientation and exploration for career purposes
- Guidelines for effective fashion buying and merchandising practices

This second edition responds to current industry techniques and to the suggestions of teachers and students who used the first edition, to whom we express our deepest gratitude. The following are some of the important revisions:

- Merchandising applications are expanded.
- Sales promotion activities include buyer guidelines for promotional events.

- Information on owning and operating an independent fashion specialty store is expanded in keeping with the current trends.
- Highlights of the fashions from 1920 to the early 1980s are related to the influences that caused them.
- The addition of a unit that explains the interrelationships of the three major sectors of the fashion industry and their effect on retail inventories.

In preparing this text, we have avoided "covering the waterfront," and deliberately omitted complete units of merchandising mathematics, the history of ready-to-wear, and analyses of the marketing practices of the textile and manufacturing sectors. These subjects, we believe, belong more properly in texts that cover them comprehensively. Our purpose is to give unencumbered focus to the assignments, responsibilities, and practices of fashion buying and merchandising. Our objectives are to assist the reader and to:

- Provide a foundation knowledge that will aid students in their discussion of current policies and procedures in fashion buying and merchandising.
- Create an awareness and an ability to express the knowledge and skill buyers need to make decisions in their day-to-day activities.
- Stimulate interest and encourage further reading regarding the profession in order to obtain a wider point of view.
- Develop the desire to observe, analyse, and criticize the fashion operations of various types of retail institutions as a para-professional as well as a customer.
- Increase the reader's confidence in his/her ability to obtain an entry-level job that leads to a merchandising position.

1983

Sidney Packard

Arthur A. Winters

Nathan Axelrod

CONTENTS

Fashion Buying
& Merchandising

part 1

ELEMENTS & IMPLICATIONS OF FASHION MERCHANDISING

The nature of fashion and its merchandising demands are far more complex than most people realize. A fashion professional knows fashion apparel as a unique product; one that reflects self-concept, lifestyle, change, a time, and a place. And above all, fashion is a result of acceptance.

Fashion merchandising is the ability to first respond to what, why, and when a style becomes a fashion; and then to determine its suitability for the particular retail operation and for what length of time. Therefore, our initial discussion focuses on fashion: definition, merchandising aspects, and background that led to current merchandising practices.

When you have finished Part One, you should be able to:

- Define fashion as it is understood by fashion authorities
- Explain how fashion responds to environmental factors
- Prove the value of merchandising
- Understand the principles of fashion merchandising
- Define marketing, retailing, merchandising, and buying
- Relate why fashion is a necessary element of American industrial and consumer life

chapter  1 FASHION CONCEPTS

INTRODUCTION

Successful fashion merchandising is based on stocking merchandise appropriate to consumer demand, a condition that leads to profitable sales. A buyer's primary role is that of a selector of merchandise for ultimate consumers. As a member of a retail team, a buyer is assigned the responsibility of building and maintaining a profit-producing stock that reflects the character and image of a retail operation. Management supports this effort by furnishing buying "tools," pertinent information, and standards of merchandising performance. A buyer is a retail executive who estimates the degree of acceptance of merchandise offered for sale by apparel producers, and then selects those styles that are most closely related to consumer demands of quality, taste, and price in such quantities that can be sold profitably.

Planning, buying, and selling fashion is the product of a well-calculated plan by an experienced, knowledgeable professional who knows customer buying habits and the meaning and implications of fashion merchandising. A successful buyer must recognize the relative importance of fashion trends, how long fashion trends will remain in importance, and when and in what depth fashion trends should be purchased.

The information that a fashion buyer accumulates in formal or on-the-job training starts with the fundamentals of:

- The Meaning of Fashion
- The Essentials of Merchandising
- The Evolution of Fashion
- How Merchandising Performance is Evaluated
- The Art of Producing A Profit in Retailing

FASHION—WHAT IS IT?

Historians and fashion experts would probably differ on the words used to define fashion, but there would be unanimous agreement that the elements of fashion are: *people, acceptance, time,* and *place.* It follows, therefore, that a fashion is anything that is *accepted* by a substantial group of *people* at a given *time,* in a given *place.* One could say that the definition covers an almost infinite range of products, ideas, practices, and attitudes. In a broad sense, fashion is the culture of a time; a set of learned beliefs, values, attitudes, habits, and forms of behavior that are shared by society, and are transmitted from generation to generation within that society. The meaning of fashion is so broad that it covers almost every aspect of human behavior.

The requirement of a substantial group of people is relative. For example, one hundred people with considerable means could purchase a yacht and make it the fashion of rich people. This fashion would be characterized as limited, restricted to those with wealth. But, on the other hand, when students in the 1960s adopted blue jeans, it had mass acceptance. In one instance substantial is one hundred people; in the other, substantial is a majority, more than half the group. Substantial can be interpreted as a group of people who have an influence on others and/or who can obtain the recognition of others.

Fashion is associated with a particular time or period. What is important today can be "old hat" tomorrow. Try this practical test— watch an old movie on television. The cars, interior decorations, clothes, and even the acting are dated. Our present lifestyle is far removed from what was accepted at the time of the film.

The *place* strongly affects what is acceptable. Different people in different places have different levels of aspiration, taste, education, and experience. Particular groups have particular guidelines for acceptance. It does not take close examination to identify food fashions of different countries and the styling of foreign automobiles. Even in the United States, different regions have different values of fashion in foods, in apparel, and in lifestyles. These are referred to as sub-cultural or regional values.

The fundamental characteristic of fashion is *acceptance.* Styles offered by producers and designers are not fashions until consumers *accept* them and *purchase* them.

THE OBSOLESCENCE FACTOR

In a society that generates an annual Gross National Product at the unprecedented figure of three trillion dollars, fashion is meaningful to manufacturers, retailers, and consumers. If we used products until they were no longer serviceable, the country's industrial rate of production would be limited to replacement. Retailers would sell merchandise less frequently, and our economy would reflect a lower standard of living. We need a constant flow of new ideas to produce new styles that age the products in the hands of the consumers. In our affluent society, consumers discard serviceable goods in favor of those that are newer. This practice is known as the consumer *obsolescence factor* and is by definition—the rejection of present ownership in favor of something newer even though the old retains utility value. How often have you discarded what you own simply because something else was newer in fashion?

As a country dedicated to mass production for mass consumption, the obsolescence factor is a key requirement to economic health. Produce, sell, redesign, sell is the marketing progression of most producers of consumer products. The industrial and consumer practice of constantly seeking the new, in economic terms, is an extravagance. However, the acquisition of the new, from a consumer's point of view, has the psychological value of making one feel good, and enjoying the pride of ownership, not to speak of the status value.

For many years an automobile was an outstanding example of a status symbol and of the design of obsolescence. Automobile manufacturers far too often brought out new models with essentially a change in styling, in silhouette, with additional chrome and more luxurious upholstery. Consumers, in turn, traded in their cars, which were in working condition, because the newer models were more fashionable and were overt evidence of financial status. Unfortunately for the industry its ability to influence consumers to practice the obsolescence factor has diminished. The high cost of oil, foreign car competition, and inflation, etc., have caused many consumers to rationalize their car purchase behavior—to consider the factors of service and cost. The automobile business in the United States is battling a loss of its share of the market. In turn, our entire economy has been affected adversely.

Television commercials can give testimony to the effectiveness of product romancing and how style causes consumer acceptance. "Buy the new and improved . . ." is a repeated message. A message that identifies one of the characteristics of fashion—change. Old becomes obsolete, even when its aging process is in a retailer's or producer's inventory. Old becomes valuable only when it is very old—an antique—an item in limited supply.

WHY PEOPLE BUY

One of the exciting areas of fashion is apparel, a very big business in the United States, one that generated approximately $100 billion at retail annually in the early 1980s. The fact is that the combined producers of fabrics and finished apparel represent the largest commercial employers in the United States, about two-and-a-half million people—and that is big business by any standards.

Why do we wear clothes? It seems like a fairly easy question, but it has more meaning than a first analysis would reveal. There has always been a need for clothing. Climate made wearing certain coverings necessary: in the Arctic furs served best; in the tropics loincloths sufficed; in the desert loose-fitting robes gave protection from the rays of the sun and heat. So primitive society's first consideration was protection.

But man is inventive. He soon learned that decorations and covering could express individuality and present an opportunity to show superiority. Covering and decorations become status symbols: kings wore crowns and robes; Roman senators wore togas; hunters displayed pelts; soldiers featured medals.

Status, authority, and wealth were reflected in the use of clothing. Uniforms were adopted by soldiers, policemen and firemen to show authority. Even political attitudes were gleaned from the use of body covering. Think of the revolutionary garb of the French Revolution and you recall peasant fashions; look at a picture of Chinese Communist men and women and invariably they will be wearing quilted cotton pants and jackets. Why? Why did the Russians give up this practice? Will Castro continue to wear fatigues and a beard? Will he continue to be emulated by his followers? Uniformity can equate with equality, but can the fashion be maintained over a long period? Do new periods bring new standards? Consider the symbolism of wearing evening clothes which lend dignity and formality; and the college graduation robes which indicate achievement.

One of the satisfactions of clothing is to assist man in asserting his authority and dominance over others. The basic need for bodily adornment or decoration to demonstrate superiority or status when civilization was a great deal younger is still common today. It would seem that wearing clothing is rooted in aesthetic and social yearning, and that the wearer secures a sense of well being and pleasure from the admiration of his fellow man. One of man's superior attributes, as compared to all other living creatures, is the ability to create and wear clothing. And herein is a psychological factor—the desire to show continued superiority over the animal kingdom. The "second skin" man acquires, which he can change at will, separates him from the animal kingdom.

The Eisenhower jacket—the modern version (see page 15).

One of the most compelling reasons for the use of clothing is to seek a state of betterment. *Better than what?* Better than we are. Better than we are endowed. Few of us are completely satisfied. We admire those with features we do not possess. When one is short, one desires to be tall. When one is fat, one desires to be slim. Clothing gives us an opportunity to improve on our natural endowments. Certain colors enhance the shades of our eyes and features. Specific silhouettes, such as a single-breasted garment, make us appear slimmer. Belted garments with a bloused effect make us appear more robust. How often do you hear, "I wear a certain type of garment because it makes me look better."

Parenthetically speaking, billions of dollars are spent by both men and women on cosmetics in their desire for self-improvement. This does not include the monies spent on beauty treatments and hair styling. It must be remembered that beauty is not created in a beauty salon, the salon merely enhances the appearance of the customer. One feels better following a beauty treatment because the improvement is largely a state of mind.

The explanation that betterment is the prime consideration may be an oversimplification. Betterment is a general term that must be put into psychological perspective and studied as to what motivates an individual to seek a state of betterment at a particular time. Also why is one garment favored over another? Our concern is to recognize that man constantly seeks change—for betterment.

We must consider that what is betterment depends on who is making the decision. A thirteen-year-old girl's interpretation of what is better for her may not be understood by her nineteen-year-old sister. Different individuals—different points of view. Is there a generation gap in clothing? Did you ever hear a father tell his son what clothing was considered appropriate in his time? Can you imagine that college students once wore white shirts and ties to classrooms? Hard to believe? What is appropriate depends upon the time and the place, and by whom. One never says never about fashion. Even crew cuts may one day return to the fashion scene—and longer hair may be out. We often reach back and embrace nostalgia and the fashions of yesterday, though never exactly as they were. There are always differences to make them adaptations of what was.

Yet fashion is evolutionary in its movement. We do not like *drastic* changes. Drastic changes may negate accepted ideas, and we do not like to give up what has been comfortable for us in ideas, clothing, or practice. As one wag once said, "Fashion is something we first find ludicrous, then smile at, eventually accept, and then fight to retain."

Complete change has economic significance. If new fashions make present ones look out-of-date, it becomes necessary to refurbish the major parts of our wardrobes. This situation is particularly annoying if our wardrobe was recently purchased.

Consumers are motivated to buy fashion apparel by a search to seek a state of betterment which could be one or a combination of the following reasons:

- Social position
- Authority
- Wealth
- Dignity
- Formality
- A second "skin" as an improvement on nature
- Conformity to peer groups
- Attitudes of conformity—rebellion, etc.
- Religious attitudes
- Aesthetic values

THE DIFFUSION OF FASHION— AN EVOLUTIONARY PROCESS

A fact of history is that artists and other innovators were seldom appreciated while they lived. The public neither appreciates nor accepts very drastic changes. It takes time for our eyes and minds to become accustomed to and to accept forward movements. The trend in this age of universal education and changing values, however, has resulted in an increased acceptability of new ideas. The acceptance of any new idea starts with the *avant garde*—the innovators, a relatively limited group of people who by reason of sophistication and/or sensitivity initiate new trends, the direction of fashion. This group is followed by early acceptors—a wider segment of the population—and later by a greater cross section. In any evolution there are some who are the laggards who never follow the fashion of the times. (The adoption process is best shown in **Figure 1–2.**)

The fashion of "down." A new material—a new look.

Who the innovators are depends on the type of fashion. Blue jeans are the most popular fashion in the world. And they did not originate in Paris (although denim fabric did originate in France as serge de Nimes). On the other hand, a great look of yesterday—The New Look— did originate in France.

Fashion can start at very high prices and trickle down to popular levels and conversely, it can start with groups having little money, rise in interest and eventually take on importance. The latter phenomenon is now due to the influence of youth on the times and their ability to make their weight felt.

High fashion was once the property of the wealthy. High fashion now refers to a limited fashion group—one that is practiced by the front runners—the early innovators—rich or poor.

The evolutionary process at one time took approximately three years—one year to rise in importance, one year to trickle down and one year for decline and final abandonment. In today's fast moving world, the process has been speeded up considerably.

CLASSIFICATION OF FASHION

The duration of a fashion's importance is a critical fashion merchandising concern. A fashion can be brief or of long duration. Once having identified this characteristic, a buyer is in a position to assess a fashion's importance to the retail inventory.

Basic or Classic

When a fashion is constant or "long-lasting," such as a long-sleeve cardigan sweater, it is called a *basic* or *classic.* It is similar to a standard in music. We do not consider the songs *Home on the Range* or *Old MacDonald Had A Farm* out of fashion. They are part of American music sung on special occasions, and part of any book covering folk music. The basic cardigan is part of the fashion scene—it does not excite a customer, but she has one or more in her wardrobe, to be worn to suit different occasions. In certain times, the basics become the most important promotable fashion, but in or out, they remain part of the fashion scene. There are many items that fall into this classification: loafer shoes, chino pants, shirtwaist dresses, pleated plaid skirts, long-sleeve slip-on sweaters in fine gauge, blue blazer jackets, corduroy separates, jumpers. There are general fashions that last for years, such as the casual look, the length of skirts, pleated skirts, and the single-breasted men's suit.

Figure 1–1. Comparative Time Values of Fashion.

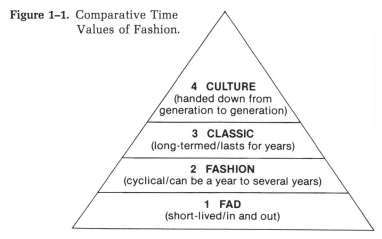

*Above-the-knee hemline fashion of the 1960s.

Fads—in and out. A harem "houri" (top right). Urban cowgirl (top left). Silver paper jumpsuit "almost instant failure" (above).

Fads

One of the most important fashion terms to be defined is *fad.* A fad is something which can either make a buyer's life more interesting or more tense. Very often something appears on the scene that captures the imagination, only to fizzle out in short order.

Two monumental past failures were the products of international designers, manufacturers, and retailers. In the late 1950s, the experts were sure that the chemise or "sack look" was headed for wide success, but the idea died quickly despite intense promotion. In the 1970s producers and retailers visualized booming business if they could make consumers accept a new fashion idea—longer hemlines. Logically, consumer obsolescence should have come into play after the extended popularity of the mini look* that favored the young. And with no opportunity to lengthen garments, consumers would have had to refurbish their wardrobes. But the experts were deceived; one of the most costly mistakes in apparel history.

More recent "flops" include the harem pant that flattered few, parrots printed on shirts, and the camouflage look. But there is hardly a season that passes that does not include a style (or styles) mistakenly touted for strong consumer acceptance.

A buyer is a selector for customers—selecting what is most likely to be accepted. Going overboard for short-lived fashions—fads—can be costly.

Style

The term *style* is a popular word in fashion and refers to a subdivision within fashion. By definition, it is that which has certain characteristics that distinguish it from other styles. For example, the fashion could be a pleated skirt, yet the style is the box pleat. It is a common fallacy to believe that famous designers create fashions. Actually, they create styles which they hope will be accepted. When and if there is consumer support, the styles then become fashion. It is repetitious but important to stress that fashion is synonymous with acceptance. **Figure 1–1** is a scale of comparative time values of fashion.

FASHION IS CYCLICAL

The term fashion cycle goes hand-in-hand with the evolutionary movement—from the beginning, the rise to the peak of popularity, and finally to the decline and abandonment of it. It is sometimes called the *arc of fashion* or the *merchandise-acceptance curve.* This movement has important meaning to the fashion business. **Figure 1–2** illustrates the dynamics of fashion apparel as well as the relationship of:

● The movement of fashion
● The acceptance by groups
● The price ranges

In this evolution, the fashions at the highest prices are adopted by early acceptors and purchased at stores with fashion leadership. If the fashion moves up, it is accepted by early followers, a much larger group than early acceptors, and purchased at specialty and department stores

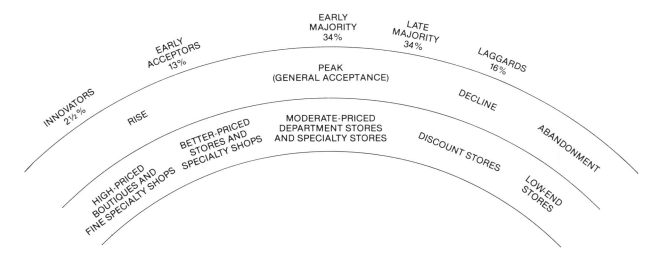

Figure 1–2. Arc of Fashion Merchandise-Acceptance Curve.

stocking medium- to high-priced goods. Later when fashion moves further up the peak, it is accepted at the broadest acceptance level, by the largest consumer group, and obtainable in the widest possible number of retail establishments at lower prices. After the peak, the fashion becomes available at the cheapest prices, often stocked at markdown racks, and in some stores at low promotional price levels before abandonment. **Figure 1–2** also points out average conditions. Fashion is not a price, it can rise from any price level. However, new fashions often start at higher prices and then trickle down to acceptance by wider segments of the population at lesser prices.

WHAT INFLUENCES FASHION

If fashion is a reflection of lifestyle, there must be certain factors in our lives which influence it. The broad influences that motivate people to purchase fashion are:

● Economics
● Social Activities
● Cultural Activities
● Technology
● Political Activities

Economics

No matter how one approaches the subject of fashion in the United States, the conclusions drawn must be that it is a luxury, and the American way is to practice the obsolescent factor. We do not buy a garment when it has been literally consumed or no longer serviceable. When a fashion is consumed, it is no longer in fashion, and the acceptance stage has passed. Because of its high income levels, the United States has viewpoints on fashion that are very different from most other countries. It is generally accepted that a family begins to have a significant interest in fashion when its income level reaches $20,000 a year. So let us briefly concentrate on the subject of the capacity to buy fashion. The following figures illustrate why America can practice the obsolescence factor, and why it will continue to be very heavily involved in the fashion business. In the late 1960s the median income family was approximately $9,300 a year. As this is being written, the median income is approximately $20,000.* Two-thirds of the world's population has a per capita income of approximately $300 a year, with 60 percent averaging less than $150

---

*In 1981 the average net worth of an American was $39,600.

per capita. This puts into perspective the fashion capacity of the United States as against that of most other countries.

Within the grasp of most Americans is the ability to live well and to seek constant replacement whether it is for refrigerators, cars, color television sets, or apparel. In countries where incomes are at subsistence levels, fashion industries operate as an insignificant facet of their existence. Our industry has almost unlimited potential for broad distribution, which affords opportunities for mass production. However, the merchandise produced must have acceptance value. Mass fashion production succeeds when the right styles are produced at the right prices for wide acceptance. Manufacturers and retailers know that styles short of acceptance must be discarded and alternatives found so that the economics of large-scale production can function.

Social Activities

The social attitudes of a country have a strong effect on its fashion institutions. There are countries of the world where interests are wholly concentrated on the home and family. This hardly makes for deep interest in apparel. Individuals in these countries will not entertain lavishly, attend the theatre, or become involved with other individuals at functions that show off clothing and status. Opening night of the ballet or opera in New York City is an example of a social function that usually merits coverage by the press of who attended and what they wore. This news is devoured by the public anxious to see what society leaders accept as the appropriate dress for such an occasion. Many of us will never attend such an opening, but we will have an occasion during the year that will require clothing of a type which is acceptable by our peers.

Social life in the United States for the most part is also a result of more leisure time created by fewer working hours. More social activity requires a greater variety of clothing—the right clothes to suit the occasion. With an increased concern for self-esteem and good health and exercise as the way to reduce weight and promote longevity, there is widespread indulgence in physical activities. Never before have so many participated in so many activities with wardrobes designed for specific purposes: golf, tennis, jogging, hiking, etc. Activewear has become a huge and profitable business—sneakers that retail for $40 and $50 a pair, jogging suits up to $200, and not to mention the popularity of sweatshirts, t-shirts, sweatsocks, denim styles, etc. Many stores have created "pro shops" and new types of specialty stores concentrate on jeans and accessories, sneakers and jogging shoes, and even t-shirts with "messages."

Casual attire and active sportswear are the most important components of our wardrobes. We have accepted them as part of our lifestyle, a way that allows us to dress as we please for almost any function. How

Current lifestyle attire.

many restaurants require men to wear ties? Where would people raise their eyebrows if someone wears jeans? The casual attitude about clothing standards has not only given fashion marketers wider opportunities, it has also helped to democratize clothing.

Cultural Activities

The cultural activities of people are reflected in their art forms. Clothing can be considered an art form. It has shape, color, and an arrangement of details. This finished product and look can be as aesthetic as a painting. What people appreciate and accept depends on their aesthetic values, shaped by their education, interest and exposure to art forms. But one art form never stands alone. It is part of a larger appreciation. It is not by accident that the French have been fashion leaders for many years. It is a corollary to their attachment for painting, sculpture, ballet, music, and gourmet cooking.

In the United States we have arts and crafts such as folk singing, handicrafts, weaving and pottery which have unique cultural values. An abundance of free schooling and our freedom for doing our "own thing" are influences that spill over into the fashions of our clothing. The result of which is that we developed, accepted, and became internationally famous for casual apparel, such as skirts, slacks, sweaters, sport suits, and sport jackets. Our designers are in the vanguard of the fashion world when the casual look assumes international importance. And the most important casual style of all time—the blue jean—is as American as "apple pie."

Technology

We are living in a world of new technology, so recently developed that of all the scientists that were ever born, 90 to 95 percent are still living.

Imagine how far our scientific knowledge has progressed. A college chemistry student might not be able to be tutored by his father, who happens to be a chemist. Space technology is relatively brand new. The technology of aeronautics has developed planes that can carry up to 400 people. The man who was the pioneer of commercial flying died in 1974—Charles Lindbergh. The wonderful world of chemistry has produced nylon, acrylic, polyester and combinations of man-made fibers with natural fibers. The consumer is deluged with textile market brand names, yet has little knowledge of textile technology. It is safe to say that we live in a world of synthetics. As evidence of that, cotton was toppled from its throne in 1968. Man-made fibers now rule in the textile industry. For young people, permanent press, soil resistance and other service features are a way of life, but these are relatively new advances which became part of our daily living and fashion just a few years ago. Wool and cotton are in the spotlight of fashion importance, but at prices that generally make them part of better-priced merchandise.

Technological strides inherent in clothing is only one phase of science in our study of fashion. Science and technology have produced the airplane and television. Through the invention of jet travel, the globe has become so small that one can reach any part of it well within a day. Reduced fares have opened travel to practically all income levels. During July and August, over 1.5 million Americans may travel to Europe. New places, exposure to different ideas and familiarity with foreign customs broadens one's scope and lays the groundwork for wider acceptance—of art forms and fashion. How can one deny the softness of Scottish cashmere, the suppleness of Spanish capeskin, the beauty of Italian shoes and handbags, the luxury of imported full-fashioned knits —just to mention a few popular categories that have become important to the American fashion scene.

How fantastic is the thought of bouncing television transmission off a man-made satellite to achieve international reception! It is now commonplace. We are exposed to the entire world within our living rooms. We are able to see kings crowned, watch wars fought, and view customs from different cultures. This exposure helps to internationalize fashion. Paris can be a flip of a dial away.

Political Activities

Political activity can inhibit or enhance the fashion of the times and is probably an influence not often considered. The most obvious examples are the restrictions which take place during wars, when the government dictates the amount of fabric used in garments in order to preserve textiles for the military. In an attempt to save fabric, it is interesting to note that men lost their vests and pants cuffs during World War II. Previously, suits were always offered with both features and not uncommonly with two pairs of pants.

Nostalgic fashion with Ralph Lauren's "Spirit of Colonial Americana."

Two nostalgic films, *The Great Gatsby* and *Bonnie and Clyde,* returned fashions (for a while) to the '20s and '30s.

World War II activity made for many fashions, some of which have become classic. Chino pants, combat boots, field jackets, field caps, Eisenhower jackets, (which were the catalyst for the single-breasted men's suit) were a few items that caught the imagination of the civilian population. In the late 1960s the youth in their role playing, adopted World War II emblems, insignias, buttons and parts of uniforms.

The cost   and degree of imports is regulated by the Federal government and if laws are enacted to curtail quantities of merchandise entering the country, it can cause a limitation on what is available in stores. Imports can be a competitive factor for domestic products, and tend to depress some domestic retail price levels.

These broad areas of influences are exerted on a constant basis, though we usually do not associate our wearing apparel with them. We are more prone to realize specific causes, such as the influence of film as a medium and the imitation of film stars. In the late 1970s, Diane Keaton set a modest trend for the "Annie Hall" look. The author of the film, Woody Allen, it should be noted, wears sneakers with formal clothing, but this practice has not "caught on" as a fashion.

Anything that occurs in our society which has an impact on the people is reflected in the art of clothing. It sometimes does not catch on or last very long. Eastern Indian influence was important after a semi-official visit by Jacqueline Kennedy, wife of President Kennedy, to the Far East. In 1970, the Japanese theme was strong since it related to the Tokyo World's Fair. A French premier's wife made a visit to this country wearing "the longuette." There was no apparent influence on American women. In this case, the public exercised its right to reject as well as to accept a fashion offering. However, in 1981 Nancy Reagan influenced the current trend to red when she wore a red outfit to the presidential inauguration. There is little question but that she will have a considerable impact on fashion in the 1980s.

The fashion business is one of the largest industries in the country. Most manufacturers and retailers make careful studies of what is currently in demand and, based on their findings, build a framework for the future. The manufacturers and retailers in this industry know that fashion changes through evolution; that a drastic change may cause resistance. Their practice is to make newer versions of the accepted and then probe with more daring styles which could provide clues to probable acceptance.

THE CONSUMER IS "KING" OF FASHION

The ready-to-wear field is a network of information exchange and feedback. Manufacturers rely on primary market (materials of fashion) people for information a year in advance of actual style development. All levels of the industry search Europe for what is being worn there, since European fashion is often six months to a year ahead of American fashion. On the other hand, young people in the United States and abroad are observed carefully, and their attitudes about wearing apparel have important meaning. Sometimes their *abuse* of fashion, such as the cutting of blue jeans or re-dyeing their clothes can *become* a fashion. Young people are wearing "their own things," and there are strong possibilities that their outfits represent some new fashion trends.

But the main thing to remember is that all research may be in vain—it is the consumer who is genuinely king and queen. Sometimes they are seemingly insensitive or fickle, but in the final analysis, they know what they want—when they want it—and in the quantities that they will absorb.

The failure rate in women's wear manufacturing is 17 percent per annum. One of the great equalizers is the inability to keep pace with consumer preference. Though stores do not fail with the same regularity, one must consider that established retailers can succumb for the same reasons. Witness the demise of DePinna's and Best & Co. in New York

City—two famous fashion stores that may have failed to recognize the times—and to redefine their customers and their new lifestyles.

On the other hand, Bloomingdale's, New York, is an example of how a department store organization was able to redefine its consumer demands and to become internationally famous for fashion expertise. After extended research, Bloomingdale's responded to new consumer attitudes by stocking prophetic and wanted fashion, creating an exciting shopping atmosphere, and packaging compelling sales promotion campaigns (see Part Four, Chapter 16). The success that followed these efforts enabled the organization to extend its operation into other trading areas. Needless to say, other retailers have and are emulating Bloomingdale's fashion marketing strategies. And its reputation was not hurt when in the course of a week, two well-known personalities shopped at the main store—the Queen of England and the then U.S. President's wife.

"There is no business like the fashion business." All fashion marketers must keep in tune with consumer wants and needs, which are always in a state of change.

SUMMARY

- The elements of fashion are people, acceptance, time, and place.
- Fashion can be regional, sub-cultural, national and international.
- Fashion is related to the length of time it is popular: *fads* are short-lived; *classics* are long-lasting; some are inherent to the society (handed down from generation to generation) and become part of the culture.
- Fashion is the effect of an evolutionary process that starts with acceptance by a relatively limited group of people, followed by its adoption by widened segments of the population.
- The dynamics of fashion apparel include: the creation of fashion, the stocking of fashion, and the acceptance by groups.
- Fashion is not a price, it can rise from any price level.
- Fashion is synonymous with change, therefore, the consumer obsolescence factor is inherent to fashion.
- The broad influences that motivate people to purchase fashion are: economics, social activities, cultural activities, technology and political activities.
- Consumer purchase behavior for fashion apparel is motivated by a search to seek a state of betterment.
- The broad influences that cause consumer acceptance of apparel include: emulation of prominent personalities; art events, foreign countries in the news, current trends of lifestyles, and job security.

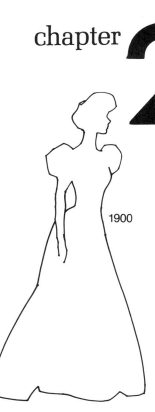

chapter

2 HOW FASHION REFLECTS LIFESTYLE

1900

INTRODUCTION

Planning is based on an analysis of past events and a judgment of what is apt to occur in the future. These considerations are of critical importance to fashion merchandising because of the cyclical nature of fashion; what was accepted in the past will reappear in due course with modifications tailored to current demand. To reinforce the periodic reappearance of fashion, the length of hemlines is said to be related to economic conditions. In a good economy, hemlines rise; during periods of economic downturns hemlines lower. It is of current interest, therefore, to note that in the last quarter of 1981, designers and manufacturers were in effect predicting an improved economic trend for the ensuing years by featuring updated versions of the mini-look of the 1960s.

Although this text concentrates on planning, buying, and selling, the material in this chapter focuses on the following objectives:

● To document highlights of the history of fashion
● To analyze why particular fashions were important in past eras
● To update recent fashion events or developments

Obviously, the material must be condensed to stay within the constraints of space, hence the discussion is limited to selected highlights. The broad influences and consumer motivations that cause fashion merchandise purchase behavior were covered in Chapter 1. This chapter focuses on how environmental conditions gave rise to particular fashions.

Our discussion begins with the era that began when ready-to-wear was "born"—*1920.*

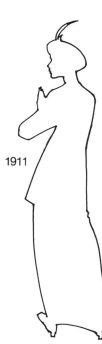

1911

THE 1920s

This was the era when the nation went on a binge. The period was "the revolution of the twenties," when there was open violation of the National Prohibition Act (Volstead Act), which was intended to outlaw the manufacture of liquor and make America dry. But home stills, cocktail parties, hip flasks, and drinking flourished. As a reaction to this legislation, America's thirst for hard liquor whetted. In this environment gangsterism became big business, and one of America's "biggest businessmen" was Al Capone.

It was a period in which many fads came into prominence such as marathon dancing, flagpole sitting, Mahjongg, and crossword puzzles; helped considerably by a new medium—radio.

One of the popular songs of the day expressed the echoes of the times, *The Best Things in Life Are Free.* And indeed, freedom ran rampant in the form of excesses: wild stock market speculation, a national spending spree, and a pervasive interest in sex.

In this atmosphere women's clothing became revealing—by 1927 skirts were knee length. It was the first time in 2,000 years of Western dress that legs were openly exposed and flesh-colored stockings replaced the traditional black or white stockings. The Puritanical values of the 19th century were ended. As a last gasp, some moral leaders tried to legislate women's clothing standards. As an example, ministers of fifteen denominations in Philadelphia proposed a moral code for dresses —loose fitting, with long sleeves, and a skirt seven and a half inches off the floor. State legislatures also tried to decree moral standard clothing. Utah's plan called for a fine for those who wore skirt three inches above the ankle. Virginia expressed dismay for a dress that permitted the display of more than two inches of throat and also decried any garment that accentuated the lines of the female figure.

As an accompanying trend, women's apparel became more suitable for office wear and travel. Simplicity and wearability became an important theme.

When golf was a genteel game.

The flapper was the pin-up girl and Clara Bow, the "It" girl. Thin was in for the first time. The fashion model was a flapper who cast aside the traditional corset and danced with abandon to jazz music.

The milieu that contributed to the revolution in women's clothing included the influences of economics (extravagance), political attitudes (women's suffrage—the right to vote), new social and cultural values, and, of course, technological advances (development of rayon, mass production, the automobile, and motion pictures).

Men's clothing, not as sensitive to influences as women's apparel, featured baggy pants with lots of excess material and the double-breasted jacket, a silhouette that remained in popularity until after World War II.

THE 1930s

During the week of October 20, 1929, the stock market collapsed from overextended buying. "Instant millionaires" were wiped out and suicides caused by financial woes were not uncommon. The new era witnessed the end of the excesses of the Roaring Twenties and the beginning of the Great Depression. A popular song of the day was, *Brother Can You Spare A Dime.*

In 1930, 1,326 banks failed. In an effort to find a means of subsistence, some idle workers turned to street vending of apples. At one point in 1930, there were six thousand apple peddlers in New York City. In the same year war veterans marched on Washington to demand a bonus, only to be beaten by Federal troops.

In 1933, Franklin Delano Roosevelt was inaugurated as the thirty-second president. In his inaugural speech he said: "The only thing we have to fear is fear itself." In the same year, Dr. Frances E. Townsend of Long Beach, California, proposed a $200 monthly retirement pension for Americans over sixty years of age. This was the root of our Social Security system, but at that time the proponent was considered a "kook."

1934 was the year when dust storms of the Southwest caused thousands to abandon their farms for the friendlier climate of California. Several years later John Steinbeck documented the plight of the Okies in his novel, *The Grapes of Wrath.*

On the international scene, on September 12, 1938, the German army invaded Czechoslovakia. In the same year, Japan overran Manchuria and invaded China. Economic unrest was leading to the ultimate crisis—a world war.

The decade finally came to a close, but the Great Depression lingered on. America survived, but many suffered from privation.

During the decade, giddy clothing disappeared. Hemlines, even for daytime, were long, almost ankle length. Evening dresses were very long, usually trailing on the ground. In coats and suits, the prominent detail was the wider shoulder, a silhouette that remained in popularity for several years. Marlene Dietrich and Katharine Hepburn, popular

Fashion forerunners: Dior's New Look, 1947 (left) and early unisex (right).

motion-pictures actresses, set the style of man-tailored slacks for casual wear. But the time was not ripe for this apparel for streetwear; it took more than three decades for their acceptance for this purpose.

Men's clothing reflected little change.

During this era American designers came into prominence with the flow of European designs cut off because of the war. Such names as Sophie of Saks 5th Avenue, Adrian, Adele Simpson, Claire Potter, and Sally Victor were among those who became well-known figures in American couture circles.

The environmental factors, mirrored by classic, lower hemlined, covered styles can be summed up as: economics (bad times); politics (war); social and cultural standards (return to more traditional values); and technology (the growing importance of radio and motion pictures).

THE 1940s

On December 7, 1941, the Japanese bombed Pearl Harbor, and the United States was forced into World War II. Although shoes were the only article of apparel rationed, clothing styles were affected dramatically because of the shortage of fabric for civilian use. Skimpy skirts were worn with long narrow jackets and blouses. Silk disappeared as the supply from the Orient was cut off. Nylon stockings, which were introduced just before the war, disappeared from the market when all nylon manufacturing was devoted to the war need. Women went barelegged in summer, but wore cotton, wool, or rayon stockings during cold weather.

With the war dragging on and the continued cutoff of foreign designer influence, American designers began to exercise their ingenuity, out of which developed the American look—sportswear . . . separates. West Coast manufacturers picked up the idea as suitable for the casual California lifestyle, and many firms located in that area gained national importance, such as Catalina, White Stag, Koret of California, and Jantzen.

As a wartime necessity, the government established clothing size standards. The result was the realization that women require size ranges to accommodate different physical endowments. In due course, the importance of junior size apparel was established. Apparel for the younger figure thus became an important segment of American fashion retailing (and 5′ 4″ and under). And out of junior sizes came another development, sizes for teenagers which became synonomous with bobby soxers—teenage girls.

With the end of World War II, France reasserted its fashion importance, and the most important innovation was Christian Dior's *New Look,* introduced in 1947. The *Look* had narrow shoulders with little or no padding, a waist that was tightly cinched, with a "long" skirt.

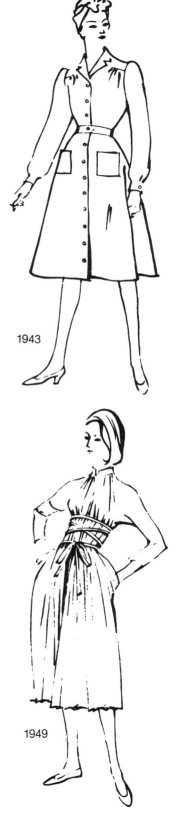

1943

1949

Men's apparel was affected considerably by wartime restrictions. Pants "lost" their cuffs and suits were produced without vests, a detail that took twenty years to return to fashion.

Political activity had the greatest impact on fashion, but other forces were also influencing their share of pressure, namely, a speeded-up economic pace, the appropriateness of more casual clothes for women who worked in plants (making war material), and the improvement of the technology of mass production (to satisfy the increased demand for uniforms), which had an effect beyond the period itself.

THE 1950s

In January, 1953, Dwight D. Eisenhower was sworn in as president. The nation was being restored to a peacetime pace. The economy was on the upswing. Television was coming of age. Rock-'n'-roll came in like gangbusters. Elvis Presley, a young singer from Memphis, Tennessee, outraged many TV viewers by the manner in which he gyrated his body from the waist down when singing.

With favorable economic conditions an unusual number of fads came to the fore. Frisbees were introduced in 1957; the hula hoop was a national craze; chlorophyll promised to make products smell pleasant-

1931   1942   1947

ly; Davy Crockett was embraced most affectionately by the young; painting by numbers made instant artists; and a morbid alternative was offered for those seeking shelter from the hydrogen bomb—fallout shelters.

The fifties unleashed one of the greatest population shifts in our history—the migration from cities to suburbia. In turn, stores followed their customers, and the result was the "retail revolution," manifestations of which were: the extension of department stores by the addition of branches, the proliferation of discount stores, shopping centers, and the increase of chain-store units.

With the influence of the move to "green acres," casual clothing assumed increased importance for men, women, and children. Among the attire that was favored were storm coats, raincoats (instead of tailored models), slacks, shirtwaist dresses, Bermuda shorts, sport jackets in single-breasted styles, blazers, and halters.

The return to prosperity and new social and cultural attitudes gave impetus to new consumer purchase attitudes—the need for increased wardrobes with greater emphasis on casual clothing. Increased leisure time as a result of a shortened work week made for more time to engage in more social activities.

The calm of the 1950s had a salutory effect on fashion—freedom for consumers and good business for retailers and producers.

1958   1959   1975

THE 1960s

With the beginning of the sixties the environment seemed to indicate reasons for national self-satisfaction. Our gross national product was starting to approach the "sound barrier" of $1 trillion annually; a new president, John Kennedy, exuded confidence and promised a "new frontier"; the average worker's wages were escalating; high technology was in place and performing "miracles"; and a substantial part of the population was seemingly secure in the knowledge that we were indeed the opulent society.

But in 1963, a relatively insignificant event took place that was the catalyst for the most turbulent era in American history. The event was the assassination of a Vietnamese politician, Ngo Dinh Diem. For reasons that are unclear, we became entangled in a war for which there was no understanding. In fact, our leaders never referred to the conflict as a war. The result of our involvement caused the polarization of groups from established institutions; over 50,000 Americans were killed; billions were spent which led to unprecedented inflation; race riots ran rampant; and even the political structure was under pressure to prove its ability to respond to a world that had become highly complex.

Among the issues of the period were the Vietnam War, sexual inequality, and the dehumanizing effect of technology.

Clothing was a means to express discontent, and what became fashion (or antifashion, which became the fashion) was revolutionary in concept. Denim, a fabric considered as work clothing material, became the symbol of democracy—the return to the principle of individual liberty. It was also an expression of discontent, an attitude that clothes do not make the person. Never before had one fashion swept the nation and the entire fashion world. The leading item of this fashion became the blue denim pants, a trend that continues in the 1980s.

Interestingly, broad influences affect all forms of art, one of which is clothing. Another art form that was deeply affected by the environment was music. The new direction concentrated on folk ballads. This art form was black music with gospel intensity, rhythmic freedom, and realistic vocal style, a trend that continues into the era of the eighties.

The "radicalizations" of apparel are so numerous it deserves indepth treatment. However, for our purpose, here are some of the effects of the era that has been characterized as the *Age of Aquarius:*

- Long hairstyles for men
- Braless look
- Topless bathing suits (fad)
- See-through blouses
- Costume jewelry for men
- Boots
- Cowhand styles

1924   1930   1947   1950   1960

1964

1975

- Unisex styles
- Afro hairstyles
- Above-the-knee hemline

On the international scene, European couture designers finally entered the arena of ready-to-wear after realizing the opportunities for a broadened audience, wider fame, and, of course, greater money-making possibilities. In France, the forerunners of the movement were Daniel Hechter, Emmanuelle Khanh, Karl Lagerfeld, and Cacharel, a firm that reached initial fame with a new shirt design, later improvised for other articles of clothing. England's contributors included Jean Muir and Mary Quant.

American designers who became household names included Norman Norell, Rudi Gernreich, Bill Blass, and Donald Brooks.

The 1960s is a keystone era in the history of fashion. It was a time when consumers showed their independence by refusing to accept the dictates of designers and manufacturers. When the market concentrated on lowered hemlines, consumers refused to buy the look. Instead, the consumer expressed a strong interest in pantsuits. The experts were proven poor prophets, and never again were they able to force a fashion on the buying public.

It was also a time when men re-entered the world of fashion by negating "timeless" styles. The "peacock revolution" of the 1960s was helped by the entry of women's clothing couturieres into the men's fashion world—such as Pierre Cardin, Donald Brooks, Bill Blass, and Yves St. Laurent.

Every general environmental influence caused its share of pressure on consumers during this hectic era.

THE 1970s

After the strife of the 1960s, Americans entered a calmer, but not particularly happy era. The Vietnam War inheritance had a high cost in terms of continued inflation and a recession. A new word was coined to describe an economic condition of too much money (supply) "chasing" too little goods—stagflation. Added to the economic woes was the escalation of oil prices, another factor that led to an increased inflation rate.

Embattled youth of the 1960s began to enter the age of maturity, and concerns turned to preparing for and entering career jobs. Mature Americans were beset by rising costs and the difficulty of maintaining a standard of living.

Although there was a continuance of the attitude that one is free to choose one's own fashion, the return to more traditional values was reflected in fashion. Hemlines were lowered below the knee, dresses were wearable for most occasions, men's suits concentrated on three-piece models in single-breasted styles, and even the button-down shirt re-entered the fashion picture. Dressing up for the occasion became more popular. And even an old standard for women's fashion—the hat—made a tentative comeback.

In general, the anti-fashion movement of the 1960s disappeared except for small pockets of dissidents. The "peacock revolution" made a strong impact; men, for the most part, continued their interest in being "properly dressed" for the occasion. Economic conditions caused considerable increases in the cost of fashion merchandise, which had the effect of reducing the frequency of consumer purchases, which in turn had an adverse effect on many manufacturing firms.

THE 1980s

The early period of the current era has consumers still reeling from the effects of a relentless inflationary spiral. Most people are concentrating their spending in one of two ways: one, by buying lower-priced merchandise, and two, by buying better products less frequently.

Since consumers are maintaining their fashion independence, fashions range from the very dressy to the very casual. Dress and pantsuits

1980

are important in silk and satin, frequently accessorized by "bronze" shoes and handbags. Separates, always a response to high prices or economic pressure, are very much in vogue. Sweaters are a definite fashion focus and hand-knit sweaters are being shown at prices that are staggering in comparison to those of recent times. In women's styles they feature lacy types, leno stitches, and other dressy versions that "pep up" an outfit. Men's sweaters are mostly in bulky types with cable stitch treatment. Men's pants are narrow, and the three-piece suit is still in trend.

The Western look has increased in importance as evidenced by the proliferation of stores that concentrate on blue jeans, denim shirts and jackets, Stetson-style hats, tooled boots, silver buckles, and other cowhand fashions. The blue jean trend continues. Designer-name styles carry labels with such names as Calvin Klein, Pierre Cardin, Sasson, and Gloria Vanderbilt. The urban cowhand outfit is high fashion and includes apparel and accessory items as boots at $700, animal skin shirts at $400, Stetson hats at $200, and silver buckles at $500. The urban cowhand never washes blue denims, they are dry-cleaned and pressed.

Apparel and accessories that express self-concept or leisure-time interest are prominent in fashions for jogging, tennis, golf, "aerobics," dancing, etc.

Difficult economic times show their effect by the acceptance of more tailored and casual clothing with counter trends of dressier styles as relief from basics.

The direction of fashion in the later years, obviously, will depend upon the influences of economics, social and cultural values, technology, and political events.

1983

SUMMARY

Fashion is an indicator of culture, the effect of influences of a particular time. History is usually related in terms of eras. Hence, it is both fascinating and necessary to know the fashions of past decades. In fact, it is a merchandising demand to have a knowledge of past fashion because of the predictability of the return in importance of what was once accepted. What and why certain fashions were once accepted arms a merchandiser with some basis to estimate the importance of new versions of returning trends.

Merchandisers who are part of institutions that have intimate relations with consumers must have a basic understanding of:

● When and why certain fashions had past importance
● What, when, why, and to what degree new versions of the old should be stocked

chapter 3
HIGHLIGHTS OF THE FASHION BUSINESS

INTRODUCTION

Fashion professionalism includes the need to know how fashion reflects current lifestyle and how the related industries contribute to the production of styles that are eventually included in retail inventories.

The processes, timing, and practices of the individual industries, which comprise the total fashion industry, should be part of the knowledge of merchandisers because these activities affect decisions of what, when, from whom, and how much merchandise should be purchased.

THE TEXTILE INDUSTRY

The requirement of most apparel is fabric. Although non-textiles share importance in the production flow of apparel and accessories, this discussion is confined to the textile industry's activities with some background of fabric development. Because of the complexities of an industry that affects almost every phase of our lives and that has a longer history of commercializing scientific developments than any other industry, it would take a most comprehensive tome to cover even its bare details. The discussion that follows focuses on:

- Textile industry segments
- Development of a fabric line
- How fabrics are marketed

Textile Industry Segments

Fabric production starts with fibers—a hairlike raw material. Fibers are spun into yarn and then either knitted or woven into fabric. There are two types of fibers: natural and man-made. Natural fibers are derived from plant or animal sources. Man-made fibers, sometimes referred to as synthetics, are produced in chemical laboratories. The three general textile segments are: (1) agricultural and chemical suppliers; (2) spinning plants that make fiber into yarn; (3) knitting and weaving mills that produce fabric from yarn.

There are essentially two ways to produce designs or color in fabrics: one in the knitting or weaving process; the other, using greige goods, which require some form of finishing, dyeing, or printing (design). Firms that convert and distribute this form of basic fabric are known as *converters.*

Woolen fabrics are most commonly made with dyed yarns, therefore the term yarn-dyed fabrics. Cotton and man-made textiles are most often produced in the greige, dyed and finished later, hence the term piece-dyed.

There are firms within the textile industry whose operations include every step in the production of fabrics from the purchase of natural and man-made fibers to the promotion and sale of finished fabric. But there are also specialists that produce specialty woven or knitted fabrics.

Figure 3–1 is a flow chart that illustrates the major segments of the fashion industry, which starts with the source of fibers. It should be noted that in the flow from fiber to finished fabric, ready for the apparel producer's process, each sector changes the nature of the product except one—the jobber. The jobber functions as a middleman by buying a product for resale. The economic purpose of a jobber is to liquidate producers' inventory and to make available out-of-production fabrics, or to make merchandise available for immediate delivery.

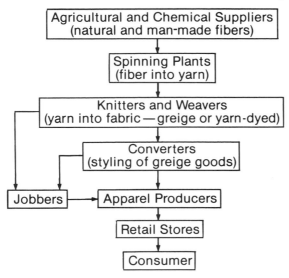

Figure 3–1. Flow Chart for Major Segments of the Fashion Industry.

Development of a Fabric Line

A textile firm is required to have expertise in three broad areas: *fashion, technology,* and *merchandising. Fashion knowledge* is gained through research—studying material and international markets in a search for what customers are most likely to accept up to two years in advance. It goes without saying, researchers are fashion experts whose specialization involves predicting trends. *Technology* is concerned with how to produce fibers and yarns. *Merchandising,* of course, is planning, buying, and selling. Planning is what to make. Buying includes the responsibilities of *when* and *how much.* Selling involves the distribution to producers of finished goods.

Once having decided future fashion trends, a textile firm concentrates on producing a line. The following are typical steps in developing a line of converted fabrics. (The styling of natural fiber fabrics, as noted, takes place before the weaving or knitting process.)

The evolution of an ancient craft. Original method of spinning (top left) and (bottom left) the current mule spinning process. Wooden loom (top right) and a modern loom (bottom right). Courtesy of The Wool Bureau Inc. and American Textile Manufacturers Institute.

1. The fashion director researches fashion trends and is the source of where fashion is headed.
2. The department manager (of a fabric type) is responsible for styling the line.
3. The stylist shapes styles into a line, puts them into salable form, or into groupings as they will be shown to customers.
4. The assistant stylist is the studio director who gives assignments to artists.
5. Artists draw designs in various patterns, often to accommodate customer requests.
6. Colorists work out color combinations of designs, particularly those required by customers.
7. The strike-off artist is the liaison between the studios and the plant. This person has the authority to modify a design or color combination to accommodate the quality or feasibility of how a fabric can be produced best.

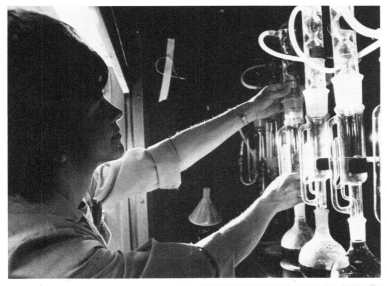

Scientific know-how is necessary in the finishing of fine fabric (top). Rotary screen printing (bottom) is one of the newest and fastest printing methods, combining the advantages of the older screen and roller printing processes. Courtesy of American Textile Manufacturers Institute.

Figure 3–2 illustrates the line of responsibility for the development of a fabric line.

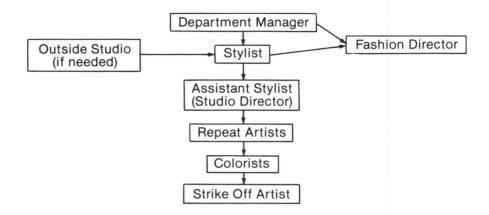

How Fabrics Are Marketed

Figure 3–3 illustrates part of a typical textile firm's chart of organization. The firm most often produces fabrics for a variety of uses, this figure shows the part of the organization wholly concerned with fabrics for apparel.

The marketing director has control of the planning, promotion, and distribution of all products. The divisional merchandiser directs and controls the personnel shown in Figure 3–2 (those involved in developing a line). The department manager is the link between the sales manager and the divisional merchandise manager, handing down instructions and following them through completion. The sales manager directs and controls the sales staff.

Salespeople are field operators. They visit manufacturers' offices to present and sell the line.

When a manufacturer is interested in a fabric(s), a fabric cut is ordered, about eight or ten yards to make a sample garment. The negotiations begin when the sample is completed and if the manufacturer decides to purchase the fabric(s). Issues are discussed by manufacturer and salesperson that involve quantity, price, delivery, and to whom the textile firm intends to deliver the same fabric. Manufacturers try to prevent making styles of fabrics that are *fords.** As a rule of thumb, the negotiated price hinges upon two factors: (1) when the order is placed and (2) in what quantity. An order placed early allows a textile

---

*Ford is a term that refers to the same style at many prices.

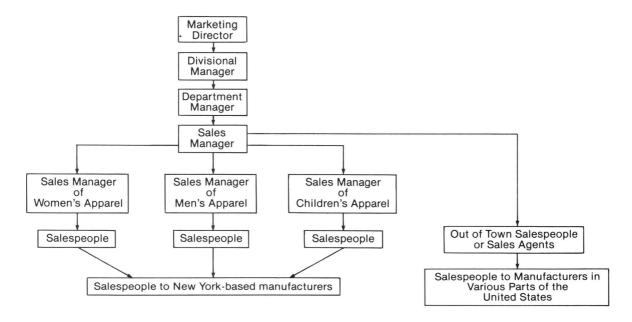

Figure 3–3. Organization Chart for Textile Firms (wholly concerned with fabrics for apparel).

producer to get an early production start. A large order keeps machinery rolling and lowers overhead. Hence, a manufacturer with a deep commitment has the advantage of obtaining a lower fabric price.

Once having taken an order, a salesperson has the responsibility of ensuring that its terms are completed as detailed by the manufacturer: in quantity, delivery date, price, and color.

MANUFACTURER/RETAILER RELATIONSHIP

Fashion marketers can be characterized by the company they keep; manufacturers by the stores they sell, retailers by their sources of merchandise. Although each operates on a different level of the industry, their common purpose is to gain ultimate consumer acceptance. The successful flow of fashion merchandising is, therefore, the production of salable styles and their placement in the hands of the right retailers, and the final distribution to the right end-users. The profitable flow requires a partnership arrangement of two parties with matching goals and abilities. The discussion that follows focuses on:

- Manufacturing industry segments
- Developing a line (or collection)
- Selling a line (or collection)

Manufacturing Industry Segments

The manufacturing industry is segmented by merchandise, sizes, prices, and geography. There is a high degree of specialization based on the product and at what price. For example, manufacturers concentrate their efforts on such narrow product lines as dresses, suits, coats, and sportswear. In effect there are sub-markets within the fashion manufacturing industry. And within these sub-markets, there is further specialization by popular, medium, and better price ranges and sizes (juniors, misses, and women's). Each sector operates in a particular building or location within a major market, by product, price level and size ranges. For example, in New York, 7th Avenue is known for better-priced merchandise, with makers clustered by merchandise type (dresses, separates, etc.). Moderate-priced dress and sportswear resources are located on Broadway, in their respective buildings. Popular-priced makers can be found on the side streets west of 7th Avenue, on 37th Street up to 40th Street. The Empire State Building houses many men's accessory firms; and men's suits are also sold from the Empire State Building and at 1290 Avenue of the Americas.

Outside of New York there are regional markets such as Dallas, Chicago, Miami, Atlanta, and Los Angeles. Also, there are areas that are known for manufacturing of apparel such as Boston for skirts, separates, and rainwear; Philadelphia as a center for women's and misses size outerwear and children's wear; Dallas and California for sportswear; and St. Louis as a junior's dress market.

Production facilities can be located almost anywhere, ranging from any region in the United States to foreign countries. (The subject of foreign producers is handled in Chapter 13.)

Developing a Line (Collection)

When a manufacturer starts to create a line or collection depends upon the required production time and price category of the merchandise (popular, moderate, or better). A knitwear line, a merchandise classification that requires a long production period, can begin six to twelve months in advance of market weeks. A popular-priced cut and sew sportswear line, on the other hand, could begin six weeks before showing dates. Additionally, popular-priced resources can copy a best seller at any time and have it added to the line in a matter of days.

Most manufacturers copy, improvise, or simply "knock off" a European couturier or a domestic manufacturer. The better market offerings are copied by moderate-priced houses; and in turn the popular-priced makers copy the moderate-priced houses. Therefore, the highest priced apparel is produced earliest—and lower priced lines later.

Manufacturers show their lines in showrooms during market weeks, when buyers visit to order merchandise for a new season, from two to four months before merchandise is received in a store (see **Figure 12–1** for a schedule of market weeks by price ranges).

Couture houses create their own styles based on the designer's sensitivity to the influences of the times. These designers shop the textile market, visit foreign fashion centers, and have good insights and experience to conceptualize what people will be prone to accept.

At price levels below the couture level, the process can vary; a line can have some degree of originality as a result of a designer's efforts, or a line can be variations of originals with styles improvised in fabric or details to make them fit certain price levels; or a line can be a series of straight copies. But whatever the price category, samples are made and put together as a line at popular and moderate price levels, as a collection at better levels.

When the line is complete, a manufacturer seeks objective advice from their customers, usually buyers important to the manufacturer. There are three reasons why advice is sought.

1. Customer's intentions are a good indication of what to put into production. The production of styles that do not sell well can be a serious loss of money and time which could have been spent on strong selling merchandise.
2. By concentrating on best sellers, a manufacturer maximizes profit.
3. Early favorable selling puts the manufacturer in a position to know what to prepare for later reorders.

It should be noted, however, that reorder availability for retailers is a matter of manufacturer's method of doing business. All manufacturers do not offer reorder merchandise. Some prefer to produce merchandise against orders, deliver it, and then offer more current styles as a new line. As a rule of thumb, popular-priced merchandise can be reordered most easily; better-priced merchandise usually cannot be reordered.

When the manufacturer has obtained buyer consensus, he/she confers with associates and an executive judgment is made—what to show for the new season. Samples are made available for selling in the showroom.

Selling the Line (Collection)

The most basic reason for being in business is to sell and realize a profit. A fashion manufacturer's aim is to produce apparel for a group of people with recognizable purchase behavior characteristics, using retailers as middlemen to reach those potential customers.

All manufacturers maintain showrooms in a major market, particularly in New York, the largest in the United States. Most manufacturers

1

2

3

4

5

6

7

8

9

From fashion concept through production stages. Courtesy of Harvé Benard Inc.

have a staff of salespeople who are assigned territories to sell stores within them. The vast majority of these sales representatives are independent agents who work on a commission basis. If a manufacturer's line has sufficient importance, exclusive sales representation is a condition of the arrangement. Therefore, some sales representatives carry merchandise of more than one manufacturer.

Salespeople start to travel well before market weeks. Some lines are "on the road" up to three and a half months before market weeks.

Receipt of orders (up to six months) in advance of delivery to retail stores gives the manufacturer the advantage of knowing what:

1. styles to put into production;
2. styles to discard;
3. colors of greatest early importance;
4. future sales can be predicted realistically.

After a sufficient number of orders are received, the manufacturer can put the styles into production which are justified by reason of sufficient early sales.

Showroom selling personnel in the meantime contact stores and resident buying offices to influence selling from the main office. It is a usual practice for the home office to work out deals for resident buying offices to send out bulletins to RBO client stores that recommend selected styles.

Retail stores place commitments with traveling salespeople who for the most part represent lines that are of importance. The advantage of placing early orders are:

- Early commitment ensures early delivery
- Not uncommonly, early delivery includes terms for additional dating (extension of date when invoice is payable)
- Early commitments cut down on a buyer's work load during market weeks

The buyer can be at a disadvantage in placing commitments before having visited the market and evaluating trends and comparing the importance of competing lines. Therefore, road commitments are made on the basis of two buyer alternatives: one, the right to change an order when in the market during market weeks, and two, to hold up the order confirmation until the market is shopped. In effect, orders given early can be an intention to do business.

Although the average manufacturer spends less than one percent of net sales for advertising, many sales promotion avenues are available to influence sales to retailers and ultimate consumers. They include:

- Market week fashion shows
- Trunk showings (showing a salesperson's line in a retail department to end-users)
- Statement enclosures (for retailers to send to their customers)
- Push money (for retail salespeople)
- Displays and other promotional aids
- Use of manufacturer personnel and EDP forms to aid in reordering staple merchandise
- Cooperative advertising

The extreme of a sales promotion program is using television, a method that is confined to giant organizations. Larger manufacturers, of course, use national advertising in fashion magazines to help to achieve national brand importance. A fairly recent practice is to purchase the right to use a designer name as "the creator" of the merchandise.

Manufacturers, naturally, are zealous in trying to gain wide and deep market penetration. However, there is the realization that saturation selling—selling anyone who will buy—carries a contingent liability. Retail stores, particularly price maintaining operations, shy away from manufacturers whose merchandise can cause unfair retail competition or is too widely distributed. Retailers realize that too much merchandise in a trading area make it vulnerable to markdowns, particularly during times when business is slow.

The relationship between a manufacturer and a retailer is evident; they both target the same ultimate consumers. One produces for, the other sells to the final judges of what becomes fashions—the consumers.

SUMMARY

The three segments of the fashion industry have their assigned responsibilities:

- To produce the materials of fashion in order to accommodate current fashions
- To manufacture consumer-wanted styles
- To stock adequate assortments and depth of what consumers are likely to demand

Hence, the total effort must have a synergistic correlation—the result of separate sectors working together. How each sector functions is related to technology, and how the methods of production and distribution effect the efficiency of the flow of merchandise from its inception to the time it becomes the possession for whom it is intended—the final consumer.

Store merchandisers, who are part of institutions with intimate relations with consumers, must have a basic understanding of:

- How the primary and secondary stages of fashion production accommodate consumer needs
- How to develop and maintain relations with merchandise resources to fill its implied promise of fashion expertise to the ultimate consumer

chapter 4 PRINCIPLES OF FASHION MERCHANDISING

INTRODUCTION

In order to understand the origins of merchandising, one must think of an uncomplicated civilization—when each individual was self-suffi-cient. Each man and woman was in a sense an individual integrated organization. As social structures became more complex individuals bartered their products and crafts—the start of trading practices. Spe-cialization came into being. As the society became more pluralistic in its form and institutions, the sphere of individual involvement nar-rowed. Retailing, the broader aspect of selling to ultimate consumers, was in its earliest stages a comparatively simple function. What was available was saleable. To express this process in modern terms—business activities at first concentrated on the production stage. There was no need for a complicated distribution system. There was an ad-vantage in the acquisition of inventory; it was worth its intrinsic value. Overproduction was not a problem.

Fashion merchandising was a relatively unimportant activity prior to 1920—the year modern ready-to-wear was born. It did not take long for retailers to realize that ready-to-wear was big business. In a very short time, fashion apparel became the most important type of merchan-dise in general department stores. The development of apparel chains and other specialty retailers helped make it even more important. As a result of the economic opportunities of fashion, a new specialization came into being—fashion merchandising. This resulted in the centrali-zation of fashion merchandising responsibility for the production of profit. The business of merchandising fashion is ultra-competitive. De-partment stores compete with chains, mail-order organizations, dis-counters, party plan companies, junior department stores, specialty shops, and other distributors. The fashion markets are available to all. There are no consumer markets that are the exclusive and permanent property of any retailer. If a retailer's stock does not contain selections that satisfy a customer's wants or needs, there are competitors seeking to take over their patronage. Fashion merchandising must compete very effectively to realize profit goals . . . and the amount of profit is based on the ability of the retailer to secure the maximum return on investment.

In order to put fashion buying and merchandising into context, the following related terms are discussed.

- Marketing
- Retailing
- Merchandising
- Buying

MARKETING

Marketing is the umbrella under which all business efforts take place, including the following:

- Managing personnel efficiently
- Planning as the basis of decision-making
- Pricing at levels that take competition into consideration
- Communicating with consumers effectively
- Achieving maximum profit

Classically, there are nine activities of marketing:

- Merchandising activities
    1. Product planning and development
    2. Standardization and grading
    3. Buying and assembling
    4. Selling
- Physical distribution activities
    5. Storage
    6. Transportation
- Supporting activities
    7. Marketing/financing
    8. Market risk-bearing
    9. Obtaining and analyzing marketing information

Since every business, regardless of size or type, practices these activities, every organization is a marketing structure. The way these activities are performed, however, do vary with an organization's purpose and product. Hence, a retail organization is involved in all the activities of marketing, with improvisions based on the particular nature of the retail business. For example, the activity of product planning and development would suggest actually making a product. A retailer's function in this activity, however, is the planning of what to buy, for whom, when, and in what quantities.

RETAILING

Retailing in economic terms serves as a channel of distribution between producers and ultimate consumers. In definitive form, retailing is the buying of goods in wholesale quantities and at wholesale costs and selling them at retail prices, which includes the operational and administrative functions of placing the goods in the hands of end users.

MERCHANDISING

The main activities of retailing are to buy and sell goods. Simply put, the retail activities are performed by merchandising—planning, buying, selling.

BUYING

Logically, therefore, buying is one of the functions of merchandising. This activity, of course, includes the search, evaluation, and selection of the right manufacturers, those who produce appropriate merchandise for the store a buyer represents.

Fashion buying and merchandising within the meaning of our subject matter refers to the activities performed by a retail executive—a buyer who plans, buys, and sells. In the chapters that follow, discussions will include the responsibilities of buyers who do not perform all three functions.

THE SEGMENTATION PROCESS

A retailer goes through a process of market segmentation. This process includes: selecting the market he desires to sell; defining the segments within the market population to whom he wishes to make his greatest appeal; developing communications and services which help to sell and maintain the patronage of the selected market sector. Bergdorf Goodman in New York City is a fine specialty shop. The merchandise it carries is specifically directed to those customers in the middle to higher income brackets. The store offers a variety of well-styled garments at medium- to higher-priced levels. It is not interested in selling tremendous quantities at lower price levels. Proper limited assortment rather than depth is the key characteristic of this operation. It offers services which include personalized selling, fine wrappings, in an atmosphere that is conducive to the enhancement of better merchandise. When one says "Bergdorf's" the listener immediately associates higher prices and modish inventory. Policies established by management shape the character of the store. The quality of merchandise carried, the price lines, the services available, and the location, are some of the considerations that management clearly establishes from the beginning, so that in the long run the mention of the store name assumes a particular meaning to the consumer.

WHY MERCHANDISING IS NECESSARY

Since you are aware of retailing as a complex business, consider the basic function of a planned operation. Managements' decisions are basically intertwined with the wants and needs of the population it serves, particularly in the fashion field. Fashion is a reflection of the culture, which is constantly being redefined. Customer wants and needs are changing as a reflection of these changes. Without the marketing approach, a store would reflect unbalanced stocks. Buyers' selections would be based on their personal likes or dislikes and not necessarily geared to the consumer. The consumers determine the fashions of the times. A buyer may consider in poor taste such items as short shorts, string ties, garish prints on pants, and metallic leather shoes. But the attitude must be put aside in planning a stock composition. The fundamental consideration of fashion merchandising is to stock what consumers are likely to accept. Management segments the customer group(s) and the buyer is charged with catering to that group's wants. The democratic process of fashion merchandising is that merchandisers "nominate" and consumers "elect."

Recognizing that fashion is a democratic process whereby the buyer selects and the consumer elects, the entire fashion merchandising approach is directed to the end result: the composition of stock reflects merchandise which includes the right styles, in the right quantities, in the right assortments, at the right prices, at the right time, based on what is right according to consumer dictates. If all these conditions could be planned, the greatest yield from stock investment would be secured. But as in all endeavors, although the plan is for the maximum, the results may be somewhat less than anticipated.

A BUYER'S EFFORTS ARE MEASURABLE

One of the most unique aspects of merchandising is that a buyer's efficiency is entirely measurable. A buyer by use of certain standards is able to establish his own efficiency. There are three ways his efforts can be measured.

- Sales
- Inventory Results
- Profit Results

Sales

At the beginning of a given period, a buyer is armed with last year's figures. He participates with his merchandise manager in setting a figure as a goal for a given period. At the end of the period it is only a matter of record to compare current results against those of the previous period. The measurement is in units and dollars. Units are expressed in numbers. In other words, if a buyer sold 5,000 units this period as against 4,500 in the previous period, there obviously has been a gain of 500 units. In the matter of dollars, this is expressed as a percentage; and as an example, if last period sales were $10,000, a 10 percent increase would result in sales of $11,000. Whether this sales improvement could be called satisfactory is dependent upon the sales volume estimated at the beginning of the period, and what was experienced by competition in the same area. In addition to competitive figures being available, there are also Federal Reserve Bank figures* which are published by the government. Both give the buyer and the merchandise manager the opportunity to compare performance with other stores.

Inventory Results

The second measure of efficiency is the inventory results. There are three sub-divisions within this category. First, the stock turn, which is actually the sales divided by the average inventory for a given period. Second, percentage of stock shortage to sales. This situation is established once a physical inventory is taken and compared with the book figure. Performances of department store buyers are measured in part by this standard; in a later chapter we will discuss why, end also indicate whether this is a measurable activity for all types of buyers. The third is the proportion of the old goods versus new goods.

---

*Federal Reserve Bank figures are given for each district of the United States, and show percent gain or loss of volume for a given period, based on selected stores' results.

Profit Results

The third measurement is that of profit results. There are several categories under this heading—initial markup, maintained markup, gross margin, and finally net operating profit (this will be further explained in their proper relationships in Chapter 11).

The main thing to remember is that merchandising activities are not a matter of guesswork. There are definite standards and operating results to prove the efficiency of every department, and therefore every buyer. Individual effort is rewarded, and the proof of efficiency can be clearly established.

STEPS A BUYER FOLLOWS IN FASHION MERCHANDISING

The planning process of fashion merchandising and its implementation are founded on consumer orientation—knowing what people want—when they want it—at the prices they will buy it—and the quantities in which they can absorb it. The following are steps a buyer follows in fashion merchandising.

- Planning
- Buying
- Selling

First Step—Planning

Since fashion is subject to change, the planning must have flexibility. Therefore our plan is in reality an estimate, or forecast, and includes provisions for constant adjustment to actual results. Now the question is—what are we planning or estimating? The plan is based on two factors—how much we expect to sell, and how much inventory it will take to secure that selling. In terms of merchandising, we are seeking to establish an expected rate of sale, and a quantity of merchandise to support that selling. Customer orientation is important throughout.

Since there is a backlog of experience, our first norm for this planning process is that which took place—our experience. We know the location of the store, the size of the store, and therefore how much merchandise could be stocked efficiently. We also know all the communication and promotional devices used in the past to help obtain a given volume. What is new for the period ahead, or for which the plan is being made, are the *anticipatory factors.* These include: economic conditions, present market strength, new style developments, store policies, new promotional plans, and any other event that is likely to affect selling for the period.

Second Step—Buying

The second step in merchandising is the actual buying, sometimes known as procurement. The plan established the dollar and unit figures that are desired for what we hope to be a "model" stock*, a condition of adequate assortment, and a proper sales/inventory relationship. These factors hopefully will provide a desired stock turn to secure maximum profit. The planning process is the basis on which stock is purchased. Buying is done by classifications, price lines, sizes, colors and quantities up to the dollar figure which has been approved by the merchandise manager.

Third Step—Selling

We have already established the first two steps in merchandising—planning and buying. The third and final step is selling (sales promotion). This activity includes communication and promotional activity. Communicating with customers can take on many different guises, but basically it is any means that accelerates sales and promotes the image of the store. Retail promotion can be newspaper ads, bill enclosures, displays, publicity trunk showings, and any other activity that will create interest and response on the part of the consumer, and influence the purchase of merchandise.

In fashion merchandising, the promotional activity takes on a different character from other categories because we are often selling emotion, and hoping to cause the consumer to practice the factor of obsolescence. Therefore we must make our promotions dramatic and strong enough so that the consumer will want to better herself and buy the merchandise offered. If a retailer does not fulfill consumer wants or needs with his merchandise offerings and methods of presentation some other store may.

The planning, buying, and selling are responsibilities of all department store buyers. Proper concentration on these responsibilities, can make for the greatest yield.

It goes without saying that a store, regardless of size, cannot and should not, stock all the merchandise available in the market. That is the crux of merchandising—selecting the merchandise with certain characteristics that are indicative of the tastes of the customers of a store, and in such assortments, depths, and price levels that make for a proper rate of sale decided upon by the customer. The one rule that guides all buying is: "That which is purchased must be sold." The purchase of the right merchandise is more than half the job of sales.

---

*There is never a model stock. This will be explained later in the text.

THE UNIQUENESS OF FASHION MERCHANDISING

We can now concentrate on the factors that make for the uniqueness of fashion merchandising, and the reasons why the study of fashion merchandising is a subject apart from the merchandising of other products. There are major differences inherent in fashion merchandising that every buyer must understand.

- Obsolescence factor
- Higher markdowns
- Faster turnover
- Seasonal factors
- Sales Promotions

Obsolescence Factor

We have defined the obsolescence factor as a process by which the consumer rejects ownership in favor of something new in an attempt to attain a state of betterment. This is despite the fact that the discarded garment is still usable. As an example, if dress lengths are raised to above-the knee, mid-calf garments will be relegated to piles of clothing to be given away. The retailer is faced with the identical situation, except his stock of the same articles has not served any end use, even though it had the same intrinsic value when originally purchased.

The dictionary defines being obsolete as: "no longer in use; or a discarded type of fashion." Unlike some commodities, styles do not improve with age. When the fashion is "used up" the retailer is in the unfortunate position of being unable to promote excellent fabric, workmanship, and wearability. In many categories of merchandise, utility value is a strong factor; but in fashion, the emotional pull is an all-consuming element. It can readily be seen that what is not accepted becomes obsolete.

Merchandise is initially priced at a level that will make for a desired profit, and when the merchandise is accepted by the consumer there is a fulfillment of the buyer's plan. However, there are often changes in styles between the time the merchandise is originally purchased by the buyer and when it is exposed to the consumer on the selling floor. When the consumer is exposed to the merchandise, they either elect or reject it. The status of the style or styles will determine whether the consumer is willing to accept what has been selected for him. The lack of acceptance means a slow or non-selling style. The buyer, recognizing that merchandise still must be sold, is given a clear mandate to establish a new selling price to move it out-of-stock. Delaying the markdown of slow-moving merchandise results in still lower price levels. It becomes apparent that the buyer's judgment was not in line with the consumer's interest. This is every buyer's dilemma. What

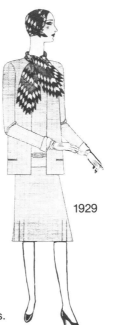

1929

Timeless classic elegance — Coco Chanel's styles.

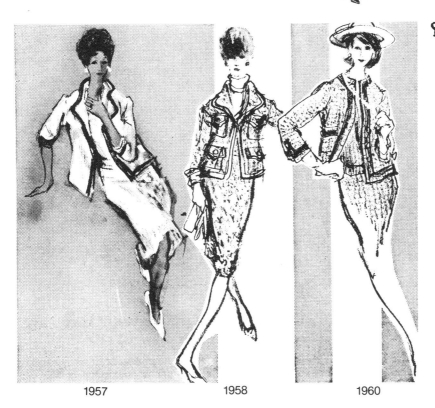

1960

1957

1958

1960

makes it more critical for the fashion buyer is the time factor because styles are as good as the acceptance level during the period of presentation.

Higher Markdowns

We could say that the obsolescence factor goes hand in hand with high markdown rate; that timing of the right merchandise at the right price levels is the key to success. You might inquire why markdowns can mean saleability. It must be understood that when merchandise is marked down, even though in the evolution of fashion the garment may be on the decline, selling is possible to the consumer who is willing to buy—if the price is right. For example, coats that were originally priced at $100.00 sold only moderately well; the buyer, in order to clear them out-of-stock marked them down to $75.00, thereby making a very strong appeal to a new set of consumers who recognize the original retail price and the value of the garment to their wardrobe. It is axiomatic in merchandising that first markdowns be deep enough so that there is an immediate appeal to consumers and that the stock can be moved out quickly.

The depth of markdowns is very often related to the time of the season. A bathing suit marked down in July is hardly earthshaking news. Customers know that July is the month when swimwear begins to take on the aspect of old age. Buyers, who are knowledgeable, markdown the poor selling styles low enough so that the price becomes attractive to consumers who are willing to buy the item at the end of the selling season either for immediate use or for use the following year. On the other hand, the same style if marked down in early June would probably not have to have a dramatic price change. Therefore, there is a strong relationship between the item and time of the season it is marked down.

Faster Turnover

Stock turnover (sales divided by average inventory), in simpler terms, is the number of times the average stock is sold over a period of time. The correlation is that since fashion is change, and by constantly changing the styles in stock, it is kept in the healthiest condition. A fact of fashion life is that consumers make it a habit of shopping in favorite departments. The consumer recognizes changes to suit her needs, obtains satisfaction from buying new styles, and also enjoyment from seeing what she would like to buy, if she were in a position to do so.

Seasonal Factors

So fashion merchandising means a constant movement of new styles, new ideas, new presentations, and always abhorring the status quo, or static position. What becomes fashionable is usually dependent upon the season of the year. Naturally in warm weather we wear lightweight clothing, and in colder weather our clothes become heavier to protect us from the elements. Generally speaking, in women's wear, there are five seasons—Spring, Summer, Transition Fall, Holiday, and Cruise. In men's wear, there are three basic seasons—Fall, Spring and Summer—although in this category particular merchandise becomes available more often. When the season is over, the merchandise fades with it. Very rarely is merchandise put in storage for the following year. It is entirely too dangerous. What is popular now may be old hat the following year, even classics change with the times. Each buyer therefore practices the established principle of that which is purchased must be sold, and there is no alternative—markdown to the price that will move the goods. Imagine the predicament a men's buyer would find himself in if he decided that since grey wool flannel trousers are classic, that there would be no need to mark them down, and that it would be wise to carefully pack them and put them in cold storage. For some years this procedure might have worked to the advantage of the buyer, even though capital would be tied up for several months, which is not a desirable situation. But what an awkward position the buyer could find himself in if there was a sudden change in styles, as was the case when pants became narrower and flared. All one has to do is to see an old movie and see Clark Gable or Spencer Tracy in grey flannel double-breasted suits with those wide pants that seemed to stand still while the star is moving forward. Classics in a general sense remain, but what changes are the particular lines and details.

In current retail practice, the variety of fabrics through technology have enhanced the seasonality of merchandise. It is a far cry from the use of only wool and cotton in men's suiting. The blends of fabrics that are available today are wide, and not totally understood by consumers. Every season the introduction of new blends makes for greater selectivity and wearability. A further complication is that mills are geared to production, and retailers are often forced into presentation of unseasonal merchandise because of market availability, and production needs. Misses' cotton dresses at highest prices are most available in January when the selection is wider and most original in styles, and prices lowest when they are in end use. This is part of market practice, and possibly will be cured some day when there is greater interest in consumer orientation; thereby giving the consumer what she wants when she needs it most.

Sales Promotion

Previously we referred to the necessity of a dramatic presentation, to encourage the consumer to better herself by buying new styles. The degree of dramatization is dependent upon the store, the price level, and its character. The name of the game is *emotion,* and causing enough of a response on the part of the consumer to do something overt, namely buy the merchandise. Lord & Taylor for example, uses a format to give an aura, rather than specifics, and hence dramatizes the merchandise so that it becomes a work of art to the beholder. The presentation is artful and in good taste. It helps sell better clothes and even more moderate clothes. The advertising in stores at lesser priced levels tends to become more specific with the lowering of price levels. Discount stores use clearly defined line art and sometimes photographs; but the appeal is at practical levels, namely the price. But in all cases, the store recognizes who its customer is, and to whom the approach is being made—the more sophisticated the store and merchandise, the more artistic the presentation. Subtlety and finesse are synonymous with the upper price levels, and the overall message to the consumer is that this is better than what you own, and we suggest you visit us to buy it. The peculiarity of retailing in the marketing process is that the transaction is consumer initiated. The store is forced to make strong appeals to the consumers to visit the establishment, to produce a bilateral arrangement—the store selects and offers, the customer overtly takes up the challenge and visits, and buys.

WHERE MERCHANDISING IS PRACTICED

Merchandising has been described as planning, buying and selling merchandise for a profit, and the examples given are related to the retailer. However, these examples have been utilized for purposes of giving simplified relationships. The fact is that merchandising takes place at several levels:

- Wholesale
- Retail
- Publications

The common denominator involved at all three levels is the need for the movement of goods—therefore planning, buying (or producing), and selling.

Wholesale and Retail Level

The *wholesale levels,* for purposes of exemplification, are grouped as one, but we know that the primary market is the one from which the materials are secured for manufacturing, and the secondary stage involves the manufacturing process. In order to keep our explanation simple we will treat both markets as one, and refer to all stages below the retailer as the wholesale market.

The wholesaler is faced with essentially the same situation as the retailer, and is concerned with two broad fields of endeavor, *sales* and *production of stock*—sometimes referred to as inventory. The difference between the wholesaler and the retailer is that the wholesaler operates at different levels. The wholesaler produces his inventory, whereas the retailer purchases it. They are both vitally concerned with the movement of goods they have either produced or bought, and selling is the objective which concerns them deeply. One might say that on both the wholesale and retail level, the sales/inventory relationship spells the level of success. Wholesalers, with the help of the retailer, are on a never ending search for that merchandise which has consumer acceptance.

One of the unique characteristics already described about the retailer is that his customer initiates the transaction; but in the case of a manufacturer, he initiates the transaction by visiting the store, or making overtures to the buyer to review, and possibly purchase his line or styles. When the rate of sale is equal to better than the norm that has been established at the beginning of the season, which is very often predicated upon production capacity, the retailer is in the throes of what he would call a successful season. It is easy to visualize a manufacturer having the capacity to make 1,000 units per week, and selling 10,000 units from March 1st to June 10th, and therefore having full production capacity for approximately two and one-half months. This would naturally ensure initial success, and with delivery to the stores, and successful consumer buying and resulting store reorders, one could easily understand that this would make for a profitable season. Conversely if 2,000 units were sold in the same period, the manufacturer would be in the awkward position of possibly overproducing. This could be disastrous because the greatest loss is suffered when unwanted merchandise is produced, since the greatest cost factor is already involved in a product, namely cost of material and overhead. It is an old cliché in the market, "I didn't go out-of-business because I undersold, I overproduced."

We have developed that merchandising activities take place at wholesale as well as retail levels, both designed for movement of goods to the ultimate consumer, and that both parties must be consumer oriented, knowing what the consumer wants, when the consumer wants it, at the price the consumer wants to pay, and how much. At both levels, there is an investment of capital in merchandise. Both levels wager on specific offerings, awaiting the acceptance of the merchandise by the consumer, and unlike political elections, there is really more than one winner. When you visit a store you see a variety of merchandise, some styles in greater depth, but most merchandise in limited assortments. If the election theory as practiced in politics were the basis of inventory, store stocks would be concentrated solely on the winners, and assortments would be very narrow and very deep. Fashions would become almost uniform, and we would all tend to look alike. But since individual tastes vary, even within fashions, stores recognize that there has to be a wide enough assortment to satisfy individual tastes.

Hence fashion stores' stocks reflect styles that have varying levels of sales appeal. A stock composition therefore consists of a well-rounded selection, one that has suitable styles for different wants and tastes. The absolute winners that we spoke about earlier are the few styles that have extremely wide appeal which stores stock in depth, and often advertise for further acceleration of sales. How deeply stock is purchased, when and how often it is advertised is all related to the store, its policies, and of course the type of customer to whom the appeal is being made.

Publications Level

The last level involved in the merchandising process is that of publication, and there are many. There are trade publications, such as *Women's Wear Daily* and *Daily News Record,* and fashion magazines such as *Vogue, Harper's Bazaar, Glamour,* and *Mademoiselle.* These publicize styles, fashions, and colors. In the case of trade publications, the information is directed to people within the industry, whereas fashion publications are sold to the consumer, and also avidly reviewed by retailers as well as wholesalers. The fashion industry is most fortunate in having a strong concentration of fashion publications and trade publications to help support their efforts. The activities are wide, and include fashion shows, in-store activities, hangtags, store-magazine relationships such as blowups of magazine ads, and contests for consumers. They center interest on selected fashion trends that very often become the fashion. Although publications do not produce goods, they are an influence on the movement of fashion merchandise. Publications' merchandising activities can be described as:

- *Planning* the selection of important themes of the season
- *Buying* specific merchandise (available from manufacturers for stores)
- *Selling* the communication of their ideas (promotion)

Therefore merchandising activities take place at the wholesale, retail, and publications levels. All attempt to secure consumer interest in styles and thereby establish fashions, which in turn can mean a desired rate of sale and profit.

SUMMARY

- A buyer is an executive of a marketing organization whose main objectives are to buy and sell goods at a profit.

- Merchandising is the planning, buying, and selling of merchandise.
- The planning, buying and selling of merchandise is the major component of the retail effort.
- Merchandising hinges on carefully calculated estimations of what consumers are likely to need and purchase.
- Merchandising results are measured in terms of sales, inventory results, and profit.
- Fashion merchandising is critical to the success of numerous retail operations because fashion volume is often the major contributor to volume and the determining factor in attaining organizational profit.
- Fashion merchandising deals with unique conditions, not the least of which is the ever-shifting moods and styles of the marketplace.
- Fashion buying and merchandising relates to a product that needs acceptance, and how that product is procured and sold.
- The "linchpin" of fashion retailing is how well the activities of merchandising are performed.

part **2**

CONSIDERING A CAREER IN FASHION MERCHANDISING

Part Two is designed to help the reader choose a career as a fashion buyer (or owner of an independent store) by explaining the competencies and personal attributes needed for a career in fashion buying and merchandising. Included in this part is a discussion of the background, organizational structure, and merchandising responsibilities associated with major retail institutions, as well as those related to resident buying and small store ownership.

When you have finished Part Two, you should be able to

- List the advantages and disadvantages of a career in fashion buying and merchandising
- Identify the types of retail institutions that employ fashion buyers
- Explain the difference between a fashion market specialist and a complete merchant
- Understand the demands of operating a small store
- Analyze your attributes and how they relate to the job requirements of a fashion buyer

chapter 5
FASHION BUYING &
MERCHANDISING AS A CAREER

INTRODUCTION

Fashion buying and merchandising and related areas have become the goal of an increasingly larger number of people of all ages and from all parts of the spectrum of our contemporary society. A recent public event bears out this statement to a remarkable degree. A one-day conference on opportunities for a career in fashion was co-sponsored by The Fashion Institute of Technology and the Office of the Mayor of New York City. Within a few days of its announcement in a single, small, newspaper advertisement in the *New York Times,* the limit of 800 people (from coast-to-coast and Canada) had been reached and 1500 others had their checks for the entrance fee returned. Although this conference was originally designed for people who were considering opening fashion-related businesses or who were in middle- or upper-management positions, young people who had not yet begun their careers also clamored for admission. This conference was so successful that it is scheduled as an annual event—an indication of the widespread interest in fashion buying and merchandising as a career. The conference leaders stressed the advisability of taking a preparatory step before entering the fashion field—comparing personal attributes to job requirements.

This chapter concentrates on the realities of fashion buying and merchandising:

- The advantages and disadvantages of fashion buying and merchandising as a career
- The personal, educational, and work-experience requirements that are essential to a career in fashion buying and merchandising
- What a fashion merchandiser should know
- Related fashion industry career opportunities

It also includes a self-evaluation examination to help you decide whether your willingness and competency match the industry's requirements.

Many students enrolled in merchandising courses want to become *buyers.* They are part of a large group who have the idea that a fashion buyer's job is glamorous—replete with travel abroad, cocktail parties, luncheons and dinners, theater-going, fashion shows, etc. They also believe that it is a career that provides rapid advancement, high pay, and constant excitement. And they are correct to some degree. However in all honesty, the fashion buyer's job demands long hours and hard work.

PERSONAL REQUIREMENTS

Management demands certain desirable traits, characteristics, and attributes. Merchandise managers like to have their fashion buyers possess some, if not all of the characteristics, that previously or currently successful practitioners of this profession exhibit.

The requirements for a buyer vary in direct relationship to an organization's function or position in the fashion marketing field. The following are some personal attributes, traits or characteristics that are commonly believed to be desirable for those who aspire to a career in fashion buying.

Expression

Buyers must express themselves easily and fluently using both the *written* and *spoken* word. The fashion buyer may be required to write fashion reports or bulletins. Buyers are required to attend, participate, or conduct meetings where the ease of verbal communication is expected.

"To Think in Numbers"

Buyers must have the ability "to think in numbers" as well as to handle figures, particularly in the rapid turnover or short life that so frequently characterizes large segments of fashion merchandise. The crux of the mathematical needs is to understand the relationship of numbers to events, merchandise developments, and profit requirements.

Getting Along With Others

Buyers, to be successful, must get along with others—their *subordinates,* their *superiors,* their *vendors,* and their *customers.* In all, the general term "human relations" is involved. It would do well for buyers in this matter to remember a simple paraphrase of The Golden Rule: "Treat others as you would like to be treated."

Enthusiasm

The ability of buyers to be enthusiastic is universally accepted as a prerequisite for success. The ability to be enthusiastic about their merchandise, their job, and their company may sound a bit old-fashioned in this day of sophistication but it is a much-desired trait.

Alertness

Buyers should develop, if they do not already possess, a keen awareness or a sense of alertness as another personal trait. Because fashion is frequently defined or is synonymous with *change*, there can be little doubt of the need of buyers to be alert to the "straws in the wind" of fashion or the changes in style.

Buyers, to be successful, must get along with others—their *subordinates*, their *superiors*, their *vendors*, and their *customers*.

Creativity

Creativity can mean the difference between a poor buyer and a good one. The meaning of creativity in this case, ranges from the ability to literally help to create or design a fashion idea, style or item to being able to recognize a style or fashion trend as it emerges. Creativity can also mean the buyer's ability to interpret things in such a way that excitement is created.

Curiosity

The ability of buyers to develop or sharpen a sense of curiosity is required. Those who can maintain this curiosity about people, events, styles, etc., will be the ones who will come out ahead time after time.

Physical Stamina and Emotional Stability

The buyer's ability to develop both physical stamina and emotional stability produces a combination that is difficult to surpass as a requirement for success in the fashion buying and merchandising field. These attributes combine to combat the daily pressures "to make figures"; to cope with frequent style changes; to deal with competition—to name a few.

A Good Memory

The ability of fashion buyers to retain what they have seen and heard is an attribute that will serve them well.

Managerial Skills

There are a number of managerial skills that are expected of successful fashion buyers. Among these are the ability to:

- *Delegate* authority and responsibility to their subordinates as well as to *follow up* on such work
- *Budget* time adequately so that the many diversions and occurrences during the working day can be taken in stride
- Be *flexible*
- Be *fair, tactful,* and *impartial* which is required by their subordinates as an essential quality in their day-to-day relationships
- Act on one's own *initiative*—which distinguishes one buyer from another, and involves the ability not only to be a self-starter, but also to carry through a project without constant supervision

You will find the attributes and other requirements needed to become a buyer restated in a checklist at the end of this chapter, and thus will be able to evaluate your candidacy for a job as a trainee in fashion buying and merchandising.

EDUCATIONAL REQUIREMENTS

It is safe to say that a college education for a career in fashion buying and merchandising has become the rule rather than the exception. It would also appear that this field of higher education may be found in community or junior colleges as well as in the upper division of many colleges and universities, both private and publicly-owned and operated.

The reason for the tremendous growth of fashion merchandising education seems to depend, in part, on the widely held premise that a college education with its inherent by-products of learning and research, generally helps to develop a young person who is able to reach intellectual maturity more readily and rapidly. There is a great deal of available statistical data to indicate that the college graduate advances in the business world faster, and earns more money sooner than secondary school graduates. During the past several decades, many marketing-oriented business organizations have given greater credence and preference to hiring college graduates from schools with programs in retailing, merchandising or marketing. Employers reason that such young people *know* what they want from the very start—a career in fashion buying and/or management. However, many leading retailing organizations are prone to accept graduates with degrees in the liberal arts areas, as well.

We must point out, however, that educational requirements for a career in fashion buying and merchandising can, and do vary with general economic conditions. When the economy is loose or booming educational requirements tend to be lower; when the economy is tight, firms tend to raise their educational criteria and are more selective. The day when a hard-working plugger, just out of grade school, starts as a stock boy and works his way up to buyer of the department, is all but gone. The educational requirement for entry jobs leading up the rungs of the executive ladder to buyer and/or merchandise manager is definitely college-oriented—only the degree or amount of education required varies.

A retail organization neither looks for nor requires people to have the greatest talent, ingenuity, or creativity. The real need is for people with intelligence, perseverance, and an ability to get along with others. Every store has a training program; the larger the store, the more sophisticated the program. Such programs may be categorized as:

- The Formal Program
- On-the-Job Training Program
- The Job Rotation Program

The Formal Program

The formal program includes classroom activities conducted by professional training personnel. Usually, the mornings are spent in class, and the afternoons on the selling floor, or in some other buyer-related activity such as receiving goods or recording data in one of the divisional merchandising offices. The trainees are also given projects, problems, or assignments to supplement this practical experience.

On-the-Job Training Program

In this type of unstructured program, the trainee is assigned to an entry-level job and learns through practical experience while under the supervision of a seasoned executive.

The Job Rotation Program

On a regularly scheduled basis, the trainee is sent to a predetermined area, division or department for a specifically designated period, which could be from several days to several weeks. Very frequently, this training program is coupled with the Formal Program. When the programs are combined, the trainee is working on the days or hours he/she is not in class. In this program, the trainee gains not only valuable experience but is also given an insight into the workings of the entire store.

Whatever the type of training program used, it is directed to the education of the beginner so that sufficient knowledge can be absorbed over a specific period, which can lead the trainee to the position of assistant buyer, and eventually to buyer. Most organizations make every effort to train the new employee to become as productive as possible as soon as possible.

WORK EXPERIENCE REQUIREMENTS

Those concerned with the recruitment and employment of buyers are in virtual agreement—previous consumer-oriented work experience is important in the job-selection process. Emphasis for job selection is placed on those individuals who began to work part-time and/or during summer vacations while still in high school in consumer-oriented jobs. Students are urged to start or continue such employment while in college, if possible.

Among those consumer-oriented occupations that enjoy favor with employment executives and the one held in the greatest esteem is *selling.* What is learned from and about customers in selling is so unique and valuable that not only retail executives prize this experience but individuals in manufacturing, advertising, and other related industries as well. The experience garnered in selling, particularly in our current consumer-geared world, is invaluable to future buyers. They learn to interpret the wants, needs, and demands of customers as well as how to act to fulfill them. There is also another valuable by-product of such selling experience—executive action experience—which will serve the future buyer/manager in good stead. It cannot fail to give the young person an insight into the everyday problems of the ordinary rank-and-file worker.

Finally, we must also be cognizant of another aspect of the need and value of work experience. There is an unmistakeable trend among young people to become entrepreneurs in the fashion business. For this type of a fashion buying and merchandising career, work experience is an absolute must. One of the greatest reasons for failure in small business is the lack of adequate experience in that business.

ADVANTAGES OF A CAREER IN FASHION BUYING & MERCHANDISING

In addition to prestige as an advantage for entering the field of fashion buying and merchandising, there are a number of other specific advantages to encourage those who are contemplating this profession as a career.

Remuneration

A buyer's salary is generally considered good, if not above average, when compared to similar positions in other industries. The important aspect of the buyer's remuneration, however, is that it is almost always directly in proportion to the buyer's level of achievement. In most cases, the buyer's earnings are measured on a sales/profit formula and thus the rewards are based on their own efforts and accomplishments.

Advancement

Opportunity for buyers to advance in rank, prestige, and pay may occur in two ways. First, they may climb the ladder of success and reach the next position in the merchandising hierarchy, which is generally *divisional merchandise manager* (the supervisor of a group of buyers in one merchandising area, e.g., sportswear). In some merchandising companies, a buyer could be promoted to a divisional manager in a branch store operation. In such cases, the next step would be promotion to divisional merchandise manager in the home store. From the divisional merchandise manager's position the field opens up, but quite narrowly of course, to the top merchandising positions; in some cases, divisional merchandise managers may also be promoted to branch store directorships.

As we pointed out, buyers are paid on their ability to produce profitable sales. The second form of promotion involves moving the buyer from one department to another department where the sales volume/profit possibilities are greater.

Opportunity for Economic Growth

There are splendid opportunities for economic growth because the knowledge and experience accumulated as a fashion buyer is often applicable to other forms of business. Buyers are sought after for marketing, sales promotion, and the sales management positions in textile and fashion manufacturing firms.

Opportunity for Personal Growth

The daily opportunities to deal with all levels of personnel; to watch people—particularly people whom the buyer is attempting to influence or to induce into some form of action—provides great mental stimulation. The need to think and reason in order to arrive at the proper course of action is a most stimulating preoccupation; the need to make decisions, which sometimes involves great sums of money is not only exciting but self-satisfying. There is a great personal satisfaction that comes from being able to live well, afford luxuries, pursue expensive hobbies, etc., because of the salary level. Life as a buyer is exciting—it is never humdrum. In fact, there are rarely two days that are alike. The buyer's job has many varied facets that preclude boredom.

Transferability

The ability of buyers to find employment is never determined by geographical boundaries or restrictions. It is a common practice for buyers to find new positions through connections "in the market" or through specialized executive search organizations in the United States or Canada. Changing jobs is relatively simple, in normal economic times, if the buyer is willing and able to relocate. Buyers' transferability frequently results in a promotion because when they do change jobs, they may often secure a better or higher-paying position elsewhere.

Travel

Most buyers have an opportunity to travel to shows and fairs, and to markets on an international as well as on a national basis. Most buyers look forward to visiting distant or foreign sources of supply because of the "fringe benefits" that travel almost always provides.

Self-expression

We have previously indicated the need for the buyer to be creative on the job as a prerequisite for success. Fashion buying itself opens many opportunities for the encouragement of creativity, because the selection of merchandise reflects a combination of intuition, knowledge, and judgment. The difference between store's fashion inventories can be a matter of buyer creativity.

Equal Opportunity

Even in these days of attempting to obtain sexual equality and the women's liberation movement, there are very few industries that can match the record of freedom from sexual prejudice that has been the case in fashion buying and merchandising. The sex of the individual rarely comes into the employment or promotion picture insofar as the buying job is concerned. In fact, if *there is* any preference shown, it generally favors women.

Lifetime Career Opportunity

Unlike many other industries which can and do experience extremely wide fluctuations of business, and sometimes even disappear from the economic scene, fashion merchandising generally provides an opportunity for a lifetime career. It can almost be said that there will always be a need for fashion buyers.

DISADVANTAGES OF A CAREER IN FASHION BUYING & MERCHANDISING

While we are more than convinced of the desirability of a career in fashion buying, it would be less than honest if some of the disadvantages of such a career were not made apparent.

Hard Work and Long Hours

The buyer's job is not an easy one; in fact, buying is *hard work.* While the hours and/or work week have been shortened considerably so that they conform to the normal industrial pattern, there are periods when longer hours are required as part of the job.

Competition

Competition is the bane of the buyer's life. In one instance there is the competition from other buyers for display space, newspaper ads, television or radio commercials, bargain tables, etc. In another sense, there is always competition for the limited spending power of the store's customers; and of course, there is competition for the store's money to make special purchases. We must not forget the constant competition for promotion or advancement among buyers.

Pressure

Buyers are ever "under the gun" insofar as their sales/profit performances are concerned. There is an ever-mounting pressure to meet and/or beat last year's figures. This pressure is always present and never subsides.

Accountability

One of the terms in current vogue in business circles is "accountability and responsibility." In the buyer's case, this not only means running a profitable department, but also being accountable and responsible for the expenditure of large sums of the store's money for merchandise, supplies, sales promotions, etc.

Travel

There are buyers who dislike travel that market visits—international and national—entail. They complain about the tremendous amount of work to be done in a short period of time; being forced to absent themselves from their families; and the burden of catching up with their work when they return.

CURRENT & FUTURE CAREER OPPORTUNITIES

Any attempt to summarize and predict current and future career opportunities is, at best, a hazardous task. There are so many variables that enter the employment picture, to name just one—the state of the national economy. However, we strongly believe that the following aspects of fashion buying and merchandising warrant consideration in embarking upon a career in this field.

1. Fashion buying is a well-paying job.
2. Fashion buying permits the individual to satisfy the desire for self-expression. It is a position where creativity and decision-making are well rewarded.
3. Fashion buying is one of the cornerstones of the gigantic retailing industry, and as such, there are a number of socio-economic factors that encourage one to believe that there is a bright future ahead.
   - The population of the United States is increasing at a steady rate. According to the 1980 U.S. Census, our population has risen to 230,000,000. By 1990 a conservative estimate indicates that there will be approximately 250,000,000 Americans available as a potential market for merchandise.
   - The population growth factor for the period 1970–1980 ranges from 9 to 11 percent (depending upon what base figure is used). Although this growth rate was the second slowest in our his-

tory, it does relate to more people with improved levels of disposable income. The prediction by knowledgeable sources is for a continual broadening and enlarging of our middle class —the most important area of our population for possible customers of fashion merchandising.

- The annual Gross National Product (GNP) exceeds $3 trillion and is heading for a $4 trillion level. Fashion apparel purchases are 8 to 10 percent of disposable income depending upon what merchandise is included in apparel. These statistics are presented merely to illustrate the size of fashion merchandising in our economy.

4. Retailing is a changing and dynamic industry. Many traditional forms of buying and selling merchandise have already left a permanent imprint on the field—the rise and decline of many discount stores and boutiques as retail institutions; the dramatic growth of shopping malls; the continuing expansion of branch stores; and the heavy population shift to the Sun Belt states are just a few examples. And it is easy to predict that the immediate future will offer similarly innovative changes which are bound to occur because consumer needs and tastes are changing.

WHAT EVERY FASHION BUYER SHOULD KNOW

The primary objective of merchandising is obviously to sell. This sounds like an oversimplification, but the fact of life is that some people opt for a fashion career because of a personal interest in clothing. They believe that a love of fashion and good taste are the prerequisites for a professional career in fashion. The real world is a commercial one in which the buyer is an agent for the ultimate consumer. It is the customer's taste that causes acceptance and therefore fashion.

The techniques and the procedures of fashion buying will be explained in later chapters, but it must be noted here that the merchandising activities are: *planning, buying and selling.* These activities are based on the knowledge *for whom* and *why* merchandise will be purchased.

The techniques and procedures are easily comprehended by a trainee. What is difficult is the part of professionalism, the specifics, that result in the assortment of merchandise that yields desired results— maximum profit within the guidelines of a store's philosophy.

This is in essence a review of the professional requirements of buyers. The most important realization is that a trainee is exposed to knowledge from the first day of employment. Professional knowledge is gained through apprenticeship. How long it takes to become a buyer depends upon the trainee's level of achievement, the opportunities available, and the evaluations of the candidate.

A buyer viewing the line.

Knowing Your Product

Every professional buyer must know the product with which he or she is dealing. The very activity of acting as an agent for the consumer implies professional understanding of merchandise offered for sale. The fashion buyer must know the elements of fashion merchandise. The specific values of fashion merchandise are:

- Silhouette
- Texture
- Color
- Details

The buyer must know why the combination of these four elements make for consumer desirability at a given time. In addition, the buyer must understand why a style is priced at a given level. In some buying practices the buyer is practically a production expert and should be aware of the various costs and expenses involved. This is particularly true of buyers who make large commitments in advance of the selling season. Examples are the buyers for J.C. Penney, Sears, or Montgomery Ward who practice specification buying. Similar situations exist for buyers who travel to other countries to develop styles (another form of specification buying).

Product knowledge in fashion merchandising is not a small subject, not when the variety of fibers and fabrics is so vast. Even experts cannot trust touch to determine the composition of fabrics. The buyer, after completing textile courses, is in the best possible situation. A curious person, without textile training, can refer to text books and secure help

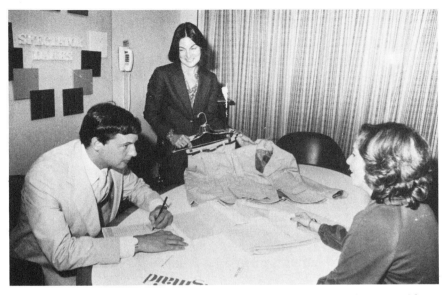

Budgeting a proposed order.

from experts in the field. What fabrics cost, how they perform, and how they are suited for specific garments are all part of a fashion buyer's professional knowledge.

One word of caution—although every buyer should be an expert about the store's customers, it does not follow that a buyer should be a designer and a fabric expert possessing more knowledge than the manufacturers. It is encumbent upon the buyer to evaluate offerings for store purposes, extend advice to important vendors when required, but not to re-do lines or purchase fabrics. It is only within the buyer's scope of duties to assume the role of "complete" expert, when buying for specification purposes. Even then, it should be a joint venture with a measure of respect extended to those who are making an investment of time, money and effort, in their areas of expertise.

Understanding Fashion Dynamics and Principles

Fashion dynamics and principles separate the beginners from the experts—one of the aspects of fashion buying and merchandising that requires knowledge and a smidgen of intuition. Fashion movement is evolutionary, the signs are always there, but the trick is to recognize them.

The evolutionary process includes a rise, peak, decline and abandonment. At what stage a style is best suited for a store is dependent upon the store's goals and relationship to their customers.

Obviously, a store that is a fashion leader needs fashion when it is on the rise; conversely, a mass merchandiser seeks merchandise that has general acceptance. The latter stage affords the opportunity to buy and sell at the desired lower price levels.

The following are considerations and principles known to fashion buyers:

1. Fashion is evolutionary.
2. Fashion is cyclical (but the return always features some newness that dates the older versions).
3. Buying is for selling.
4. Customers make fashion.
5. Acceptance levels of fashion vary (fad, fashion, classic).
6. Different fashion for different customers (i.e. young styles vs. mature styles).
7. Price is not fashion.
8. Fashion depends on place.
9. The nature of fashion is change.
10. Fashion can filter down or seep up.
11. Fashion does not improve with age.
12. The cardinal sin of fashion merchandising is to be out of trend.
13. Maximum fashion selling requires a communication process which includes: display, accessorization, advertising and personal selling.
14. Fashion reflects lifestyles.
15. Timing of fashion stocking is dependent upon who you are (the store).

The overriding consideration is that fashion is for people, and their acceptance of it is really what it is all about.

Knowing Your Customer

As a professional, the buyer's knowledge of the customers and their wants and needs should be examined constantly and reevaluated. Knowing customers from a statistical point of view is relatively easy. There are numerous sources and materials that can make any beginner an expert. Demographics (vital statistics about people such as age, income or education) afford the opportunity to realize the quantitative and qualitative factors of the population to be served.

In this era, the buyer is faced with a new dimension—opinions, attitudes and beliefs of customers. This study, psychographics, is a relatively new one and important to the buyer. Briefly, the lifestyle of people has changed dramatically during the past several years. How people view themselves, how they wish to express themselves, and how they want people to see them, are attitudes that have surfaced and have become important to so many people. These values have resulted in new definitions for the wearing of clothing and the polarization of fashion attitudes.

A buyer must also consider that a large segment of potential customers are female heads of families, career women and financially independent. The degree of role playing for women has changed and has created new attitudes towards apparel.

One must come to the conclusion that fashion reflects the affluence of a society. A society on the "go" demands fashion that reflects the style of individuals of a group activity. Role playing is not confined to any group, an examination will reveal pertinence to almost every class or group of society. The difference from former eras is that we have more, do more, and want more.

Naturally, rules or principles cannot cover all conditions about people. There is only one group that is not affected by new conditions—people who do not care about style and buy only for service needs.

The crux in fashion is change because people change. The difficulty is that the changes are really not overt in the sense that they are apparent and easily discerned.

In today's world of fashion the professional must be concerned with the signs that point to new trends and eventually new fashion ideas. It is important for the practitioner to understand what people do and what they will wear when they do it.

This leads us back to a fashion term—*consumer orientation.* How does one study the consumer?

A buyer must be involved in life; read newspapers and periodicals; attend events, whose audiences are the store's customers as well as the customers of other stores. In other words the buyer must be an aware, well-rounded individual.

Knowing Your Resources

Fashion markets are located in many cities of the United States, but the biggest and most important is located in New York City.

One of the advantages of the United States fashion merchandising structure is the communication system at every market level: information from the textile market to manufacturers, from manufacturers to retailers and finally, from retailers to consumers. There is no other fashion communication system like it in the world.

Part of the communication system is the availability of publications, including free pamphlets, that list all the manufacturers for every classification of fashion merchandise. Some booklets list the tenants of specific buildings in the fashion market. So, there is no secret of who makes what.

Knowing what manufacturers make is not the answer to a store's needs. Each store must build its own list of manufacturers that best serves its purposes. Although stores have many resources in common, there are no two stores that buy from the identical roster of manufacturers. Resources may have similar characteristics but there are reasons why one will be favored over another (the reasons for selection of resources will be discussed later).

Buyers are usually familiar with most major markets. Some visit and buy from several, although New York City is the one utilized by all. In addition, many buyers use and visit resources in foreign countries. Of course, stores provide the buyer with a list of resources through past records, resident buying offices, and information exchanged with sister stores, to mention a few.

Obtaining names and locations of resources is as easy as reading. Professionalism involves knowing how to best use the best resources for the store. It is the buyer's job to search, evaluate, select, negotiate and review resources to establish profitable relationships.

Understanding Management Goals and Policies

Every store tries to appeal to and to attract a desired segment of customers. The practical application is what is often referred to as the *marketing mix.* The marketing mix is a combination of elements that include:

- The location of the stores and its physical attributes
- The merchandising policies—assortments, depth, prices, timing
- The policies of personnel availability, services, and all communications to customers.

Buyers are made aware of the store's goals, practices and customers at the beginning of their employment. This information is initially implanted by the training department and later by the merchandise manager. Every store, therefore, has its own policy that is spelled out by the management based on their interpretations of the patronage motives of their customers. Mass merchandisers utilize mass-marketing techniques (price appeal, lack of service, etc.), but higher-priced stores utilize their own marketing techniques (fashion timing, designer names, etc.) designed to appeal to the characteristics inherent in their targeted marketing group's value system. Among the policies that are spelled out are those merchandise attitudes affecting:

- Price levels (price points)
- Price zoning (price ranges of most importance)
- Assortment of stock (variety of customer choices)
- Depth of stock (amount of stock)
- When and how to promote merchandise (includes what and why)
- Markup
- Markdown (difference between original and new lower price levels)

The reader can easily establish the difference in marketing techniques by visiting different stores and doing observational research. It is recommended that a student of fashion merchandising observe one store from each of the following store categories:

- Discount store
- Fine specialty shop
- Department store
- Variety store
- Apparel chain store

It will become apparent that top-level management must capture a certain segment of business through selected strategies and tactics. The fashion buyer once educated to the goals of the store's category must stay within the parameters established by management.

Understanding Basic Merchandising Arithmetic

The aim of business is to make a profit. Profit can only be achieved if the retail price is sufficiently higher than the cost of merchandise. This is basic. An important decision is how much higher shall the retail price be than the cost of merchandise. In a well-operated retail establishment, all phases of merchandising are calculated mathematically and expressed in percentages and ratios. The retail price is determined by a planned percentage that will include the cost of merchandise and various costs of doing business. The reason for using percentages is to establish norms or standards that are easily calculated and evaluated. Management is in the position to easily judge performance against standards.

One does not have to be a mathematical genius, but it is necessary to have a facility with numbers in order to understand relationships. Following are some important areas that require an understanding of mathematical relationships.

1. Return of merchandise
2. Markup
3. Markdown
4. Stock turnover
5. Stock/sales ratio
6. Cost of goods sold
7. Gross margin
8. Operating expenses
9. Net return
10. Merchandise classification importance

All of these terms are relevant to sales and show either a goal, standard, or level of achievement.

RELATED FASHION INDUSTRY CAREER OPPORTUNITIES

In addition to fashion buying and merchandising, there are numerous entry-level opportunities in the fashion industry that could be considered as rewarding alternatives for those with special talent or preference for merchandising-related positions. **Figure 5–1** lists the numerous entry-level jobs in various aspects of the fashion industry as a whole, including retailing (which will be discussed in detail within this text).

Entry-Level Opportunities in the Textile Industry

ASSISTANT STYLIST Sets up appointments for the stylist; acts as liaison with mills; works with clients and salespeople in the stylist's absence; keeps records.

ASSISTANT CONVERTOR Assists the convertor in supervising the various processes in the conversion of greige (grey) goods to the finished fabric; maintains production and inventory records; acts as liaison with mills; expedites shipments and flow of goods; follows up on work, especially by telephone. Requirement—good at details and figures.

QUALITY CONTROL TRAINEE Checks fibers, yarns, fabrics, and apparel to see that specifications are being observed; identifies problems and works with production personnel to correct them. Requirements—an analytically minded person, good at details and follow-up.

SALES TRAINEE Jobs in the fiber, yarn and finished fabric aspects of the textile industry. Training programs are built around either formal classes, on-the-job training, job rotation, or a combination of several methods (learn by checking customer orders insofar as deliveries are concerned). Accompanies sales personnel to clients or assists sales personnel in the showroom; works with swatches.

Entry-Level Opportunities in the Apparel Industry

SHOWROOM SALES TRAINEE May also act as a receptionist; deals with buyers on the telephone and in person; writes and follows up on orders; keeps records; shows and sells garments; occasionally models garments.

ROAD SALES TRAINEE Duties are quite similar to showroom sales trainee; must be able to cope with the problems and demands of traveling alone and acting independently.

MARKET LEVEL	PRIMARY PRODUCERS (fibers & textiles)	SECONDARY PRODUCERS (apparel manufacturers)	RETAILERS
Merchandising Related	Assistant Color Coordinator Market Research Assistant Public Relations Assistant Advertising Department Assistant Trade Association Aides (e.g. Wool Bureau, Cotton Council)	Showroom Model Assistant and/or Showroom Sales Assistant to Marketing Sales Manager Assistant Public Relations Department Assistant Advertising Department	Assistant to Market Research Manager Research Department Assistant
Marketing Staff or Selling Related	Assistant Stylist Production Assistant Mill Liaison Assistant Fashion Office Assistant	Assistant Stylist Assistant to Merchandise Manager Assistant to Piece Goods & Trimmings Buyer Assistant Fashion Coordinator	Executive Trainee Assistant to Assistant Buyer Assistant to Buyer/Department Manager Assistant to Branch Store Coordinator/Department Assistant Head of stock Buyer Office Assistant Buyer Chain-Distributor/Planner Trainee Assistant Fashion Coordinator
Sales Promotion Related	Advertising Department Public Relations Trainee Junior Copywriter Direct Mail Assistant Media Trainee Advertising Agency Liaison Trainee	Sales Department Trainee Advertising Department Trainee Public Relations Department Trainee Sales Promotion Assistant Junior Copywriter	Junior Copywriter Special Events Assistant Public Relations Assistant Display Assistant Sales Promotion Assistant

Figure 5–1. Entry-Level Opportunities in the Fashion Business.

Figure 5–2. List of Auxiliary Careers in the Fashion Business.

Assistant to Account Executive
Junior Media Analyst
Public Relations' Assistant
Junior-Trade Paper Reporter
Junior Magazine Reporter
Assistant to Fashion Consultant
Junior Copywriter

A SELF-EVALUATION CHECKLIST

This self-evaluation checklist concludes this chapter and is an opportunity for you to compare your personal attributes with those required for fashion buying and merchandising. You set a passing grade!

	Yes	No
Are you generally able to speak freely before a group?	—	—
Are your verbal skills adequate?	—	—
Is your written English adequate for communicating with your peers and your superiors?	—	—
Do you consider yourself a person who has good analytical ability?	—	—
Can you think in numbers as well as in words?	—	—
Do you have a command of basic arithmetic skills?	—	—
Do you get along with others? With your peers? With your superiors?	—	—
Do you consider yourself an enthusiastic person, particularly when you are doing things that you like?	—	—
Do you believe that you are alert most of the time?	—	—
Are you generally aware of change around you?	—	—
Do you frequently come up with creative ideas?	—	—
Are you curious about things in your surroundings?	—	—
Do you have good physical stamina?	—	—

Do you believe that you are emotionally stable? — —

Do you feel that you can work under pressure? — —

Can you meet deadlines? — —

Do you have a good memory? — —

Do you readily assume responsibility? — —

Do you believe that a supervisor should be able to delegate authority to others without difficulty? — —

Do you believe that the easiest way to get things done is to do them yourself? — —

When it comes to ideas or changes, are you flexible? — —

Can you budget your time to the best advantage? — —

Do you consider yourself to be fair and impartial? — —

Are you a tactful person? — —

Do you frequently take the initiative in social or business affairs? — —

Do you believe you have or are now pursuing an educational course that will lead you to achieve your present career goals? — —

Have you gained enough experience in your chosen career field to help you achieve a good background? — —

SUMMARY

Fashion merchandising offers the dedicated person an opportunity for a viable career. The rewards are numerous and self-satisfying, but like every activity in life, one must be willing to pay the price. In this case, the price is dedication, hard work, and the willingness to learn the "calendar." This last involvement takes time, because there are up to six calendar seasons to a year; once around means one exposure per season. It takes several exposures to understand the dynamics under different conditions; hence, the time for real training takes years, not days or months.

The decision to enter the field of fashion merchandising should be based on objective information. The fundamental considerations of a fashion merchandising career should be an investigation of job responsibilities, job description, and above all, a self-analysis.

chapter 6

THE ORGANIZATION OF A LARGE RETAIL STORE

INTRODUCTION

The previous chapters concentrated on an understanding of the meaning of fashion and its concepts and an orientation of the career aspects of buying and merchandising, including what it takes to be a successful buyer. This chapter, after focusing on the organization structure of large fashion enterprises, furnishes a relatively complete survey of where various types of buyers are employed and their responsibilities.

The growth of the fashion industry, the increase in sales volume, the frequency of style changes, the influence of the national economy and lifestyles on the attitudes of fashion were factors in the change of the size of stores. The size of stores grew into the large specialty and/or department store that is familiar to us today.

Figure 6–1. A Large Retail Store Pyramid.

OWNERS
(stockholders and
board of directors)

TOP MANAGEMENT
(president and
vice presidents)

MIDDLE MANAGEMENT
(divisional merchandise
managers and buyers)

FRONT LINE SUPERVISORS
(department managers)

RANK AND FILE EMPLOYEES
(sales supportive personnel
and sales personnel)

At the completion of this chapter, there should be an awareness of the importance of the organizational structure for a large retail establishment. The material in this chapter examines:

- The difference between a *line* and a *line and staff* organization
- The major divisions of a large store
- The growth and importance of the branch store
- The need, importance and role that the several staff supportive services play in buying and merchandising activities
- The buyer's relationship to non-merchandising activities such as receiving and marking.

Figure 6–1, exemplifies the broad levels of a large retail organization as two structures—*line* and *staff.*

THE LINE ORGANIZATION

To understand how a large fashion retailing establishment is conducted, study the typical line organization structure in **Figure 6–2,** which has been adopted by many companies with variations to suit that company. The purpose of such an organization chart is to show the lines of authority and responsibility for each of the six divisions, the relationship of one division and its personnel to each of the other five—the interaction of people and jobs.

The line of an organization is a position or department with assigned responsibilities required to carry out the main functions of a business. In **Figure 6–2,** the line divisions are:

- Finance or Control
- Sales Promotion
- Personnel
- Operations
- Merchandising
- Branch Store

The line concept was modified later to separate the main division into two sectors: *line and staff* (discussed later in this chapter).

Let us now examine this organization chart. We begin at the very top of the chart where for simplicity sake we have grouped the stockholders (if any), the board of directors, and the major officers of the company under *Top Management.* We feel that this is sufficient for this text since it is not intended to be used in a course of business organization and management. Now, reading from left to right, let's examine each division and its relationship to the other divisions.

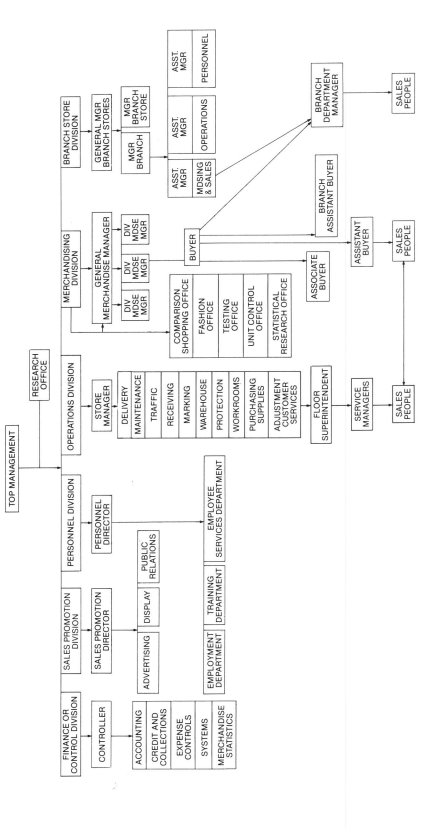

Figure 6–2. Organization Chart for a Large Department and Specialty Store (adapted from Mazur Plan).

Finance or Control Division

The finance or control division is usually headed by a *controller* or *treasurer;* broadly speaking, it has five main areas of responsibility:

1. *Accounting*—handling such details as accounts payable, payroll, insurance and taxes.
2. *Credit and Collections*—handling accounts receivable (charge accounts and other credit plans; charge authorizations; bill adjustments).
3. *Merchandising Statistics*—for those who need to make decisions —such as buyers—department profit and loss statements; open-to-buy figures.
4. *Research and Development Systems*—of the forms and other systems used throughout the store.
5. *Expense Control*—concerned principally with controlling the spending activities, advising on current budget status, and keeping the departments or divisions within their allotted funds.

Sales Promotion Division

The sales promotion division is headed by a *sales promotion manager.* This division has three main areas of responsibility which usually are handled as three separate departments.

1. *Advertising*—working with the buyer and/or the divisional merchandise manager to plan all the sales promotion events, using newspapers, mailing pieces, radio, television, etc.
2. *Display*—working frequently in coordination with the advertising department and the buyer, to plan and execute window and interior displays; to execute the signs used throughout the store.
3. *Public Relations*—this is a broadly based department that handles the news releases, which make up the publicity function. Special events that invite free publicity, and involve the store and the public, are also handled by this department, e.g. art shows, contests, school relations, women's clubs or parades.

The sales promotion division works principally with the merchandising division in promoting the *merchandise* that the store has to sale. However, another important function of this division is to promote the *character* and *image* of the store as a whole.

Personnel Division

The personnel division is involved with every division and department in the store. It is headed by a *personnel director* and usually consists of three major departments.

1. *Employment Department*—recruiting, screening, interviewing, selecting, and placing all new applicants for employment. In addition, this department frequently handles all the employee records, employee evaluations and ratings, promotions, transfers, dismissals, etc.
2. *Training Department*—training the newly hired employees in the store's policies, systems and procedures, rules and regulations, benefits, selling techniques, etc. Also concerned with re-training regular employees and training those who have been selected for promotion.
3. *Employee Services Department*—sometimes called Employee Benefits Department. This department handles such activities as the store's house organ, employee special events, hospitalization, pension plans, and similar fringe benefit areas.

The personnel division's relationship to all the other divisions on our organization chart is obvious. It is concerned with staffing all the departments of the store, training these employees and servicing them once they have been employed.

Operations Division

The operations division, sometimes called the management division, is headed by the *store manager,* who has the task of handling a myriad of store activities:

1. Delivery, wrapping, and packing goods purchased by customers.
2. Building maintenance—which includes repairs, alterations, cleaning, and other housekeeping jobs.
3. Receiving, marking, and traffic—preparing incoming merchandise for sale.
4. Warehousing—both resale merchandise and supplies which are needed to run the store.
5. Protection—supervises the security forces that protect the store's property, merchandise, customers and employees.
6. Workrooms—those areas that alter, repair, or manufacture goods for the store's customers.
7. Purchasing supplies and services, fixtures, etc.
8. Customer Services—through the floor superintendents and/or the service managers; handles such customer relations as refunds, adjustments, exchanges, and complaints. In addition, these service executives control such activities related to salespeople as their working hours, lunch hours, days off, and vacations.

In its relationship to the other divisions, the operations division affects the merchandising division the most, but the services it provides touches all aspects of the store by its maintenance and supply purchasing functions.

Merchandising Division

Since this is a book dealing with merchandising and since this division is primarily concerned with planning, buying and selling, it should come as no surprise to the reader that your authors regard this as the most important division on the organization chart.

This division is headed by the general merchandise manager, who in turn, delegates some of his immediate supervisory responsibilities to a number of *divisional merchandise managers.* Each divisional merchandise manager is in charge of a group of departments that are generally related, e.g., mens' and boys' sportswear. Each divisional merchandise manager therefore supervises the activities of a number of buyers, each of whom head a merchandise department. In large department or specialty department stores where the emphasis is on fashion merchandise, instead of one sportswear department with one buyer in charge, there could be several departments, each with its own buyer,

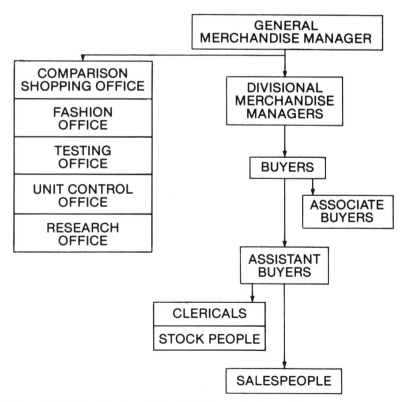

Figure 6–3. The Merchandising Division of a Large Store.

such as junior sportswear, budget, sportswear, and swimwear. Most departments will have a number of junior executives assisting the buyer. The buyer has varying degrees of responsibilities for the salespeople upon whom this entire pyramid rests, as exemplified in **Figure 6–3** of a typical merchandising department.

The merchandising division has a number of important, primary functions:

- Planning
- Buying
- Pricing
- Promoting
- Selling

In relation to the other divisions, the merchandising division touches and is touched by them all. In fact, it can almost be said that they all exist primarily to serve the merchandising division.

Branch Stores Division

The branch stores division is generally headed by a *manager or vice-president for branch stores* who, in turn, supervises the activities and responsibilities of each *branch store manager.* The branch store usually has three major departments each headed by an assistant store manager who reports to the branch store manager.

1. Operations Division
2. Personnel Division
3. Merchandising and Sales Division

The *operations division* performs many of the same functions discussed previously. Other functions such as purchasing of supplies, receiving and marking are handled by the main store.

The functions of the *personnel division* are practically identical with those discussed previously.

In the *merchandising* and *sales division,* the main store buyer most often does all of the buying for both the branch and main stores. Merchandising activities are conducted from the main store through the branch store assistant buyer who works with the branch store department manager. The branch store department manager is the first-line supervisor responsible for sales in one or more departments in the branch and who directly supervises the activities of the department's sales personnel.

Figure 6–4. Organization Chart for a Large Store Using Line and Staff Concept (three-division plan).

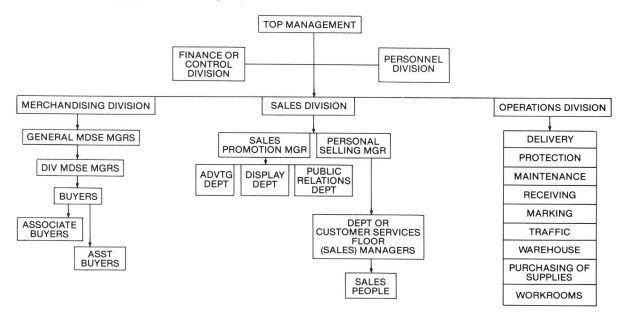

THE LINE & STAFF ORGANIZATION

There is another version of store organization that deserves our attention following the previous study of a line organization. This is called the *line and staff organization plan.* **Figure 6–4** is an example of such an organization chart for a large store.

As we did in our previous evaluation of the line organization, let us examine **Figure 6–4**—the *line and staff organization.* Again we have consolidated the owners of the store and its major officers into *Top Management* at the top of the chart. Reporting to top management, but devoting all their time and effort as staff organizations to servicing, assisting, and advising the other three main divisions are the *finance or control* and the *personnel divisions.* Their activities and functions are identical to those previously discussed under the line organization, but in this instance they are both divisions designated as staff organization. Therefore, the modification of line and staff identifies the line as that part of the organization that is involved in the main activities of the business: buying, planning, and selling; the staff are those store divisions that act as advisory units to aid the line, viz: personnel and control.

In this study, we are chiefly concerned with the activities of the *merchandising, sales* and *operations* divisions.

Merchandising Division

The merchandising division is organized almost the way it was organized under the *line* and *staff* plan with one major exception: it is no longer responsible for the supervision of the salespeople and their activities.

Operations Division

The operations division is also organized almost the way it was under the *line* and *staff* plan with two major exceptions—it is also not responsible for supervising salespeople nor for customer services.

Sales Division

The sales division emerges as a relatively new concept and is composed of those functions involved in the sale of merchandise. It should be noted that the sales promotion division which had equal status on the *line* and *staff* plan has disappeared from the chart and is now a function of the sales activities. However, the sales promotion area has the same responsibilities and the same three subdivisions—advertising, display, and public relations.

It is in the area of personal selling that a new concept is emerging. Here, the responsibility for selling, formerly shared by or split between the merchandising and operations divisions, is now an independent organization whose first line supervisors are in charge of both customer service and the salespeople.

BRANCH STORES

The branch store is a post-World War II phenomenon that had a profound effect on the size of a department store, the manner of operation, and the responsibilities of merchandising. (This subject is handled in great detail in Chapter 7.)

SUPPORTIVE STAFF SERVICES

As indicated earlier in the large department store organization chart, there are a number of staff services that assist the fashion buyer in making better buying and merchandising decisions. The following is an examination of the functions of these staff-assisting services.

Fashion Office

The Fashion Office, headed by a *fashion director,* is usually found in most department stores and larger specialty department stores where a good part of the store's volume is derived from the sale of fashion merchandise.

The fashion director and assistants are charged with the task of collecting fashion information from every obtainable source. This information is then summarized into usable data by which the merchandising and sales promotion executives can be made aware of fashion trends or fashion forecasts.

Another aspect of the Fashion Office's work entails planning, directing, and producing fashion shows for various departments, particularly as a prelude to their major selling seasons. Such fashion shows are given not only at the store but also at women's clubs, luncheons, etc.

The Fashion Office also tries to educate sales personnel who have the final responsibility of passing on fashion information to the store's customers. This is usually done by holding department or division meetings with the salespeople, preparing bulletins, or fashion shows.

Finally, the Fashion Office attempts to produce a coordinated fashion story or image for the entire store. Otherwise, the store would emerge as a series of fashion departments, each headed by a buyer who is in business with a fashion idea of her or his own. The fashion director works hard at presenting a single fashion story to the store's customers and sees to it, for example, that there are shoes, bags, gloves, and other accessories to coordinate with the dresses, coats, and sportswear.

Steeped in the fashion trends of the time, the fashion coordinator and the staff in the Fashion Office try to influence and assist the buyer in purchasing those styles to suit the clientele for which they are being bought.

Unit Control Office

Since the details of unit control will be discussed in Part Three of this text, the purpose here is to make the reader realize that in large stores there is a staff bureau that gathers information from sales tags and from stock figures and by the use of electronic data processing equipment to furnish the buyer with daily information on inventory, selling results, merchandise receipts, purchases, etc. It should be noted, however, that stores use this centralized unit control office to give the buyer and management information that can be useful in helping to determine merchandising and buying courses of action. In smaller stores, the buyer is responsible for gathering and keeping the department's own records to determine their buying patterns.

Comparison Office

Most large stores prefer to set up an independent staff of shoppers whose primary job is to check the various departments of their own store and compare their merchandise, stock assortments, prices, services, etc. to those of competing stores. The results of the comparison shopper's investigation are reported to the buyer and/or the divisional merchandise manager who then has an objective point-of-view about his departments.

It is then left to the buyer and divisional merchandise manager to take such action as they deem necessary. In addition to this actual comparison work, these shoppers may also bring in new, different or out-of-the-ordinary merchandise that they may have spotted in competitive or other stores. As part of their regular procedure, comparison shoppers frequently buy merchandise with previously provided funds to illustrate or prove their point.

In smaller department stores, where there is no provision for a comparison shopping office, the buyer may delegate these duties to the assistant buyer or to a senior salesperson.

• Testing and Standards Office

Only the largest stores and chains can afford the expense that a testing bureau requires. And even those who did maintain such an office, with its expensive equipment, have closed their own facilities and use outside, commercial or college testing laboratories. Among the leading proponents of the use of this facility are: J. C. Penney, Montgomery Ward, and Sears, who use it as a merchandising strength.

Whether the store has its own testing office or resorts to professional testing firms, the need for such services exists to:

1. Help the buyer set specifications and standards for use by vendors in manufacturing merchandise that is acceptable, particularly if the merchandise is labeled with the store's own brand.
2. Help develop new variations of products or to improve existing ones.
3. Help to train salespeople by giving the buyers information on government regulations, labeling, etc.
4. Help police the store's sales promotion claims for merchandise offered to the public.
5. Test merchandise constantly for defects in order to reduce or avert customer complaints.

✍ Research Office

Again, only the largest stores, chains, and buying offices can afford the expense entailed in establishing and maintaining a research office. As a rule, there is no limit to the breadth and scope of the research office's work where they do exist. Among the services rendered may be:

1. Population and income surveys on the possibility of locating a new branch store in any given area.
2. Store layout designs.
3. Store and/or department customer traffic studies.
4. Analysis of the statistical data resulting from store merchandising and operating activities.
5. Studies of customer preferences in good and services.
6. Revision of, or developing new forms, systems, or procedures that make up the paperwork needed in merchandising and operations.

Where there is no research office in the store, the services are shifted to the particular office or department that is most affected by the need for such research. But a specially created office, manned by trained, experienced, skillful research personnel who are not troubled with the every day operation of a merchandising or management department, can be much more effective.

Resident Buying Office

A thorough study and evaluation of the resident buying office will be discussed later, however for this section, suffice it to say that the resident buying office should be regarded as a supportive staff service in the same vein as the preceding supportive staff services.

ACTIVITIES RELATED TO THE MANAGEMENT OF MERCHANDISE

In the final section of this chapter we have a need to examine some non-merchandising activities. In writing the purchase order, the buyer, sets into motion a number of activities related to the management of merchandise that directly or indirectly involves the buyer as well as those who assist him. This section will examine the following such management activities:

- Traffic
- Receiving
- Marking
- Distribution

Traffic

The buyer has a definite responsibility when completing the purchase order for specifying the means of transportation of the merchandise from the vendor to the store. Traffic (management) is the title given to

Neiman - Marcus, October 1913

Macy's, New York, 1940s (facing page, top).

Neiman-Marcus, Dallas, 1913 (facing page, bottom).

Bloomingdales, New York, 1931 (top).

this phase of retail management in order to bring these goods into the store quickly, safely, and as inexpensively as possible. Incidentally, the Traffic Department also handles the R.T.V. (Returns to Vendor) which involves merchandise that could not or should not be sold for a variety of reasons. If the buyer's responsibility for traffic is puzzling to the reader, it is easily clarified. First, the buyer must consider the cost of transportation as an additional cost of merchandise. Secondly, there are many occasions when speed in delivery is helpful, if not mandatory, and the proper routing or the type of transportation is thus essential. Actually, however, these two reasons can conflict because in giving the vendor transportation instructions, the buyer has to consider the need for speed versus economy.

The Traffic Department, where it exists in large stores, is generally part of the Receiving Department; if there is no Traffic Department, the Receiving Manager or one of his assistants usually performs this function. The principal duties of the Traffic Management Office include:

1. Working with buyers in standardizing incoming merchandise shipments. They can literally teach the buyer how to use that part of the store's merchandise purchase order that provides for shipping instructions and to do so with a combination of speed and economy.

2. Working with the buyer (and sometimes directly with the buyer's vendors) on packing as well as shipping instructions. For example, a knowledge of less-than-carload rates can save the department considerable transportation charges if small shipments are consolidated. A good traffic staff knows a great many other packing and shipping methods that could be very helpful in reducing costs.

3. Creating written shipping guides for use by both the buyers and the store's regular sources so that when an order is placed with one of these vendors, there is no need for detailed shipping instructions. The buyer can merely refer the vendor to these standardized shipping instructions on the buying order, e.g. "as per Bennett Department Store Shipping Guide." The manufacturer is then automatically held responsible for obeying these instructions regarding packing, routing, shipping, insurance, etc.

4. Investigating and filing claims against the vendor, the shipper, or both, when notified by the buyer or by the receiving room that merchandise has been damaged or lost in an incoming shipment. Settling such claims is important to the buyer because merchandise, and therefore the department's money, are involved.

5. Saving the department and the store considerable money by a continual watch on transportation charges on incoming shipments. In this phase of traffic management, the buyer's order and/or the store's standard shipping guide are compared to the

vendor's following those instructions. Where the manufacturer fails to follow shipping instructions, the Traffic Department enters a credit against the manufacturer's invoice and the difference is deducted before payment is made.

Those stores that give sufficient attention to the matter of proper traffic management will find this area of the retail management of merchandise to be rewarding in many ways.

Receiving

Once the merchandise is ordered and the shipping and packing order issued, the buyer must wait for the goods to arrive at the store. In all but the smallest stores, this next activity is called receiving and the Receiving Department, while actually part of the Operations Division is nevertheless a heavily merchandising-oriented function. It must be apparent that merchandise ordered by the buyer for resale to the store's customers must first be received at the store; next the order must be sorted and counted; and then price marked in accordance with the buyer's instructions; and finally brought to the sales area.

Another aspect of this merchandising-connected store function is the need for the best possible system for physically receiving and checking incoming merchandise because:

1. A good receiving system will insure that the merchandise will be guarded from possible theft or pilferage, and preserved from being soiled or damaged until it is sent to the buyer's department.
2. A good receiving system will prevent merchandise from being kept too long where it cannot be sold and thus cause potential markdowns or loss of sales volume. It has the necessary flexibility built in to get the merchandise to the floor on time.
3. A good receiving system will never delay the payment of invoices so that the buyer will always be able to take legitimate cash discounts and anticipation where permitted.
4. A good receiving system will prevent poorly made or damaged merchandise from reaching both the sales floor and the customer by accurately checking all incoming goods. This will eliminate customer returns and the ill will they frequently engender.

While there are no typical receiving procedures that can be labeled as models that all can follow, the following centralized receiving department principles are generally accepted by the industry:

1. The receiving department manager reports to the store manager as head of the Operations Division. But in checking the merchandise, he has a relationship to the Finance or Control Division

whose function it is to pay the invoice once it is approved by both the buyer and receiving room personnel. Another liaison is with the Merchandising Division in marking the goods and getting it to the selling floor.

2. In the actual, physical act of receiving the merchandise shipment, the following procedures are usually observed:

   A. The receiving clerk checks the merchandise in its cartons or on hangers against the freight bill of lading or memorandum that accompanies the shipment. If the number of cartons or hanging pieces tally, and they appear to be in good condition, the driver is given a receipted copy of the bill and the truck is permitted to leave.

      If there is an apparent shortage or if the merchandise is damaged, the proper form is completed or a notation made on the bill of lading and acknowledged by the trucker. This is used at a later time to make a claim by someone in the Traffic Department.

   B. Whenever possible, the receiving clerk should weigh the total shipment to check on the freight charges.

   C. The receiving clerk, after entering the shipment on the permanent record of the department, prepares a receiving record which is sometimes called an *apron.* This is also frequently attached to the bill of lading and all the information available concerning the shipment is entered on it as the receiving process progresses.

   D. The shipment is then assigned to a section of the receiving department for actual checking of the merchandise, which is done by first opening the cartons; then sorting the merchandise by type, size, style number, etc.; and finally the merchandise is examined for its conformity to the quality standards of the store.

   E. There are several methods of checking or counting the merchandise and the method used by one store can vary greatly from that used by another. The following are some of the choices available:

      (1) *Blind Check Method*—The clerk lists all the merchandise in the shipment on a blank form. This is checked against the invoice, which he has not seen up to this point because the invoice is usually mailed by the manufacturer as the shipment leaves his plant. Those who advocate this system believe it has many advantages but they are especially impressed with the fact that the Blind Check insures accuracy, since it prevents clerks from accepting the manufacturer's figures—the clerk never really knows what to expect and must be doubly careful.

(2) *The Invoice Method*—The clerk uses the manufacturer's invoice which either comes with the shipment or has already arrived by mail and is on file. The clerk merely verifies the count of the merchandise against the invoice. It is a simple and quick way to check the merchandise and it requires little or no experience.

(3) *The Buyer's Order System*—The clerk uses a copy of the buyer's purchase order which is on file in the receiving department. The clerk checks the incoming merchandise against this order copy. Where the shipment is complete the clerk signs the copy indicating this fact. Where only a partial order is received (a normal occurrence) this is indicated in the proper space on the order so that an actual record is kept on the order until it is completed.

A well-organized receiving department is one that is laid out carefully and efficiently to insure a rapid and smooth flow of merchandise from receiving dock to the sales floor. This involves a well-engineered, spacious layout complete with good marking tables and other equipment for counting and marking. In the larger department stores there is the possibility that some of this work can be mechanized by use of conveyor belts.

Marking

Once the merchandise has been received and checked, it is ready to be price marked. It is the buyer's responsibility to give the marking personnel the information necessary for the price ticket; of course, the first order of business is the price of the merchandise itself. All other information such as size, color, style number, manufacturer's number, classification of style, is readily available from the buyer's order copy. The size and type of store as well as the merchandise it carries will be among the considerations given to determining which type of price marking is best suited for the store or for that type of merchandise. However, there are several generally accepted rules for marking goods:

1. It should be easily removed once the customer has purchased the item and intends to keep it; it should not damage merchandise.
2. It should be easily and inexpensively done.
3. It should be clear, easily read, and identifiable with the store and the department.
4. It should contain sufficient information in code to enable the Unit Control Office to secure the information easily and satisfactorily.
5. It should provide the ability for easy remarking.

There are a number of ways to mark merchandise and this again may vary greatly even within the store or the department, depending upon a variety of factors. These marking methods include:

1. *Bulk Marking*—no prices or tags are affixed to the merchandise itself for several reasons, e.g., it is too small, too inexpensive, a price rise is expected. The merchandise is priced by a sign which is placed over the bin, rack, counter, etc. that holds merchandise.

2. *Hand Marking*—may be done either in the department or in the receiving room. The merchandise is marked by hand by crayon, pen, pencil, rubber stamp, gummed labels or by hand-attached pin or string tickets.

3. *Machine Marking*—a number of machines automatically print and affix folding pin tickets to the merchandise. There are also machines that print hangtags primarily for larger garments, which are affixed by special tools to the merchandise.

4. *Manufacturer's Markings*—also known as *pre-marking* or *pre-ticketing*—a method whereby the store either sends the manufacturer tickets that were previously printed in the store to be attached to the garments before shipment or the manufacturer uses his own ticketing. Manufacturers frequently extend this service because the item may be specially packaged, and adding tickets in the store after it is factory packed could necessitate spoiling the packaging.

5. *Professional Marking*—an innovation in the marking field. This relatively new system came about with the establishment of professional marking companies such as Posners and Gilberts. These companies, for a fee, will receive, check, and mark incoming fashion merchandise, on hangers or in boxes, and consolidate the merchandise from different manufacturers into one large shipment to the store. They usually give fast service and this is especially valuable for fashion merchandise where speed in getting these goods to the floor is so essential. It also can eliminate the need for a receiving and marking area and staff or reduce them to a minimum.

6. *Re-marking*—the process of either changing the price by raising it (additional markon) or lowering it (markdown); or an item may require re-marking because the original price tag has been damaged, lost, or become shopworn. The re-marking process differs from store to store. Some stores centralize this process and require the merchandise, with proper paperwork attached, to be returned to the marking room for new ticketing. Other stores have new tickets made up to be attached to the merchandise in the department itself. There are special hand-held machines available for use on tickets which have enough space to print a new price and clip off the old one in a single operation.

Distribution

After the merchandise has been marked, it has to be moved out of the receiving area to make room for other incoming merchandise and to avoid congestion and confusion. The already-marked merchandise has for its objective the selling floor, for immediate integration into the department's stock; or it may be destined for the store's various branches in conformance with the buyer's orders; or it may be necessary, for a number of reasons, to put these newly-marked goods into a forward or reserve stock area for future use; or it may be stored elsewhere for much later use, perhaps because the merchandise was bought at a special price inducement for early delivery.

Another aspect of distribution in this era of multi-branch stores is the process of transferring merchandise from branch to branch, or from branch to main store or vice versa. The proper use of the unit control system can give the buyer and those who assist in the buying a relatively rapid idea of what merchandise is selling well and where. It is not an uncommon practice towards the end of the selling season to consolidate remaining merchandise at one branch or at the main store for clearance purposes rather than to leave bits and pieces of a previously full line of merchandise.

SUMMARY

This chapter should have familiarized the reader with the manifold operations necessary to run a large department store and, additionally, enumerated the number of jobs available in such structures. It should be clear that a large retail organization demands interrelationships of all personnel to make available the kind of merchandise that suit customers' needs and services.

A large retail organization, of necessity, demands the assignment of responsibilities to different divisions and their personnel. The *line* and *staff* evolved to assure the concentration on corporate objectives and the evaluation of efforts to achieve them. To establish the most efficient operating conditions, *staff* departments are designated responsibilities to aid the *line* to reach established business goals.

An interested reader should study the typical organizational chart included in the chapter to see the interrelationships of departments, personnel, and to identify a position or department as a possible career goal.

The buyer is part of the retail *line* because the major responsibility of planning, buying, and selling—basically the main features of a retail organization.

7 THE FASHION BUYER'S RESPONSIBILITIES IN A LARGE RETAIL STORE

INTRODUCTION

A buyer is a merchandising executive, one of whose major responsibilities is to pick and maintain a stock of appropriate merchandise for the store's customers. Obviously, the type and size of the organization that employs the buyer will make a great difference. Not only in regard to the selection of merchandise, but also in regard to the many other responsibilities that make up the buyer's total job.

We shall examine and analyze the buyer's responsibilities* as a whole from the viewpoint of the *larger* store. We have selected the larger retail store for two reasons:

1. There can be little doubt that this classification of buyer offers the most job possibilities.
2. The larger store usually requires the greatest number of responsibilities and gives us the opportunity to study the subject from the widest aspect.

PLANNING

Although a buyer's job is that of a merchandising executive who is charged with selecting merchandise for customers, a critical evaluation of the buyer's work reveals that there are many more responsibilities. One of the most important of these is her responsibility for *merchandise planning*, which will be discussed in detail in a subsequent chapter. However, some mention need be made here of some of the buyer's major

---

*The buyer's responsibilities in working with the resident buying office are discussed in detail in Chapter 9 and will not be covered in this chapter.

planning responsibilities. Working with the merchandise manager and in keeping with general store policies, the buyer must plan stocks, both in the main store and in its branches, so that the character of the department and its merchandise objectives are achieved. The buyer is also responsible for input in the preparation of the Six-Month Buying Plan by maintaining a knowledge of updated fashion trends; current market conditions; economic factors in the community served by the store; an analysis of the department's unit control and other records of the previous seasons; and the demographics and psychographics of the store's present and potential customers.

BUYING

The buyer is responsible for the actual buying process, which includes choosing the resource, selecting the merchandise, securing the best terms, and actually placing the order. As a corollary to these responsibilities, the buyer is also charged with the duty of following-up on the delivery of the merchandise ordered. The buyer is responsible for determining not only *what* and *when* to buy, but also *where* and *how much to spend.*

1. To purchase merchandise in accordance with the approved buying plans and within the limits of the currently available open-to-buy.
2. To maintain balanced stocks of fashion-right merchandise desired by the store's customers, at the right price and time, and in assortments consistent with the maintenance of the department's image and character.
3. To establish and maintain effective buying relationships with approved merchandise resources.
4. To deal with merchandise resources in the fairest and most ethical manner.
5. To obtain the most advantageous terms compatible with legal and trade restrictions.
6. To secure the participation of resources for important special events by obtaining merchandise that is specially priced, with advertising allowances, etc.
7. To arrange to have the store's name included in the credits or by-lines of the resources' national advertising, if part of the store's policy.
8. To seek the cooperation of the resources to obtain the most favorable terms for the payment of invoices, a means to add profit to the department.
9. To secure manufacturer's selling aids such as hangtags, merchandise labels, informative brochures, and ad mats.

10. To organize the trip to the market.
11. To keep in contact with the resident buying office. (The buyer's responsibilities in working with the resident buying office are discussed in Chapter 9.)

PRICING & PROFIT

A major area of the buyer's responsibility revolves around pricing and profit factors. Thus, the buyer's responsibility for securing the best possible markup on all purchases as well as for markdowns and other price changes, in order to keep them within the approved standards. In line with the store's policies, the buyer's responsibility also extends to adequately stocking the department's price lines and price zones. In order to have accurate merchandise figures, the buyer's responsibility involves keeping the department's book inventory as correct as possible and to supervise the semi-annual physical inventory as well as any stock counts that may be made from time to time to verify the accuracy of the stock records.

BUDGET

Another responsibility of the buyer concerns the department's *merchandise budget* activities. The buyer is responsible for submitting plans to the merchandise manager to revise merchandise plans when the department's stock and sales figures, market conditions, and any other factors indicate a need for such a revision.

CREDIT

The current American way of life is solidly built on a foundation of *credit*—particularly *retail credit.*

In view of this widely held concept of giving customers instant purchasing ability, coupled with a promise to pay later, the American consumer has immediate possession and use of merchandise. The buyer therefore must have both a knowledge and an understanding of the reasons for the use of credit by the store's customers. Since credit has become so essential an adjunct to selling the department's merchandise, the buyer must not only know about the store's credit operation but also must be able to communicate this information to the department's salespeople. The buyer is responsible for training the salespeople to suggest the use of charge or credit plans in order to close the sale or to increase the size of the sale. Salespeople also need to be trained to encourage customers to open a credit or charge account, which helps to influence customer patronage.

SELLING

In general, the buyer is responsible for the *selling* activities of the department. Although there has been some movement in retailing circles to separate buying from selling, particularly in stores with multi-branch operations, the buyer is still responsible for department sales. It is expected that the buyer will provide merchandise information such as new styles, new colors and new materials, as well as guide the department's salespeople in professional sales techniques. This will be done primarily through meetings with the department's personnel on a regular basis.

In other areas involving selling activities, some buyers have the responsibility of providing proper customer coverage by obtaining sufficient salespeople for the department. It is the buyer's responsibility to secure sales aids from merchandise resources such as point-of-sales displays and to arrange visits by their vendors' salespeople to stimulate sales in their own lines.

SALES PROMOTION

We will examine the buyer's responsibilities for sales promotion in greater detail in Part Four of this text. However, this section on the buyer's responsibilities would not be complete if we did not examine, albeit briefly, the buyer's sales promotion responsibilities.

1. To plan and supervise the execution and maintain effective departmental displays of timely fashion items, using appropriate fixtures, coordinated display techniques, and effective signs. (Permanent displays or fixtures are designed and approved by the display department and merchandise manager, respectively. Reference is made to approved movable displays commonly used by fashion departments.)
2. To be aware of fashion items that lend themselves to sales promotion.
3. To select merchandise for advertising and displays and to provide both the advertising and display departments with enough information, sufficiently in advance, to enable them to make a proper presentation.
4. To check advertising proofs and department signs to verify prices and descriptive information; to be certain that the merchandise information is in compliance with Federal Trade Commission regulations and Better Business Bureau standards.
5. To make every effort possible to ensure that the merchandise being advertised or on display is in stock in the department in an assortment adequate to meet reasonable customer demands.

6. To take steps to ensure that the department's salespeople, as well as the sales supporting staff, are informed in advance of all sales promotion activities, such as advertisements, window displays, newspaper and magazine publicity, television and radio ads. The staff should be in possession of information regarding merchandise assortments, merchandise facts, selling points, deliveries, and other pertinent information.
7. To evaluate response to the promotion, maintain records of the department's advertisements and the sales response in order to use such information in planning future promotions.
8. To cooperate with and to use the information and services provided by the Fashion Office.
9. To work with the sales promotion department and the divisional merchandise manager in planning for the department's sales promotions.

INVENTORY SHORTAGES

The buyer has a responsibility for *protecting* the department's merchandise from loss by training salespeople to be alert insofar as merchandise thefts are concerned, as well as to prevent damage to merchandise by its improper handling by customers. The buyer is required to supervise personnel in order to assure that the department's stock is properly handled and accounted for during movement in the department's stock areas, on the selling floor, in the marking and receiving room, and finally, to the delivery department.

One of the buyer's principal responsibilities is that arising from *inventory shortages* and methods of controlling them. While it is true that inventory shortages are caused by a multiplicity of factors, some of which are entirely out of the buyer's ability to control them, the net result of such shortages is reflected in the gross margin of the department's profit and loss statement. This is one of the standards used by management to appraise the buyer's worth to the store.

With the increase of multi-branch stores, the buyer's ability to personally supervise efforts to lower inventory shortages has become almost impossible. Not only has the buyer and those who assist the buyer much more to do in the buying and merchandising areas, but time and distance factors only permit one major avenue of pursuit—exercising as much supervision and guidance to all concerned, to be constantly aware of where and how inventory shortages occur and to try to reduce them.

Many inventory shortages are caused by clerical work—manual or electronic-data-processing—involved in keeping the perpetual inventory records of the department. The buyer's job here is to exercise constant vigilance in supervising this paperwork and impressing those concerned with it to be careful and accurate. There are so many places where transfers of merchandise; poor receiving practices; return-to-vendor records; markdown record, etc., can contribute to possible shortages that it boggles the mind.

The department's salespeople can also contribute to the inventory shortage problem by mistakes involving lost price tags. A buyer's vigilance in this area can reap large rewards. Putting the wrong price on saleschecks, where used, is one more factor arising from selling floor errors. Most large retail firms take a storewide physical inventory semi-annually and it is when this actual count of the merchandise is compared to the *book* or *perpetual* inventory that shortages become apparent. It is certainly to the buyer's advantage that such department inventories be done with meticulous care. There are so many opportunities for lax or tired people to omit items or to take the amounts on closed boxes for granted, for example, that the buyer must exercise a tight-ship discipline or face potential trouble.

While all of the previous causes of inventory shortages probably account for most of the potential shortages, we must not overlook the possibility of theft of the department's merchandise, by customers (shoplifters) or by employees (pilferers). Consultation with the store's security organization can frequently be helpful in tightening weak spots.

VENDOR RELATIONS

While it is an established truism that good merchandise resources belong to the store, not to the buyer, nevertheless, the buyer's responsibility for good *vendor relations* is clear. It is common knowledge that a buyer is as good as the vendors who make up the department's sources of merchandise. In any given merchandising segment, vendors will come and go but the new buyer will discover what the older buyer already knows: The department's principal sources of merchandise are usually firms who have had a long and profitable tenure with the store. It stands to reason that such resources must have been doing something right all along to withstand the ravages of time in such a highly volatile industry. Alexander Pope, the famous 18th century English poet, said it very well more than two hundred years ago: "Be not the first the new to try nor the last the old to put aside."

If it becomes necessary for a buyer to discard an old resource, there should be valid reasons apparent to the buyer and vendor. In general, the buyer should avoid favoritism; for example when a buyer sees sales personnel in the store's sample rooms or at the buying office when in the market. Another safeguard for good vendor relations is making a comprehensive department merchandise resource plan with the approval of the divisional merchandise manager. Such a plan lists a number of basic vendors for each major segmentation of the department's merchandise. This plan not only ensures proper merchandise coverage to support the character of the department but it also helps to establish closer working ties with vendors. Another aspect of vendor relations is in the matter of merchandise returns. While vendors never appreciate returns, they tend to take them in stride if they are fair; however, unfair returns by which a buyer tends to rid her stocks of poor- or slow-selling merchandise which was bought in good faith, can cause serious repercussions.

When all is said and done, however. key resources should be developed and nurtured for as long a period of time as they are reciprocally profitable. If the vendor loses his "touch," the buyer has an obligation to give the vendor helpful criticism; if there is no appreciable improvement, then the buyer must replace his key resource.

PRIVATE LABEL MERCHANDISE

Another modern merchandising responsibility concerns private label (brand) merchandise. Until quite recently, many customers preferred nationally branded merchandise which they had gotten to know and trust over a period of time. They believed that they knew the manufacturer and could depend upon the firm's reputation to stand behind its products. Of course, this confidence was accomplished through frequent use of sales promotion media.

Now, however, many major retailers and/or their buying organizations have developed private label merchandise—sellers' brands—backed by the retailer's reputation in the community of its customers. The customer is often inclined to act favorably towards the store or private brand, not only because it is frequently lower in price, but it can be higher in quality than the national brand.

The buyer must study the sales performance of the branded merchandise in the department and be aware of its growth or decline.

BRANCH STORES

One of the great changes in recent years in fashion merchandising has been the growth, both in number and importance, of the *branch store.* The post-World War II population explosion that led to the growth and development of large suburban areas by most large cities of the United States, also created the need for large retail stores located in the central city areas to move with their customers. In these past thirty-five years the growth of the branch store has been nothing short of phenomenal. Accordingly, a study of this area of fashion merchandising is deemed an essential part of this discussion on the large retail store.

As central city shopping districts decline in importance and the outlying or suburban areas continue to grow, buying fashion merchandise for these branches becomes an increasingly important responsibility of the buyer. For example, Burdine's Department Stores, an important division of Federated Department Stores in Miami, Florida, has established a large number of branches and continues to open new ones as this Sunbelt area continues to expand. One branch alone known as the Dadeland Mall now has an annual volume of over $100 million. This branch store is so large that it is run by 84 department managers, whereas the typical Burdine's branch has just 24 department managers; its work force which averages about 1,900 far surpasses employment levels at the other Burdine's stores which typically have 300 workers. Thus it can be said that the buyer's responsibility for branch stores is a relatively new, flexible area that demands new alternatives to new problems.

The following discussions illustrate some of the types of branch stores' organization plans currently in effect.

Basic Main Store System or "The Brood Hen and Chick" System

The N.R.M.A. has classified one type of branch store organization as the Basic Main Store System. Informally, this is also known as "the brood hen and chick" method. Under this system, the main or downtown store is conceived as the "hen" and the branches are visualized as her "chicks." Chronologically this was one of the first forms of branch store organization and the branch stores were merely treated as if they were more like members of a chain. This chainlike image was carried out by having the branches centrally controlled in all phases of merchandising and operations. This brood hen and chick idea also depends on the fact that in such a setup, there are not many branches involved; the branches are relatively modest in size; and that they are all within a reasonably short distance from the main store. The entire merchandising operation is completely centralized with the buyer at the main store.

Multi-Unit System

The N.R.M.A. has given the title of Multi-Unit System to another type of branch store organization. This plan involves some degree of autonomy for each branch store, because there is good probability that some, if not all, of the branches are located quite a distance from the main store. In some instances involving this autonomous unit system, it is quite possible that the branch store has approximately the same sales volume as the parent store. J. L. Hudson, Detroit; Abraham & Straus, New York; Burdine's, Florida, are several examples of leading department stores who have such high sales volume branches. The Multi-Unit

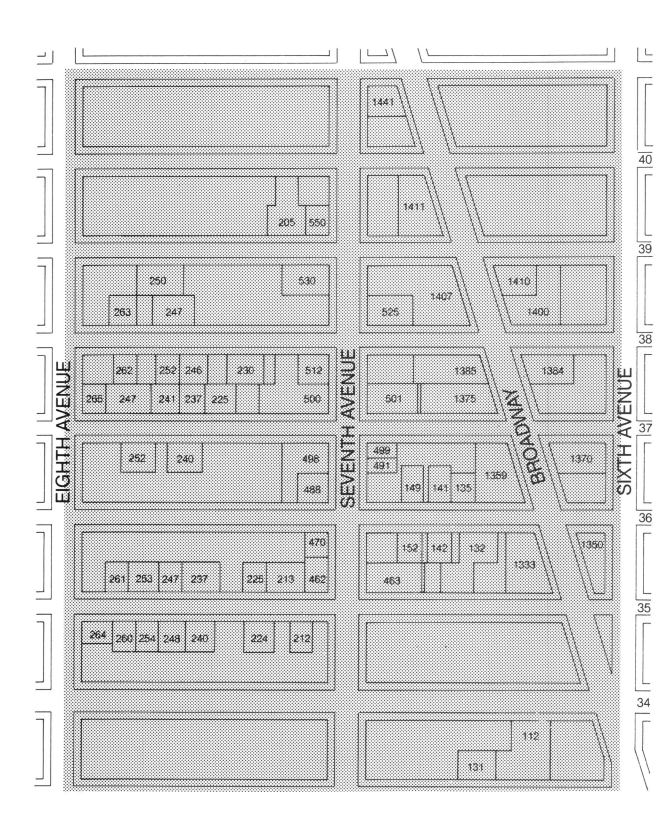

System is also used when there are too many branches for a brood hen and chick setup—the main store buyer just could not physically handle the job.

While there is a great deal of variation in the autonomous branch store setup, it can be safely said that the following generally applies:

1. In its highest form, the branch store can have its own buyers, for a number of departments; and in reality, the branch is big enough to be an independent store.
2. More commonly, however, the main store buyer is in charge, but acts in a merchandising capacity; each branch has department heads for each department and they have varying amounts of autonomy in merchandise selection. For example, there are arrangements that allow the branch store department to re-order; select merchandise that best suits the branch store's customers; and prepare local sales events.

A map of New York City's garment center. Shaded area (here and on facing page) indicates the various manufacturer's offices and showrooms available to buyers of men's, women's and children's wear.

Centralized Administration System

There is another type of branch store organization that is commonly known as the Centralized Administration System. It is in use in stores with many branches. The main store buyer is primarily concerned with buying and merchandising and is *indirectly* involved with other responsibilities commonly assumed by department store buyers. Two large retail organizations—Hecht's, Washington, D.C., and Macy's, New York, are examples of operations within this type of branch store organization. Under this centralized administration system, the main store buyer's responsibilities include:

1. Securing suitable merchandise for all the branches, if necessary, on an individual basis, to meet local needs.
2. Distributing merchandise to the branches in accordance with a continual flow of unit control information.
3. Planning and buying merchandise for the branch stores for group sales promotions and/or individual branch store local sales promotions.
4. Managing the inventory at each store in a profitable manner.

The top management of the store will decide which of the three types of branch store organizations is best suited for the company; and they may make changes or variations as the situations or the times dictate. Since there is no apparent industry-wide movement for branch store standardization, the buyer will have to learn to accommodate to the method chosen by management.

As we indicated at the start of this section, branch store buying and merchandising patterns are still in a flux and in unstandardized form. It will take more time for this era of expansion to end.

The buyer should learn by careful analysis of each branch's figures how they differ not only from the main store, but also from each other. There can be radical differences from branch to branch due to such factors as the income levels, ethnic makeup, color and/or size preferences of the customer; recreational or leisure-time and cultural activities of the customer; and competition from local stores or branches of other retail organizations.

The buyer should set up good communications between the main store or "flagship" store and the branches. Such communication is particularly improved by the buyer's attempts to visit the branches regularly, in order to meet personally with the branch store manager, department manager, and the sales and sales-supporting staff. Such visits are necessary to supplement the information culled from statistics and telephone conversations. The buyer is able to generate excitement, give praise when due, offer constructive criticism, and give advice if needed.

The branch store presents special merchandising problems of which the buyer must be aware. For example, there must be sufficient backup merchandise of advertised sale merchandise as well as adequate stock at all times so that customers are not given the impression that branch store stocks are incomplete or skimpy. The buyer must also keep a sharp lookout at the sales movement of basic stock items. Another responsibility would be to recall and/or transfer slow-selling merchandise to the main store or to other branches where the merchandise might sell better or where it might make one big clearance sale. Finally, the buyer must advise and supervise the flow of all necessary information about scheduled promotional events, and merchandise details to support effective selling.

RECEIVING

Previously, we discussed how a large store is required to have well-organized receiving and marking departments as part of their operations division. Here, in discussing the buyer's responsibilities, we must observe the buyer's involvement in this phase of merchandise handling. For example, when merchandise is received, the buyer is given "professional" assistance in determining whether or not the quantities on the purchase order and the manufacturer's invoice are correct; if the merchandise is "as ordered" and there is no substitution in sizes or colors; and here shortages and/or damages are discovered and returned for credit.

Marking the merchandise.

The buyer and those who assist in buying are required to be in contact with the receiving room several times during the day. This liaison can be helpful if required information on orders is clear and complete; "badly needed merchandise" requests are factual, not a ploy to get out-of-turn delivery service; and plans are made for receipt of large shipments that require additional personnel. In addition, the following are some of the buyer's specific responsibilities in the receiving and marking processes:

1. To spot check incoming merchandise in order to ascertain if it is as ordered insofar as style, fabric, workmanship, etc.
2. To provide marking room personnel with all the information needed for proper preparation of the stubs (selling tickets on the garments).
3. To give the receiving room personnel a distribution plan of the merchandise received for either shipment to the branches, delivery to the selling floor and/or for storage in stockrooms.
4. To authorize the payment of the invoice after the merchandise is

received and checked in order to permit the controller's division to take the permitted cash discounts and anticipation.

5. To cooperate with the receiving room manager in order to help equalize that area's work force. This involves planning and timing the arrival of special or large volume purchases which can put an undue strain on the normal operation of the receiving room.
6. To deliver merchandise to departments. Merchandise should be checked for style, size and quantity delivered and a record made of it (particularly if statistical records are challenged).

TRAFFIC

Closely allied to the buyer's responsibilities for receiving and marking merchandise, and a more direct part of the buying process, is the buyer's responsibilities involving *traffic.* The buyer knows transportation costs reduce departmental profit. Therefore, the buyer assumes the responsibility of providing instructions to the vendor as to how to ship merchandise. It is the buyer's responsibility to ship merchandise as requested by the store. It is obvious that the department's profits can be adversely affected by poor transportation instructions, which can result in higher than necessary shipping costs, undue delays in shipping time, etc. In large retail organizations the buyer is assisted by a traffic department or by knowledgeable personnel in the receiving department.

The following are some specific traffic responsibilities which are particularly important to fashion buyers:

- Every buying order must indicate unequivocally how the merchandise is to be shipped.
- The buyer must avoid general terms such as "fastest way" or "cheapest way." The interpretation of these terms is frequently left to workers employed in the manufacturer's shipping department and they are apt to send it the "easiest way" for their own purposes.
- The buyer should always refer to the store's shipping guide which spells out the means of transportation for various situations. This will assure the selection of the fastest and lowest cost method.
- The buyer should understand the cost of frequent small deliveries. This is especially true with special orders, although if it requires many small orders from different resources (e.g., boutique-type operations) the buyer should ensure the use of consolidation or freight-forwarding service, a method always used by medium- or large-sized stores.
- The buyer should realize the cost of shipping merchandise the fastest way. Air freight, for example, can be expensive and should be used only when the importance of the delivery demands it, such

as a reorder for merchandise needed to support customer response to an ad.

- While it is considered a standard trade practice for the store to pay for the cost of transporting the merchandise it has purchased, the buyer should always try to secure more favorable shipping terms as part of the bargaining process. F.O.B. factory is the normal shipping term but if the buyer can obtain F.O.B. store terms, the cost of shipping would be paid by the manufacturer—a considerable savings. A buyer realizes the advantages that accrue from store designated merchandise carriers:
    1. Improved profit.
    2. Faster delivery.
    3. Proper handling of merchandise.
    4. Easier location of shipment (where goods are delayed on route).
    5. Maintenance of goodwill with both manufacturer's and store's management.

PERSONNEL

The buyer has the overall responsibility for the *personnel* of the department. Basically, the buyer, in addition to her merchandising and buying responsibilities, is the department manager. In fact, some large stores use this latter title rather than "buyer." We have seen this in many of the responsibilities we have already discussed, but it is in the area of personnel (which involves handling people) that emphasizes the buyer's managerial talent and skill. The buyer's *personnel* responsibilities as head of the department may be divided into the following categories:

- Trainer (Teacher)
- Communicator
- Delegator
- Supervisor

Trainer (Teacher)

The buyer has the responsibility of training all the people in the department. The job of devising and maintaining a training program for the department may, however, be delegated to one of the buyer's assistants. Among the areas found in a typical fashion merchandising department's training program the buyer may review:

- Store policies
- Selling techniques
- Merchandise information

- Advertising and other sales promotion information
- Systems and procedures
- Store rules and regulations

Communicator

The good buyer is one who realizes that communication is one of the most pressing problems of present-day management. There are several factors that have influenced this focus on the need for better communication including:

1. The growth in size and power of unions.
2. People are thinking more independently and are thus demanding more democratic and less autocratic actions and attitudes from their supervisors.
3. The increase in the level of both formal and informal education (radio and television, etc.).

In addition to the need for better communication between the buyer and subordinates, there is the job of acting as the liaison between top management and subordinates. The buyer must review and express new, or existing store policies, featured advertising, etc. The buyer must also communicate enthusiasm for the merchandise purchased to the sales force who must sell it.

Delegator

Thus far, we have discussed the buyer's many responsibilities and the enormous amounts of work a buyer must do. It therefore becomes advantageous to the buyer to delegate various parts of these many responsibilities to various subordinates. The buyer has to remember to:

1. Select the right person who knows how and is capable of doing the job.
2. Assign both the authority and the responsibility for the work to such a person in a clear, concise manner.
3. Follow up to see that the work was done correctly.

Supervisor

A buyer is a department head and is thus the *supervisor*. It is generally agreed that a simple definition of supervision is: *"Getting work done through people."* This merely means that the buyer has been given the authority to direct the work of those in the department, and is in turn now responsible for their output. Within this framework:

1. The buyer selects someone to do a specific job.
2. The buyer should then motivate the employee to do the job well. If it is necessary the employee should be trained to do the job.
3. The buyer must evaluate the job performance and give praise when due or correct any errors.
4. The buyer, at regular intervals, should evaluate the job performance and, over the long term, reward the employee; or where required transfer, discipline or dismiss the employee.

FAMILIARITY WITH LEGAL REGULATIONS

The buyer is frequently confronted with legal responsibilities arising primarily from Federal laws regulating the labeling of the fabric content in fashion merchandise; the necessity for care in advertising merchandise, especially in making claims for its serviceability and use; making buying arrangements with vendors. It should be noted that the buyer is not expected to be an attorney. The store will simplify the laws and give practical guidelines on how to comply with all marketing and consumer protection legislation requirements.

Briefly, the buyer should be aware of the following legal areas in exercising regular merchandising responsibilities.

The Sherman Antitrust Act

This Act prohibits combinations, contracts, or understandings that stifle or tend to stifle competition. The most notable case involved three of America's most prestigious high-fashion stores that pleaded "no contest" to charges of violating this Act. The stores were fined and agreed to cease and desist acts against competitors.

The Clayton Act

The Clayton Act refines the Sherman Antitrust Act by specifically extending the bans on the exclusivity of merchandise, price discrimination, etc., which lead to monopolies.

The Robinson-Patman Act

An amendment to the Clayton Act, outlaws price discrimination in selling, so that large scale purchases cannot obtain unfair price advantages.

Buyers must also be thoroughly familiar with the laws that directly influence the purchase of fashion goods.

- Wool Products Labeling Act
- Fur Products Labeling Act
- Textile Fiber Products Identification Act
- Flammable Fabrics Act
- Country of Origin

In addition, buyers must be familiar with the Federal Trade Commission's legal interpretations as promulgated in its *Trade Practice Rules or Guides,* which comprise several hundred rules applicable to the deceptive or fraudulent wording in retail store advertising.

There are other legal restraints, such as state or local ordinances, with which the buyer must be familiar.

STOCKKEEPING

Those who assist the buyer deal primarily with the actual aspects of stockkeeping. But the buyer has the real responsibility for this duty as with everything else that concerns the running of the department.

Broadly speaking these stockkeeping responsibilities involve:

1. Arranging the merchandise so that it is convenient for the customer to inspect and handle, e.g., by size, by color.
2. Placing "hot items" or advertised merchandise in a prominent selling position in the department.
3. Arranging stock attractively.
4. Arranging related items conveniently close by; similarly for items that can be sold in multiple units; e.g., $5.95 each, two for $11.
5. Keeping stock clean, properly folded or hung and protected from soiling, in other words reflecting the store's respect for the merchandise.
6. Maintaining a constant flow of merchandise from the receiving and marking areas to the stockroom or selling area is part of the stockkeeping responsibilities.
7. Removing stock from fitting rooms constantly and returning it to the floor in salable condition.

Some fifty years ago, Nystrom said, "Customers want clean, fresh, well-assorted stocks of goods and this is, after all, the prime objective of retailing."

HOUSEKEEPING

Housekeeping is sometimes thought of synonymously with stockkeeping, and that is quite understandable. Keeping the department's stock in good order and well arranged is a primary consideration for good sales production. But the buyer's responsibility must go beyond merely good merchandise display. The following is a list of rules for a buyer to observe where housekeeping of a good fashion department is concerned.

1. Fitting rooms should be kept neat and clean; unwanted merchandise should be removed immediately; and a limited number of items of merchandise permitted per customer for each try-on.
2. Counters should always be *immaculately* clean.
3. Showcases should be sparkling at the start of each day and periodically given some attention.
4. Merchandise displays should always be neat, tidy and well coordinated.
5. Flat merchandise should be carefully folded and should not be permitted to become jumbled up or crushed.
6. Hanging merchandise should be well centered on individual hangers.
7. Salespeople should be taught to be alert to merchandise that may have been dropped on the floor by careless customers. Dirty floors damage the merchandise and create the opportunity for customers to ask for cleaning allowances on the cost of the item.
8. Belts, after try-ons, should be replaced rather than be permitted to hang awry.
9. Dusting shelves and fixtures should be a daily routine.
10. Signs should be clean and clear both as to their intent and appearance.

SUMMARY

A buyer is a merchandising executive at the sub-middle management level and as such is responsible for planning, buying and selling. The planning and selling activities obviously involve other people. The planning must be approved by higher echelon, e.g., divisional merchandise manager; selling involves salespeople as well as the sales promotion division. In addition, a buyer has responsibilities related to retail operations with impact into the activities of receiving goods, marking goods, delivery of goods, etc. Finally, in order to perform most effectively, a buyer must be a teacher (trainer), communicator, delegator, and supervisor.

The buyer's most basic role is to act as a purchasing agent for the customer. In this role, many hats are worn. It can be exciting, rewarding, and fulfilling.

chapter 8
FASHION BUYING FOR A CENTRAL CHAIN & MAIL-ORDER ORGANIZATION

INTRODUCTION

This chapter deals with two different types of fashion buyer (or buying) —the chain and the mail-order organization. The discussion that follows focuses on:

- The difference between the various types and classifications of chains
- How a typical fashion chain is organized
- How chains are merchandised
- How mail-order organizations operate
- Why mail-order merchandising continues to grow and prosper despite its seeming anachronism

CENTRAL CHAIN ORGANIZATION

A *chain* is a group of four or more stores selling essentially the same merchandise; centrally owned and managed; and centrally merchandised from an office located in a major market. (Some authorities use the figure three or more stores; the Federal Census has defined it as two or more.) Chains also exhibit the following distinguishing characteristics:

1. There is usually a separation of the *buying* and *selling* functions, and the buyer, therefore, is a market specialist.
2. Chains generally employ a number of highly specialized personnel who are available to all levels of the organization in an advisory as well as a functional capacity.
3. Chains can usually affect economies by increasing the number of stores because they are able to:
   A. purchase larger quantities of merchandise and enjoy the advantages that accrue;

B. spread overhead costs among many units;

C. the cost of the merchandise staff is similarly absorbed by the stores.

4. There is frequently a marked tendency towards standardization in merchandise offerings, store layout, store front, fixtures, display and advertising.

5. Chains with numerous stores have huge purchasing power and by effecting purchase terms to save manufacturers' costs (legal according to the Robinson-Patman Act) are able to secure lower prices from manufacturers.

6. Chains, because of their arrangement, are inclined to buy merchandise that can move rapidly—high turnover goods.

While some marketing authorities trace the beginning of chain stores in the United States to the mid-19th century, chains actually became an important factor in the distribution of fashion merchandise after World War I (1919). There was a period of growth at that time both in the nation's population as well as in its capacity to mass produce a large variety of goods.

Between 1929 and 1946, which included the Great Depression, the New Deal and World War II, the development of the chain was greatly hindered. The major chains, however, did strengthen their position by closing unprofitable stores and enlarging and renovating profitable ones. After 1946 and continuing to the present, chains were quick to follow the trend to the suburbs, opening stores in the rapidly growing shopping centers, or as developers and landlords frequently creating shopping plazas for not only their own stores but for other chains as well. In addition, many chains rebuilt or renovated their older stores and added broader and larger merchandise lines. Some of the big national chains became multi-national in character, opening stores in foreign countries. Chains today continue to occupy an important part of the American marketing economy as a channel of distribution.

Chains may be classified into three major categories:

1. Ownership
2. Geography
3. Merchandise Categories (fashion related)

Ownership

CORPORATE CHAINS Chains of every type may be owned or operated by a corporation.

FRANCHISE CHAINS A franchise is a legal agreement by which the franchiser, who has developed a successful plan of operation, sells this format to individuals or to independent chains. In addition to the cost of the franchise, there is generally a royalty charge on sales volume because the franchiser regularly conducts national sales promotion campaigns on behalf of the entire franchise chain and sells the merchandise to the franchisee.

LEASED DEPARTMENT CHAINS A leased department is a department in a large department, specialty, or chain store which is leased space and furnished needed facilities to an outside firm for which the store receives a percentage of sales. It is not uncommon for leased departments to be owned and managed by a chain organization with units in many stores. Typical leased departments include shoes, furs, millinery, beauty salons, cosmetics.

VOLUNTARY CHAINS Chains usually formed by wholesalers or manufacturers and are made up of independent stores who voluntarily agree to take part in merchandising and sales promotion programs sponsored by the vendor, who agree to provide the stores with various services and advice. In return, the stores agree to buy a certain proportion of merchandise from the wholesaler.

MANUFACTURERS CHAINS A group owned and operated by a manufacturer who is interested in greater distribution of his merchandise. In the fashion field, there are a number of such chains in men's clothing, women's hosiery, and in men's, women's and children's shoes.

Geography

MULTI-NATIONAL CHAINS Stores in foreign countries in addition to the United States.

NATIONAL CHAINS Stores throughout the country from coast-to-coast and border-to-border.

REGIONAL CHAINS Stores confined to one region of the United States, e.g., the South, the Midwest.

METROPOLITAN AREA CHAINS Stores located in and around a major city and its suburbs, e.g., New York, Boston, Los Angeles and Miami.

LOCAL CHAINS Stores saturate a major central area of either an entire city or a principal locale within the city, e.g., Long Island, the Wall Street or Grand Central areas in New York City.

Merchandise Categories (fashion related)

GENERAL MERCHANDISE CHAIN This type of chain carries all types of goods including apparel and accessories. Examples: J.C. Penney, Sears, Roebuck.

SHOE CHAINS Shoe chains carry men's and boys' or women's and girls' shoes and accessories. Examples: National Shoes, I. Miller, Kinney.

SPECIALTY STORE CHAINS These chains carry women's apparel and accessories. Example: Lerner's, Winkelmans.

MEN'S WEAR CHAINS Men's wear chains carry men's wear and men's furnishing's. Examples: Wallachs, Bond Stores.

INFANTS' AND CHILDREN'S WEAR CHAINS Chains carry merchandise for children from layettes to early teens. Examples: Cornells' Apparel, Brody's.

How Chains Are Organized

As we have seen the organizational structure of a business has a strong relationship to its ability to succeed. The structure of a typical chain in the fashion field bears some resemblance to that of a large department or specialty store in that there are several similar functional divisions such as control, merchandising, and personnel; but the lines of authority and responsibility differ greatly as an examination of **Figure 8–1** will reveal. The separation of buying from selling alone requires a different divisional setup. While some of our largest department stores with big branch store programs might have a real estate department, this is a requirement in the chain, not an option.

Central Buying Plans

One of the chain's chief characteristics is that it has central planning, buying, and merchandising. The chain's headquarters is located in what was originally the center of the chain's geographical area. Buyers are located in a central market city, such as New York, so that they can have rapid and convenient access to vendors. Most chains maintain elaborate and expensive electronic data processing installations that use pre-punched price tags, which are stubbed or detached from the merchandise at the time of sale. Other systems involve the use of data processing cash registers that are hooked up to terminals in centers hundreds of miles from the stores. By analyzing these reports, usually

Figure 8–1. Organization Chart of Apparel Chain.

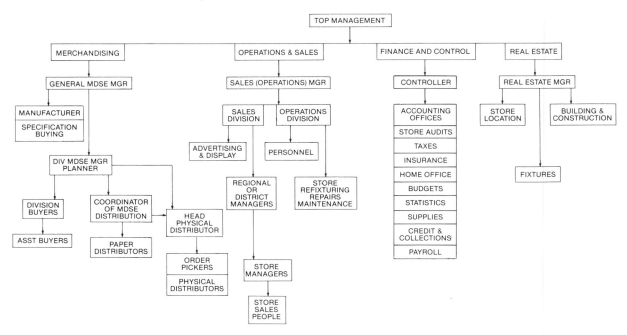

the merchandise manager is able to make buying plans not only for the chain as a whole, but also for the special needs of chains in specific regions and individual stores or groups of stores. The vast buying power inherent in a central buying system gives the company extra buying clout. While there are some differences in the approach, method and philosophy of the central buying function, there are several variations that require examination.

1. The Central Merchandising Plan
2. The Central Purchase with Merchandise-Requisition Plan
3. The Listing or Price Agreement Plan

THE CENTRAL MERCHANDISING PLAN In fashion merchandise chains, although it is by no means confined to them alone, there is a tendency to keep a tight control on the entire buying and merchandising process. The central buying office of the chain by means of a continuous flow of information from each store, consisting of reports, dealing with the movement of merchandise including colors, sizes, and styles, knows what is happening in each store at all times. (Note: Follow the lines of authority and responsibility of a typical chain operating on the *central merchandising plan* in **Figure 8–2.**)

Heading this system is a *general merchandise manager.* A divisional merchandise manager or divisional planner, as they are frequently called, heads each major merchandise category, e.g., dresses, sportswear. Each division has one or more buyers, depending upon the size of the chain and the degree of segmentation or specialization that the chain desires. Most buyers have at least one assistant buyer, again depending upon the size of the operation, the market coverage desired, etc.

Once the merchandise is ordered by the buyer, general plans for distributing that merchandise to the individual stores are made by the distribution branch of each division. There is usually a divisional coordinator who is in charge of one or more head paper distributors. Each head paper distributor has a number of paper distributors and each of these is usually assigned to a limited number of stores, sometimes on a geographic basis, which he gets to know well. The work of the paper distributor is to take the reports of the merchandise actually received and marked in the home office warehouse facilities at any one time, and using available unit control and other records, make a paper breakdown of each style by colors and sizes for shipment to the stores. Such shipments are either designed as new numbers for initial sale or as fill-ins for the current stock. The divisional coordinator also supervises the activities of the physical distributors, whose job is to take the paper distributor's plans and physically pick the colors and sizes specified for each store. The physical distributor then moves each store's "order" to the packing area of the shipping department of this central warehouse for ultimate delivery to each store involved.

This is a brief explanation of a fairly typical Central Merchandising Plan in operation although there may be variations possible to suit the merchandising needs of the chain or its subdivisions. It has certain advantages built into it by virtue of the policies of the organization, because the chain is able to seek and employ highly skilled buying personnel with expertise in a very narrow segment of the market, if that is desirable. Added to this fact of being able to secure very knowledgeable buyers is the inherent buying power of great amounts of merchandise as compared to independent stores of any size. The central buyer is a *market specialist* whose primary job is to cover the market segment assigned by spending a great part of the working day there. This normally results in the chain's ability to secure quicker deliveries as well as the purchase of timely merchandise and/or basic stock fill-ins on a steady basis.

The central merchandising plan also lends itself to specification buying; to contract manufacturing by the buyer or the chain; and to private label or chain brands. In addition to quantity discounts, due to volume buying, the chain buyer is frequently in a position to demand and to secure exclusivity on a particular item or line. In fact, the chain can frequently take the manufacturer's entire output.

If the unit control records are accurate, and the use of the most modern E.D.P. equipment provides the hope that accuracy will be assured, then there will be an opportunity for the buyer with the assistance of the distribution section to keep all the stores in a well-balanced stock position. The chain's merchandising lifeline depends on good record keeping and everything possible is done to see to it that it remains accurate. Finally, it should be noted here once again that the central buyer has no other real responsibilities than buying; planning and sales promotion, and all other responsibilities that we have detailed for other buyers are performed by specialists in their respective fields.

Of course, there are limitations in every plan or system and the central merchandising plan is no exception. With the necessity for separating buying from selling, and with selling activities concentrated in the hands of the district manager, the store manager, and the salespeople, all this hundreds of miles away from the home office, it is commonplace for those on the selling line to be critical of some of the merchandise shipped to them. This situation of being shipped merchandise by a distant, faceless buying organization becomes more aggravated if the merchandise does not sell well. Some chains try to offset this disadvantage by having the buyer, the planner, and sometimes even the distributors travel to the stores whenever possible. In many chains the buyer's office is responsible for the production of bulletins giving sales information to be used by the store's personnel. Some chains also provide an opportunity for periodic visits by store managers to the home office, particularly to have them act in an advisory capacity to the central buying staff.

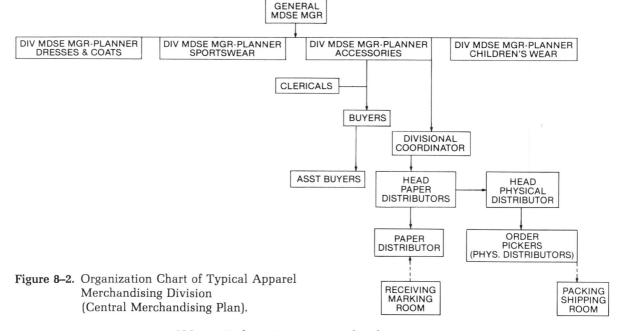

Figure 8–2. Organization Chart of Typical Apparel
Merchandising Division
(Central Merchandising Plan).

Another disadvantage of the Central Merchandising Plan arising from the separation of buying and selling, is the acrimony that can arise if merchandise selected by the central staff and shipped by the home office does not sell. There is a tendency for the central buyer to blame a possibly unenthusiastic store manager for the failure; and vice versa, the store people become disgruntled and blame the buyer for the poor choice of merchandise that they did not ask for in the first place. Some chains have attempted to open lines of communication to the central buying office that permits suggestions of merchandise to be bought or shipped that is apparently doing well elsewhere in their community.

It is very difficult to merchandise by statistical records alone. It takes a personal knowledge and an almost innate feeling to know and understand local conditions and merchandise peculiarities that mere records find difficult to reveal.

THE CENTRAL PURCHASE WITH MERCHANDISE-REQUISITION PLAN This plan of central buying and merchandising, tries to eliminate some of the limitations of the Central Merchandising Plan. The store manager and/or his duly-designated subordinates, such as department managers, are given an opportunity to control the amount and classifications of merchandise shipped to their store for resale to their customers.

Simply stated, this plan is used primarily for *basic* stocks. The central buyer purchases large amounts of merchandise at good quantity discounts and stores the merchandise in a distribution center (some national chains use regional distribution centers). Each store is supplied with a stock checklist and the merchandise is requisitioned from the center where the central buyer maintains an adequate inventory from which to select. When the store requisition reaches the distribution center, it is filled and the merchandise is shipped to the store. While the individual store manager has no voice in the store's original inventory, he may select or choose items from the center's checklists that he feels will sell best in his location, omitting those about which he has doubts. The manager is expected to keep his inventory at peak levels so as to avoid running out of stock of basic items between deliveries.

It is quite obvious that the store manager under this plan has more freedom of choice in managing his selling activities than under the Central Merchandising Plan. In cases of local, regional, or national sales promotion events, stores must stock the items on sale if they are listed as participating stores. The Central Purchase with Merchandise-Requisition Plan helps to eliminate some of the disgruntlement that is engendered by the central buying office's normal activities. In case of poor sales the store manager has no one to blame at the home office. This technique also assures faster delivery for replacing basic items.

THE LISTING OR PRICE AGREEMENT PLAN The most sophisticated central buying plan, insofar as the store manager's autonomy is concerned, is known either as the *Price Agreement* or the *Listing Plan* (sometimes as Price List and Agreement).

The central buying office prepares catalogues wherein the merchandise is sketched, photographed and described. This list has been culled from the market by the central buyer based upon past sales and current trends in the fashion field. The buyer makes commitments with manufacturers based upon his best scientific estimates. The manufacturer produces the merchandise, which is now owned by the chain, and awaits shipping instructions. The individual store managers, upon receipt of the catalogues which are frequently updated, are then able to order directly from the manufacturers listed, at the prices and other terms agreed upon between the central buyer and the manufacturer. The central buying office receives a copy of each store's orders to each resource in order to keep track of these store "purchases" against the initial orders. The manufacturer ships the merchandise directly to the stores. This method is called *drop ship.* The store manager is free to "buy" from these approved resources or not. Frequently there is even authority to buy from local resources of his own choosing without home office approval.

Of course, there is always the possibility of the buyer's misjudgment as to the potential sale of any one item or line and thus stock could remain in the manufacturer's warehouse after the season is over; this is a frequent occurrence. The merchandise is owned by the chain and the buyer must make some arrangement to dispose of such "remainders." He has a number of alternatives:

1. Sell it to a jobber or to a discount operator at a closeout price.
2. Offer it to the individual stores of the chain at a lower price (markdown) and thus have the central office take the loss.
3. Attempt to sell it back to the manufacturer, at a loss.
4. Ask the manufacturer to become a "partner" to the loss and have the manufacturer attempt to sell it to a third party.
5. Pressure the manufacturer to accept a complete return of the goods for credit.

The central buyer, therefore, frequently makes provision in determining the cost of the merchandise to the members of the chain to cover the possible loss arising from the possibility of having goods left over.

Career Opportunities

As a result of an examination of the central buying office system, we can now add several career opportunities to the ones discussed in Chapter 5. The chain store merchandising organization contains several new titles such as paper distributor, head paper distributor, and divisional merchandise planner. Some chains use the distribution wing of the merchandising division from which to recruit merchandising executives. Salaries in chains are on a par with and in some instances better than department stores and certainly much higher than the resident buying office.

Summary—Central Chain Organization

The overall responsibilities of central chain buyers' include:

- They are market specialists who perform the buying for a classification of merchandise or for a department.
- They work in an office and have no relationship to stores or selling activities except to buy for them.
- They have a direct relationship to a whole group of specialists who help to plan purchases and to distribute the merchandise to stores once it arrives from the vendor. With the aid of the divisional planner and the merchandise distributors, they formulate seasonal budgets.
- They must be knowledgeable about climate and geographic considerations; ethnic and other demographic factors in buying for many far-flung areas.
- They have a keen interest in securing the best prices for the merchandise they purchase and which because of their vast purchasing power, they can legitimately secure, in addition to other favorable terms.
- They can undertake manufacturing, specification buying and confining lines to the chain because of the great amount of merchandise they need for normal use and/or special promotional events. They frequently seek special merchandise for such activities.
- They motivate the store manager and his salespeople to sell the merchandise they have bought for the store by personal visits and by regular bulletins giving merchandise information.

MAIL-ORDER ORGANIZATION

A mail-order house is a retail organization that solicits its business and seeks its customers through the use of catalogues or other forms of the printed media, usually sent to the prospective customer by "mail"; and it makes its sales by delivering the merchandise to the customer by "mail." It should be noted at the outset, however, that the original concept of only using the United States mails for both solicitation and delivery is no longer true. The increasing cost of catalogue mailing and parcel post delivery, particularly since the U. S. Post Office became a

Non-store retailing.

The easy way to travel

D. The Deluxe
Square
Rigger Set.

quasi-public governmental agency, has forced mail-order houses to use private industry for both ends of the mail-order business. These private enterprise delivery systems have generally been faster and less expensive than the official Post Office.

Mail-order houses fall into several main classifications:

GENERAL MERCHANDISE FIRMS Such companies as Sears, J. C. Penney, Montgomery Ward, Spiegel's, offer a department store-like wide line of products for sale through their catalogues.

SPECIALIZED MERCHANDISE FIRMS There are literally thousands of mail-order houses who are engaged in the business of offering a narrow line of goods for sale through mail orders. Included in this area are those who specialize in one or more aspects of fashion merchandise, books, fruit, records, garden specialties, etc.

MAIL-ORDER DEPARTMENTS OF LARGE DEPARTMENT AND SPECIALTY STORES Practically all of the country's large stores are in the mail-order business using catalogues at regular intervals during the year, with Christmas being the biggest period of the year. This is in addition to their almost daily use of mail-order coupons in their newspaper ads or by including a by-line in either the printed or audio-visual media which solicits telephone or mail-order business.

MEDIA MAIL-ORDER SHOPPING Here, too, there are an untold number of mail-order enterprises which use newspapers, magazines, radio and television and which deliver the merchandise ordered by mail or a private delivery system.

History & Development

The history and development of the United States in the last quarter of the 19th century is responsible in part for the growth and development of the mail-order house as an important retail institution. Both Montgomery Ward and Sears, the pioneers in this field, are greatly indebted to such historical developments as the completion of the transcontinental railroad from Chicago to the Pacific Coast, (Chicago therefore became the headquarters of most mail-order houses and the center of the mail-order industry because it was the railroad center of the nation with its express package service); the beginning of rural free mail delivery; and the establishment of the United States Parcel Post System. With the popularization of the automobile in the 1920s and the building of roads suitable for such vehicular travel, the mail-order houses saw the handwriting on the wall and began to open stores. While the big mail-order organizations now derive a great deal of their sales volume from their retail outlets, the contributions of the mail-order division to their sales volume and profits is still very sizable. As a matter of fact, every Sears, Montgomery Ward, or J. C. Penney store has a mail-order catalogue desk. And both Sears and Montgomery Ward, among others, have thousands of catalogue stores scattered all over the country where the principal fixtures are counters with mail-order catalogues on them and clerks to take their orders; some have a few samples of currently featured items. Currently available statistics indicate that contrary to a widely held but completely erroneously belief, that the mail-order business is an anachronism that has long since seen its best days, it is actually holding its own as a multi-billion dollar phase of American retailing, despite chain, branch store, and shopping center expansion. In fact, there are some authorities who feel that the full cycle of history will swing back to the mail-order house despite the growth of highways and automobiles. The American consumer is getting more and more irritated with the hassle of heavy traffic, high gasoline prices, parking difficulties, etc., and may predictably turn to the comfort of shopping from a catalogue in their own home. Another factor that must be taken into consideration is the continued growth of women in industry which limits the time available for personal shopping. So while it is an understandable fact that the big mail-order firms have indeed become chains, they are still in the mail-order business with both feet and will be there for as long as people will welcome their catalogues into their homes with sufficient sales resulting to remain profitable.

Mail-Order Merchandising

Today, the large mail-order house is in reality a dual operation. As a chain with hundreds of stores, many of department store size and scope, the mail-order house often uses the *Listing or Price Agreement Plan* for particular categories of goods. In the mail-order phase of their business, they and those firms that have no stores alike, use an entirely different approach to buying and merchandising. Unlike the chain buyer whose purchase planning and methodology is quite similar to the department store buyer, the mail-order buyer must plan about a year in advance of the selling period. The mail-order buyer requires this lead time because the production of the catalogues takes considerable time. A mere glance

In the beginning: Sears, Roebuck's first retail store, 1917 (left). Montgomery Ward & Co. (right) established in 1872 as a mail-order business.

at any of the major mail-order firms main catalogues will suffice to prove the enormity of the merchandising task. In addition, the large variety of merchandise and the depth of the stock carried requires a great amount of market work by the buying organization. To this must be added the problem of "guessing" what customer preferences will be so far in advance and whether they will accept the selection of styles as well as colors. While it is true that catalogue fashion always centered around the more basic styles or "fords," new consumer attitudes have made it necessary for fashions to be more sophisticated. The mail-order buyer must make huge commitments far in advance chronologically of the store competitors. They, too, rely a great deal on past sales records gathered by highly sophisticated E.D.P. equipment. To help overcome their time handicap, Sears and the others have hired big name fashion designers and consultants in an effort to lend glamour to their catalogues.

Once the merchandise is ordered and it is received at the mail-order headquarters or their regional distribution points, customers' orders from the mails, catalogue stores, or counters are processed with speed and dispatched to avoid customer impatience and dissatisfaction. Failure to have merchandise for a customer's order for current goods is known as an "omission" and is considered a bad mistake on the part of the merchandise staff.

Summary—Mail-Order Organization

To conclude this discussion on the mail-order organization, it would do well to summarize the advantages and disadvantages of the mail-order house as a contemporary fashion merchandising institution.

ADVANTAGES

1. It provides a convenient form of shopping for a broad spectrum of the American public that has limited time to devote to personal shopping.
2. Over the years, the mail-order business has built up a reputation for integrity in merchandising from the specifications in the manufacturing of the merchandise and quality control; to the pricing structure; and to the willingness and even encouragement of guaranteed satisfaction from a liberal return policy.
3. The size and scope of the variety of offerings in all merchandise categories is frequently staggering. This gives customers a wide choice in many merchandise categories.
4. Customers generally believe that values are usually on par or better than those available from conventional retailers and that the mail-order firms are able to pass on price savings through their huge purchasing powers.

5. To help maintain a desired price structure and to ensure the delivery of vast amounts of merchandise to the warehouse, the mail order firms have lead in exercising some form of control of many of their merchandise resources.
6. As a business, mail order enjoys the advantage of lower overhead due to inexpensive rentals, no displays, no fixtures, practically no customer services, other than delivery for which the customer pays, and advertising limited to the catalogues.
7. The price of gasoline, hassle of heavy traffic, parking difficulties, etc.
8. Women now make up at least half of the work force and have limited time to "shop"; they need easier ways to "shop."

DISADVANTAGES

1. Obviously, one of the big problems involved in the mail-order business is the publication of two major catalogues each year plus smaller ones that assist in keeping the merchandise operation up-to-date. In addition, there is usually a special Christmas catalogue featuring gift purchases, a Back-to-School catalogue, and several clearance catalogues to move overstocked merchandise or slow sellers. Since most catalogues today feature fashion from cover-to-cover, the cost of producing this catalogue has risen. When this catalogue cost and its distribution expense is added to other costs of doing business, even if they are lower than stores, it is clear that the catalogue must bring in a sizable annual sales volume per book to justify itself.
2. Despite all the scientific devices of modern business, the time-tried and proven adage of "having the right merchandise at the right time" can be an aggravating factor in mail-order selling. Customers are impatient people and the time between placing the order and the arrival of the merchandise is frequently annoying.
3. The necessity for buying large quantities of merchandise so far in advance in order to be able to have a good assortment of merchandise on hand for a much longer period than stores means that there is a stronger possibility of markdowns and clearance merchandise.

Quite obviously, the advantages outweigh the disadvantages. It is safe to conclude that the mail-order house will continue to maintain its place in the retail picture of this country for the forseeable future. With Sears alone having a catalogue sales volume of several billion dollars and with an estimated national sales volume of the mail-order business at almost $29 billion, we believe that there is a bright future ahead for those in this field.

chapter 9 THE RESIDENT BUYING OFFICE

INTRODUCTION

The *resident buying office* plays a vital role in the flow of merchandise from producer to ultimate consumer. It is an indispensable institution in a society characterized by mass production for mass acceptance.

Included in this chapter are discussions that relate to the need and importance of resident buying to retail fashion merchandising, with explanations of:

- The different types of resident buying offices and the types of retail organizations that constitute their probable clients
- The services performed by resident buying offices
- The role of the assistant buyer in the resident buying office
- How to select the right resident buying office for the individual store

We have already indicated that the resident buying office can be considered as one of the staff* services of a store. Here we will examine its operation emphasizing the activities related to fashion merchandising.

A resident buying office is an organization located in a major market for the purpose of representing member stores that have their own complement of buyers. It should be clearly understood that the primary function of a resident buying office is to *render a service.* The term buying office is almost a misnomer. Many offices use the term "representatives," which more accurately describes its function. The offices or representatives can buy for stores only under special circumstances: by request, or with permission, of the store buyers, who are responsible for merchandise budgets. There can be an arrangement which provides for the resident office to merchandise a department within a store. This arrangement is based on a contractual agreement for the inclusion of an

---

*Although the RBO is not an internal department it is a "team" member of the merchandising staff and therefore functions as a staff department.

extra service—central buying, sometimes called unit control service, for which the office receives additional compensation.

In order not to confuse resident buying with central buying consider the service function area. In central buying, the responsibility of merchandising is in the hands of buyers who are located in a major market and buy for member stores. Store personnel is primarily responsible for carrying out instructions from the home office. Resident buying offices offer a service to stores to help their buyers who operate from store locations.

Since New York City is the major fashion market of the United States, it has by far the greatest number of resident offices. There are some offices in other fashion markets, particularly in Los Angeles and Miami. With the advent of the importance of markets, it is necessary for some large organizations to have national and global market representation. Some large offices therefore have branches or affiliates in Los Angeles; and in some instances maintain foreign offices. The Associated Merchandising Corp., the largest office in the country, has offices in Barcelona, Brussels, Copenhagen, Dublin, Florence, London, Milan, Munich, Naples, Paris, Vienna, Zurich, Manila, Osaka, and Tokyo. Another giant organization, Allied Stores, similarly has global coverage. The larger the organization, the wider the coverage.

Another point that should be understood is that an office establishes a membership of stores that is non-competitive. That is not to say that a small office cannot represent several clients in a larger city, in non-competitive areas.

HISTORY & DEVELOPMENT

The *resident buying office* is an outgrowth of a number of socio-economic factors that came into being following World War I; it might also be said that the resident buying office started with the birth of modern ready-to-wear about the same time—1920. There were a number of events that led to the development of both the resident buying office and ready-to-wear as we know it today. In the first place, the need for uniforms that arose during World War I caused the growth in the productive capacity of the garment industry. As always, mass production led to the need for mass acceptance. Up to that time, home sewers, seamstresses or custom tailors were the major sources for women's and children's clothing.

Another important factor was the change in the traditional women's role. The feminist movement demanded equality of rights for women and women entered the work force, particularly into jobs that had been traditionally barred to women. With it a new attitude about women's clothing began to develop—the importance, the variety, and the function. Clothing for women began to make sense, the concept of

Early production—home sewers, seamstresses or custom tailors were the major sources for women's and children's apparel.

how and when it was to be worn was considered important, and the new or active life required clothing that permitted greater mobility.

One of the primary developments at this time was the increasing availability of rayon—garment manufacturers possessed an inexpensive fabric which permitted the making of dresses at popular prices for the masses. Up to this date, a dress was actually a cotton shirtwaist attached to a skirt. Any fabric other than cotton was called silk. Rayon, the first man-made fabric, was the catalyst for a new approach to fashion by manufacturers and customers.

The ability of manufacturers to produce inexpensive dresses gave rise to stores that concentrated on selling popular priced ready-to-wear —the chain store. In their early years they were dress shops located in major cities. The best known organization that started at that time, and which is today still very much in business is Lerners. The period of

1920–1930 is known as the "Chain Store Age." This new upstart sector of retailing was a disturbance to the entrenched retailers for several reasons. The chains used central buyers who were able to:

1. Buy directly from manufacturers.
2. Feed stores new styling on a constant basis, since the buyers were market specialists.
3. Secure merchandise at special prices in exchange for quantity orders.

The establishment was in a vulnerable position because traditional buying was from jobbers. Purchases were in sufficient depth to cover needs for a designated period.

Enterprising people in the market, New York, organized a new institution and sold a market service to counteract the chain advantage —market presence or representation—which afforded information and if necessary, buying. The advantage of chains was made largely available through membership of a buying office. To this day, it is not uncommon for some resident buying offices to maintain greatest personnel depth in the dress area. Sportswear importance of recent years has tended to change the balance considerably.

The year 1920 also marks the date when the rural population began to move to urban areas in considerable numbers. This population shift laid the groundwork for more mass acceptance—people in sufficient numbers with similar attitudes. Two additional factors started to operate at this time that helped bring about the potential for the large-scale marketing of fashion. One was the growing influence of the motion picture and the tendency of many people to emulate prominent personalities—motion pictures incidentally brought the latest news about fashion to housewives. The other was the coming of age of the automobile which afforded greater mobility and more social opportunities for everyone creating a need for different clothing for different functions. All of these events helped to bring about the necessary changes for the ready-to-wear business.

The resident buying office played a big role in the development of ready-to-wear. It was a major link between manufacturers and stores, its founding afforded a communication system that would accommodate fashion needs as practiced in the United States—change, speed, educational process, and promotional support.

CLASSIFICATION OF RESIDENT BUYING OFFICES

It can be easily understood why a resident office is a requirement for a store doing even a modest volume. Without representation in the fashion market, a buyer is isolated from developments necessary to be current in a business characterized by change. Fashion merchandising is practiced by a wide variety of types of stores which differ in size, services, volume, personnel, ownership, location, and customers.

There is a need for market representation that best suits the requirements consistent with the characteristics of the store. Thus, there are different resident offices to service organizations with different needs. Resident offices are classified into five different categories:

- The independently owned office (clients pay a fee)
- The cooperatively owned office (stores own office and share expenses)
- The corporatively owned office (ownership by a syndicated store organization)
- The individually owned office (an office within an office)
- The merchandise brokers or commission office (no charge to stores, manufacturers pay commission to office)

Figure 9–1. The Line Part of the Organization for a Moderate- to Large-Sized Resident Buying Office.

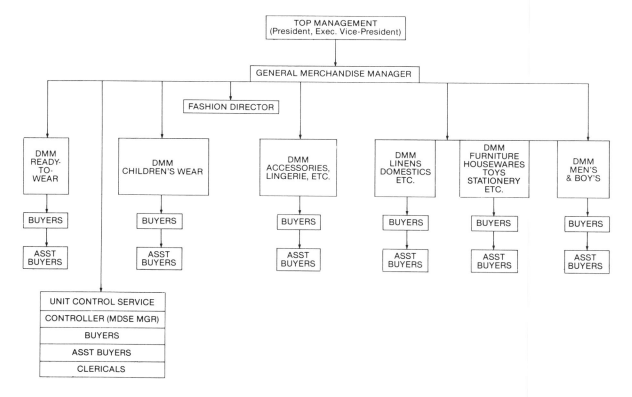

The Independently Owned Office

Numerically, the independently owned office, which is also known in the trade as either the *salaried, fee,* or *paid* office, is the most numerous.

Stores who affiliate themselves with a "paid office" establish a contractual obligation with a market representative firm, that receives a fee for its services. Originally, the independently owned resident buying office charged an annual fee based on a percentage of the store's annual sales, paid in monthly installments. Today, especially for the smaller store, the trend is definitely toward fees being set by negotiation on a flat monthly rate.

Many "fee" offices use all sorts of sales promotion methods to constantly secure new store clients, for example: direct mail, telephone, personal solicitation by the office's principals, trade paper advertisements. It should be noted that most independently owned resident buying offices cover all the fashion (apparel and accessory) markets.

Some of the prominent firms include Independent Retailers Syndicate (I.R.S.) and Felix Lilienthal Co. There are some independent offices that specialize such as Youth Fashion Guild, specializing in infants', children's and teen apparel.

The Cooperatively Owned Office

While the cooperative office, which is also frequently called the *associated* office, is numerically the smallest one in our resident buying office classification list, the size, sales volume, and prestige of its member stores cannot be overlooked. Two leading offices of this type are Associated Merchandising Corporation (A.M.C.) and Frederick Atkins Co. As the trade name indicates these offices are cooperatively owned by their member stores, which are among the biggest in the United States. While there is little information available on the actual cost of belonging to a cooperative office, it is generally believed that the charges involved for such market representation is a direct reflection of the sales volume of each member store. Another interesting sidelight concerning stores who are members of a cooperatively owned buying office, is that they are primarily stores who can afford to pay for the most intensive market representation. Some of them had previously maintained private offices, which they found to be expensive; now they are able to enjoy the benefits of their required services by sharing expenses with stores on their own level with similar interests. Among the outstanding nationally known stores affiliated with the A.M.C. are Bloomingdale's, Abraham & Straus, Lazarus, and Filene's. The greatest number of their member stores are part of the Federated Department Store chain.

The Corporatively Owned Office

The corporative buying office, sometimes referred to as the *syndicate* office is a resident buying office of which there are relatively few. As we have just pointed out in the cooperative resident buying office the size, sales volume, and prestige of the stores represented is enormous. In this case, the resident buying office is owned by the parent corporation whose stores are the only members represented. Thus, The May Company Buying Office; the Macy's Corporate Buying Office; the Gimbel's Corporate Buying Office; the Allied Stores Marketing Corp. or the Associated Dry Goods Association Buying Office service stores owned by the parent corporation. The corporation that owns and controls the stores provides another service for their subsidiary companies—market representation.

The Individually Owned Office

This type of office is best described as an office within an office. Many retail organizations, usually larger ones, deem it necessary to have personnel in the major market to fulfill tasks that are peculiar to their stores. For example, the placement and follow-through on a bridal order, which has time importance. Although the resident buying office has a bridal buyer, who can and will handle the request, some stores feel more comfortable when the responsibility is placed with individuals who have no function but those related to their stores. A resident buyer receives many daily requests and must establish a work priority. Personalized service becomes a reality with the employment and maintenance of a person, or persons, in a private office within the resident buying office.

The Associated Merchandising Corp., the largest cooperative buying office, is not typical, but best exemplifies the practice of the private office. Every member store (thirty-one domestic store organizations as of this writing) maintains a private office with one or two people employed by the stores. These employees concentrate their efforts on requests of their respective stores. Where one person mans the office, it is customary for all activity to take place on the premises. The private office employee does not visit resources. Where there are two or three people, it is usual for one of the staff to visit resources when the occasions demand personal attention.

There are a few retail organizations that maintain a private resident buying office for their own merchandising activities, exemplified by Neiman Marcus. However, this type of RBO represents a small part of the buying office sector.

The Merchandise Brokers or Commission Office

In all of the preceding resident buying office classifications, the store clients directly or indirectly paid for the use of market representation.

In the case of the commission office—now known officially and legally as merchandise brokers—the store does *not* pay the resident buying office any fee. The merchandise broker collects his remuneration from cooperating manufacturers in the form of a commission based upon a percentage of orders placed for their clients. While there is a conflict of interest, in that it appears that the merchandise broker is more involved with the interests of the manufacturer rather than the store's, this apparently has not been too great a handicap for a good commission office to overcome. There are many such small commission offices operating, and they are a blessing to the small fashion store whose annual sales volume would not permit them to pay for the services of any of the other classifications of resident buying offices discussed. One of the largest merchandise brokers is Apparel Alliance which lists hundreds of stores as clients. One might ask, "Suppose an order is received by the merchandise broker and the manufacturer is non-cooperative, refuses to pay a commission"? The answer is that a good merchandise broker will place the order and waive the commission, as a necessary service to the store.

SERVICES PERFORMED BY RESIDENT BUYING OFFICES

The following is provided to enable the student to understand and the store owner to select more efficiently the buying office best suited to his needs in the market. In our discussion of the classifications of buying offices, we indirectly referred to *cost.* In addition to considering the cost involved in a specific resident office and its buying service, a store would do well to investigate the following services which are or should be available through the resident buying office.

Market Coverage

The buying office must provide not only market coverage in all classifications of fashion merchandise, but must relate the value of the merchandise to store needs. In other words, the market representatives in reviewing a fashion item should do so in terms of "How will it sell in the store"? In addition, the resident buying office, wherever possible, should actually blanket the market area in order to save the store buyers time, money, and effort when they come to the market. Above all, the coverage should accommodate the needs of the member stores.

Market Reporting

As a result of the market coverage, where the market representative is acting as the "eyes and ears" of the store buyer, this information must be communicated to the store buyer primarily in the form of regularly and/or specially written reports. In a good resident buying office, each day's market activities are recorded by the market representatives, screened, edited, and in a series of written media are sent to the member stores in a steady, correlated flow of information.

Although the titles of this type of regular media coverage may vary from buying office to buying office the following are some typical, self-explanatory bulletin titles:

- Merchandise News
- Special Attention (Special Item)
- Re-ordering Now!
- Immediate Action Required!
- Private Brand
- Group Action News
- Fashion Activity
- Special bulletins for anniversary sales, January specials, Mother's Day, Father's Day, Founder's Day, etc.

Bulletins, such as these, and other variations of communication are produced on a regular basis by each merchandise department in order to keep the store buyers up-to-date and to show them the general direction of the market.

Seasonal Preview Clinics

At the opening of each market's major selling season, the resident buying office should arrange for a clinic and/or a preview of the leading resources' merchandise at the buying office or at a hotel in the market area. The market representative is required to make a merchandise presentation for each merchandise classification which depicts trends and strengths which will influence business for the coming season. Recommendations are made for opening inventories by classification, type, price line, and resource. These pre-season clinics also allow for exchange of information and ideas between all the attending buyers from all the other member stores.

Providing A Variety of Personal Services

When the store informs the resident buying office that the buyers of any of its departments are going to the market, the resident buying office is expected to provide personal services for the store buyers:

1. To notify the "Buyers' Arrivals" column of the local newspapers, e.g. *The New York Times;* and trade papers such as *Women's Wear Daily,* of the buyers expected presence at the buying office (if desired).

RE-ORDER RECAP

THE FOLLOWING ITEMS ARE CURRENTLY RE-ORDERING AND HAVE
A CONTINUED SELLING LIFE IN MOST AREAS OF THE COUNTRY.

-2-

DIVISION: HOUSEWARES

DEPT.	RESOURCE	STYLE # AND DESCRIPTION	COST	DELIVERY	COMMENT
Luggage	Henry Rosenfield Net 20 Days FOB: No. Bergen, New Jersey	Safari Collection.			
Drapery	Rodless Decorations Net 30 FOB: New York	Floral Bouquet Barclay Squares - In One price pr	$18.75 to 37.50	3 wks ROO	Bloomingdale's promoted 5 styles N.Y. Times, Sunday 4/12. Reorders from advertisement were a total of $15,900 in two weeks.
Linens		Twin			

WESTERN HATS - PICK YOUR FABRICATION....

Cowboy Hat has proven to be an important accessory for girls. Many
's have reported strong sales, especially when displayed with Western
, jeans and belts.

n now pick from fabrications of felt, corduroy, denim and suede in a cut
n Western style hat with band and feather trim.

ACTION OPPORTUNITY

THE "PRAIRIE SKIRT"

FOR THE URBAN COWGIRL...

The prairie skirt is not new to
the West. The re-emergence of
the American way, the re-
laxed Western look is becoming
apparent for Spring, Summer
and will be a definite way of
life for '81. The prairie
skirt already reordering
in the "Better" contemporary market in most major
cities. This skirt
incentively priced at
$13.60, regular price
$17.50 in 9½ oz.
washed indigo
denim.

This item should be
featured on T-stand
in all updated misses
departments....

#9130

SPRING INTO ACTION

DEPT.: UPDATED SPTS -
MERCHANDISE: Skirt
RESOURCE: VIA WEST SPT P
TERMS: 8/10 EOM
DELIVERY: A/R 1/30 Comp'
F.O.B.: New York City
DEPT. HEAD: BILL FRIEDM/
BUYER: RITA CHILDS
NUMBER: 4-2-4405-4
DATE: 1/12/81
ck

Juniors will be
ready for action in
poly/cotton interlock
short sets
from:
ANGEL MILLS.....

#9126

 TE INC.

MARKET MEMO

DEPT.:
MERCHANDISE: SPORTSWEAR - Jr.
RESOURCE: Short Sets
TERMS: ANGEL MILLS
DELIVERY: Net 10 EOM
1/15 - 2/28

The most important
fabrication in the most
important silhouettes!

© 1980 INDEPENDENT RETAILERS SYNDICATE

(OVER PLEASE)

F.O.B.: Georgia
DEPT. HEAD: BILL FRIEDMA
BUYER: DEBBIE RC
NUMBER: 4-3-
DATE:

Communications (or bulle-
tins) that typify the information sent by resident buying
offices to member stores.

buyers' arrivals

ANSTENDIG, BLITSTEIN & GILLENSON, INC.
Alliance, Ohio — Lingenfelter Brill: B. Cardinal, ready to wear.
DuBois, Pa. — Patricia's: P. Godek, ready to wear.
St. Charles, Ill. — Clothes Tree: K. Nelson, ready to wear.

ATLAS BUYING CORP.
Chicago, Ill. — Goldberg's: Yvonne Maling, all budget sportswear, junior, missy.
Johnstown, Pa. — Glosser Bros., Inc.: Dave Levenson, mdse mgr accessories; Michael Engel, mdse mgr infants', children's, girls', teens', students' wear, juvenile furniture; Lee Sakony, infants', children's, girls' wear; Murray Meltzer, girls', teens wear; Jules Sloane, women's coats; Carol Sullivan, mdse mgr women's better sportswear, dresses, off price, brand merchandise.
Middletown, N.Y. — Playtog's, Inc.: Allen Klash, infants', toddlers' wear.
Needham, Mass. — Lee Shops: Leo

Taunton, Mass. — New York Lace: M. Makowski, ready to wear.

Klein, mdse mgr ready to wear.
INDEPENDENT RETAILERS SYNDICATE, INC.
Carson, Calif. — Boston Store: Anna Johnson, misses' sportswear; Trudy Rasmussen, misses' dresses, coats.
Huntington Park, Calif. — Wineman's Dept. Store: Yolanda Arredondo, intimate apparel; Lois Head, sportswear; Irene Navarro, junior sportswear, junior budget apparel.

FELIX LILIENTHAL & CO., INC.
Greenville, S.C. — Meyers-Arnold Co.: Ken Hall, mdse mgr coats, suits, dresses, sportswear.
Omaha, Neb. — Richman-Gordman Stores: Judy Hassenstab, lingerie, jewelry; E. Brazzle, infants' basics, furniture.

Tulsa, Okla. — The Froug Co., Inc.: Bob McMurtrey, gen mdse mgr; Gary Eminger, dresses, coats.
LOWETH-NATIONAL BUYING SERVICE
Detroit, Mich. — Annis Furs: Glen Kraske, gen mdse mgr.

OWN OFFICE
McKeesport, Pa. — G.C. Murphy Co.: M.J. McNeal, 3rd., home improvements, paint; B.M. Balawajder, housewares; R.K. Fowler, Jr., seasonal goods; F.J. Remaley, electronics; G.B. Gose, kitchen, dinnerwares; J.R. Turner, curtains, draperies; W.F. Riddle, Jr., home furnishings; T.C. Siple, novelties.
Reading, Pa. — Boscov's: Barbara Andruzak, lingerie; Walter Brandt, junior sportswear; Norman Burton, gifts; Dace Cate, handbags; Saul Eisenberg, cosmetics; Ann Grubbs, misses' coordinates, bottoms, active playwear, better sportswear; Arnold Heicklen, girls' wear; Jean Hulock, women's sportswear; Ann Merkle, maternity wear, uniforms; Betty Majesky, draperies; Tom Mosko, shoes; Phyllis Nonnemacher, pre-teens' wear;

Audrey Rentschler, infants' wear; Arthur Salhanick, misses', women's, petite misses', daytime dresses; Morty Tittelbaum, misses' tops, blouses, shirts; Shawn Walker, jewelry; Edwina Wentzel, little girls' wear; Rubin Yablin, coats; Alex Miller, accessories, hosiery; Bill Hearn, fabrics; Sam Flamholz, mdse mgr dresses; Bill Gallagher, mdse mgr hard lines; Gil Snyder, mdse mgr draperies fabrics, domestics; Paul Levy, mdse mgr accessories; George Weiss, mdse mgr toys, hobbies, sporting goods; Terry Kasoff, gen mdse mgr women's apparel; Albert R. Boscov, president; Morty Morrow, mdse mgr.
West New York, N.J. — Rainbow Shops: Irene Sachs, sportswear tops; Elaine Eisner, lingerie, intimate apparel; Harriet Napier, dresses, sportswear bottoms; Joyce Wurtzel, accessories; Harriet Russell, foundations; Marty Stein, shoes.
York, Pa. — McCrory Stores: G. Murphy, women's, junior, misses' dresses, uniforms, dusters, robes, loungewear, smocks, women's coats, jackets, blazers.

4 apparel stores closed by K Young

NEW YORK (FNS) — The K Young Corp. told a creditors' meeting it has closed four of its six women's and children's apparel stores in the Baltimore area, paving the way to a profitable future beginning in December.

Jeffrey M. Sherman, attorney for the debtor, said at the New York Credit Men's Adjustment Bureau that Young is aided by a good working relationship with its bank, which is allowing it to use the cash collateral.

The bank, the First National Bank of Maryland, has a lien on all the assets to secure $70,000 in loans. Young also owes the trade $275,000 to $300,000. Wage claims are $3,000 to $5,000; $28,000 to $30,000 is owed for taxes.

Young, trading as the Better Look Stores, filed a Chapter 11 petition Aug. 11 with bankruptcy judge James F. Schneider Baltimore.

Siegel, Sommers & Schwart

represents the creditors' committee; Richard A. Eisner & Co. is its accountant: Glenn Heller of the adjustmen ... is secretary. Sherman ...baum & Gins, W? ...tes is the 'bank...' The committee is represented by Hahn & Hessen.

2. To provide telephone, mail, office or desk space, sample room, and if possible, secretarial or clerical help, for the store buyers during their stay at the buying office.
3. To secure transportation reservations and hotel accommodations; admission tickets to fashion shows or to manufacturers; and in some cases arrange for the store buyer's entertainment (to be paid for by either the store or the buyer. Entertainment costs are borne by the buyer.)

Providing A Variety of Buying Services

When the buyer is away from the market and does not contemplate any market trips for whatever reason, the market representative at the resident buying office should provide the following buying services for the store buyer:

1. The market representative at the buying office should have received a copy of every order placed by the store buyer to the resources. These orders are followed up by the market representative or assistants and efforts are made continually to prod the manufacturers, to ship on time or to speed up lagging deliveries.
2. The market representative at the resident buying office in certain, restricted, and carefully regulated instances may place merchandise orders for the store buyer.

Providing Special Counselling Services

The good resident buying office is one that attempts despite its size, large or small, to render personalized service to each of its store clients. To do so requires a knowledge of each store's unique character, clientele, and its own merchandising problems and needs; and the resident buying office through its top management must endeavor to get to know them. The following are some concrete forms of special, personalized merchandising counselling services that a good resident buying office should provide:

1. The market representatives who are in their individual, segmented markets each day should try to share their extensive market knowledge with the store buyers on a one-to-one basis in addition to the normal store bulletins that are constantly being mailed to all clients. To accomplish such an ideal liaison, the market representatives should encourage the store buyers to use the telephone regularly (at the store's expense), to check on market information, review their merchandise classifications, resources, price lines, turnover, etc.
2. In the event that the store people—buyers, merchandise manag-

ers or principals—feel that they have merchandising problems, they should be able to feel that they have a friend and ally at their resident buying office. This feeling can only be engendered if the resident buying office principals have made it clear that they are willing and able to help the store develop strategies and solutions to major problems.

3. There should be a continuous line of communication between the resident buying office representative and the store buyer so that information of any kind may be easily understood for proper representative execution.

4. The resident buying office should be willing and able to conduct all types of buying, merchandising, or training sessions either at the store or at their own offices for any client store's buying staff.

5. The resident buying office market representatives should be available to accompany the store buyer to the market upon that buyer's request. This is especially necessary when a new buyer is coming to the market for the first time, either as a buyer for that store or with that buying office. This would also be helpful if the buying office has located or developed new manufacturing resources. Accompanying visiting store buyers during peak market weeks is difficult, a buyer may accompany a group of buyers with common interests. A new buyer should arrive in New York before the influx in order to receive maximum attention from the office representative.

6. The resident buying office should make provision for at least one meeting a year for store principals, preferably in some well-known resort-like area away from the market place, where the heads of stores may be able to meet without the pressures of business in order to analyze major trends, exchange ideas and information, and chart future common policies and programs. The resident buying office, with a steering committee of store heads, should prepare an agenda and in general plan, organize and conduct the meeting.

Group Buying Programs

Whether the resident buying office represents large or small stores, the good buying office (other than private and merchandise brokers) is one that engages in, has facilities for, or provides leadership for a variety of group buying activities. This can help their member stores to compete with the giant chains whose multi-billion dollar volume and tremendous buying power gives them a large edge over their competitors. The group buying activities should include arranging and coordinating group buying programs, which have been the resident buying offices' primary objectives since the inception of the buying office concept more than a half century ago. The task of group buying is handled by the department's market representative and a committee of store buyers (steering committee), in merchandise categories best suited for such an enterprise. Not only are there price reduction benefits inherent in quantity or mass purchasing, but also some additional benefits.

1. Specification buying—wherein the group buyer arranges with certain resources to manufacture these items to their own specifications or to build in special features not ordinarily available to regular buyers.
2. Better delivery and availability of goods to the group because production of fashion merchandise, which nominally requires a cutting ticket with a minimum amount, can usually be met by any normal group order.
3. Better freight rates may be obtained by the group particularly if it is possible to use a carload lot shipping arrangement with partial load dropoff along the line.
4. It may be possible to get exclusivity or confining of certain parts of the manufacturer's line to the group if their orders are large enough to warrant it.
5. The group may be able to secure cooperative advertising money or such other sales promotional aids as, free advertising mat services; direct mail inserts; display materials; store listings in national ads either in print or in broadcast media.

Wholesaling Activities

Frequently coupled with group buying activities are wholesale or jobber activities that can be conducted by the buying office, by which their member stores are able to buy good staple fashion merchandise at a price that can assure them a better markup than similar merchandise purchased on the open market. Such wholesale activities can also assure better and faster delivery and to some degree, exclusiveness of the lines carried.

WHOLESALE SUBSIDIARIES For good and sufficient legal reasons, many of the larger buying offices have set up separate wholesale divisions. These wholesale companies not only use specification buying and quantity buying, but can also act as jobbers in selling closeouts or irregulars that they obtain directly from the manufacturer or from the mill. They generally operate on a volume basis with a low markup to their member stores, who in turn are able to retail such merchandise at either substantially higher markons or to pass this merchandise on to the consumer at lower prices in the form of "sale" items.

This wholesaling or jobbing operation functions in several ways. In some cases, arrangements are made to sell the merchandise from samples and then have the merchandise dropshipped directly to the member store. In other instances, the wholesale division takes title to the merchandise, warehouses it, and ships it on order or demand to the store for a stated sum, usually a percentage fee.

UNIT CONTROL SERVICES Many buying offices offer their member stores an opportunity to operate one or more of their large volume, popular-priced departments such as a large apparel or a discount chain. For many years, this merchandising activity was confined to the "downstairs store" dress business and as such is still referred to as a C.D.O. (Central Dress Operation) by some offices. The broader term is *Unit Control Service.* As indicated, the system works as if the department was a division of a chain and depends entirely on daily unit control figures for successful operation. The store's department is stocked by purchases made by the UCS buyer in New York. As sales, as well as returns occur, they are tallied (or most probably there is an I.B.M. or other E.D.P. method of ticketing). These figures are then sent to the Unit Control Service for tallying and analysis on a nationwide basis from all the member store departments subscribing to this service. The UCS buyer is thus quickly able to find style trends, reorder good items, and to phase out poor numbers in the inventory.

PRIVATE BRAND PROGRAMS It is quite common to find, (in conjunction with a group buying and/or a wholesale division and perhaps even a Unit Control Service) that a buying office may frequently sponsor a Private Brand Program. Such a plan, of course, must be integrated or coordinated with the national branded merchandise that the store probably carries. Therefore the buying office has to be extremely careful in selecting the items to be branded. A continual search for exclusive items from good resources that can provide a higher markup (if desired, private branding can be used for higher markups; better quality, customer patronage motive, or lower retail prices) must be a part of the buying office's market representative's job. Also involved in this phase of merchandising may be packaging or designing some form of wrapping or packaging; quality control and testing; and an easily handled promotional program to enable the store's customers to recognize and to buy the private brand.

FOREIGN BUYING With the tremendous growth of importing and the easier flow of merchandise from abroad, due to low tariffs or free trade policies, the matter of foreign buying has become one of great importance in all phases of fashion merchandising. The resident buying offices have been involved in foreign buying for many years and this increase in imports has only strengthened their role in it. Among the ways that the resident buying offices are active in foreign buying are:

1. The larger buying offices, particularly corporative and coopera-

tive types, maintain their own foreign offices or branches in the leading commercial or manufacturing centers of the world. These offices perform some of the same services that their domestic counterparts do in the United States.

2. Most buying offices within all the classifications are affiliated with independent, foreign buying offices who are known as *commissionaires.* These commissionaires render services to the store clients of the New York based buying offices to ensure production, quality, transportation, and filing of necessary government forms.

3. Many of the larger resident buying offices maintain a special section on their premises and frequently employ a special foreign buying expert. In this area, there may be a showroom where imported merchandise samples are on display.

Sales Promotion Services

There is an old adage in retailing that "nothing happens until something is sold." It is quite logical therefore that member stores should expect the resident buying office to assist them in the sale of the goods that the buying office helped them to select and buy. The good buying office should be in a position to help their store clients with the following sales stimulation efforts:

- "Ad Mats"
- Statement Enclosures
- Sales Promotion Calendars
- Displays
- Catalogues
- Merchandise Bulletins
- Fashion Office

"AD MATS" A newspaper advertising matrice ("ad mat") is a device which enables the buying office to provide their member stores with a finished newspaper advertisement, complete with art and copy on merchandise which the buying office has recommended for purchase. The ad mat is a lightweight composition material which has been pressed like a mold from an original metal engraving of an advertisement. It is much lower in cost than the original (quantities can be bought for $0.15–$0.20 each) and they can be sent to stores at a low mailing cost. The newspaper running the store's advertising can recast from these ad mat molds, a facsimile of the original. These ad mats are frequently sent to stores on a weekly basis at no charge. In addition, a consolidated and classified "mat" book is often sent to the stores at the beginning of each season featuring office selected styles of market importance.

STATEMENT ENCLOSURES Since most fashion stores encourage charge accounts, it is a time-honored custom to enclose direct mail advertising pieces with the monthly statement. These statement enclosures are usually prepared by manufacturers but the resident buying office frequently arranges, at a small cost, for these mail "stuffers" to be imprinted with the individual names and prices of their member stores.

SALES PROMOTION CALENDARS The sales promotion department of the resident buying office is expected to recommend long range store sales promotion planning. This usually takes the form of a six month or a year sales promotion calendar including promotion themes, as well as specific creative ideas for advertising, display, publicity, and special events based on traditional and innovative sales objectives.

DISPLAYS Taking a leaf from the national chains' centralized display services, the alert resident buying office can provide display assistance for many major promotions to their store clients such as:

1. Major theme model window displays designed and executed at the buying office, which are then photographed or sketched, and mailed to the stores.
2. Backgrounds, props, mannequins, etc., designed by the sales promotion department and arrangements made with display manufacturers to produce for the store clients.
3. Copy written for window signs and samples; sometimes arrangements are made with sign manufacturers to prepare the finished product for sale to the stores.
4. Lighting plans are designed and are then sketched, prior to distribution to store clients.

CATALOGUES The sales promotion department of the resident buying office is expected to design and produce merchandise catalogues geared to important seasonal events and merchandise categories such as Christmas, Back-to-School, January White Sales. The merchandise featured in these catalogues reflect the coordinated buying efforts for member stores who will be offering this merchandise for sale. The resident buying office will arrange to imprint the individual store's name, logo, special message, and prices, on their order of catalogues so that it would certainly appear to the customer that this catalogue was the store's own promotion and production.

MERCHANDISE BULLETINS While the information for the daily resident buying office bulletin services is gathered and written primarily by each department's market representative, the final preparation and production is done by the sales promotion department. They will often add new ideas for advertising, display, and promotion of the merchandise being reported. In these bulletins there are also case histories, success stories, and reorder reports which should indicate what could be promoted. The bulletin also could indicate whether an ad mat and/or statement enclosure would be available for the stores' use.

FASHION OFFICE To assist their store members, the resident buying office like the department or large specialty store, generally has a fashion office headed by a fashion director or coordinator, whose job here is to devise ideas for fashion shows and other special events by the store. The fashion office prepares themes and "how-to's" in the form of fashion promotion kits, which are filled with ideas for advertising, display, publicity, shows, and events for major fashion trends. The buying office's fashion director should be able to provide a capsule fashion show for each seasonal preview in every major merchandise category. Fashion directors of large resident buying offices make regularly scheduled tours at the request of member stores. The store provides the clothing and the amateur models and amidst much excitement stages a fashion show in the store's auditorium or local theatre. The fashion-minded public is invited by ticket to view the forthcoming seasonal new trends and highlights. In some cities, women's clubs use these events as fund-raising efforts for a worthy cause or charity, thus engendering goodwill as well as sales.

Miscellaneous Services

The following miscellaneous services are frequently available but cannot be categorized under any one heading:

EXCHANGES, CANCELLATIONS, AND ADJUSTMENTS It is quite obvious that store personnel could simply and easily do the routine business such as the cancellation of unfilled or late orders; wrong merchandise shipments; exchanges, and other normal complaints that may arise from any business transaction. But the store is probably hundreds if not thousands of miles away from the market and such actions could cost the store time, effort and money in the form of long distance calls and written correspondence. Simple instructions to the market representative can usually settle any adjustment with the manufacturer through personal conversation. This is particularly true where the market representative and the buying office has influence in the form of the buying power of a large group of stores.

SAMPLE ROOMS Each buying office representative assembles a good-size collection of samples from cooperating resources for buyers to preview on their market visits. These samples are available for inspection throughout the buying season and are very helpful in saving the store buyers' time and effort during the rush of market week.

CONSULTATION SERVICES In addition to counseling services discussed earlier, the well-organized resident buying office generally offers merchandise/management consultation services for in-store diagnosis and cures by the buying office's teams of officers and experts. On request, such resident buying office personnel will visit the store and conduct an on-the-spot analysis of the problem. This service can frequently be highly effective because the consultants are able to use an outsider-looking-inside point of view. The costs of such visits are paid by the stores.

MERCHANDISE MANAGEMENT ASSISTANCE There is also generally available long-range merchandise management assistance. This usually takes the form of coordinated campaigns by buying office executives working with the store's merchandising executives, to improve individual departments as well as the store as a whole. Such assistance usually has as its goals: more volume, fewer markdowns, and faster stock turnover. The buying office attempts to implement these goals by strategically diversifying stocks, weeding out unprofitable resources, and by overhauling the store's advertising and sales promotion plans and methods. There is also a monthly review of sales, and inventory to attain maximum stock-to-sales ratio.

CONFIDENTIAL DATA EXCHANGE Under the leadership of the resident buying office's research personnel, a spirit of mutual assistance and cooperation is often generated which enables the buying office's analysts to collect, on a regular basis, all sorts of vital, statistical data from their non-competing member stores. Careful compilation and analysis of such data as operating expenses, sales promotion costs, department markup and markdown figures, can be of invaluable use to the stores' executives in comparing their own departments, or the entire store's operation, to the figures of a similar or comparable group of stores.

STORE EXECUTIVE RECRUITMENT Because the resident buying office is located generally in the heart of the principal fashion marketplace, one of its natural, if not frequently used services, is to act as a personnel consultant to its member stores when they are in need of hiring merchandising or management executives. While the larger, cooperatively owned and corporatively owned buying offices can afford the luxury of an actual executive recruitment office, the hundreds of other buying offices perform this service in an indirect and informal way. In some instances, the buying office employs the service of an executive search organization (or employment agency) on behalf of their store clients; in other cases, they may pass the word around the market using key manufacturing resources, to attract the attention of executives from other stores who might be interested in making a change; or the resident buying office might insert an advertisement in the local public or trade press and screen any applicants.

SELECTING A RESIDENT BUYING OFFICE

Much of the material previously discussed can be condensed into the following questionnaire or checklist and used to help in selecting the appropriate resident buying office. It is merely a series of questions based on facts and data that require research and thought designed to facilitate a decision. In the United States Government's Small Business Administration Marketers Aids, Pamphlet No. 116, Ernest A. Miller has summarized a number of factors to aid the retailer, who is away from the primary fashion markets in New York, in screening the possibilities, narrowing the field, and avoiding selecting a buying office which is not compatible or suitable for the store. The following is a synthesis of that summary:

1. Is the resident buying office known for its popular-priced and promotional merchandise connections; or is it a specialist in the medium or higher-priced fashion field? In other words: Does its retail thinking agree basically with the store's?
2. How does the size (sales volume) of the store fit in with the resident buying office's actions and services? Basically, it boils down to: Is the store too small (or too large) for the resident buying office?
3. How do the principals and staff of the buying office strike the store's executives and buyers? Are they the kind of people the store feels that it can do business with on a close and continuing basis?
4. Is the resident buying office's staff sufficient in size to give adequate service? Is there at least one buyer for each major fashion classification or does one buyer cover a number of markets or categories?
5. What business references can the resident buying office give the prospective store member? Can they be checked easily and can the general business and financial reputation of the buying office be ascertained?
6. Who are the buying office's current store clientele? Are these stores generally similar in size and scope to the prospective member?
7. Is it possible to speak to the heads of some of the other store clients to give *their* opinion of the buying office? How much credence can be given to the opinions in view of their selection by the buying office principals?
8. Can the prospective store client secure a list of manufacturers that the resident buying office staff deals with regularly? (To this

list can be added other prominent fashion resources.) Can the opinion of these manufacturers about the competency of the resident buying office staff and the office's general reputation in the market be considered valid?

9. What standard, regular services can the store expect that will help it save time, avoid needless market trips, and offer professional buying assistance?
10. Does the resident buying office offer auxiliary services such as pre-season clinics, fashion coordination, figure analyses?
11. Can the store purchase from the buying office sales promotion aids such as mailing pieces, catalogues?
12. Does the resident buying office have a wholesale operation and/or act as a jobber on staple merchandise?
13. Does the resident buying office maintain a private brand buying program?
14. Does the resident buying office have a central buying operation? In what merchandise categories?
15. What will joining the resident buying office cost? What is the fee and how is it determined?

THE ROLE OF THE ASSISTANT BUYER IN A RESIDENT BUYING OFFICE

Little mention has been made of the role played and the responsibilities assumed by the assistant buyer in the resident buying office. Of course, the role will differ depending upon a variety of factors, such as the size and type of buying office, store clientele. Unlike the store assistant buyer, who generally begins as an executive trainee and then is promoted to the position of assistant buyer, the resident buying office novice to begin with usually assumes the title of assistant buyer. While this beginner is frequently literally thrown into the marketplace, there is usually an apprenticeship or on-the-job training until the newcomer actually learns the principal resources in a particular market. The learning process is usually accomplished by assigning the new assistant buyer to the *follow-up* tasks previously discussed in this chapter. From this point on, the assistant buyer is given the opportunity to place special orders, reorders, and finally, open orders.

In the larger resident buying office, (cooperatively owned, corporatively owned, or independently owned), each buyer usually has at least one assistant. In the smaller buying office, it is a common practice for several buyers to share one assistant.

In the matter of career building, the assistant buyer, who is employed by a buying office, finds promotion to buyer to be easier and quicker than contemporaries working in stores. But as in the case of the resident buyer versus the store buyer, the buying office assistant buyer is paid less for better hours, fewer working days, and has fewer responsibilities.

SUMMARY

This chapter, should have performed two functions:

1. to acquaint the reader with the role of an office;
2. to offer sufficient information to help the reader decide whether this is the sector of the industry that affords career opportunities.

The resident buying office, department by department, is arranged on an organizational structure similar to the stores it services. This very feature of paralleling merchandise categories or classifications is responsible for the trade slogan that the buying office is truly "the eyes, ears and legs" of the store buyer.

The resident buying office must keep the store buyer informed at all times of what is happening in each segment of the vast fashion market. At the same time, the market representatives are also constantly maintaining good vendor relationships for their store clients with those manufacturer resources that will best serve their client stores.

In essence, buying offices perform three major functions:

● Researching
● Buying (with permission)
● Helping stores promote goods

The following should be considered: resident buying is a service business and therefore does not remunerate employees, as those engaged in merchandising where there is direct responsibility for profit. Resident buying does not include responsibility for either sales or selling. It does offer its own aspects of working conditions and satisfactions. As a resident office buyer, one works with (and for) people from all over the country, sometimes with (and in) foreign countries. One of the main activities is to digest market conditions and render reports that help stores generate sales and profits. This can be a highly creative endeavor. The work week is five days, with Saturdays and Sundays free.

For a person interested in people, resident buying offers a wide assortment of them and under circumstances that can result in a great deal of self satisfaction.

chapter 10

FASHION BUYING FOR
THE SMALL INDEPENDENT STORE

INTRODUCTION

There are believed to be somewhat less than two million stores in the United States (a more exact figure centers around a million and three quarters, according to the last business census figures available). Of this number, there is also estimated that the overwhelming number of them —a million and a half—are considered to be *small* stores. Further beliefs make it seem probable that about ten percent of these stores can be linked to the fashion business.

One of the most difficult terms to define is what makes a store a *small* one. How much sales volume is required to define it as a small store or as a medium-size store? There is some agreement among marketing authorities that the low figure of $100,000 is an acceptable one; on the other end, a maximum of $2,000,000 has achieved general acceptability. The word "independent" is more readily understood to be that form of retail establishment that is a one-store operation. It may seem peculiar that in the present era of multi-billion dollar conglomerates and giant retail chains, that the small store has as great an opportunity as ever. In the language of the current vernacular and for many of today's consumers, being big can be a "turnoff," synonymous with impersonal or no-service, pushing crowds, and the general limitations associated with mass merchandising.

While this text was written for use in a course in fashion buying and merchandising, we recognize the need to include information beyond fashion buying and merchandising for the ever-increasing number who have that great American dream—to be their own boss. Many believe that going into the retail fashion business is not difficult if they want to work hard; if they have some creativity; and what they believe to be sufficient financial backing to start. Hopefully, most of these aspiring entrepreneurs have had several years of experience working in the field.

In order to be entirely accurate, this chapter will also have to include factors that involve the thinking and planning prior to opening of the store as well as a brief examination of the requirements needed to open the store, and the pitfalls that must be avoided.

WHO IS THE SMALL INDEPENDENT STORE OWNER?

The following may be considered as a profile of the person(s) whose personal characteristics augur well for success in this field:

1. The owner manages a single, independent store.
2. The owner is a generalist, rather than a specialist—the complete merchant, wearing many hats such as buyer, salesperson and janitor. In other words, there is no specific organizational chart in the small, independent store with its division of authority and responsibility such as is found in the larger store.
3. The owner has gained sufficient working experience in a similar small business and/or a large retail fashion firm, working for somebody else while accumulating sufficient capital to open his/her own business (95 percent of all failures arise from a lack of experience and undercapitalization).
4. The owner excels in what is known as "the personal touch." He is truly the purchasing agent for his little community because he believes he knows his customers and what they will need, want, and buy. And that the store is located as conveniently as possible to those customers.
5. The owner has the ability to assess potential profit, capital need, and an understanding of government requirements and regulations, primarily because of in-depth consultations with both his accountant and his attorney.

HISTORY & DEVELOPMENT

Recent archaeological findings reveal that retail trade existed even earlier than was originally believed in ancient history. Every history student knows about stores that were discovered in the ruins of ancient Greece and Rome and down through the Middle Ages. Insofar as the United States is concerned, hardly had the first settlers arrived when trading posts were established. The evolution of the trading post into the general store and the era of the itinerant peddler are also well known, as is the fact that most of our leading department stores started as small independent stores. Chains frequently evolved from the expansion of an independent store by a successful, ambitious proprietor.

An interesting development of the small, independent store was the establishment of the boutique which first began as a modern version of the small independent store. The boutique then became a department in a large department store, and sometimes evolved into a chain operation, sometimes as a result of a franchising operation. The boutique came into being in the 1960s and its customers were particularly affluent people or were those who demanded "different" merchandise and could afford it. These customers were those who reacted strongly against "bigness" and who looked for individuality versus mass production in fashion merchandise. Thus, during the 1960s, the boutique in decor and ambience as well as merchandise became the symbol of fun, and excitement in merchandising. Unfortunately, this form of independent store has had a high rate of failure due to a variety of reasons, among which are: inexperience of owners, the state of the economy in the 1970s, and undercapitalization.

MERCHANDISE POLICIES FOR THE SMALL INDEPENDENT FASHION STORE

In reality, a small store is a retail operation that carries a limited number of price lines, in limited space, with limited buying power for a limited number of potential customers. As in every retailing endeavor no matter what size, the most fundamental activities are buying merchandise and re-selling it to customers. This, however, is too simplistic a statement because merchandising requires the owner to know *what* type of merchandise is to be handled; in *what* quantity; *when* it is to be stocked; and *how* it is to be sold. Involved in the *stock* phase is the well-established principle that it should be balanced—in assortment (style variations that are attuned to customer preferences) and in depth (how many of each as projected by careful planning).

The merchant must also decide if the store should carry nationally branded merchandise, if available. Such a decision must weigh the pros: good markup; well-known quality; a responsible manufacturer; time-proven specifications; and generally favorable reception by customers. The cons: the branded merchandise manufacturer usually requires in-depth purchases, thus constricting both in merchandise budget dollars and in the narrowing range of offerings, to a few resources. The other disadvantage centers around the general area of the wide distribution that nationally branded merchandise has with the large retailer, such as the department or specialty store, who carry large stocks, thus putting the small store in competition with the giant—an unfair, and unneeded situation.

Another phase of merchandising which requires setting of policies relates to the pricing of the merchandise stocked at levels that will attract and hold a certain group of customers. Of course, the average small store can afford only a limited range of price zones—those which interest most of its customers. This tends to help the store to keep its merchandise moving rapidly, and makes for narrow rather than broad assortments. It has been said that such policies tend to limit customers' choices, but on the other hand, it does help to build the store's image and character, and it is a big reason why many customers prefer to shop in small stores with a definite fashion viewpoint.

The biggest advantage a small store has is its policy that here the customer can get personal selling service, something that has practically disappeared in this age of "bigness." Other services revolve around policies regarding the alterations, delivery, gift wrapping, etc., of the merchandise purchased. The whole area of promoting the store and its merchandise also require policies which delineate how and when to use such media as local newspapers, telephone selling, local radio, TV, and direct mail.

PLANNING & CONTROLLING MERCHANDISE

Unlike large fashion operations with their sophisticated E.D.P. systems, the small independent store owner has neither the money, time, nor necessity for complicated control methods. This means that the small store must institute meaningful manual recording of merchandise that can give the owner sufficient information for effective planning and control.* We have already indicated, but it bears repetition, that in an operation of limited scope, merchandise must be confined to a well-selected assortment of styles, price lines, colors and sizes but still be consistent with the probable demand of the store's clientele. This helps to assure that there will be a minimum of investment and a maximum rate of sale.

The details on how to establish an effective system for planning and controlling merchandise is relatively the same for a small store as for a large store—only the scale of operations is different (see Chapters 11 and 12).

BUYING

In addition to planning the small independent store's stock, by dollars and units, the owner/buyer also needs to be prepared at all times to determine what will be "in fashion" for the store's clientele based on the volatile nature of fashion (as defined in Chapter 1): "that which is accepted by a substantial group of people at *any given time* and *place*." The American woman has been conditioned to expect that generally what she is wearing now will be obsolete in a relatively short time.

The owner must also be aware that the fashion calendar calls for up to six seasons and that this requires that the store's stock has to "turn

*Computers are available for small store use, and there are computer firms that handle data for small stores.

over" (be replaced) rather rapidly. Therefore, the small store "buyer" must have a keen awareness of fashion trends, customer motivation, and what these customers are likely to want, when, in what quantities, and in what price ranges.

To secure such information and knowledge, the independent store owner must keep accurate records that reveal customer preferences of merchandise types, price levels, resources, colors, sizes, etc. (If this is for the opening of a new store, perhaps these facts can be secured from a friendly non-competitor.) However, much of this information can be secured by affiliating with a good resident buying office, one that is known for its services to small stores (see Chapter 9). For additional information, the merchant can turn to such channels as:

FASHION MAGAZINES *Vogue, Bazaar, Mademoiselle, Seventeen, Glamour,* etc.

TRADE PUBLICATIONS Women's Wear Daily, Retail Week, *W,* etc.

DAILY NEWSPAPERS The women's page(s) or fashion section of the leading newspapers in all large cities; advertisements that show the fashion offerings of the leading stores in that city. (By studying the fashion offerings in the Miami, Florida, and the Los Angeles, California, newspapers, the small store owner in northern sections of the country can get a preview of the forthcoming season which is different due to climatic conditions.)

THE APPAREL MARKET Manufacturers, wholesalers, and their sales representatives.

THE TEXTILE MARKET Illustrations of fabrics in use are generally made into sample garments to promote the new fabrics and colors and gives an insight to future developments in fashion.

COMPETING STORES Visiting and studying their stock.

The careful planning previously referred to is all in preparation for actually buying merchandise which will hopefully result in the customer's approval as indicated by their purchasing the store's merchandise. The fashion store owner can complete the buying function primarily by going to the main fashion markets in New York and/or by visiting regional markets. In addition, many manufacturers have traveling sales representatives in territories that cover most of the country. Also, as we indicated in Chapter 9, the store's resident buying office can be empowered to buy for the store; re-orders can be placed by mail or phone or by the R.B.O.

One of the disadvantages of being a small independent store in the buying function is that its smallness prevents it from buying in large enough quantities to make any impression on important vendors. In fact, there may be times that such resources may even refuse to sell or to ship to small stores. In some areas of buying, it is also possible that small stores may not be able to buy directly from the manufacturer but must resort to wholesalers or jobbers. Of course, the small store is frequently at a disadvantage from the preferential treatment given to larger stores when it comes to exclusivity of the best numbers of the manufacturer's line.

However, the small store merchant who knows his customers—and many do, very well—does not have to employ the "buckshot" technique used by larger stores in their merchandise selections in order to cover their customers' range. The independent store owner can buy so carefully that at times, he can even have specific customers in mind. This is a particularly important aspect in the fashion business because it indicates to those customers the personal touch in the store's merchandising that is so important. Most customers are appreciative when they receive a call from their local fashion store that they have some new merchandise which was bought especially with them in mind; and many sales result from such personal selling.

Unfortunately, when it comes to buying and merchandising matters, the small store owner is frequently tied up with simple, daily duties to plan or he has no training or ability to make merchandise budgets; to watch for slow-selling merchandise in order to make markdowns on time; or to watch inventories to prevent overstocking, etc. Because the small store certainly has limited traffic, it is much more difficult to get rid of buying "mistakes." It is no easy task to pinpoint a highly selective and salable stock.

SALES PROMOTION

In the retailing sequence, sales promotion is the process that follows planning and buying to hopefully make for profit. Actually, sales promotion (commonly called advertising) will be discussed in great detail in Part Four of this book, covers a wide range of activities many of which are precluded to the small store owner because of their cost in time, money, and lack of proper personnel.

While there are many forms of sales promotion such as newspaper ads, local radio and television spots, direct-mail, publicity releases, and fashion shows, many of these, most of the time, are not within the small store's budget. However, by means of window and interior displays, telephone selling, circulars or flyers, signs, and some direct mail (post cards), the promotion of the store and its merchandise can be accomplished without undue financial strain. Some areas are fortunate enough to have one or more small, local newspapers whose advertising rates are within the reach of the average small store, and this can supplement the sales promotion program.

As a rule, however, the small store owner will find the mail and the telephone to be the best sales promotion tools available. It would be advantageous for the owner to keep accurate records of the store's regular customers or to obtain by purchasing from the local telephone company block-by-block names and addresses and telephone numbers of good prospective customers. The merchant can then use the telephone to good advantage to describe what is felt that particular customer might find of interest by a visit to the store. The use of inexpensive, direct-mail pieces are equally helpful in securing sales.

SO YOU WANT TO OWN YOUR OWN BUSINESS!

The following guidelines are presented for examination by those who feel that they owe it to themselves to be among the hopefuls who open new stores every year.

Ownership

The form of business ownership that the small store will have depends on a number of factors including financial status; business knowledge; size and scope of the enterprise; the ability, the need, and the desire to co-exist with a partner, etc. For all intents and purposes, for most ventures, the choice can be made from going it alone—(sole proprietorship), partnership, or corporation.

SOLE PROPRIETORSHIP The store's assets are owned by one individual or a family. This form of ownership has the advantage of simplicity of organization; the ability of the owner to make all the decisions; to enjoy all the profits; and to get out of business easily, if necessary or desirable. On the other hand, the limitations or difficulties include the problem of raising money; the unlimited liability for all risks and debts; the limited life of the firm—the great probability that the store will be forced to close with the death or total disability of the owner, etc.

PARTNERSHIP Two or more persons voluntarily agree to associate as the co-owners and operators of the store. The rights, responsibilities, and duties of the partners are specifically set forth in the articles of partnership, drawn up by a mutually agreed upon attorney or by separate attorneys. The partnership brings definite advantages to the ownership because it frequently ensures combined skills, talents, and experience to the operation of the business. It almost always brings the greater availability of capital and with that, greater potential borrowing power. The partnership's limitations are quite similar to that of the individual proprietorship in that all partners are still liable for all the risks and debts of the store (albeit any losses are divided equally); and the life of the partnership ends with the death or total disability of one of the partners (although this may be offset by insurance). In addition, there is the factor that the business can be disrupted by disagreement among the partners and by the danger of the divided authority that this form of ownership might engender.

CORPORATION A business entity which can operate as a legal "person" and as such may own assets and be subject to debts contracted by the corporation. The most important advantage of incorporating is that it removes the burden of personal liability for the debts and risks of the firm from the individuals who comprise the ownership of the corporation's stock and limits that liability to the value of the shares held. The other advantages include the assurance that the death of any of the owners will not terminate the business—perpetual life; the readiness of transfering ownership to others—by selling the stock; the greater ability to raise capital—by selling stock in the corporation; and depending upon certain circumstances—tax advantages. The limitations of organizing a corporate form of enterprise include government regulations of corporations which are not applicable to single proprietorships or partnerships; the expense (legal and state fees) of incorporating—important to those with low capital budgets; various corporation taxes—depending on Federal, state, and local laws; periodic time-consuming legal paperwork created by bureaucratic control of corporations, regardless of size; and finally, restrictions set up by the corporation charter which limit the freedom of business activity to those outlined in the charter.

Acquisition

After making a decision on the form of *ownership* described above, the next decisive step to be taken by the prospective store owner is how such a business is to be acquired. One way is, after careful investigation, to *buy a going concern.* Another method, if applicable, is *to buy a franchise* from a manufacturer, wholesaler, or franchise promoter. But the most common form of acquisition is to start the new store from "scratch" after determining that there is a real need for such a store.

Financing

Actually, everything we have discussed thus far in this chapter and all the factors yet to be examined hereafter, hinge on one final question—

can the prospective small store owner secure sufficient capital, no matter from what source, not only to open the store but also to keep it going for at least one year no matter what business problems may occur. Among the items to include in determining the size of such a start-up fund are rent and security; purchasing of fixtures and equipment; procuring merchandise for resale; installing telephone and other utilities; cleaning and painting the premises; repairs to the building if needed; supplies of all kinds including business forms and stationery; opening a checking account with an adequate cash balance; advertising and promotion for the store's opening and continuance; establish credit facilities for customers; and salaries if full or part-time employee(s) are needed. Starting a new business can easily consume unusually large sums of money during a very short period of time. Without sufficient funds, the proprietor can be forced out of business almost before the business begins. *Undercapitalization* ranks near the top of the causes of small business failures.

Location

Determining the right location for the store is a prerequisite for its survival and ultimate success. Only the merchant who offers one or more very important inducements such as consumer-satisfying prices, extraordinary service, and unique products, can convince sufficient numbers of potential customers to go out of their way; all others must offer the customer the right merchandise, at the right price, and at the *right place*—a convenient one. Thus, the retailer must select a trading area in which it has been determined there is a sufficiently large enough population that makes one feel quite certain that the merchandise offerings will attract adequate numbers of customers. This determination was arrived at because a study was made about these potential customers' income level, age groups, educational background, fashion apparel preferences, etc.

Once the general geographic area or region is fixed, then the city, town or village therein is pinpointed; next, the neighborhood in that city, town or village is decided on; and finally, the exact site within that community is selected. It should be made clear that in order for the prospective store owner to be certain that the location selected will help to secure success, basic research on that location must be undertaken. As a result of such a study, the owner must feel that the location will be able to support the store; that the current competition is not overwhelming and that the new store could survive that kind of competition and yet prosper; that the location is in an adequate growth situation; and that the location is not saturated with similar stores. A word about the latter—people like to shop where there is ample choice available and where there is a large number of similar stores in a relatively small area; which is another way of saying that competition attracts traffic—customers believe that comparison proves value.

A final word about store location involves this age of the automobile—America on wheels. It is not an isolated fact that stores have been forced to close because parking was scarce and customer competition for the parking spaces was too keen. There are very few things more frustrating to shoppers than a lack of adequate and convenient parking.

Physical Plant

Once the store's location has been determined, choosing the actual building in which the store is to be housed or in the shopping center or mall, is the next consideration. The building should be of good construction and in good physical condition; if it is not in good condition and in need of repair, it should be clearly understood as to who will be responsible for such reconstruction. The appearance of the building is another aspect that merits thought—it should be both functional and pleasing to all senses. The building's exterior should also, if at all possible, reflect the character and personality of the store; or at least, give the customer a feeling that it is a solid, dependable, honest place to do business with. Not many people really want to deal with a sleazy-looking, fly-by-night store. The basic appurtenances which enable the store to be properly heated and/or cooled should be in place; provision for adequate lighting and safety factors such as sprinklers should be considered.

The size of the building is directly concerned with the physical plant and the image the store conveys to the public. If the building is too large or too ornate or too plain, it could have a ludicrous or harmful effect on the store's image. The same thing holds true if the building is too small—the cramped atmosphere that would be created would seem to stifle the customer and would have an adverse effect on the message that the merchandise should be conveying to the customer.

Finally, from the physical plant viewpoint, the building must be as safe as possible from fire and other natural hazards. It should afford the merchandise and the entire investment adequate protection from burglary and other crimes.

Store Layout and Decor

The interior space of the store should be handled in such a way that an atmosphere of friendliness, enthusiasm, and stimulation is created in the selling and various service areas, and that this spirit is easily felt by both the public and the store's personnel. To do otherwise would be setting up a handicap that the merchandise and those concerned with its sale, would find it very difficult to overcome. This means that the interior needs to be attractively laid out; styled to its potential customers' taste; efficiently fixtured; economically but interestingly illuminated; and effectively using color to enhance the merchandise.

The store's front is both a part of its interior and its exterior. The windows and signs are both intended to communicate a message to the customer to come in and find merchandise to suit them.

In this day and age, it can be said with some degree of surety that customers are generally not attracted to or interested in shopping for fashion merchandise in warehouse-like buildings and factory-like interiors. The failure of the giant Robert Hall, the national family apparel chain as well as the S. Klein Stores, is clear proof that pipe-racks are out and that our affluent society seeks pleasant, bright, cheerful, relaxing surroundings when they do their shopping.

Credit Facilities

Retail trade in the United States has been operating in a credit economy for several decades and the new small independent store must be alert to that fact from the very beginning. Many customers expect—even demand—a wide variety of credit services. Extension of credit may be accomplished in several ways, but the store with a very good financial situation may elect to "carry its own paper"—handle its own accounts receivable.

CHARGE ACCOUNTS The customer's financial background is checked and a monthly charge limit is determined. The customer then can charge goods up to that limit and is billed every month with the expectation that all charges will be paid in full, monthly. There is no charge for this service if payments are made within a specified time.

INSTALLMENT CREDIT While this is used primarily for "big ticket" items, many small stores allow their customers to accumulate a predetermined amount during a given period and then repay the total in regular installments over a fixed period of time, e.g., six or twelve months. There is always an interest or service charge for this type of credit and it is generally a profitable business because the store is dealing with lower income families who need this form of credit in order to enjoy immediate possession of the goods.

REVOLVING CREDIT The customer is given a credit limit and is expected to pay for all charged purchases on a monthly basis. However, upon presentation of the monthly statement, the customer may elect to pay a stated minimum amount of the total due and carry over the balance at a substantial interest charge, (now at *least* 1½ percent per month or 18 percent per annum) with privilege of paying off the entire amount at any time.

If the store is unable or unwilling to tie up funds in order to finance its own credit facilities, then it may elect to sell its accounts receivable to a bank or factoring firm. Under this arrangement, the store receives cash from the purchaser of accounts receivable in advance of due date for which it pays a fee. However, many independent small stores arrange for their customers to use nationally accepted credit card systems such as *Visa, Mastercard, American Express,* or *local group charge cards.* This also gives the store practically overnight cash flow since it can deposit these credit transaction slips with their local bank. Of course this eliminates the need for collection procedures since the credit card companies bill the customer directly. However, accepting credit cards reduces the margin of profit since the retailer must pay a small percentage of the sale to the organization that finances the card system.

There are two widely practiced retail policies that are related to credit facilities. One is the *layaway promotion,* a merchandising technique to sell new merchandise prior to the coming season. Merchandise is sold for future delivery. Customers usually pay a small percentage of the purchase price with the remainder paid in installments or in full when delivery is made. A variation to this practice is "buy now and you will not be charged until . . . ," often sixty days after purchase. Summer coat sales are examples of this technique. The second policy concerns the *return of goods.* Large stores offer a liberal return-of-goods policy, they take back goods for cash or credit to a charge account. Many small stores, however, confine the exchange to a credit memo—customer credit for the purchase of merchandise.

Policies

Everything that is done from the inception of the idea to open the store to the actual operation of the business is determined by various principles, objectives, or policies which the owner(s) of the business have determined to be correct for that business. Thus, the selection of a site for the store is determined by a policy which decides whom the store owners wish to serve; a policy as to price lines to carry; a policy concerning what credit facilities, if any, to offer—and the list is endless. Thus, these policies are the way by which those who conduct the business decide how the business will run and what image the store will have in the eyes of its customers.

Many stores feel the need to have the public—their customers and potential customers—know what certain store policies are in addition to those store policies that are used merely as guides for the store's owner(s). Such policies are then used in the *store's advertising,* e.g., "We will not be undersold!"; *on signs,* e.g., "No exchanges or refunds without a receipt"; and *in mailings* to the store's customers, e.g., "Regular charge customers will be able to purchase this merchandise before it is put on sale next week."

A small store—a regional market (see pages 231–234). Courtesy California Mart.

CALIFORNIA MART PRESENTS

the BIG SHOW

Large Size Market
October 10-12, 1982
Sunday, Monday, Tuesday

LARGE SIZE MARKET October 10, 11, 12, 1982 at the California Mart-Market Mezzanine, Market hours: Sunday. 10:00 a.m. to 5:00 p.m. Monday and Tuesday. 9:00 a.m. to 5:00 p.m.

FASHION SHOW/BRUNCH Sunday, October 10, 1982, 10:00 a.m. in the Fashion Theatre.

COCKTAIL PARTY Monday, October 11, 1982, 5:00 to 7:00 p.m. Fashion Theatre.

SEMINAR/CONTINENTAL BREAKFAST Tuesday, October 12, 1982. 8:30 a.m. Buyer Forum, Market Mezzanine 2.

FOR YOUR CONVENIENCE, ALL LINES WILL BE SHOWING ON THE MARKET MEZZANINE

YES, I WILL ATTEND Please pre-register me and send:
_____tickets for the Fashion Show/Brunch, October 10, 1982, 10:00 a.m.
_____tickets for the October 11, 1982 Cocktail Party, 5:00 p.m.
_____tickets for the October 12, 1982 Buyer Forum, 8:30 a.m.

RETURN TO: Large Size Market, California Mart, 110 E. 9th Street, Suite A727 Los Angeles, California 90079. (213) 620-0260
Name _____
Store Name _____
Street _____
City_____ State _____ Zip _____

110 E. Ninth Street, Los Angeles, CA 90079

California Mart
where the action is!

It is necessary that policies be flexible—that they change to fit new circumstances, to meet competition, and to enhance the store's image.

Professional Assistance

From the very beginning of planning the new store, the need for professional assistance is a necessity. For example, there is an immediate need to choose an attorney to help determine which form of ownership to use in organizing the store. The need to select a qualified accountant in order to get the best assistance possible in the proper financing of the new venture. The following ideas or problems need to be discussed with the appropriate professional.

Attorney

- Government requirements
- Insurance coverage
- Real estate leasing or purchase
- Form of business enterprise
- Collection of delinquent accounts
- Contracts for building construction
- Lawsuits

Accountant

- Required business records
- Working capital
- Stock turnover
- Level of sales required
- Tax returns
- Monthly balance sheet and Profit and Loss statements

In those instances where the entrepreneur is required or feels compelled to build his own building to house the store, a registered architect and/or a store designer should also be engaged.

Government

We have already inferred that there are times when various government agencies are involved in the running of a small business. The mere mention of taxes, licenses, permits, etc. brings that problem into immediate focus. There are literally thousands of Federal, state and local laws, regulations, and ordinances that affect the daily operation of the store; and ignorance of any statute is no defense. The following is a brief list of government controls that are part of the store owner's every day's activities:

- Advertising claims—F.T.C.
- Labeling laws
- Credit charges
- Withholding and Social Security Taxes
- Sales taxes
- Unemployment insurance

- Labor laws
- Workmen's Compensation and Disability Insurance
- Civil Rights Laws
- Pricing agreements (antitrust)

There is no business so small that the owner can ever escape contact with some government agency.

Risk-Taking and Insurance

Taking a risk is part of everyday life and in business as well. Therefore, one must first understand that there is a difference between taking a gamble and taking a risk. A gamble is a situation where the element of loss is accepted in advance and the degree of risk is difficult to predict; a risk may frequently be calculated quite accurately as to the possibility of success or failure.

So, in business, the kinds of insurance and the amounts of coverage to offset the normal risks the store may be subjected to are quite predictable to a high degree of accuracy. To become more specific, we must first examine the principal areas of the business where risk is involved; namely, loss or damage to the physical plant, merchandise, supplies, and fixtures; loss of income due to interruption of business; and personal injury to customers and employees.

The following types of specific insurance coverage are available to the small independent store owner:

- Fire and general property
- Plateglass
- Burglary
- Public liability
- Product liability
- Workmen's compensation
- Business interruption
- Fraud/Bad Check

Personnel

This chapter began with the general assumption that an estimated more than one-third of all the small stores in the United States did not even have one person, with the exception of the owner(s) employed. However, for the remaining two-thirds, mention should be made here of the personnel factor that could be part of the new enterprise from the beginning, or later on, as the business grows. It is an accepted fact that a well-selected, well-treated employee(s) can be detected easily by the store's clientele as indicated by their demeanor; their enthusiasm for the merchandise; and their general attitude toward their employer and to the public. It is another corollary that any customer can tell you that if the management is good and decent, those working for them will reflect this—good labor relations always lead to good public relations. Briefly, the personnel responsibilities faced by the owner(s) include:

1. A formal or informal *job analysis, job description,* and *job specification* should be made—so that everyone involved knows what the position is all about.
2. A knowledge of the *employment process*—which includes recruiting; screening, using application forms and/or tests; interviewing the applicant; checking references; and then placing the employee on the specific job.
3. *Training* the new employee; re-training the old employee; training people for supervisory jobs, when required.
4. *Evaluating* the employee's performance—for advancement, salary adjustment, transfer, or termination.
5. Understanding *salary* scales and *wage* payments.
6. Understanding the need for *grievance* handling; *human relations,* and other morale building techniques.
7. Keeping adequate *employment records.*

A store's personnel can either become one of its most valuable assets or a deterrent to success. The successful handling of the personnel factor by the small independent store owner can give the business an edge over its giant retail rivals so frequently found nearby.

SUMMARY

In essence, the small independent fashion store is a small scale version of a larger specialty store. We have seen that there are numerous areas of concern involved in opening and operating such a store and that all these responsibilities plus the planning, buying, and promotion of the merchandise falls on the shoulders of the owner(s). Yet, all of this is being met and handled successfully by hundreds of thousands of independent merchants. The pitfalls are great; the rewards are many, one of which is the grand feeling that you are your own boss—with no one to report to!

part **3**

TWO FUNCTIONS OF MERCHANDISING: PLANNING & BUYING

Up to now we have been concerned with *what* fashion buying and merchandising is about: its place in retailing; the qualifications of applicants; the practices of buying for different organizations; and explanations of merchandising terms and concepts.

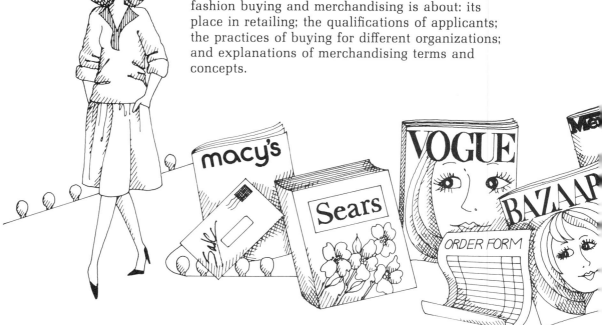

Part Three will be devoted to *planning* and *buying,* two of the major functions of merchandising.

Every buyer who is a complete merchant, is involved in all phases of merchandising—planning, buying, and selling. The degree and areas of responsibility of the buyer are dependent upon the type of organization and its policies, as discussed in Part Two.

If there is a science to buying, it must be in the planning process. And the buyer is a key figure in the planning process.

When you have finished Part Three you should be able to:

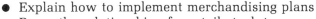

- Explain the elements of a dollar plan
- Compute and explain the importance of stockturn to fashion merchandising
- Explain how merchandising events affect the stock level a buyer may prepare
- Respond to the question of why the retail inventory system is used by most retailers
- Relate how a fashion buyer obtains information to plan and buy a stock composition consistent with store policies, anticipated sales, and probable consumer demand
- Explain how to implement merchandising plans
- Prove the relationship of a retail stock to a segmented customer group
- Explain the meaning of a balanced stock
- List the criteria for resource selection
- Express the manner in which a buyer should conduct relations with vendors

chapter 11

DOLLAR PLANNING & CONTROL

INTRODUCTION

Profit is not an accidental occurrence. It is the result of a carefully planned course of action.

The goal of a business plan is to minimize the use of capital and maximize profit. The *merchandise plan* is one of the most important "tools" to support this effort. It is often referred to as the *six-month merchandising plan* or *dollar plan.*

The merchandise plan consists of two major elements (1) an estimation of merchandise needed and (2) a control method to regulate stock levels. As in the case of most business plans, estimates vary from results. Therefore, in addition to estimating merchandising objectives, the plan establishes corrective measures when actual events prove the need for adjustment. Hence, the terms *planning* and *control* describe the techniques used with the plan to make dollar investment in merchandise that will be most responsive to consumer demand or—how inventories are expanded or contracted as circumstances and sales occur.

The larger the organization, the greater the need for a plan. Large stores, where there are layers of responsibilities and the need for large capital outlay, require sophisticated plans and controls, without which they would be vulnerable and unable to function profitably. In some small stores, especially where ownership plays a dual role—buyer and manager—formal plans are not often utilized. Investments are mentally weighed and developed or planned on a handy piece of paper. Obviously, the small-store operator is totally involved and completely conversant with all of the store's activities and able to plan and execute action from personal experience and knowledge. The responsibility for profit is contained, there is no accounting to higher echelon.

The merchandise plan is the means of *budgeting merchandise activities in terms of dollars.* This blueprint does not regulate units, assortments, or quantities.

From the viewpoint of the retail institution, the planning process is a management tool to estimate the value of inventory to be carried in each department of the store for a given period. On the other hand, a plan has important advantages for the buyer.

Plans start at the departmental level and are eventually collated into a master store plan.

THE RELATIONSHIP OF A
DOLLAR PLAN & CONTROL

The dollar plan is actually a budget which balances *planned* sales and *planned* stocks in terms of dollars. It also includes standards, if achieved, which should result in a *planned* profit.

The control feature is known as the *open-to-buy*—the dollars that a buyer may spend for delivery of goods within a given period. Dollar planning and control consists of:

1. A prediction of customer demand for each month of the plan.
2. An estimate of the inventory need for each month of the plan.
3. The maintenance of planned inventory levels by means of a control feature (the regulation of how much a buyer can purchase based on merchandising events).

The form and information required of a plan will vary with the organization, but the buyer's main objective is to be guided in purchasing the correct amounts of merchandise at the right time. The best time is, obviously, when customers want it. The following must be emphasized.

The Plan

1. All planning starts with sales.
2. All stock needs are related to sales.
3. Merchandising activities can be evaluated (by establishing standards and comparing results).

The Control Feature

1. The difference between the *planned* beginning of the month stock and the *actual* beginning of the month stock is caused by a variation from plan of sales, purchases, and markdowns that occurred in the previous month.
2. The open-to-buy is a resultant figure.

RESPONSIBILITIES FOR A DOLLAR PLAN

The responsibility for the dollar plan is dependent upon the organization's viewpoint and the nature of the operation. In a chain operation the responsibility for dollar planning is most often the divisional merchandise manager's, with the aid or consultation of the buyer. Giant mail-order chains invariably assign this responsibility to divisional merchandise managers, as well, and use the buyers as sources of information. The buyer in a department store is assigned a part of the planning and in some cases is called upon to submit an entire plan to the divisional merchandise manager.

Regardless of who initiates the plan, it is scrutinized by several levels of the management and ends up in the hands of the controller and/or treasurer for the total store plan.

What is of paramount importance is the submission and approval of a realistic plan at such time that it can be used as an effective tool in controlling budget requirements.

REQUIREMENTS OF A DOLLAR PLAN

A good plan is one that is developed through the efforts of those who are responsible for the achievements and evaluations of the merchandising activities. Therefore there must be cooperation from all levels of management: the buyer (the performer), the merchandise manager (the controller), and top level management (the evaluator). Team concept is evidenced with an understanding of goals, responsibilities and interests at all levels.

A plan is an estimate and subject to constant revision and possible use of new tactics. The plan should be under close watch by both the buyer and the merchandise manager, exchanging views and evaluations.

APPROACH TO A DOLLAR PLAN

The planning requires gathering all pertinent and available information in advance of the effective date of the plan's operation. Management supplies each department with the past year's records which become part of the plan.

In order for the merchandise manager to control and implement the plan, information relative to economic conditions, intended store applications of marketing techniques, advertising, etc., as well as any information that could affect the merchandising activities, principally the selling levels, is required.

Preliminary work sheets are used and temporary plans established at the buyer or merchandise manager level. These temporary plans are later finalized and submitted to the general merchandise manager for revision or approval. They are then returned to the divisional merchan-

Figure 11–1. Example of Six-Month Merchandise Plan.

Department Name_____ Department No. _____

		PLAN (This Year)	ACTUAL (Last Year)
SIX MONTH MERCHANDISING PLAN	Workroom cost		
	Cash discount %		
	Season stock turnover		
	Shortage %		
	Average Stock		
	Markdown %		

SPRING 19-		FEB.	MAR.	APR.	MAY	JUNE	JULY	SEASON TOTAL
FALL 19-		AUG.	SEP.	OCT.	NOV.	DEC.	JAN.	
SALES $	Last Year							
	Plan							
	Percent of Increase							
	Revised							
	Actual							
RETAIL STOCK (BOM) $	Last Year							
	Plan							
	Revised							
	Actual							
MARKDOWNS $	Last Year							
	Plan (dollars)							
	Plan (percent)							
	Revised							
	Actual							
RETAIL PURCHASES	Last Year							
	Plan							
	Revised							
	Actual							
PERCENT OF INITIAL MARKON	Last Year							
	Plan							
	Revised							
	Actual							
ENDING STOCK July 31 Jan. 31	Last Year							
	Plan							
	Revised							
	Actual							

Comments

Merchandise Manager_____ Buyer_____

Controller_____

dise manager, who in turn works with the buyer who then plans the stock composition within the framework of the established figures. The *required lead time* to a large measure depends upon the size, nature and location of the operation.

ELEMENTS OF THE DOLLAR PLAN

All activities of merchandising are planned in advance and standards are established by management in order to evaluate performance levels of each area. **Figure 11-1** is an example of a *dollar plan*, also called *six-month plan, merchandise plan, six-month merchandising plan.* Organizations can use different forms, however, the one used here as an example contains all the elements commonly found in a dollar plan broken down into monthly units.

The dollar plan requires an estimate of sales and a provision for an inventory of proper stock size to support it. The essential figures or elements of a plan are:

- *Planned Sales* —estimates for each month and the period
- *Planned Stock* —estimated inventory need at the beginning of each month
- *Planned Markdowns* —estimated inventory reduction for each month
- *Planned Purchases* —estimated purchase budget to be spent during a given period

Since a plan is also a set of financial goals, it may include planned figures for:

- *Workroom Cost* —cost of alterations and repairs of garments that are charged to the department. This can be a dollar or a percentage figure, or both. When a percentage figure is required, it represents a ratio to net sales.
- *Cash Discounts* —percentage of the period's cost purchases (discounts earned through early or prepayment of accounts payable). The ratio is a percentage of the department net sales.
- *Season Stock Turnover*—net sales divided by the average inventory.
- *Shortage*—difference between book inventory at retail (usually the retail inventory system) and the physical inventory in terms of retail values. The shortage (or overage) is a percentage of net sales.
- *Average Stock*—beginning of the month inventories divided by the number of months of the period.
- *Markdown* —dollar reductions from originally set retail prices of merchandise, a percentage of the net sales.

- *Percentage of Initial Markon*—difference between the costs and first retail prices, expressed as a percentage.
- *Newspaper Advertising*—shown in dollars or as a percentage of net sales, or both.
- *Gross Margin Percentage*—difference between the cost of goods and the amount of sales, expressed as a percentage.

For each merchandise activity there is a provision for a *planned* and an *actual* figure. The actual figure is the performance, and can only be filled in during the period of operation, after the results. For example, the actual sales figure for February can be shown on March 1. There is also provision for figure revisions. If events develop that necessitate new estimates, the buyer discusses these events with the divisional merchandise manager and establishes new figures.

All planned goal figures are expressed as a ratio to sales figures. It must be emphasized that the standards for each department will vary— the merchandise, trade practices, and consumer expectancies make for a different set of circumstances.

Note that there are two different periods: February through July and August through January. These periods are widely used because the starting dates are in periods of low inventory and each period contains two major merchandising seasons—spring and summer, fall and winter. As a corollary, retailers usually operate on a fiscal rather than a calendar year, (the fiscal year ending January 31).

Planned Sales

The first consideration in planning is forecasting sales for the period and then for each month of the period. The planner starts by filling in the sales for each corresponding period of the previous year, the base or starting point. These figures are provided by the organization.

It is then necessary to estimate the increase or decrease for each period of the plan. Last year's levels afford an area of probability. Therefore sales forecasting is a combination of two considerations— experience plus anticipation.

The factors of anticipation are many, but the following discussion explains the most usual. Obviously when the economy is healthy and the people have confidence in it they buy more freely. So, the first consideration is *the economic climate of the country, the region, and the trading area.* This information can be secured from many sources, such as:

1. the store's figures;
2. the department's volume trend;
3. Federal Reserve Bank figures;
4. trade statistics;

5. trade associations;
6. business magazines;
7. bank economic forecasts.

There is a myriad of sources available to determine what direction business is going. The main point, however, is that expert opinions are obtainable. This type of information is usually secured by a store's management level and related to the merchandise manager, who in turn advises the buyer.

The planner must be aware of another anticipatory factor. It is not uncommon for departments to be enlarged, in which case there might be a need to increase planned sales. There could be a realignment of price levels, perhaps the elimination of lower price points, which might have an adverse effect on the number of units that can be sold. A situation that comes to mind is a nationally known department store that had a well-developed ladies sportswear operation that did over $2,000,000 a year. Management decided to change the price ranges, establishing new higher prices and eliminating lower ones. A budget department, with a new buyer, was created on the same floor, in fact adjoining the existing department. The buyer who remained with the new better department had to plan a decrease in sales. The store benefited from two departments, but the buyer had to work temporarily at a lower sales level, at least until the department established a track record.

Scheduled promotional activity must be studied carefully since the desired effect would be accelerated selling. This information is secured from the merchandise manager, and probable sales increases are estimated by both the buyer and the divisional merchandise manager.

An important consideration is any change in the competitive situation; additional stores competing for the same customers could dictate a more cautious approach. Just imagine a new shopping center with many stores carrying competitive merchandise, opening within one's trading area. In a major area on Long Island in New York many merchants were forced out of business with the opening of a branch of a well-known department store.

One of the buyer's main contributions to a good plan is the proper assessment of market strength. This ability marks a fashion professional. It goes without saying that if the market offerings of a new season appear to be highly saleable, the plan should express optimistic sales estimates. On the other hand, if the market lacks newness, caution would be expressed in modest estimates.

The buyer has an additional source to help in planning sales. Many buyers maintain a daily diary, noting the volume for each day and any comments that affected the sales such as a promotion, trend, or the weather. If weather conditions were extremely bad and resulted in poor sales for a given period, it is probable that the same period for the following year would not be so affected. A promotion that generated strong sales puts the buyer under pressure to plan a means of beating these figures during the period of the plan.

These are some of the evaluations that are included in the process of estimating sales. Naturally, it takes experience and judgment to arrive at realistic figures. In summary, planning is estimating and that no plan is rigid, it is subject to change. A good plan is one that is based on realistic figures with small margins for errors.

Planned Stock

Once sales have been estimated, the next step is to set inventory figures to accommodate these figures. The question is: How much stock should be planned to support planned sales? It is clear that to sell $10,000 in one month, the stock position must be greater. How much *more* is the problem. The buyer recognizes that at the beginning of the month there must be an adequate depth and assortment of stock to provide an adequate selection for the customer. Management sets up guidelines within which the buyer must work. The fundamental goal is to balance stock to sales. In reality there is never a perfect condition, but management's concern is to get as close to a state where there is reasonable balance. There are two guidelines to follow for balancing stock to sales:

- Stock Turnover
- Stock/Sales Ratio

STOCK TURNOVER The first guideline is stock turnover. This is a method that is useful in planning the total size of the inventory. It is computed using the following formula:

$$\frac{\textbf{Planned Sales (for a period)}}{\substack{\textbf{Planned Average Inventory}\\ \textbf{(for the period)}}} = \textbf{Stock Turnover}$$

This result is a ratio that measures the speed of merchandise in and out of the store over a given period. It is a measurement of efficiency and it is usually calculated for a period of six months or a year. Every department has its own stock turnover rate since different merchandise requires different levels of selling speed. Going from one extreme to the other, certain dairy products require a turnover rate of 60 times a year, but toys can operate efficiently on approximately 3 turns. In fashion merchandise a typical shoe department probably could be considered doing well with 2½ turns a year, while a budget dress department standard should approximate 6 turns. From management's point of view stock turnover indicates a level of capital usage, turning money into inventory, inventory into money, and repeating the process. Although it is a valuable figure, it has its shortcomings. The greatest deficiency is that it does not show stock at particular times, it is an average, and therefore does not reveal shallow or excessive depths at particular times.

STOCK/SALES RATIO The second guideline is the ratio of stock to sales. This is a method that establishes a ratio at a given time usually at the beginning of the month. If sales are estimated at $10,000, and the established store ratio for the department is 4, the planned stock as of the beginning of the month would be $40,000. It is calculated as follows:

$$\frac{\text{Retail Stock (as of a specific date)}}{\text{Sales for a given period (a month)}} = \text{Stock/Sales Ratio}$$

The guidelines used to establish a ratio are usually based on the experience of the department. In addition there are store exchange groups that share their experiences, plus industry organizations that publish consensus figures. Different norms are set for each of the six months of the period. When selling is at the low volume ebb of the season, the ratio is increased because it is necessary to maintain an adequate selection of merchandise despite lowered selling levels. **Figure 11–2** illustrates a typical monthly stock/sales ratio.

WOMENS AND MISSES COATS AND SUITS											
FEB 3.2	MARCH 1.8	APRIL 2.4	MAY 2.7	JUNE 5.2	JULY 5.5	AUG 3.5	SEPT 3.5	OCT 2.7	NOV 2.5	DEC 2.7	JAN 2.9
LADIES ACCESSORIES											
4.0	3.0	3.3	2.9	3.2	4.1	3.9	3.2	3.6	3.3	1.8	4.4

Figure 11–2. A typical monthly stock/sales ratio.

The Relationship between Stock Turnover and Stock/Sales Ratio

Stock turnover and stock/sales ratio are valuable statistical guides used by management to obtain a proper balance of stock to sales, as noted in the preceding discussion. During the months when selling is at the low volume ebb, the ratio is increased because it is necessary to maintain an adequate selection of merchandise despite lowered selling levels. The following example shows that the stock turnover can be the basis for the stock/sales ratio: If the desired stock turnover is 6 times per year, the stock/sales ratio would be an average of 2 for each month. As previously explained, in practice the stock/sales ratio would be different for each month, but the average figure for the period would be 2.

The planned stock figure is known as *stock beginning of month,* or *stock BOM.* Conversely, *EOM* means *end of month.*

The difference in the two approaches then is that the stock/sales ratio is a figure at a given time, whereas the planned stock turnover is an average figure for a period.

In calculating the average inventory for stock turnover purposes, it is usual to use 2 inventories of the last month of the period. For a six-month period, 7 inventories are added, the beginning inventory of each month plus the ending inventory of the last month. For a period of a year (12 months), 13 inventories are used. This method results in the best possible average. For example:

STEP 1   **PLANNED BOM INVENTORIES**

February	$ 1,000
March	1,500
April	1,800
May	1,500
June	2,000
July	3,000
August	2,500
September	3,500
October	2,000
November	1,500
December	1,800
January	2,000

$24,100

Inventory Jan 31 + 1,200

Total Inventories $25,300

STEP 2

12 BOM Inventories + 1 EOM Inventory

$$\frac{\text{Jan. 31} = \$25,300}{13} = \$1,946 \text{ (Average Inventory)}$$

STEP 3

$$\frac{\text{Sales for the Period—\$10,000}}{\text{Average Inventory—\$1,946}} = 5.14 \text{ Stock Turn}$$

Stock turnover and stock/sales ratio are guides to help control the amount of stock requirements in relation to sales and are based on the experience of the department and industry norms. The degree of balance reflects the proper usage of money and a means to achieve desired profit.

RETAIL INVENTORY METHOD

Stores carry a wide assortment of merchandise which can add up to huge quantities. To achieve effective dollar control some kind of *book inventory* must be established. It can be a system that operates at cost or retail values. Most large organizations use the *retail method.* In this method, an accounting method, all merchandise is carried at retail values. Merchandising activities for purposes of evaluation, are then based on retail sales results. Since markup percentage is also a statistic, the approximate cost of merchandise can be obtained easily. All figures in the dollar planning and control system are shown in retail sums.

Advantages of the Retail Inventory Method

1. The ease of making comparisons with figures of other stores.
2. A relatively efficient means of determining gross margin and net profit.
3. The ability to determine cost of merchandise by the application of a percentage, the cumulative markup percent (cumulative markup on all goods).
4. The ability to maintain close supervision of all merchandising functions.
5. The maintenance of a book inventory of all merchandise on hand.

Applications of the Retail Inventory Method

The following are some common applications of retail figures:

COMPARING MERCHANDISING PERFORMANCE An increase or decrease in sales volume compared to a comparable period or plan is expressed as a percentage.

EXAMPLE   To find an *increase* of actual sales over planned sales:

FORMULA

$$
\begin{array}{lr}
\text{Actual Sales This Month} & \$100,000 \\
\text{Planned Sales This Month} & \underline{95,000} \\
\text{Difference} & \$5,000
\end{array}
\quad = \dfrac{\$\,5,000}{\$95,000}
$$

$$
\$95,000\;\overline{)\,\$5,000.\,00}^{\;.053\ \text{(Rounded)}}
$$

$$
\text{Increase} \qquad\qquad 5.3\%
$$

DETERMINING MARKUP Markup is figured as a percentage of the retail price.

EXAMPLE To calculate the retail price of a $49.75 garment with a 45 percent *markup*:

FORMULA

$$
\begin{array}{lrr}
\text{Cost} & \$49.75 & = 55\% \\
\text{Markup} & 40.70 & = 45\% \\
\hline
\text{Retail} & \$90.45 & 100\%
\end{array}
$$

or

$$
55\% \;\overline{\smash{)}\;\dfrac{90.45 \quad \text{(Retail)}}{\$49.75}}
$$

The retail price could be rounded to $90.00 to fit into a department's price range structure.

COMPUTING PROFIT Merchandising plans and results are related to sales and expressed as percentages. The following is a departmental profit and loss statement, the base for figuring merchandising results in terms of percentages.

EXAMPLE Net sales are $500,000, the cost of merchandise sold is $300,000, and operating expenses are $150,000.

FORMULA

Net sales	$500,000 =	100%
Cost of goods sold	300,000 =	60%
Gross margin	$200,000 =	40%
Operating Expenses	150,000 =	30%
Net Profit	$ 50,000 =	10%

$300,000	$200,000	$150,000	$ 50,000
$500,000	$500,000	$500,000	$500,000

The figures are based on the department's profit and loss statement.

Gross Sales	$520,000
—Returns and Allowances	20,000
Net Sales	$500,000

Opening Inventory (cost)	$185,000
+Purchases (cost)	300,000
Total Merchandise Handled	$485,000
−Returns and Allowances	6,000
	$479,000
+Cost of Transportation	9,000
	$488,000
−Ending Inventory (cost)	192,000
	$296,000
−Cash Discounts	18,000
	$278,000
+Alterations and Workroom Cost	22,000
Cost of Goods Sold	$300,000
Gross Margin	$200,000
Operating Expenses	$150,000
Net Profit	$ 50,000

CALCULATING MARKDOWN PERCENTAGE Markdowns are retail price reductions, which are one of the measures of merchandising efficiency.

EXAMPLE Net sales are $5,000, markdowns are $450.

FORMULA

$$\frac{\text{Markdowns}}{\text{Net Sales}} \quad \frac{\$450}{5,000} \quad \frac{.09}{450.00}$$

Markdowns 9%

A store's statistical department maintains current records of all inventory movement in terms of dollars, which permits a retailer to determine the on-hand value of all merchandise without taking an inventory count and also provides a base for merchandising standards. Naturally, a retailer takes periodic inventory counts to verify the accuracy of the book figures. The following is an illustration of how merchandising events are recorded to maintain a book inventory:

Opening Inventory
+Retail Purchases
 Total Merchandise Handled
−Net Sales
−Markdowns (or price changes)

- —Employees Discounts
- —Returns-to-Vendors
- —Merchandise Transfers (out of stock)
  - Total Deductions
- =Book Inventory

THE DOLLAR PLAN IN ACTION

Figure 11–3 illustrates a dollar plan with most of the essential figures filled in for the purpose of explanation.

Step One is to fill in last year's figures. The total sales for the period were $24,800. Based on experience, we have concluded that the modest 5 percent increase for the period is in order, or sales projection of

Figure 11–3. Example of Six-Month Merchandise Plan in Action.

Department Name_____ Department No. _____

SIX MONTH MERCHANDISING PLAN		PLAN (This Year)	ACTUAL (Last Year)
	Workroom cost		
	Cash discount %		
	Season stock turnover		
	Shortage %		
	Average Stock		
	Markdown %		

SPRING 19- ~~FALL 19-~~		FEB. AUG.	MAR. SEP.	APR. OCT.	MAY NOV.	JUNE DEC.	JULY JAN.	SEASON TOTAL
SALES $	Last Year	3100	4000	3500	5000	5500	3700	24,800
	Plan	3300	4100	3600	5100	6000	3940	26040
	Percent of Increase	6	3	3	2	9	7	5 %
	Revised							
	Actual	3000						
RETAIL STOCK (BOM) $	Last Year	6000	8100	6900	9800	10000	7200	
	Plan	6600	8200	7200	102000	122000	8000	
	Revised							
	Actual	6600	8530					
MARKDOWNS $	Last Year	420	567	450	828	791	501	
	Plan (dollars)	390	500	400	795	700	425	
	Plan (percent)							
	Revised							
	Actual	370						
RETAIL PURCHASES	Last Year	5620	3367	6850	6028	3491	3351	
	Plan	5290	3600	7000	7895	2600	3625	
	Revised							
	Actual	5300						
PERCENT OF INITIAL MARKON	Last Year							
	Plan							
	Revised							
	Actual							
ENDING STOCK July 31 Jan. 31	Last Year							6350
	Plan							7200
	Revised							
	Actual							

Comments

Merchandise Manager_____ Buyer_____

Controller_____

$26,040. Each month was considered and increases were assigned based on the anticipated conditions. Each month has a different rate of increase, but the overall percentage is 5 percent.

The stock/sales ratio, in order to establish a BOM for each month, was calculated on the basis of 2, therefore the monthly sales were multiplied by that number. February planned sales of $3,300 multiplied by 2 ratio equals planned BOM stock of $6,600. As previously noted, the stock ratio usually varies from month to month.

The following is an illustration of how to arrive at planned retail purchases, using February as an example.

Planned sales—February	$ 3,300
Planned stock—end of February	8,200
Planned markdowns—February	390
Total provision requirement	$11,890
Less planned stock—beginning of February	6,600
Planned retail purchases—February	$ 5,290

It should be noted that all figures are in round sums since all calculations are, at best, estimates. The reader may be puzzled about finding the ending inventory for the month of February, but the answer is that the opening inventory for March is actually the closing inventory for February.

The illustration takes into account the stock need. First, to sell $3,300 worth of stock it is necessary to have that much inventory. Then a store must have a stock position at the end of the month which is the opening inventory of the next month. Markdowns must be deducted from the requirements because they lessen the available inventory. And finally, the stock on hand at the start of the period is already part of the preparation and must be subtracted from the planned stock preparation for the month.

THE CONTROL SYSTEM

Assume that the plan is in operation and the date is March 1. We are in the position of figuring our stock needs for March.

Let us see what happened during February. Sales were $3,000 for the month against a plan of $3,300, therefore we are $300.00 below estimate. The markdowns were $370.00 or $20.00 less than anticipated, which means that the actual inventory will be affected by $20.00. And finally, we bought about even with our calculations, or $10.00 more, which adds to the difference between planned and actual figures. Add these differences up and they total $330.00 more than planned.

Now let us illustrate the formula to see how the control system can put a brake on the buyer or afford a greater budget if the circumstances were reversed—where sales, purchases and markdowns were greater than the plan. In which case the buyer would be allowed an increase over the planned budget in order to bring the actual inventory up to the planned stock.

MARCH

Planned Sales	$ 4,100
Planned EOM Stock	7,200
Planned Markdowns	500
Total Provisions Required	$11,800
Less Planned Inventory BOM	8,200
Planned Retail Purchases	$ 3,600
Less Stock Variation	330
Total	$ 3,270
Less Unfilled Order for Delivery This Month	700
Open-to-Buy* This Month	$ 2,570

Examination of our merchandise plan will show that it called for a BOM stock of $8,200 and that it is actually $8,530; therefore an over-bought position as of March 1, the sum of $330.00, which must be deducted. If the actual stock was less than plan, the difference would be added to the planned purchases because the stock position would be in an underbought condition.

It is evident that the control system involves three factors: *sales, purchases* and *markdowns.* Any variances during a month from the figures planned for each factor will result in a difference between the planned BOM stock and the actual BOM stock. This *difference* is the *control element.* A deduction or addition, as discussed. We suggest that the reader review the events of February that resulted in the $330 variation as shown in the plan in action.

The deduction of $700 is a compilation of orders at retail figures which have been placed with manufacturers for delivery during the month. In other words, part of the buyer's commitment has been made but not received. These unfilled orders are obtained from the buyer's records. Unfilled orders are often kept on a clipboard for easy reference.

*A budget for the purchase of merchandise for delivery within a given period.

CONTROLS & FASHION CONSIDERATIONS

Occasionally buyers find themselves in an overbought position, where there is no open-to-buy. The buyer made some miscalculation that resulted in more merchandise than planned, when there is improper stock/sales balance. According to the book no further monies can be spent without permission from the merchandise manager. This situation is not a rarity by any means.

If the economic situation is bad, it is possible that no monies would be available to the buyer. Top management could put a temporary lid on all new purchases to bring the store inventory level into line with selling trends. However, if normal business conditions prevail, both the buyer and the division merchandise manager, are cognizant of one fact, "to be out of trend is a cardinal sin of fashion merchandising." Hence, if the buyer's stock does not include a new important trend, despite an overbought condition, there would be an accommodation to make money available for what the customers would have a right to expect in the store.

It would appear that the faster the stock turn the greater the profit, and that is true. However, a stock turn that is too fast can be a negative factor. It can lead to holes in stock, that is, absence of sizes, colors, etc., of which customers could take a dim view. In a budget dress department a normal turn per year is 6, but an ambitious buyer might speed it up to 8, especially when market deliveries can support this rate. Management would undoubtedly clamp down on the buyer in several ways. One way is to increase planned sales considerably and maintain the original stock/sales ratio. Another method would require increased quantities of merchandise at the highest price levels of the department, which will tend to slow down the turnover rate.

Planning and control is the key to a sound retail operation. A buyer is part of an institution that has many guidelines. There are few organizations that have more definitive methods of controlling the activities of the members of the organization.

In this chapter the planning and control centered on dollar planning. A seasoned fashion buyer knows that fashion is constantly changing. He is in a position to mentally calculate the control system. Knowing the approximate inventory levels permits a knowledge of the relationship of inventory to sales. For example, if a month's sales are projected for $25,000, the buyer knows a daily rate of $1,000 is not going to better the planned figures. So the purchasing is restrained. If the sales are $2,000 a day, the buyer knows that it is necessary to revise the predicted sales which will make more open-to-buy available.

The wise buyer is always flexible, rarely spending all the money available. Fashion takes funny bounces, sometimes fast developments take place after market visits and being open-to-buy is the key to taking advantage of the situation.

SUMMARY

The dollar plan (six-month plan or six-month merchandising plan) is one of the most important merchandising "tools." The major purposes of the dollar plan are to assure the most efficient use of capital, maintain a balance between stock and sales, and provide standards of merchandising events. It is a flexible plan that can be adjusted to respond to actual or newly anticipated merchandising developments or external conditions.

The plan starts with a sales estimation of each month of operation, followed by the determination of an inventory level for each planned sales figure. When actual sales, purchases, and markdowns vary from planned figures, they cause a variation of the succeeding month's planned opening inventory, which necessitates a change in planned purchases. Hence, the resultant figures of the plan is the open-to-buy—the controlling factor of the planning process.

The plan is wholly concerned with dollars in retail terms—a method referred to as the retail inventory system—by which goods are charged into a department at retail—permanent inventories are carried at retail—merchandise is marked down at retail—goods are sold at retail—and merchandise results are expressed as percentages of retail sales.

A fashion buyer has deep concern for the department's stock turnover rate, essentially the number of times during a period merchandise is stocked, sold, and replenished. Generally, high turnover stocks yield high profits and those with low turnover are likely to require high markdowns. A rate of stock turnover is established by management, based on retailing standards for different classifications of merchandise. Most buyers, however, think and plan in terms of stock/sales ratio, the stock depth needed to support planned sales of a period, usually a month. The meaning of both terms is essentially the same, but stock turnover is figured for a period, whereas the stock/sales relationship is at a given point in time, such as at the beginning of the month.

The most fundamental business considerations are the need of capital and how it can be put to best use—to earn the greatest return. The dollar plan abets these efforts and gives management the opportunity to assess capital need and to assure a proper relationship between stock and sales.

chapter 12
MERCHANDISE ASSORTMENT PLANNING

INTRODUCTION

Successful fashion merchandising requires a stock that is in harmony with consumer demand. A buyer, after having obtained an approved dollar plan, determines how and when to stock balanced proportions of style assortment, depth price, sizes, and fabrics. The nature and timing of a fashion stock varies with different types of stores, but what all buyers practice is purchasing the appropriate merchandise that their consumer group will probably buy.

Management selects the consumer group and establishes the merchandising policies, while the buyer selects resources and anticipated customer-satisfying merchandise. A variation to this relationship is when management exercises the option to approve or disapprove a proposed commitment, for example, with a nationally branded manufacturer. The reason for this possibility is discussed in this chapter.

A buyer uses many sources of information, within and outside the store, before concluding what fashion trends are worthy of stock inclusion. As in dollar planning, the broad planning approach is based on two factors—experience and anticipation. The former is obtained from internal records, sometimes called unit control, more recently, merchandising by classification. But whatever method is used, consumer acceptance of specific styles and fashion trends are a matter of record of every well-run fashion operation. In a time characterized as the computer age, a buyer, most often, has available current computerized information of how consumers are reacting to merchandise, a considerable advantage in a business in which time is always of the essence.

A buyer considers the following as important principles of merchandising assortment planning:

- An inventory must relate to a customer group selected by management.
- An inventory must be consistent with policies established by management.

- Profit is a result of customer-satisfying merchandise.
- The character of the merchandise in all fashion departments of an organization must be related (compatability of prices, colors, sizes, fabrics, and silhouettes).
- Profit-producing inventory is the result of organized and systematic planning.

STORE POLICIES THAT INFLUENCE ASSORTMENT PLANNING

Every type of store in its attempt to appeal to a targeted consumer group uses selected merchandising policies. Therefore from the beginning certain guidelines are made known to the buyer. The following policies are important and affect the planning process.

- To stock *national brands* or *irregulars*
- Exclusivity of Merchandise
- Pricing
- Sales Promotion
- Service
- Mail Order

National Brands

Fashion goods are available from manufacturers who have ultimate customer identification. For some stores, these are recognized advantages: ample markup, known quality, proven specifications, resource responsibility, and favorable predisposition of some customers. Many stores operate on the basis that a wide selection of national brands make for a wanted stock position. There is one well-known New York department store that has almost an entire department stocked with nationally identified merchandise. The management's interpretation is that this is what their customers desire and need. On the other hand, some New York Fifth Avenue stores maintain fashion departments with limited manufacturer identification. The stores are interested in one brand—the names of their stores. Their attitude is that customers buy from the store, not from the manufacturer. A difference in philosophy. In fashion merchandise a designer name is considered a brand name. The inclusion of goods that carry the designer's name becomes the tactic of the store in its attempt to appeal to its audience.

What must be considered is that a brand requirement necessitates a certain amount of stock each season and that overstocking brands limits money available for market development of unbranded resources. Another thought is that brands are usually widely distributed and that stores selling higher-priced fashion do not want the same goods as stores having lower-priced levels, even though retail prices are controlled or maintained.* A matter of prestige is at stake. Still another matter of concern is when a brand is dropped, or the resource decides to sell to competition. Whatever goodwill established by a store could accrue to the benefit of a competitor.

Irregulars

Irregulars are slight mistakes in the manufacturing process which do not affect the wearability of a garment. In today's affluent society, fashion departments are not concerned with irregulars. This is a subject more closely related to traditional basement fashion departments. In instances where stores stock fashion merchandise irregulars, the strategy is an appeal to price-conscious customers—a tactic to widen the store's consumer base. However, one department that invests in irregulars is home furnishings. January White Sales, for example, feature irregulars, particularly because of the profusion of prints, where colors bleed but do not affect usage.

It is interesting to note that some discount stores do not carry irregular merchandise because regular lower-priced merchandise might be interpreted by the customers as irregulars.

The term *seconds* should be noted, because some low-priced stores use them. This merchandise can be described as having holes, tears, or defects that require repair by the customer.

Exclusivity of Merchandise

It is axiomatic that when goods sell at a rapid rate a store does not like competition—if it can help it—because, competition means sharing the market. In the ordinary course of events a manufacturer does not like to give in to stores' demands, if it can be helped. Distribution is the manufacturer's life blood. However, some stores can and do get exclusivity in their trading areas if they are important and give the manufacturer some selling advantage. Exclusivity may be for a period of time within a trading area, part of the line or part of the time.

Exclusivity imposes the necessity of purchasing sufficient goods to give adequate manufacturer representation in the trading area.

Stores that carry higher priced fashion merchandise, that which is in the rise of the fashion arc, do not wish to pioneer for competition. Exclusivity of fashion merchandise is obviously desired by fashion stores since it enhances their images, but most of all, exclusivity of

---

*This can be considered as another disadvantage since the store has no control over price levels and price break dates are dictated by branded resources.

Exclusivity—a merchandising strategy as illustrated by this ad.

fashion merchandise appeals to a customer group that is interested in forward styled merchandise, at an early stage of fashion acceptance (refer to Chapter 1, **Figure 1–2**). But the practice is not confined to this group. Even discount stores will request exclusivity for a closeout deal. When the offered quantity is great they may ask the option of buying the entire lot after running an ad to prove the saleability of the merchandise.

Pricing

The merchandise price levels reflect part of the store's strategy to attract certain types of customers. Consumer income is one of the yardsticks in target marketing.

A buyer must stay within the price ranges established for the department (the range being the lowest to the highest price) and concentrate on those price zones (price areas of greatest importance) to be compatible with the rest of the store. Customers who buy cloth coats for $300 do not usually buy long sleeve sweaters for $10. Every department's price range must accommodate the store's image.

Right prices are a matter of right customers. For example, a better quality store can alienate customers with low-priced merchandise. Of what significance is a $1 lipstick to the average Neiman Marcus customer? On the other hand, high-priced merchandise can turn off customers of popular- and moderate-priced stores (and departments).

Sales Promotion

How, when and why a store promotes is part of the communication process that will be handled in depth in Part Four. Considerations for promotional events include: newness of merchandise, price levels, timing, and quantity of merchandise to support the activities. These factors come within the precincts of store policy because they affect customer attitudes.

Stores designate certain times for special events, institutional and product, which feature the merchandise of many departments. Such events include: Anniversary Sales, Opportunity Days, Clearance Events, Back-to-School Days, Fashion Shows, and others too many to mention. Of concern is that the buyer must participate in these events and make stock preparation. The events become part of the buying plan.

A store's policy may dictate specific types of institutional fashion ads above best selling price levels to enhance its image. Many stores use bill enclosures (in monthly customer statements) which require planned purchase depth.

Store clearance sales held during designated periods also have rules concerning: stock characteristics, how much, what markup, and advertising space allotment (or time allotment for radio and television).

Management is aware that advertising is part of the marketing effort and that it has to be realistic, consistent, and representative of what the store is about. The buyer plans the department's promotional activity within the store's policies. The buyer's responsibility is to make sure that the merchandise supports the efforts.

One aspect of sales promotion is a fashion show, which many stores present regularly. The buyer is consulted about themes and specific merchandise, which the buyer makes available for the event.

Every store has a philosophy of what the sales promotional activity should consist of and what results are sought. Some stores look for immediate sales returns based on low prices; other stores may use the activity for prestige purposes. These aims are passed on to the buyer who works the stock requirements into merchandise plans.

Service

Stores offer a variety of services such as personal shoppers, refund on demand, delivery, gift wrapping, credit facilities and merchandise location information. They have some influence on the quality and quantity of what is bought, but primarily the service that affects the buyers attitude most in planning stock composition is the availability of selling help, a strong influence in the stock preparation. In modern retailing the most costly customer service is the cost of sales personnel. The fact is that there has been a deterioration of quantity and quality of service, due to many reasons. The major reason being that it is the highest cost of doing business outside the cost of the merchandise. It is true, to a large extent, that we have learned to do with little or none of it.

Merchandise is inanimate and can look "dumb" on a hanger. With proper salespeople, merchandise can come alive—a person talking for it. Where high-priced fashion is sold there is a need for sales personnel, in fact it is demanded, because the customer is paying for it. At lower-priced levels the customer is often given little or no help, dependent upon a store's practice. The buyer recognizes the type of merchandise that needs the benefit of selling help, even when the store does not offer the service. Some merchandise has hanger appeal, or broad enough appeal to sell by itself. Hence, when there is absence of service, the buyer will try to buy common denominator merchandise that is in high consumer demand, avoiding merchandise that requires explanation and the need for sales personnel. Stores that offer no customer help concentrate on merchandise of greatest appeal, omitting limited selling styles completely.

Another factor that a buyer takes into account is the availability of an *alterations department.* In a department not affording this service, the styles offered must have specifications that are sufficiently ample to fit most customers. Garments that are skimpy are potential markdown styles with or without an alterations department. In a medium- to better-priced store an alterations department is always available. Most men's departments, regardless of price levels, maintain this service. In the lower-priced stores, alterations are charged to the customer. The buyer makes strong attempts to purchase styles, which include suits, jackets, and pants, that come in proportioned lengths. Naturally, it means carrying greater stock depth, but the means can justify the end.

Mail Order

Despite increased leisure time and customer mobility, there is an increased effort by stores to do impersonal selling through the means of newspaper ads, radio, television, and direct mail. There is reason to believe that this form of selling will continue to become more important.

What is unique about the practice is that the customer buys without seeing the merchandise. The first inspection of an article takes place in the customer's home. It goes without saying, that copy can make styles more appealing than they are in reality and can whet the appetite of the customer to the extent that there might be a letdown on receipt of the goods. The buyer is faced with the problems of how much to buy and the knowledge that customer returns average about thirty percent of sales.

Since mail orders must be covered adequately by merchandise in sufficient depth, the buyer must exercise care in planning, taking into account the degree of style acceptability and the nature and force of the promotional effort.

This type of selling is comparatively easier for mail-order houses that have the means of providing goods to customers during a relatively long period. Arrangements are made with manufacturers for coverage over a period of months. The store buyer, however, does not have this same time advantage. A competent buyer works with an established resource and tries to secure some leverage in the form of back-up merchandise and limitation of size of original commitment. The size of an ad, where it appears, (news section or magazine supplement, radio or television), the form (black and white or color), what price level, fashion acceptability, the customer means of ordering it (mail or telephone), are all relevant to the amount of planned purchases.

This is a sophisticated area of planning which takes careful consideration and a steady hand.

• LIKES & DISLIKES OF CONSUMER GROUPS

Within any large group, there are people of different ethnic backgrounds, religions, ages, lifestyles, social positions, etc. All of these characteristics are considered when interpreting the meaning of fashion, which must be considered for planning stock.

A specialty shop appeals to a narrow customer segment and has the least difficulty in understanding the stock requirements of its customers. The large store with a much wider audience, on the other hand, must take into account the varied characteristics inherent in their targeted customer group.

Climate and regional differences are important to a store and a buyer. For example, Burdines, a Florida department store organization of twenty stores, must stock merchandise based on the sub-cultural or regional values of a sub-tropical climate. Wool garments, most dark colors, and men's ties are examples of merchandise of relative insignificance. A further complication is that their customers are not homogeneous, branch store customers vary in their sets of value and demographic characteristics. These conditions require plans to accommodate different customers with different merchandise choices—style-wise, price-wise, and timing-wise.

Listed here are some likes and dislikes of customer groups, and in some cases, the merchandising effects.

1. Customers want adequate stock assortments as comparisons of value and types for the purpose of validating choice. A merchandising rule—always stock sufficient merchandise above best selling price levels.
2. Increased black population in cities have caused some stores to stock ethnic styles. The black population makes up approximate-

ly twelve percent of the United States population and some of the youth prefer merchandise of their ethnic origin.

3. Older females look for styles that cover the signs of aging around the neck. Scarfs are a boon to this group.

4. People of Central European origin with limited funds buy very high-priced wedding gowns. To them, a wedding is one of the most eventful days of a lifetime.

5. Slavic background groups accept lilac and purple tones in quantity when these colors are of limited fashion importance.

6. Groups with lower incomes tend to purchase brighter fashion shades.

7. Young people are prone to accept fashion newness earliest. Their fashion attitude can reflect a "fad."

8. Men favor specialty shops, but women buy a substantial percentage of men's furnishings.

9. Some older people are laggards in fashion and prefer price and serviceability, rather than newness.

10. "Smart" shoppers enjoy comparison shopping and are conscious of price levels of the same and similar styles carried by stores.

11. Brand loyalty is important to many customers, but each resource must be examined carefully. A generalization about brand loyalty of different groups is hard to make, the times make for different degrees of interest. It can be said that the young are reputed to be less loyal, but repeated purchase of certain labeled blue jeans are reflected in astronomical figures.

12. Mature females prefer wearable clothing and complain about faddish attitudes built into present offerings.

13. Customers do not like to buy fashion that has a short life span. They do not like a style to become a *ford* * shortly after purchase.

14. Customers always prefer fashions that are distinctive or flattering to the figure. In the long run, despite pressures from manufacturers or stores customers will not accept merchandise that does not offer a state of betterment.

15. Most people complain about the quality levels of fashion merchandise. It is true that mass production does not have the fineness of the handwork but guilt is to be placed on both manufacturers and stores. The absence of quality levels has had a measure of influence in causing some people to change patronage motives.

16. Many customers would like to buy fashions closer to the period of merchandise need, not when it accommodates the manufacturer or the store. In some organizations, transitional clothes (light-

*Ford is a term for a style produced by many manufacturers at different price lines simultaneously.

weight fabrics for late summer and early fall) are promoted in preference to heavier fall clothes in periods formerly called the back-to-school period.

17. Customers are annoyed at lateness of delivery of special orders or promised new fashion groups. A store safeguards proper stock preparation to support promotional events. Not having merchandise for a promotion is an unforgiveable sin in the eyes of management.

18. Classic merchandise is expected to be stocked for the convenience of the customer. When a basic item is not available, the customer finds it a source of annoyance and may look to competition for satisfaction.

19. Customers resent when a department stocks merchandise that is not compatible with styles offered by other departments (in price, timing, styles, etc.). When a customer buys a coat in one department she should be able to buy a pair of shoes and/or a blouse to accessorize it in another department. Merchandise categories and departments are part of the store which hopes to service total customer wants.

20. Customer patronage is offered to the store where the customer is comfortable. A state of comfort in the area of merchandising is achieved when the prices, styles, assortments, depth, timing, stockkeeping, and services are positioned for the convenience of the customer.

REPEATED SEASONAL BUYING PATTERNS OF CONSUMERS

Stock peaks and ebbs are of extreme importance in the planning process. When heavy selling is expected there must be sufficient goods on hand, when there are low levels of selling the stock must be reduced.

Expected selling levels are based on experience and anticipation, as discussed. Reference to past records will disclose the customer buying patterns that have developed and have been practiced over the years. Customers expect certain price levels, assortments, and depth at particular times. And by the same token, the buyer knows when customers will be motivated to shop and buy goods based on the calendar.

The merchandise customer calendar includes the following expectations and store practices.

1. January is a clearance month, stores offer merchandise at promotional price levels. The buyer is anxious to dispose of old goods and bring inventory down to a low level because January 31 is the end of the fiscal period.

2. The heaviest spring customer buying is in the weeks immediately preceding Easter.

3. Post Easter is usually the spring clearance period.

4. Post Easter is the start of summer.

5. July is the price promotional period for summer goods (many stores promote off-price fashion in late June).

6. Immediately following July 4 the fall season begins for many stores, especially in the South where the summer period is long.

7. August and September are the strong consumer buying periods for fall merchandise. August store stocks offer wide assortments to determine the "winners."

8. October is a clearance month for many stores and is the month of lowest volume of the last quarter.

9. December is the period for Christmas shopping and represents the best month of the year for departments offering merchandise suitable for gifts. Generally, ready-to-wear selling is not accelerated during this period (sportswear enjoys the best month of the year).

10. Repeated holiday selling patterns are exemplified by Mother's Day and Father's Day for which gift-type merchandise must be prepared at levels of expected demands. Preparation for each of the periods is dependent upon the type of merchandise that has increased or decreased seasonal demand.

Figure 12–1 is a fashion calendar of the selling season used by buyers (with variations for climate and regional differences).

PERIOD	SELLING SEASON
Cruise and Resort (better-priced stores)	December, January, February
Spring	January until Easter
Summer	after Easter through July
Fall (including back-to-school where it still exists)	July, August, September, October
Transitional	July, August
Holiday	November, December

Figure 12–1. Fashion Calendar for Selling Season.

MAINTENANCE OF BALANCED ASSORTMENTS

The amount of choices offered customers is known as *the breadth of stock.* The quantity behind each choice is *the depth.* The assortment factor is dependent upon the nature and size of the department, and the type of the store. A mass distributor who offers broadly accepted styles at the top of the arc of fashion (mass acceptance level) might have limited assortment but in tremendous depth. At the other end of the spectrum, a fine specialty shop may have wide assortments but very little depth. Assortment and depth are related to the nature of the operation, a store policy. There is no such thing as a model stock. No one attains perfection. What is sought is a balanced stock containing all the "rights" of appropriateness for the customers.

A well-balanced assortment is important to attract customers. What is the proper assortment is often suggested as the right merchandise, at the right time, in the right quantities, at the prices that consumers are willing and able to pay.

In fashion merchandising what is right depends upon who is being served. A fine specialty store might seek styles from Paris because the income and taste levels of their customer group shows, by past experience, that is what is wanted. On the other hand, a mass distributor might interpret the fashion demand as sweatshirts with slogans emblazoned on the fronts. Different fashions are for different people.

The buyer must, within the guidelines of store policies and marketing offerings, predict what customers will accept—the key to fashion merchandising. Price levels do not indicate fashion, acceptance is the key.

In every store that carries fashion merchandise the buyer must understand what is new and wanted by a customer group. And there must be further understanding, that there are different fashions for different people. All people do not accept the same things at the same times, some prefer to stay with the "tried and true." A well-planned stock reflects what is newest to the season, what is evolving and what is classic or basic. There must be a combination to best serve that all important group—customers. What is of paramount importance is for whom and why. There is no rule for a balance of newness verses proven, it is all relevant to circumstances.

It is true that the nature of fashion is change, but even classics are affected by seasonal variations. Moreover, in the evaluation of fashion, customers may not realize the changes that are taking place. Severe changes are accepted by innovators (not a substantial group). In the acceptance stages of a fashion only 2½ percent of the population can be considered as innovators; 13½ percent early adapters, 16 percent laggards and 34 percent each for the early and late majorities (refer to **Figure 1–2,** Chapter 1). It is apparent that a store catering to a broad base of the trading area must concentrate its efforts to the people below the group of innovators.

Limited and volume selling merchandise must be planned to round out a stock suitable for the width of the audience. In any important merchandise category there should be an adequate selection made up of type and price level. With the most important present fashion in the world, jeans, a store will have the most important style in real depth. It will not, however, forget other styles featuring different details and prices, giving customers the opportunity of choice. One branded blue jean may consist of 90 percent of the sales, but the merchant knows other styles may help sell the big reorder number and offers a security blanket for the consumer. In a dress department, featuring styles that sell freely at $100, there should be some stock at $125 and $150 which will sell at a lesser rate to give price composition to the department and prove difference in value. Naturally there is stock representation under $100.

Probably the best example is the "loafer" shoe, once part of a college student's uniform. In today's world it is not a volume selling fashion, but it can be purchased in any well-stocked store. It is not carried in depth, but it is available for those who want it. There is a demand, even if limited.

INTERNAL SOURCES USED TO PREDICT CONSUMER DEMANDS & FASHION TRENDS

Part of the study to determine the characteristics of the desired merchandise takes place *in* the store. The following sources are used:

- Salespeople
- Buyer Floor Contact and Observation
- Sales Records
- Want Slips (in stores where salespeople are available)
- Trends in Related Departments
- Consumer Surveys
- Consumer Advisory Panels
- Civic Groups
- Fashion Directors

Salespeople

The firing line of the merchandising activity is on the selling floor where there is a face-to-face encounter with the people for whom fashion is all about. Salespeople are the stores' personal representatives. They are in the position to do primary research. Salespeople are part of a relationship that is either affirmative or negative.

Selling is not the entire story. Information can sometimes be as valuable as a sale, especially if it is sufficiently important to cause the buyer to change or seek a new direction. Personal selling is an effective way to receive immediate consumer feedback, with detailed pros and cons. Records give levels of achievement, but they cannot ask questions or request particulars. Interested salespeople are worth their weight in gold, if handled properly.

It is common practice for buyers to hold one or two meetings a week with salespeople to discuss incoming merchandise, trends and customer's attitudes. It does not take long for the perceptive buyer to learn which salespeople are most incisive and able to offer genuine feedback about acceptance or non-acceptance of merchandise in stock.

Buyer Floor Contact and Observation

When retail structures were less complicated, management demanded that a buyer spend a considerable portion of the work week on the selling floor. The theory, a good one, is that personal experience is required to obtain incisive consumer feedback. In this era of large retail structures, with multiple units, it is impossible for a buyer to practice personal selling in depth or to be on the selling floor to the same degree as when stores were single units.

The single-unit store buyer does enjoy an advantage and is often able to satisfy customer's needs more accurately. In small stores buying purchases are often made with particular customers in mind.

A great deal of the buyer's customer relationship is secondhand, relying, for the most part, on salespeople and sales records. Many organizations require buyers to be present on the floor at least once a week, usually on traffic days like Saturday. A wise buyer will manage to spend sufficient time on the floor to observe the action firsthand.

Mass merchandisers, without sales personnel and stores spread over wide areas, must rely on department managers and records.

Sales Records

Every retail operation keeps records and can be the source of judging trends and fashions. The clues are always there but it is necessary to finger the desired information. It is like a detective story that necessitates the ability to discern the meaning of the clues.

It is obvious that a department's sales volume will indicate a level of achievement. Naturally, sales by themselves tell only part of the story. Sales volume records are kept on a daily, weekly, monthly, and yearly basis. Comparisons for every time interval are available. When selling is off the buyer knows it. Sometimes the reasons are obvious, other times the reasons are more difficult to assess. In addition to departmental figures, there are records for every style and classification

A buyer (right) educates store personnel.

of merchandise. With the utilization of a perpetual inventory system every style is open to continuous examination and the rate of sale can be judged at a glance.

The acceptance of fashion merchandise can be graphed and it is not unlikely for records to indicate late in the season demands that may become important fashions of the future. This is one path to fashion prediction, the experience factor.

Want Slips

Want slips are forms used in some stores by sales personnel to note customer requests for merchandise not in stock. At the end of each day want slips are submitted to the buyer, who analyzes the requests for possible stock inclusion. This method can be efficient, if there is proper direction and control. If it is to be a successful tool, there must be meetings during which the importance of the requests must be stressed, followed by an explanation of intended buyer action. Efficient use of want slips can be an important channel of information about stock omissions.

Trends in Related Departments

All styles and fashions are related, and eventually end up on the person of the ultimate consumer. Manufacturers practice consumer orientation and attempt to produce styles that suit customers' preferences of silhouettes, colors, textures, and details. One category of merchandise is not separated in the customer's mind—it is the store that isolates merchandise groups. It is the buyer's responsibility to study other classifications of merchandise to learn of any trends that can or should be considered for present or future stock.

The fashion buyer should make periodic examinations of all fashion departments in the store and in the competitions' stores. It is not unusual for a buyer, who has seen a trend from another sector of the market, to go to a favored resource and report this trend. The manufacturer will very often include the trend in his line. The buyer may decide that the importance of the trend demands store concentration and might develop an exclusive style with the manufacturer, for regular stock or for a promotional event. Designers continually review related categories of fashion in the development of their lines.

Consumer Surveys

Consumer surveys can take several shapes. The easiest one can be effected on the selling floor since customers are usually vocal about what they like or dislike. Salespeople, assistant buyers, or associate buyers can hold informal talks with potential customers. On occasion stores resort to formal surveys through personal contact, telephone or mail. These methods are usually conducted by the store personnel, but a research organization can be employed for the same purpose, affording an objective point of view. The most widely known fashion research firm is Kurt Salmon Associates, Inc., New York. Research, on informal or formal surveys, *must* be evaluated carefully. Store surveys are much broader than the subject of fashion merchandising and most often include service factors. In-depth research projects are more often practiced by manufacturers or trade associations and results given to stores.

An excellent example is a demographic and psychographic survey conducted by a Detroit research firm for a West Palm Beach newspaper. The research identified the size of the fashion market by county, the number of dwellings, and consumer store preference for men's wear, women's wear, and children's wear. Armed with this information, alert merchants were able to evaluate and modify their retail mix (location and ambience, fashion merchandising policies, and communication and services).

Consumer Advisory Panels

In this age of consumerism, consumer advisory panels are manifold and consumers are eager to express their feelings about merchandise—the styling, pricing, and quality.

The enlightened store affords the buyer opportunities to secure opinions of different age groups. Age groups can be varied and most often reflect the views of the more mature fashion customer. College Boards still exist in many stores. The young people who serve on the Boards play several roles—as advisors, salespeople, and models. Perhaps their opinions were more important when a college-bound student prepared a complete wardrobe. The wardrobe assortment for the college-bound student has been compressed, but attitudes of young people must be considered, particularly since they have given fashion leadership in so many areas. Teen Boards have been part of the activities of stores for many years. These young groups function at the same levels as college boards. They are concerned with social, school and charitable functions. The buyer can study them, seek their present preferences, and possibly establish attitudes for the future, when they are both consumer and user of fashion merchandise.

Civic Groups

Many stores have relationships with organizations to maintain goodwill and secure institutional benefits. These organizations are articulate and mirror the standards of their peer groups. Civic groups afford the opportunity for stores to put on fashion shows, which give an immediate response to fashion offerings. Fashion shows frequently attract wide audiences in certain regions, particularly when they are a regular occurrence. Sometimes famous designers or personalities are featured to build traffic. Within fashion show activities is a trunk showing, a manufacturer's display in the selling department of a new line, not yet stocked, on live models. Excellent response in the form of special orders taken after the show can establish clues of fashion rightness and importance of a line, style, color or manufacturer.

Fashion Directors

Every store (of fair size) has one or more fashion director. Fashion directors are trained fashion experts whose services are available to fashion buyers. They are familiar with the dynamics of fashion, its history, and are students of current developments. They are in a position to guide buyers concerning trends, appropriateness of merchandise to the total store fashion thrust, to help with displays, to prepare and participate in fashion shows, and to express opinions about the most suitable merchandise for advertising.

EXTERNAL SOURCES USED TO PREDICT CONSUMER DEMANDS & FASHION TRENDS

There is a wide variety of sources *outside* the stores that offer information for the buyer to form a base of what should be important for merchandise planning. These sources include:

- Resident Buying Office
- Advisory Fashion Consultants
- Resources
- Primary Market
- Competing and Non-Competing Stores
- Publications (Consumer and Trade)
- Television and Film
- Lifestyle

Resident Buying Office

This arm of the buyer serves the store and is often referred to as a part of the staff of the organization (see Chapter 9).

The relationship between the buying office representative and the store buyer is usually maintained by constant correspondence. The resident buyer is constantly digesting market developments and advising store buyers. In turn, the store buyer examines and evaluates the offerings for immediate or future use. The bulletins that come out of the resident buying office not only convey news about new style developments, but also relate current retail events, so that the store buyer can evaluate present stock for fashion rightness, retail values, and future promotions.

During market visits the store buyer holds interviews with the resident office counterpart and is brought up-to-date for specific needs. It is normal procedure for the store buyer to obtain printed recommendations about resource developments, new trends, price levels, merchandise availability, and other stores' activities. Added to this information, the office usually holds office fashion shows for visiting store members.

The buying office fashion coordinator also relates fashion news and recommendations from her frame of reference, usually accompanied by particulars detailing manufacturers, styles, colors and delivery.

Advisory Fashion Consultants

There are professional people who sell fashion services to stores. The oldest and best known is the Tobé Service founded in 1927. Tobé Coburn developed a syndicated service to which stores all over the country subscribed. Her reports were digests of the fashion market recommending styles and suggesting promotional themes. The organization still exists and sells a service that interprets market offerings and suggested promotional points of view.

Amos Parrish & Company is another advisory service, reporting on store operations and supplying some fashion advice. Kurt Salmon Associates, Inc., mentioned previously as a research firm, also prepares studies of consumer attitudes as they affect fashion merchandising.

I.M. International is one of the largest international fashion and textile forecasting companies in the world. I.M. reports on fashion trends in all markets—Paris, Milan, London, Hamburg, New York, etc.

Eleanor Lambert and Estelle Hamburger are among the fashion experts who can be engaged for the purpose of giving an objective fashion viewpoint or performing various activities related to fashion merchandising.

Resources

A manufacturer's life blood is the distribution system, the people he sells. He is more than anxious to be an important part of a store's operation. The relationship includes the exchange of ideas between both parties.

Important resources of a store can be a fund of knowledge, particularly because there is an investment in fashion, which took place after research. A good relationship with several top resources in one merchandise category can result in a buyer's perspective of where the market is going insofar as style, price, and color. The relationship often avails the buyer the opportunity to look in the "kitchen" (before the line

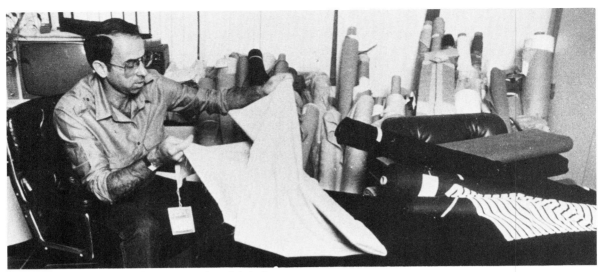

To develop his line, a designer can select fabric from
bolts of fabric (above) or samples of fabric (below).

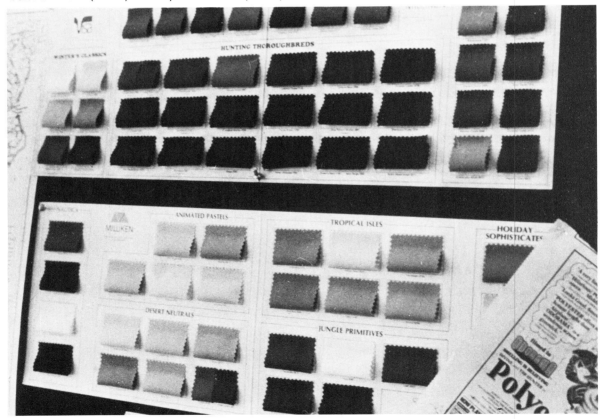

is shown to all buyers), and to view a collection that represents the viewpoints of both the designer and the seasoned maker of fashion. Successful manufacturers in a highly competitive market have much to add to the buyer's research, particularly at the beginning of a season, when research is deepest and most subjective.

During the selling season, important resources commonly call cooperating stores, local or long distance, to inform them about their best selling styles, which gives the buyer another assessment of the store stock. A conduit for information from resources is often the sales person who can relate the same information plus current developments about competitors and non-competitors. Not infrequently their information includes news of events in trading areas beyond those of the store's, and this is valuable when it pertains to sections noted for early fashion acceptance.

In a previous chapter, we stated that the ability to relate to people is a necessary buyer attribute. This in one area where it comes into play.

Primary Market

The textile industry must develop products earlier than any other sector of the fashion industry. Textile producers are thinking and working on their plans a year in advance. This market must be consumer oriented and must do intensive research to determine what fabrics and colors are likely to be in fashion long before collections are shown. Accordingly, this research is done by the fashion director although some buyers do their own legwork. Large chain store buyers usually make it a practice to do intensive studies in this market.

Another section of the primary market that develops early is the leather industry, which supplies the material for accessories and shoes. Since their colors accessorize apparel and relate to major color themes, it is an excellent source for color information. This area also requires long lead time for production and works one year in advance of seasons.

Publications (Consumer and Trade)

Publications are part of the communication system of fashion merchandising. Although consumer magazines direct their information to the ultimate consumer, they work with manufacturers and stores. Fashion points-of-view are expressed to their readers.

Every magazine has a merchandising department which shops the market prior to each season. Information about their fashion stance for a new season includes color and fabric selection, anticipated readership demand, are all available to the buyer. In fact, new season's color charts and other professional material are available to the buyer at a small cost.

Communicators of fashion information.

Magazines additionally hold shows during market weeks for visiting store buyers, which are previews of what will be advertised and what the magazines believe are the major fashion trends. Some magazines have showrooms to exhibit merchandise that will appear in the advertisements issued for end users readership.

Trade publications are another source of professional news—about the industry developments. Some of the major publications are: *Women's Wear Daily, Daily News Record, Boot and Shoe Recorder.* There is no fashion level that is not represented by trade papers.

Fashion buyers read several publications to keep up with current events that relate style developments, resource information, cost factors, and other news that makes for professional knowledge and understanding.

Most buyers subscribe to all local newspapers, some read important out-of-town periodicals. Stores located in Texas will subscribe to Chicago and New York papers to keep abreast of what important stores in these major trading areas are supporting. Additionally, merchandising activities can be seen in *Retail News Bureau,* which reports advertising results of selected store advertisements.

Another side of this coin, is that news makes fashion. What happens in the world affects what will be accepted. Fashion is an expression of attitudes and news affects attitudes, a fashion buyer therefore must be aware of the events of the world.

Competing and Non-competing Stores

Macy's may never tell Gimbel's, but it may tell Marshall Field. One of the many services available to stores provides for the exchange of merchandising information. There are professional organizations that compile information and make it available to non-competing organizations.

One of the largest buying offices in the United States, Associated Merchandising Corp., offers information to their stores about the membership achievements.

Buyers often relate their findings and directions to buyers of non-competing stores when they meet during market weeks. If a buyer has a problem, a telephone call to a buyer friend may be the means to clarify that problem.

The ways to secure information from a competing store is somewhat different. Stores will never tell competition about future plans, that goes without saying! Once merchandise is placed on the selling floor, the merchandising direction is unfolded. It is necessary to constantly shop competition to see what they believe the customer prefers and how it will make its appeal: by manufacturer, assortment, depth and price levels. A seasoned buyer can walk through a store and see a complete story.

Newspaper ads are excellent indicators of competitive stores' merchandising tactics.

Television and Film

The world in which we live is reflected in television and in movies. People are affected by what they see in these media, particularly when clothes are worn by people who they admire and who they want to emulate.

Lifestyle

Lifestyle is a rather well-worn term which describes the mores of a society—another term for culture. How people live, what their order of priorities and what they think are basically the reasons for the study of psychographics—the study of sociological and psychological factors, a word that is now well used by retailers in projecting merchandising plans.

The buyer must be aware that the ever-changing world requires changes in clothing. The point is that the buyer must visit the places people attend, see them in action, and how they dress. There must be a conceptualization of what apparel does for people, why they want certain adornments, and why they will not accept others.

It is evident that the fashion buyer does not have to make a lonely decision, there is a great deal of aid. But, the final decisions must be made by the buyer.

UNIT CONTROL: DEFINITION & REASONS FOR ITS USE

The overriding consideration of merchandising is the need to make available the specific merchandise that a store's customers want. Assortment and depth are store requirements to serve a broad base of people, but particular customers have specific needs. How often have you heard a person say, "I visited "X" store and it has nothing!" What was meant was that the offerings did not include a desired style or type of merchandise.

As we have seen, experience is a strong factor in the planning process. One of the most important sources of past and current information about customers' preferences is *unit control*—a recording system that shows the movement of specific merchandise. The system provides a record, of the following, in *number of units:*

- Price lines
- Styles

- Sizes
- Colors
- Vendors
- Classifications
- Other desired information

In its broadest aspect unit control helps the buyer achieve a balance between sales and types of merchandise, the specifics—the number of prices or units bought, sold, on hand or on order.

In the strictest sense, although it is called unit control, it is not a control system; it is a recording method which affords the buyer an opportunity to exercise some form of control over specific merchandise. The buyer is armed with information used to make merchandising *decisions.*

Stores use different systems, and the systems can vary even within a store, where departments have different information needs. The unit control system will vary dependent upon:

- What kind of information is needed
- How information is collected
- How is the information recorded
- What forms are used to record the information

The unit control system is tailored to the department, and the term *programming* is widely used.

As previously noted, the buyer in a small store often does not use any records. More than likely, planning and control are done by observation, by eyeball. Such individuals are close to the scene and are able to determine what is needed for whom, how much, and when, all by observation.

But this is a visual system. In a large store where there is a multitude of goods this visual system could not work, certainly not efficiently. Factors of modern retailing that prevent eyeball merchandising include:

- Many buyers handle more than one department within a store.
- Branch stores or multiple operations do not allow the buyer sufficient time to be present in all the stores.
- Some merchandising must be done from records. For example: chain store operations where there are many stores, some in widely scattered areas, requiring different types of merchandise.

Large organizations, and even small stores, require records of reasonable accuracy on which to base planned stock requirements, without which merchandising could be tantamount to "blind flying" and mistakes could be of major proportions.

There are essentially two types of unit control systems:

- Perpetual Unit Control System
- Physical Unit Control System

Our major concern is with the perpetual unit control system, because the nature of fashion merchandise requires constant up-to-date, specific information. Other departments that have the same needs also use this system.

The Perpetual Unit Control System

A perpetual inventory system can be maintained by hand or by computer. Obviously, large organizations use computers. The discussion that follows focuses on a hand-collated system because:

1. the flow and meaning of the system's information can be more easily traced;
2. the recorded information can be identical.

The perpetual inventory system starts when an order is placed. A clerk fills out a card for each style purchased. Each style card contains the following information:

- Department Number
- Manufacturer's Name
- Manufacturer's Style Number
- Style Classification
- Cost Price
- Retail Price
- Number of Pieces Ordered
- Colors
- Sizes

The style card is placed in a file of similar merchandise. The clerk will make a dot or line in pencil in the proper box for each piece of merchandise *on order.* When merchandise is *received,* the penciled dot or line becomes an ink line. Each line therefore represents one piece of merchandise. When merchandise is sold, each line is superimposed with a diagonal line (✕) or a circle (⌀).

All forms of movement for each piece of merchandise are recorded with an appropriate mark. Other forms of movement include:

1. customer returns;
2. merchandise on loan (to other departments);
3. manufacturer returns;
4. merchandise transfers.

Different color inks can be used to show the different forms of movement.

MANUFACTURER: The James Co. CODE: 105	STYLE # 158	CLASSIFICATION SSC	COST PRICE $4.75	RETAIL PRICE $8.98	MARKDOWN			Daily Sales						
								Week	$^4/_1$	$^4/_8$	$^4/_{15}$	$^4/_{22}$	$^4/_{29}$	
Description: short sleeve, crew neck wool slipover								M	3					
Color/Sizes	34	36	38	40				T	8					
White	/ X	// X X	/// X	/ X				W	2					
Red	/ X	/// X	X X X X	//				T						
Navy	//	/ X X /	////	//				F						
Brown	//	////	////	//				S						
								Net Sales	13					
Order Date	$^3/_{10}$						Dept 57	Rec'd	48 $^3/_{25}$					
Quantity	48							On hand	35					

Figure 12–2. Style activity card used in a manually operated system.

Figure 12–2 is a style activity card used in a manually operated system. This card can be conformed to include an account of any required information. The form of the card and where the information is noted, is a matter of store preference. What is important is that the information can be read easily and is sufficient for merchandising needs.

Referring to **Figure 12–2** note that on March 10 an order was placed for 48 pieces of a short sleeve, crew neck wool sweater. A total of 48 pieces where received on March 25 and a line for each piece was placed in the appropriate box. During the week of April 1 a total of 13 pieces were sold. Notice that the buyer was able to determine early color and size preference. The card actually provides for a case history of each piece of merchandise.

COMPILING THE SALES DATA One of the important phases of the perpetual inventory system is determining what has been sold at the time the sale occurs, so that the style activity cards can be filled in with the necessary information.

In stores of limited size where the system is relatively modest, or the nature of the merchandise requires it, the information is obtained from sales checks. At the end of the day, duplicates of all sales checks are summarized and recorded on unit control forms. This method is slow and is dependent upon the accuracy of the salespeople.

A much easier method of collecting sales data is through the use of ticket stubs, part of the price tickets attached to individual garments. The store receiving department attaches a ticket to every item received. The information for the ticket is taken from a copy of the order placed by the buyer. The hangtag usually comes in three parts, one of which

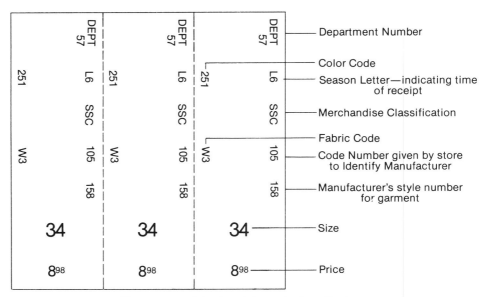

Figure 12–3. Hangtag used in the stub-control method.

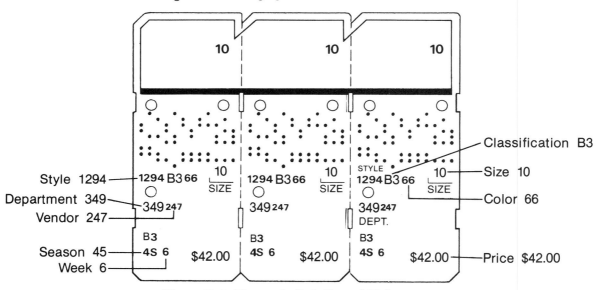

Figure 12–4. Electronic Stub-Control Ticket.

is torn or chopped off at the time of sale and deposited in a box provided for all sales personnel of the department. The tickets are usually collected by a clerk at the end of the day and then summarized for later recording. Tickets can be picked up or scrutinized at any time of the day by the clerk or any interested merchandising person. A buyer can tell the direction of the "winds" on a busy selling day a few hours after store opening.

Figure 12-3 is an illustration of a hangtag used in the stub control method. Note that all the information required for the style activity card is easily available. This is possible through the use of codes which reduce each unit of information to a few numbers.

ELECTRONIC DATA PROCESSING AND THE PERPETUAL UNIT CONTROL SYSTEM The reader may wonder about the stub control system since most hangtags on price tickets are not as illustrated. The fact is that we are living in an electronic age and computers are utilized to collect, record, and even analyze data. In modern retailing, computers are used widely and are maintained for unit control purposes; therefore, the retail price tags are in such form as to accommodate them. **Figure 12-4** is an illustration of an electronic stub control ticket that serves the identical purpose of the ticket previously illustrated. The difference is in the method and recording of the information. It goes without saying that using electronic data processing (E.D.P.) is a fast and accurate means of obtaining, recording, and later analyzing sales data.

Speed is an advantage in fashion merchandise, which is an area of fast change. The greatest advantage and greatest practice of E.D.P. is in larger operations where more sophisticated records are needed. The disadvantage is the high cost of maintenance.

Another application of E.D.P. is point-of-sale registers which are used at wrapping desks. A sales clerk presses keys on a machine that records unit control data at the time of sale. The information is collected centrally and is used by larger stores and those with branches. This system is here for many and a wave of the future for others.

Still another system is the use of hand-held wands which feed information (inventory on-hand) into the computer system. This system, used widely by supermarkets, also records sales and gives customers the individual and the total cost of their purchase.*

CONSIDERATIONS IN THE PERPETUAL UNIT CONTROL SYSTEM In theory, the perpetual inventory method should show the amount of stock on hand at all times. The total figure of recorded merchandise is known as *book inventory.* Errors of omission or commission and stock pilferage can create either stock shortages or overages*. Recognizing that no system is foolproof and that the book records will reflect some errors, periodic physical inventories are taken and any errors of book

---

*Cashier passes price-coded products over scanning device.
*Stock shortage affects profit. It is a sub-division in the measurement of a buyer's efficiency. The reason is that there is some buyer control of shortages and overages. The latter is caused by buyer unawareness of accounting mistakes. Shortage control can be minimized by: checking records, judicious placement of floor stock, and overseeing personnel (a difficult task in today's world).

Figure 12–5. Daily Sales Report.

records are adjusted. In fact, careful buyers after receiving style cards or computer printouts may check floor inventory against the balances of stock shown. Sometimes the eye will see what records will not show: shoplifting, wrong tickets used on merchandise, or merchandise improperly received (error in the receiving process).

The Physical Unit Control System

Another system is known as the *physical control* or *sales resultant system.* In using this system a stock count is taken and recorded. When additional merchandise is received, the amount is added to the inventory. At a given date another stock count is taken and this result is subtracted from the total inventory. The difference between the two inventories is assumed to be the result of the selling of merchandise during the period since the original count. This system does not record sales as they occur, does not show a perpetual unit control figure, and requires taking repeated physical inventories.

WEEKLY SALES AND STOCK REPORT

SK 900-01 (REV 8/73)

DEPT.	TERMINATION CODE	STYLE GROUP CLASS OR SCHEMATIC GROUP	PRICE POINT	MAT	STYLE	VENDOR	NAME OF STYLE AND VENDOR OF REPORT	WEEK ENDED
420		E 21					XXXXX XXXXX BREAKDOWN XXXXX NO. / SALES XX BY SIZE BREAKDOWN XXXXX SIZE NO.	01-18

PRICE HISTORY: COST — ORIGINAL RETAIL — CURRENT RETAIL

STOCK ON ORDR OWNRSHIP SALES

STORE NO. OR STYLE NO.	3RD PRIOR SALES	STOCK	2ND PRIOR SALES	STOCK	LAST SALES	STOCK	CURRENT SALES	STOCK	ON ORDER	TOTAL OWNER-SHIP	CUM. SALES REG.	MD.	STOCK %	ON ORDR %	OWNRSHIP %	SALES %
1		1		1		1		1	1	1	1		.2	.2	.2	.7
2	2	49	1	48	3	45	2	43	43	43	27	1	9.6	9.6	9.6	17.9
3		20	1	19		19		19	19	19	5		4.2	4.2	4.2	3.3
4		16		16	1	15	1	15	15	15	9		3.3	3.3	3.3	6.0
5	2	42		42	1	41	2	39	39	39	9		8.7	8.7	8.7	6.0
6		34	1	34	2	34	3	34	34	34	2	2	7.6	7.6	7.6	1.3
7	1	35	-1	36		34		34	34	34	14		7.6	7.6	7.6	9.3
8	1	29		29	1	29	3	26	26	26	10		5.8	5.8	5.8	6.6
10		39		39	1	38		38	38	38	10		8.5	8.5	8.5	6.6
11		18		18		18		18	18	18	6		4.0	4.0	4.0	4.0
12		21		21		21	1	20	20	20	4		4.5	4.5	4.5	2.6
14		23		23	1	23	1	22	22	22	2		4.9	4.9	4.9	1.3
15		33	2	31	1	30		30	30	30	18		6.7	6.7	6.7	11.9
16	1	38	2	38	1	38	3	35	35	35	13		7.8	7.8	7.8	8.6
17		17		17	1	16		16	16	16	8		3.6	3.6	3.6	5.3
18		19		19		19		19	19	19	5		4.2	4.2	4.2	3.3
21	1	19		19		19	1	18	18	18	6		4.0	4.0	4.0	4.0
22		23		23	1	22	1	22	22	22	2		4.9	4.9	4.9	1.3

WEEKLY TOTALS / THIS WEEK (RCVD RTM TSFD, ORDERED)

MERCHANDISE DIVISION	3RD PRIOR SALES	STOCK	2ND PRIOR SALES	STOCK	LAST SALES	STOCK	CURRENT SALES	STOCK	ON ORDER	TOTAL OWNERSHIP	CUM. SALES REG	MD	THIS WEEK RCVD RTM TSFD	ORDERED	STOCK	ON ORDR	OWNRSHIP	SALES
209	8	476	3	473	11	462	13	449		449	151				100.1	.0	100.1	100.0

STOCK BY SIZE BREAKDOWN - SIZE NO.

0	1	2	3	4	5	6	7	8	9
100.1			.0	100.1		100.0			

TOTALS (UNITS)

	CANCLD ORDERS	RECEIPTS	WEEK SINCE FIRST RCVD	LAST RCVD

COLOR		CURRENT	CUMUL.	STOCK
SALES				

PAGE 3974

Figure 12-6. Weekly Sales and Stock Report.

Reserve Requisition Control

Another system that is used for staple goods such as canned groceries, drugs, hardware is the *reserve requisition control.* This system provides for a warehouse or reserve stock area where merchandise is kept. A department requests or requisitions merchandise. These requisitions are maintained as the selling records. This obviously is not a unit control system that should be used for fashion merchandising.

Information Obtained from Unit Control

The amount of information that is obtainable from a unit control system is almost infinite. A well-developed merchandising system will include all reports that are required for detailed analysis.

Figure 12–5 is a form that is a valuable buyer guide and is received the day following sales activity. It is an objective record of the events of a day in terms of what has sold with reference to: manufacturers, price levels, style numbers, sizes, colors, and classifications. This form is used in a manually operated system.

Figure 12–6 is a form used by an organization that uses an E.D.P. system. Note that it is a compilation of style cards having somewhat more information then provided for on the manually operated card.

Another advantage of E.D.P. is the additional information that can be programmed into the system.

Unit control is like a cardiogram that measures every beat of the heart of retailing—the rate of selling—and affords the experience of knowing what people prefer. Good planning always starts with what happened before, where you were before going forward.

But no system is without its disadvantages. Unit controls involve substantial costs in setting up and maintaining. In a manual operation there is a certain amount of inaccuracy based on human error and carelessness; in electronic systems they can only operate as expertly as the systems were planned and the information that is fed into them. The one great disadvantage is that it will not show a record of anything that is missing from stock; the record is confined to selling of what is owned.

CLASSIFICATION MERCHANDISING

Without question a unit control system is a necessity for fashion merchandising. In order to benefit planning, the information should reach the buyer as soon as possible following the selling experience. As in some organizations if the information does not reach the buyer the time gaps are harmful to the buyer's efforts to plan with precision.

In fashion merchandising, unit control offers details about individual styles which need interpretation, since trends represent a direction in which the stock should be planned. Individual style or styles may not give clues necessary to make *major* stock investments.

As a companion to unit control another dimension is added—*classification merchandising,* or merchandising by classification. A classification is a unit of consumer demand, one that permits coupling of any one or a combination of end use requirements into one class. It is also referred to as an assortment of items, all of which are reasonably suitable for each other to the customer.

These definitions sound rather academic, and they are. For example, in a mens' sportswear department classifications would be sweaters, jackets, shorts, sport shirts, and pants. These should be stocked according to customer expectations and requirements.

The Classification System

The buyer must estimate the relative importance of the number of choices and depth of each classification so that there is an adequate supply. An order of priority is established and a budget established for each. At all times the buyer is working with a total budget (OTB) for the entire department, so it is necessary to come as close as possible to proper proportions of stock needs. Otherwise there will be an imbalance, when goods are not relevant to demand and can cause customer's dissatisfaction and poor departmental performance. As an example, the buyer in an effort to achieve a proper stock balance could establish the following plan:

Sweaters	20%
Jackets	20%
Shorts	15%
Sportswear	30%
Pants	15%

In a well-developed department these classifications may be too broad, possibly defeating the very purpose of the system. These broad classifications by refining consumer demands, do not give a proper representation of goods. So, the system includes sub-classifications, particularly when the demand warrants greater variety and depth.

For example, sweaters can be broken down into the following sub-classifications: long sleeve crew neck, long sleeve turtleneck, sleeveless V-neck, long sleeve cardigan. If sweaters are selling in volume and conditions warrant, the sub-classifications can be further defined into yarn types. At one time when men's sweaters were relatively unimportant, there was one classification, "sweaters." The stock contained three or four styles and the buyer planned each style by price level, such as: long sleeve slip-on, sleeveless V-neck, and long sleeve cardigan. Each type was a different price, so the planning was easy. In today's world, sweaters are important and are available in many variations. There are many sub-classifications which are established to ensure proper representation in the total sweater stock.

Sub-classifications permit the buyer to plan, and later evaluate, the performances of narrower important units of consumer demands.

Classifications can change from season to season, be expanded into sub-classifications, or eliminated as fashion suggests.

Some of the reasons for the classification system are: the ability to plan sales/stock ratio with reasonable accuracy; the development of a practical open-to-buy position; the evaluation of performance of narrow segments of departmental merchandise; trend spotting, and avoidance of duplication of goods.

Flexibility of Classifications

Although the classification system tends to remain relatively the same from season to season, sub-classifications cannot be finally determined until there is an evaluation of all market offerings. Important characteristics of silhouette, styles, materials, colors, price lines, and any other merchandise qualities, are studied and then listed in *fashion acceptance* and *importance.* If circumstances warrant, new sub-classifications are added which affect the assortment of the future selling season. Old classifications can be eliminated if they have no value. Sub-classifications therefore are based less on past performance as in the case of merchandise carried in departments of staple merchandise which tend to be the same season after season.

SUMMARY

Many fashion principles have been incorporated in this chapter. Merchandise acceptance has different levels for different groups of people. The buyer, in accordance with store policy, must know where fashion is on the arc of fashion acceptance. A store selling high-priced merchandise requires styles when they are new, and often eliminates them once they are in more popular demand. The medium-priced store waits for a style to reach an acceptance level that their customers understand, can afford, and want. A variety store often waits for a fashion to get into late majority acceptance and buys it at an attractive price that is in proportion to the retail levels of other goods stocked.

These are generalizations made with the realization that in today's world, there are many styles that seem to be developed and accepted almost instantaneously. They are available in a vast assortment of sizes, fashion names, materials, and prices.

The fact of life is that the customer who can pay a higher price wants the luxury of certain characteristics of merchandise, one of which is the limitation of supply.

Timing is one of the important aspects of merchandise; the right merchandise at the right time: too early or too late can be equally bad for the merchant. Too early often means poor selling and a reluctance to try again, a double loss. The trend might have been too early for a particular store, yet it might have sold if the merchandise were stocked at the right time. The penalty for lateness is always a lower price—markdown.

Some thought must be given to the terms of quality and detailing. The former value is often related to price. Higher priced merchandise should have higher levels of quality inherent in a garment. Stores do and should have standards. There is recognition that the one ingredient that cannot be "knocked off" is *quality.* The simplest style is the hardest to copy, the material and the needle are what make the garment. On the other hand, profuse detailing offers the best opportunity for copying at lower prices.

The influences that affect fashion—economic, social and cultural values, technology, political events, and governmental constraints—are part of the planning process. Fashion is a reflection of the way people live. This day of immediate communication brings the world into living rooms through the medium of television and one trait of human behavior is imitation. What is happening and who is wearing what are vital concerns of the fashion merchandiser. Evaluation of those we admire causes people to imitate.

The main consideration is that merchandise must be stocked within the character and the expectations of customers—the segmentation process dictates what fashions for whom.

There is no mystique about the planning process as part of merchandising. The avenues are clear and delineated, it is a constant awareness (and good management techniques) that keep the buyer attuned to the world of consumers—what they want—what they will probably want. The sources of information are: the world of the consumer; the textile industry; the manufacturing sector; the retailing sector; the store.

chapter 13

SELECTION OF RESOURCES

INTRODUCTION

The most basic role of the buyer is to seek, evaluate, select, cultivate, and develop resources from whom suitable stock and information can be secured for the benefit of the store. As a representative of a retail organization the buyer establishes relationships between the retailer and manufacturers.

Following the birth of modern ready-to-wear in 1920 fashion became the major volume producer of numerous retail organizations—and fashion merchandising became a specialization. Fashion merchandising achieved big-business status and the wholesale market expanded —manufacturers became more numerous and widespread. Two developments that occurred in the market are significant in how and where resources are selected.

- Foreign Markets
- Regional Markets

Since the end of World War II, retailers have dramatically increased purchases of *foreign-produced merchandise.* The current yearly retail sales of foreign-made apparel are approximately $30 billion, approximately one of three garments sold (one of two pairs of shoes sold) are foreign-made. The impact of import volume level has made fashion merchandising more complicated. Commitments for foreign apparel alter the manner in which orders are placed, and when merchandise is received and placed in stock.

In the last ten years, numerous *regional markets* have been constructed in strategically located cities that have become significant competitors of the New York market, the acknowledged capitol of mass-produced apparel. This trend has made purchasing less costly and more convenient, particularly for limited-scale retailers. These regional markets additionally offer merchandisers the opportunity to review lines and fashion trends before visiting New York.

The criteria for resource selection are directly related to the type of retail organization and its segmented customer group—potential customers. A buyer rates manufacturers by their degree of importance, which has a bearing on when and how much business will probably be transacted with them.

Among the considerations for selecting resources is the question of how many resources are necessary to achieve merchandising goals. Two resource-selection-policy extremes are: one, to concentrate on as few as possible, and two, to spread commitments on the basis of profit opportunity or broadened stock assortments. Guidelines for selecting resources, however, are a matter of executive judgment—decided by the general merchandise manager, controlled by the divisional merchandise manager, and executed by the buyer.

A well-selected group of manufacturers is critical to merchandising success, since the fundamental purpose of a retailer is to act as a means by which goods pass from the producer to the ultimate consumer. Obtaining the right goods from the right manufacturers is the assigned, basic responsibility of a buyer.

In the final analysis, strip away the details of what makes a top-notch fashion buyer and you have a perceptive person who knows what people want and when and where to obtain it.

SUPPLIERS OF FASHION GOODS

Suppliers of fashion goods with offices in major markets can be grouped into three categories.

- Manufacturers
- Wholesalers or Jobbers
- Importers

Manufacturers

The most numerous and important suppliers of fashion goods are firms that make or contract for goods. They are categorized as manufacturers even though a firm that uses contractors is really a jobber.

Wholesalers or Jobbers

The second group is a small segment of companies called wholesalers or jobbers. Wholesalers should not be confused with manufacturers (in a previous chapter the term wholesale market was referred to as all areas below the retailer). Wholesalers buy in large quantities from manufacturers and resell to smaller stores which visit markets infrequently or not at all, mostly "Mom and Pop" stores. The wholesaler can work on an 8 percent profit, the trade discount of women's fashion merchandise. The store pays the wholesaler the listed price and loses the discount, which would have been available had the store purchased directly from the manufacturer. Reasons for this practice are that merchandise is available faster with little transportation charges and that merchandise is available from large manufacturers who are unwilling to accept small orders. This type of distribution is on the wane. Another type of wholesaler/jobber offers stores the opportunity to buy close out or promotional goods. Distributors of this type solicit manufacturers and buy remainder goods at the end of a season. Since they buy from many sources they are in a position to make promotional packages at advantageous prices for basement, main floor, and sometimes upstairs stores (principally when stores offer promotionally priced goods). The jobber serves the market by "washing" stock. The manufacturer sells to the jobber at low prices, usually at a substantial loss, but the advantage is in disposing an entire lot of goods, in every size and color remaining. Manufacturer remainders are mostly broken sizes and colors and, usually, cannot be sold or shipped to regular customers. Another reason for this practice is that the lot will invariably have poorer selling styles, which are mixed with the good. If the manufacturer has sold his line well and the lot is a nominal quantity, he is happy to take the loss. And at the same time the buyer, in weighing a promotional purchase, is aware of the conditions and offers low prices (this will be discussed in Chapter 14).

Importer

The third type of supplier with offices in the United States' major markets is the importer. His method of doing business is similar to that of a domestic supplier, the difference is that goods are made overseas. Merchandise is produced in foreign countries, delivered to the United States, shown in an office in New York, and distributed on the same terms and conditions as a firm producing goods in this country. One firm of this kind had a volume of $150,000,000 in the early 1980s. The company is owned by a Japanese trading company, has a New York office staffed with former merchandisers of United States retail stores who style and sell the merchandise. What is most fascinating is that the merchandise is produced in any Oriental country, not necessarily Japan, that offers advantageous labor prices. Imagine then: merchandise styled in New York ("knocked off"), taken to the Orient where it is made, delivered to New York, and sold and distributed to stores around the United States. Small world!

In this same category are exporters who sometimes have agents in this country and can sell particular styles or request store styles to be made abroad and delivered directly to the store.

METHODS OF OBTAINING DOMESTIC MERCHANDISE

The prime method of obtaining merchandise is through personal visits to the market. When and how often a buyer visits the market are determined by the size of the department, the speed with which a market develops new styles, the lead time a market requires for delivery, and the distance of the store from the market. A large store requires high inventory levels, therefore, buying trips are relatively frequent. However, the most important reason for the number of required market visits is the development of new styles. The better dress market ($200 retail and up) offers seasonal collections, and merchandise is set throughout the season, until the presentation of the collection for the next period. The popular-priced dress market ($25 to $35 retail) develops styling on a constant basis, so a buyer may be in the market in some instances every second week, depending on the location of the store. Buyers from stores that are considerable distances from the markets, for the most part, arrive about a week or two before the general influx. A buyer from a California store visiting New York City, for example, must contend with transportation conditions, which require lead time for proper delivery of stock.

Timing of market visits is also related to the price levels of merchandise: highest priced offerings are developed earliest, moderate-priced garments later, and popular-priced merchandise last. This is part of the dynamics of fashion development: moderate houses watch and copy the styles of better-priced houses, and popular manufacturers "knock off" the medium houses. All perfectly legal and accepted—the name of the fashion game.

Figure 13–1 is a calendar of fashion buyer visits to New York. The popular market dates are not precise since there are constant style

Figure 13–1. Calendar of Market Visits to New York.

SEASON	BETTER & HIGH PRICED	MODERATE PRICED	POPULAR PRICED
Fall	April/May	June	July
Holiday	Sept	Sept/Oct 15	Oct
Resort & Cruise	Sept 15/Oct	---	---
Spring	Oct 15/Nov	Oct 15/Nov	Nov
Summer	Jan	Jan/Feb	March/April*
Transition	May	May/June	---

*These markets start showing in those periods, but continue style developments throughout the selling season.

developments and store needs for promotional events. Another feature is that New York City, the major fashion market, has the greatest influx for better goods and fall merchandise. Other seasons of the year require stores of certain locales to support regional markets. For example, a store in Texas could consider the Dallas and California markets as important areas for the holiday, spring and summer seasons.

Store buyers are not market specialists and, therefore, cannot be in the market on a constant basis. They require support from people who act as their eyes and ears. The resident buying office personnel fills this role. But one must be careful in defining the *buying* function of a resident representative. The responsibility for the open-to-buy belongs to the store buyer, no one else. The resident buyer can only buy with the permission of the store buyer. Hence, when a requisition by a store buyer is sent to New York, the appropriate resident office representative is charged with order placement. Orders sent by store buyers can be in several forms.

- Open Order
- Specific Order
- Distribution Order
- Sample Order

OPEN ORDER An open order contains limited detailing against which the resident representative exercises judgment. The order is usually in the form of: ". . . buy 25 coats to retail at $50.00, in the best colors." The resource is discretionary.

SPECIFIC ORDER A specific order includes all details: manufacturers, styles, colors, and sizes. The order is often placed by an assistant buyer, or follow-up person (trainee).

DISTRIBUTION ORDER A distribution order is one that the resident office representative sends to selected stores because the merchandise represents market newness. If the store buyer feels it has a place in stock and has open-to-buy for it, a confirmation order is sent to the resident representative for placement with the manufacturer. Until the confirmation is received from the store buyer there is no commitment with the manufacturer for the store.

SAMPLE ORDER A sample order is dependent upon the relationship between the store and the resident office representatives. If the store buyer has confidence in the resident office representative, limited order discretion is given, so that if there is anything new in the market that deserves stock representation, an order of modest size can be placed without specific approval. An example is an open order for six pieces of any selected style on a semi- or weekly basis. If the department's open-to-buy becomes limited or non-existent, the sample rights arrangement is terminated by the store buyer.

The majority of fashion firms have representatives who are largely commission sales agents or traveling salespersons and who visit stores for the purpose of obtaining orders. They travel on the average of thirty-nine weeks a year and cover designated trading areas, with territorial rights (commissions for all orders taken in a fixed geographic area). Over a period of time they establish relationships with buyers and are able to offer advice about styles and/or trends. Representatives of well-known lines have an easier time of securing early order placement. Salespersons travel to the stores previous to market weeks, in the case of some forms of knitwear as early as late February, early March, for fall orders. Naturally the merchandise represents long-term production goods.

The practice of selling on the road has been affected considerably by the development of regional apparel markets. Some marts are brand new; others have been doing business for twenty or more years. Hundreds of thousands of apparel manufacturers and buyers are attracted to these regional markets annually because they allow manufacturers the opportunity to maintain continuous contact with buyers across the nation, and offer retailers the advantages of "one stop shopping," reduced traveling cost, and convenience. Sales representatives are able to avoid the need to travel from 30,000 to 60,000 miles a year in large cars needed to transport sample line(s), a cost that must be added to the expense of spending 160 nights annually in hotels and motels.

There are good reasons to encourage continued growth of regional markets. However, even regional market executives agree that despite New York's loss of their market share, New York will retain its number one market position. There are regional apparel markets in Atlanta, Georgia; Dallas and Houston, Texas; Denver, Colorado; Miami, Florida; Los Angeles and San Francisco, California; Chicago, Illinois; Seattle, Washington; Portland, Oregon; New Orleans, Louisiana; Boston, Massachusetts; etc. Major manufacturers also have regional showrooms in Minneapolis, Minnesota; Charlotte, North Carolina; Pittsburgh and Philadelphia, Pennsylvania; Cincinnati, Ohio; Memphis, Tennessee.

The following are cited as examples of the dimension of regional markets:

- Dallas attracted 126,000 buyers in August, 1980, for its showing of spring/holiday women's and children's apparel. In October, over 17,000 buyers viewed spring offerings. The complex consists of 2 million square feet of space. It was originally designed to do business in a twelve-state area, but in August, 1980, 400 buyers from overseas visited the mart.

Marketing areas of fashion merchandise. Courtesy California Mart.

As a meeting place, The California Mart is conveniently located in "The *Center Of Everything*". The freeways are easily accessible and we are centrally located in Los Angeles and Southern California. In-house parking facilities are available, and a mini-bus ride and ten minutes of your time will take you to all the hotels and points of interest in "center" Los Angeles. The California Mart . . . where facilities are built with you in mind.

For more information please call the California Mart, (213) 620-0260 and ask for meeting room reservations.

California Mart
(213) 620-0260
110 E. 9th Street,
Suite A727,
Los Angeles, California 90079

- The new seven-story structure, in the heart of Atlanta, encompasses 1.2 million square feet of exhibit space, offers 1000 permanent showrooms and 120,000 square feet of temporary exhibit space. Nearly 3500 different manufacturers are represented in the new mart.
- Chicago's Apparel Center offers exhibitors 1,300,000 square feet of display area, including over 850 permanent showrooms, plus a 140,000 square foot Expo center exhibit hall. Over 4000 lines are shown covering domestic and foreign-made merchandise, covering every merchandise classification of men's, women's and children's apparel.
- The California Mart has over 2 million square feet, 2000 showrooms and features close to 10,000 apparel lines. It features apparel lines not only from around the United States, but also from foreign countries.

Apparel marts have become veritable "cities" where buyers can select resources in an environment that contains theatres, restaurants, medical facilities, living quarters, parking garages, transportation, and public service agencies. However, fashion marketers look to New York for its creativity, quality, and fashion direction.

Other methods of obtaining goods are through telephone, mail and telegraph services. These means are confined to reorders. When a style sells well and a buyer wants goods fast or needs delivery information, the quickest and most efficient method is calling the manufacturer long distance.

METHODS OF OBTAINING FOREIGN MERCHANDISE

The easiest way to secure foreign merchandise is to buy from an importer who stocks goods in the United States. The advantages are that there is limited transportation costs, shorter delivery terms, and responsibility for the goods. The disadvantages are that the merchandise is available to other stores and additional markup cannot be obtained. As discussed, exporters do have New York offices and buying arrangements can be made there. However, this type of buying often requires inspection of facilities and dealings with management on the scene. With the importance of foreign merchandise, resident buying offices have become part of the international buying practice. They solicit their clients for an open-to-buy for stated classifications and send one of their representatives (or a group) to Europe, or the Orient, to develop styles for the participating stores. This has become a widespread practice among large- and medium-sized offices. Some of the larger offices maintain foreign offices in cities such as London, Milan, Tokyo, and Paris, staffed with people who take care of necessary papers, transportation, meetings with manufacturers, quality control, and delivery of merchandise.

The larger stores send their buyers to foreign markets but make sure that they are thoroughly experienced. In some cases, the divisional merchandise manager accompanies a team of buyers. The first step of the trip is to draw up a foreign purchase plan which specifies the merchandise, the transportation costs, and approximate land cost. This enables the retail values to be established. If there is a foreign buying office the buyer works with familiar personnel; in the absence of an office, a commissionaire (foreign buying agent) is hired to help the buyer make contacts, negotiate transactions, and follow the goods through delivery. It must be stated that merchandise is bought on the basis of buyer specifications, lines as shown in the United States is not the custom.

Prêt-à-porter, Paris.

Objections to Foreign Markets

Although there are important advantages to using foreign fashion markets and the practice has become widespread, there are disadvantages that must be considered—particularly in merchandise classifications that are vulnerable to fast change, for example, blouses or coordinates. The following are major objections to the use of foreign markets.

1. Extended trips mean extended absences of the buyer from the store and the store may suffer during the period.
2. It is a costly venture that includes air fare, meals, accommodations, and other expenses for living and traveling.
3. Commitments are for long periods and a merchandise pipeline is created, not required for domestic purchasing. Reorders cannot be filled for timely selling.

4. Specifications of foreign merchandise are not always made for American consumption, although this disadvantage has been cured to a large degree.
5. Because of the required lead time, a buyer must predict fashion acceptance, a job the domestic manufacturer undertakes.
6. The exclusivity of foreign merchandise enjoyed initially is not available to the same extent because the practice has become so widespread.
7. A store takes on the responsibilities of a manufacturer and must be dependent upon the buyer's ability to handle the hazards involved: inaccurate assessment of future fashion trends, deep commitment, long delivery lead time, and the contingency of heavy markdowns.

DOMESTIC MANUFACTURERS VERSUS FOREIGN MANUFACTURERS

There are approximately 25,000 manufacturers of fashion apparel in the United States, which affords a long roster of suppliers from which a store can select. The following list represents advantages in using domestic manufacturers without invoking patriotism and concern for our economy.

1. delivery;
2. proven specifications of merchandise;
3. relationships with manufacturers that result in certain advantages (to be discussed fully);
4. availability of merchandise in selected quantities;
5. availability of reorders;
6. responsibility for merchandise received;
7. ability to test selling rate;
8. opportunity to weigh line importance to total market;
9. planning and control of stock are comparatively easy;
10. permits stock adjustment to new trends.

However, the following advantages are enjoyed when a store buys from a foreign market (when the buyer visits the country of origin).

1. Prices can be cheaper, making promotionally priced goods available.
2. Mass distributors who cannot buy from better houses have sources of supply, who do not recognize stores' status or pressure.
3. Certain products are not available in the United States because foreign markets offer certain arts, crafts, or machinery know-how. For example: Parisian styling, Scottish cashmere sweaters, Norwegian hand knits, Spanish leathers, Italian knits.

4. Exclusivity of styling based on specification merchandising offers a store improved markup potential.
5. Certain foreign merchandise has status meaning.
6. Merchandise offers an opportunity for stores to offer a wider variety of merchandise.

Whatever the values, stores recognize the present need for both types of resources, with a heavier concentration on the domestic scene for the reasons listed. It must be recognized that despite everything the United States is the leader, by far of mass-produced ready-to-wear. Specific pockets of manufacturing, the shoe industry for example, have been hurt badly and have been reduced to lower levels of production. The markets in general became global after World War II and caused product dislocation in many areas. Japanese manufacturers, for example, have taken advantage of a fertile American market for a host of products, which range from matches to automobiles. It is a new world in which countries can use comparative advantages for commercial value.

One might wonder about the relationship of dollar control and foreign buying, since the definition of open-to-buy is a budget for delivery of goods within a specified time. Adjustments are made for the money by improvising the Six-Month Plan and knowing approximately when the goods will arrive with acceptance at an earlier than needed date.

CRITERIA FOR SELECTING RESOURCES

There are many sources of information available to learn where resources are located, what they manufacture, and their level of success. Sources of information follow the patterns outlined in Chapter 12 devoted to determining what to buy, which are here listed without explanation, but the reasoning is the same.

1. Resident buying office
2. Competing stores
3. Reporting services
4. Other buyers
5. Market centers
6. Trade advertising
7. Trade directories
8. Observation at events, affairs, etc.
9. Want slips

The unit control records reveal a complete record of every manufacturer used by a store and includes information on delivery, selling, customer returns, maintained markup and markdowns. The measuring rod of the system is complete. However, before a buyer makes a commitment with a resource, certain standards or criteria must be met. The following are the most important factors a buyer considers in the selection of resources, and some combinations of them will influence a buyer to choose one resource over another.

- Appropriate merchandise for the customer group
- Manufacturer's distribution policies
- Timing—Fashion leader or fashion follower (depending upon the store's customer group)
- Specifications
- Retail price maintenance
- Clearance policies
- Delivery policies
- Advertising policies
- Prices and terms
- Brand identification

Appropriate Merchandise for the Customer Group

A buyer selects resources based on what the resource can offer the customers of the department, such as quality, styling, and price ranges. The merchandise, whether for a large or small consumer group, must embody some style distinctiveness which consumers see as relatively important to them.

Manufacturer's Distribution Policies

Just as a store segments its customers, a manufacturer segments its audience. Therefore which stores have the same goods is of paramount concern. The higher priced store wants exclusivity or some form of insurance that the competition will be fair, limited, or as desired. The medium-priced store is equally concerned about any competitive edge that will lessen its status in the eyes of its customers. Even the discount store often looks for a manufacturer who will cooperate and offer competitive advantages. As discussed in Chapter 7, there are Federal laws* that bar a manufacturer and a retailer from acting in collusion to inhibit another retailer from purchasing the same goods and prohibit certain practices which may substantially lessen competition.

---

*A series of seven acts starting with the Sherman Antitrust Act (1890), Federal Trade Commission Act (1914); Clayton Act (1914); Robinson-Patman Act (1936); Miller-Tydings Act (1937); Wheeler-Lea Act (1938); Antitrust Procedures and Penalty Act (1974).

There are three general distribution policies followed by manufacturers:

1. franchise;
2. selected;
3. open.

Franchise applies to a limited number of stores, sometimes on an exclusive basis in the trading area, time, or part of line. *Selected* distribution policy involves a controlled number of stores within a trading area, usually based on population and potential volume availability. *Open* distribution policy means anyone with good credit rating can buy.

It follows that one of the first points a buyer makes to a manufacturer is "Who do you sell in my area?" One of the largest cities in the United States has two giant retailers on the same street who will not share resources from whom they buy in quantity. They will not advertise the merchandise of a shared resource, although they both stock goods from many of the same manufacturers. This case is indicative—the greater the investment the closer the inspection of competition.

Timing—Fashion Leader or Fashion Follower

Manufacturers develop merchandise to appeal to stores which are located in different positions of the fashion arc. Designer-name manufacturers are supported by retailers whose customers spend large sums of money and are part of the early-acceptance group on the fashion arc. This manufacturer must have styles that show fashion leadership. As noted, medium-priced vendors follow the leaders, popular-priced vendors follow the styles with majority acceptance. The buyer must evaluate to what degree is fashion leadership expressed by the vendor's line and where do his customers stand on the fashion arc.

Another timing evaluation for the store is the reorder policy of the vendor. Some vendors produce a line, deliver commitments, and have little or no merchandise available for reorder. This causes limited selling of well-accepted styles and prevents advertising of proven best sellers for the stores. Buyers will attempt to gain information about the distribution strategy of a given vendor, especially if the store policy requires a rate of sale as a condition for sales promotion. A successful style in most stores is one that sells well initially and can be reordered for restocking, advertising, and special orders.

Specifications

Despite the scope of the industry, the government has made studies of men's and women's figure types. However, garment sizes vary with manufacturers. Customers recognize the vendors whose garments fit them—in some cases in a different size than they are accustomed to wearing. The characteristics of fit, quality, and style are inherent values that represent know-how. When there is any question about fit, a buyer can secure several garments and try them on salespeople whose sizes are representative of customers. Dressmaker forms are not used for this purpose, though they are part of the manufacturing process, because groups of people do not possess model figures. Popular-priced buyers must exercise care as well, because budget manufacturers tend to make garments in less than ample proportions in order to save material cost.

Retail Price Maintenance

The store's reputation depends upon retail prices that are competitive for the same goods. Off-price selling by a competitor is a matter of deep concern. A manufacturer who permits or is part of a scheme that allows competition to sell below agreed retail levels will be dropped. There are no fair trade laws in ready-to-wear that require price maintenance, in fact, a Federal Act* terminated all interstate fair-trade regulations as of March 11, 1976. As a rule, retail price maintenance is directly related to the selling rate of goods. A poor selling style will be marked down despite any arrangement. When the markdown will take place depends upon the policy of the store, the amount of merchandise stocked, and the time of the year. A manufacturer with a record of poor sales will go out-of-business or sell stock overages to discount stores. Many stores will not use a resource whose goods can be found in a discount store. As a matter of maintaining customer satisfaction, stores will avoid suppliers of discount and popular-priced stores even if it can be proven that prices will be maintained. The only exception is the foreign manufacturer who develops goods for anyone with money. As stated previously, this is a reason why many mass merchandisers buy a profusion of goods from foreign markets. This practice avails the widest assortment of goods at cheaper prices, with no retail price restrictions.

Clearance Policies

No merchant at the manufacturing or retail levels can sell all the goods handled. Quantities are left over. The retailer uses store promotional events to dispose of stock remainders. The manufacturer sells disposable goods to stores or jobbers, depending upon his distribution policy, the quantity, and the nature of goods.

The buyer is concerned with the stores that offer off-price goods— When will they be stocked? At what prices? These are important factors because they affect the value of goods in the store's stock and sets up a level of competition. Having an ample supply of regular-priced mer-

*Consumer Goods Pricing Act, 1975.

chandise on hand when a competitor breaks prices can cause heavy markdowns.

Delivery Policies

There are two delivery situations that are uppermost in the buyer's mind. The first is when the original orders are delivered and in what quantity; and the second situation has been discussed—time for reordering.

Theoretically, orders are delivered on a first come, first serve basis. In practice this does not hold up because the trading area often permits important stores to obtain merchandise almost when available, to the detriment of the smaller retailer.

If the manufacturer does not have some anticipatory system, reorders will be nonexistent or in minimal quantities. The truth is, initial store selling success determines the amount of goods the manufacturer will have available for reordering. Therefore, the availability of reorder merchandise is dependent upon either strong early retail selling or poor selling. The manufacturer knows that stock preparation for reorders without early retail success is hazardous.

A manufacturer sometimes delivers goods to stores willing to accept merchandise early, disregarding the delivery date on the order. The ploy, which puts the manufacturers in an advantageous position, is to receive early payments and to avoid packing and holding goods until the agreed delivery dates. The result is that the manufacturer's inventory is depleted and delivery may be made on a partial basis. This sometimes puts the buyer in the position of having to experience late delivery or to agree to early delivery. In the case of goods purchased abroad, the buyer has less control over when merchandise is received.

A store dislikes broken shipments of colors and sizes which result in customer dissatisfaction. The need is for a retail stock of complete colors and sizes to satisfy the wants of customers and to establish a rate of sale.

Delivery experience often illustrates the manufacturer's respect for the buyer and the store. A manufacturer shows a respect for the store when deliveries are made on time and in the quantities, sizes, and colors ordered.

Advertising Policies

In this age of competition, millions of dollars are available in the form of cooperative advertising, which is supplied to a large degree by giant companies and trade associations of the textile market. The offer of advertising money is a strong influence on a buyer in the face of a limited store advertising program. A retail truth is that a buyer should never buy advertising—goods should be bought on merit.

The wise buyer applies the first rules of buying—what is well bought is half sold, and *then* looks to what cooperative advertising is available. (Cooperative advertising will be discussed in detail in Chapter 16.)

Advertising should be discussed *following* the selection of goods as a plus factor, and care should be exercised not to go overboard on the amount of goods ordered based on the available co-op money.

Prices and Terms

The prices of all the garments shown in manufacturers' showrooms are firm. There is no bargaining. It is the buyer's job to evaluate the level of the offerings, thereby determining whether the goods are competitively priced. The buyer is not essentially interested in cheaper prices. His concern is whether the customers will know that the styles are set at fair retail prices and are not available at lower price levels from competition. However, off-price or promotional goods prices are not firm and are subject to negotiation by both price maintaining and discount stores.

Advantageous terms can always be sought because they can be the means to added profit. (This subject will be discussed in Chapter 14.)

Brand Identification

This subject was discussed in the previous chapter. Brand name importance is a matter of store policy therefore it is an area of concern and decision-making for the merchandise manager.

In conclusion the buyer must weigh the following:

- The appropriateness of merchandise and its compatibility with store policies (and relationships)
- The growth potential of resources
- The availability of merchandise and the competitive conditions
- The profitability of merchandise

CLASSIFICATION OF RESOURCES

Like people, stores are rated by the company they keep. An important marketing strategy is the value of the resource to the store, since this relationship is one of the essential reasons for customer patronage. A buyer cognizant of the value of resources establishes levels of resource importance. The following discussions deal with the various classifications of resources available to buyers.

Key or Preferred Resources

These resources are important in terms of volume of sales, they are the most profitable moneymakers of the department. An added dimension is that they shape the character or prestige for the department, providing goods that are desired by a large segment of loyal customers. In a sense a partnership arrangement is maintained between the store and the resource and each plans on doing some business season after season, and year after year. A strong department has at least several key resources that give distinction and/or flavor to it as a unit of the store. A department without key resources does not operate at a maximum level.

Stock Resources

The success of these resources is solid and is stocked on a fairly consistent basis. Satisfactory profit is made, but the level is somewhat lower than a key resource.

Item Resources

This type of resource is used for specific styles, types or specific events, dependent upon fashion or promotional needs. For example, in a sweater department a "jeweled sweater" is made by specialists who are used when the item is in fashion. Or a better example, there are firms that are famous for blue jeans but offer complete sportswear lines. The buyer may buy one item, the jean, and bypass all other items. The house (resource) is used as an item resource.

Classification Resources

These resources are specialists in given classifications: bathing suits, sweaters, shirts, pants, leather jackets, or any other classification of merchandise.

Secondary Resources

Resources that are shopped and used on a sporadic basis, when styles are suitable for being included in stock.

Shopping Resources

Shopping resources are good resources, who show suitable merchandise but with whom there is no reason to do current business. In the long run, there is hope on the part of the manufacturer that "the ice" will be broken.

Trouble Resources

Manufacturers with whom the store has difficulty in terms of merchandise adjustments, excessive quality defects in delivered merchandise, and any rupture in business dealings. The buyer omits them from the shopping list, sometimes by order of the merchandise manager.

CONCENTRATION ON RESOURCES

As previously stated, a store's highest return from a manufacturer's goods is a combination of profit and prestige. By limiting the number of resources a store uses, a relationship can be established in which there is an exchange of fashion information. Early and well-researched information from resources supported by the investment of time and money must be taken seriously. Another important advantage of such a relationship will include preferential deliveries for both original orders and subsequent reorders—no small advantage in an opportunistic business where speed is of the essence. Also a key resource will avail coop advertising for loyal stores. Some other benefits that might be derived from a close relationship between a store and resources are:

1. markdown money for styles that sold poorly (many manufacturers are not prone to accede to this practice);
2. returns of poor selling styles (sometimes);
3. manufacturer fashion shows in stores (trunk showings);
4. inducements for salespeople (push money);
5. interior displays (racks, blowups of ads, etc.);
6. specification merchandise made exclusively for the store.

However, there can be disadvantages to limiting the number of resources used. Severely narrowing your resources and placing substantial orders with them can limit stock assortment. Little opportunity is given to new resources in a business where manufacturers come and go. In other words, important styles can be lost until established resources catch up, if ever. Also chances are not afforded to new firms on the way up, so competition gains the advantage of newer or more exciting styles. There is an old song that says, ". . . you always hurt the one you love." Paraphrasing these words, problems can arise because of overconfidence in resources such as:

1. Merchandise can be delivered *not* as ordered—styles, colors, quantities, etc.
2. The manufacturer, certain of arrangements, may look for new worlds to conquer and flirt with competition. This puts the buyer and store in a poor position. (Competition is in a position to take away a share of the market.)

3. The buyer becomes lethargic and makes little attempt to seek and cultivate new resources. New trends escape attention because of lack of market exposure; information about new trends is obtained from a relatively short list of manufacturers.

SUMMARY

Buying success or failure, to a large extent, depends upon the ability to develop and maintain desirable relationships with suitable resources. Over the years, the choices of resources has widened and includes foreign producers. With the development of regional markets, central locations are now available for buyer and seller to meet more frequently.

Because of the consumer's acceptance of foreign merchandise and its merchandising advantages, buyers, to a considerable degree, are increasingly engaged in foreign trade. What and how deeply foreign merchandise should be stocked is a matter of executive judgment. However, a market penetration of 30 percent, which is apt to increase, indicates future deeper buyer involvement in international trading.

Continuing established resource relationships is a matter of results. When retail records prove a manufacturer's capacity for creating profits, by delivering salable styles, a buyer continues the relationship; when selling is poor, the relationship is discontinued. Criteria for the selection of a new resource is based on the suitability of merchandise and the manner in which a manufacturer conducts business.

In the fashion business there are many resources making the same or similar goods, the competition is intense, and a good measure of a buyer's professionalism is exhibited by the selection of resources. The type of store and its strategies will dictate to what extent:

1. trips to the New York market are made;
2. regional marts are visited;
3. foreign markets will be used;
4. fashion leadership is exercised;
5. merchandise is delivered (early or late peaking);
6. brands are maintained;
7. resources are limited (to those with the best probability of selling success).

Resources are the means of obtaining merchandise, including purchases according to specifications, in which case the manufacturer acts as a contractor for the store.

Above all, the buyer is the one who is responsible for the relationship with the resources.

chapter 14

FASHION BUYING PRACTICES & TECHNIQUES

INTRODUCTION

Effective merchandising—maximizing profit and minimizing investment —includes realistic planning followed by its implementation in a manner that leads to the procurement and maintenance of a consumer-satisfying inventory. It follows, therefore, that a buyer must respond effectively to the questions:

- How much to buy?
- What to buy?
- Where to buy?
- When to buy?
- How to buy?
- How to maintain resource relationships?

The first three questions have been discussed, respectively, in the three preceding chapters; this chapter will deal with the last three questions, which cover the broad subject of fashion buying practices and techniques.

The preceding discussions concentrated largely on planning and buying for a period—a new season. However, a buyer also purchases merchandise at various times during a month. Most retailers provide buyers with information to calculate a current open-to-buy. A weekly merchandise report is distributed to buyers every week or ten days which permits a buyer to easily compute a current open-to-buy position as of a given date. With information on specific merchandise such as the date when style was received, its selling record, and its inventory level, a buyer can decide how much should be spent for reorders or for newly developed styles.

As a review of the previously discussed strategies, the following data and tactics are planned:

- A budget plan—the open-to-buy (OTB).
- A breakdown of merchandise needs in terms of units at price levels

within classifications and sub-classifications (there is a strong possibility of some changes after market research).

- An allocation in terms of money for classifications (although market offerings may dictate establishment of new sub-classifications or deletion of some).
- The entire OTB will not be spent.
- Stock should be peaked just prior to the period of strong consumer selling of the new season, and that is when it should consist of the widest assortment to establish the "winners" on which heavier depth will be placed, possibly for promotions.

Open-to-buy is a resultant figure subject to modification by actual merchandising events or revising plan figures. It is increased or decreased by:

- Actual Events
- Sales
  Markdowns
  Purchases
  Shortage
  Return to Vendors
- Revised Plans
  Sales
  Markdowns
  E.O.M.
  Cancelled Orders
  Postponed Orders

WHEN TO BUY

Fashion buyers must build new stock assortments for all the seasons depending upon the nature of their operation. For example a mass discounter certainly shows little or no interest in the cruise season and has small regard for the transitional season. The major seasons—spring, summer, fall, and holiday—the universally covered periods that comprise the merchandise calendar. Regardless of the nature of the operation, price levels, quality, composition, and location, there are four minimum visits to the market. (The location of the markets and the frequency of visits were covered previously.)

The following situations permit the buyer to purchase goods within the guidelines of a plan and control system.

- Store Policies
- Rate of Sale
- Sales/Inventory Relationship

- Market Conditions
- General Business Conditions

When to buy depends upon a series of considerations with the strong influence of—for whom the buying is being done—the customer group.

Store Policies

The store's policies play a strong role in establishing "when to buy," such as:

1. *When the stock is to be peaked (greatest assortment and depth).* Retail price levels, fashion leadership, and store location are definite considerations in timing and in line with store policies. Stores that concentrate on high-price apparel (fashion leadership) want early retail stock. Their customers tend to buy earliest.

    Store location can be exemplified by stores in the south that like to peak fall stocks as early as possible because of the extended warm weather period which makes for customer apathy for lightweight clothing. Many stores try to achieve high stock levels in July. On the other hand, some New York City stores will not permit peak levels until the middle of August. The feeling is that proximity to the market and weather conditions favor later peaking.

2. *Use of foreign markets.* As indicated previously, specification merchandising abroad does not permit pin-pointing delivery. In many instances delivery must be accepted very early. For example, Italian knits for the fall season may be delivered in April, long before the season. Do you remember ads in April, May or June featuring this type of merchandise? The reasons are apparent; the store must either put these goods in a stockroom or on the selling floor. The decision is often in favor of the latter since it represents fashion in a rise position and creates additional business.

3. Domestic manufacturers sometimes offer *special inducements for stores to accept goods earlier than needed.* The incentive is typically dating delivery in April as of June 25. This makes the bill due August 10 (the 25th of the month is considered as the first of the month following). Normally this requires permission from the divisional merchandise manager, a change in policy. For example, seasonal manufacturers, such as for sweaters or swimwear, build inventories early in the year to allow for timely deliveries. In order to lower high inventories and to avoid the higher cost of delivering during a compressed delivery period, they offer stores an incentive to accept merchandise earlier than needed or than

as detailed on store orders. Management sometimes alters its policy and accepts the inducement because, in many instances, the extension of extended payment terms allows a store to sell the merchandise before payment is due. In effect, when payment terms are extended, the manufacturer helps to finance the retailer's operation.

Rate of Sale

When a style sells well it is a reason to reorder—to restock more of the same merchandise. This is always an affirmative action and the perceived reason for the initial purchase. But like many principles, it cannot be invoked without some qualifications. The buyer must weigh the following:

- How long is the reorder delivery period?
- Will the demand continue when the reorder is received?
- Has the style been "knocked off" and is it available at lower prices?
- What is the seasonal cut off date? Remember that spring immediately follows Easter, and fall begins the day after July 4.

There is an old buyer saying: "It was the last reorder that 'killed' me." Discretion may dictate concentration on newer styles, forgetting present selling success. There is more than just a selling rate as the criterion for reordering. Reordering is a matter of relationships that an experienced buyer understands.

Stock/Sales Relationship

Here is a familiar term. You will recall that when selling is above plan, other factors not considered, it creates additional open-to-buy. Sales and stock must be in balance; when selling is above plan more stock is required to re-establish the norm of stock/sales ratio. Let us assume that the planned EOM is $25,000 (really the BOM for the next period) and that $10,000 more goods were sold than planned. The result will be BOM stock of $15,000, or $10,000 less than needed. Consequently the buyer watches the flash figures (the unaudited gross sales of the department submitted to the accounting office at the end of each day) and can tell the way the balance of stock/sales is being affected on a daily basis.

If you have worked in a store you probably heard the buyer ask "How are we doing?", or observed frequent references to the stubs of items sold. Why? The buyer knows that the stock/sales equilibrium is based on making estimated daily sales. Not making the figures creates an overbought condition, an imbalance of stock for the current rate of sales.

Market Conditions

When the market reflects strength, merchandise that in the buyer's judgment means highly salable fashion trends, substantial sums of money are invested in goods, with an adequate supply saved for future developments. When the market is weak, the buyer will hold back and place minimum requirements, hoping that it will readjust itself. Insecurity may cause a hand-to-mouth buying practice with continued placement of small orders. This is a costly procedure to the department because it necessitates frequent orders, many receiving processes, extra transportation charges, and shallow stock. The latter condition is not customer desired, particularly in major selling periods. It is a tendency of some new buyers who lack confidence.

What percentage of the open-to-buy is spent at a given time depends upon several factors, one of which is *market strength*. When a market is assessed as being weak, a buyer will retain a fair share of the open-to-buy with the realization that manufacturers will develop more salable styles during the season. As a rule, maintaining liquidity, having open-to-buy, is the best tactic when a season's trends are evaluated and they lack sufficient newness or fashion excitement.

General Business Conditions

Sometimes a business condition arises when no buying or limited buying becomes the policy. For example, with several hundred thousand automobile workers laid off because of the industry's loss of market share to foreign producers, stores in Michigan, our automobile producing capital, are wary about their merchandise investments. Tight control over stock/sales ratio is enforced.

When economic conditions cause management to order maintenance of minimum stock levels, it could have the effect of assortments of shallow depth. Despite budget restrictions, however, a fashion buyer must be permitted to stock what is new and desired by his customers. Failure to stock consumer wants is a reason for loss of patronage, a condition no store wants to face.

TYPES OF ORDERS

Merchandise is purchased for different purposes and on different terms. For example, a reorder can be placed for immediate delivery. On the other hand, some orders can require a delivery lead time of six months. The reason for this extended delivery term can be one of three reasons or a combination of two reasons: one, the order is for merchandise specified by the retailer (exclusive style characteristics requiring the manufacturer to schedule and produce special cuttings for the store);

two, the retailer must accommodate the production and delivery schedule of highly rated manufacturers; and three, the merchandise requires a long production period. As a case in point, Burdine's, a southern Florida-based department store chain, ensures timely delivery to accommodate its climatic needs by placing orders in advance for two seasons during each major buying trip. In effect, they write orders eight months in advance; they place commitments in June for needs the following early spring.

The following types of orders are discussed in this unit:

- Stock Orders
- Reorders
- Special Orders
- Advance Orders
- Blanket Orders
- Promotional Orders
- Open Orders
- Special-Purpose Orders
- Back Orders

Stock Orders

Stock orders are given to the vendors for stock requirements with full specifications of style numbers, quantities, delivery dates, sizes, and colors.

Reorders

Reorders are additional orders based on successful selling with full details of style numbers, quantities, delivery dates, sizes, and colors. The buyer will pressure for fast delivery in order to maintain adequate stock for continued good selling.

Special Orders

Orders placed to satisfy an individual customer, usually the customer's name and an order number are attached for later identification. (The style is earmarked for the customer and not put in stock.)

Advance Orders

Advance orders are given to vendors with the same details supplied as on stock orders. The difference, however, is the delivery date, which is a longer term. Here are some reasons for giving orders with extended delivery terms.

1. *Long Production Goods*—For example, men's suits that are bought five or six months before retail selling; ladies' knits that are featured in February/March for July/August delivery. These goods require long-term planning and production.

2. *Specification Buying*—A manufacturer concentrates on a retailer's order which specifies exclusive style characteristics. In this case the manufacturer must stop production on styles shown in the showroom and produce special goods for a particular retailer. Mail-order houses place orders at least six months in advance of delivery.

3. *Promotional Needs*—A buyer may place an order with a key resource in June for off-price goods to be delivered in time for an October promotional event.

4. *Foreign Goods*—bought on specification terms.

Blanket Orders

Blanket orders are really promises to do business with a manufacturer over a period of time. Sometimes used by resident representative*, but rarely used by store buyers. They do not detail colors, sizes, or manner of shipment (therefore goods cannot be shipped). The blanket order requires detailing or placing a new order against the blanket. It can work as follows: a particular style is estimated to be in great demand in the future. The buyer is wary of market deliveries. A favored resource is selected and the buyer gives the manufacturer an estimate of the need for an entire season or year, which the vendor agrees to supply. For example, a blanket order is made for 1,000 dozen with the stipulation that stock orders will be placed on specific dates, with some delivery terms noted. The 1,000 dozen can then be worked perhaps in 5 orders of 200 dozen each.

Promotional Orders

These orders are for merchandise in larger quantities than stock orders. The size of the order is relevant to the store policy and the intended promotional force and anticipated volume potential. The merchandise is listed separately because it must fill a need for a planned promotional event. It requires that a buyer is aware and follows up to insure timely delivery.

Open Orders

Open orders are ordinarily sent to the resident buyer who uses discretion in determining which manufacturer to use. When there is a very

---

*In anticipation of receiving orders from member or client stores.

close relationship between buyer and manufacturer, the buyer may send an open order without detailing of styles or colors which is filled in and delivered. This can be a dangerous practice, but it is on occasion used to secure a "hot" selling line and when there is reason for confidence. The manufacturer can be uncomfortable with this situation, if the delivered merchandise sells poorly or otherwise is not desireable. In this instance the buyer probably would exert strong pressure to return goods.

Special-Purpose Orders

Special-purpose orders are commitments for fashion shows, window displays, or for any special event that requires one or several pieces of a style.

Back Orders

Orders that have not been filled either in full or in part within the time specified. They are still in the manufacturer's files to fill and have not been cancelled by the buyer.

—THE MARKET TRIP

The market trip is of prime importance because it encompasses two vital concerns for the buyer:

1. to obtain the best market offerings for the store;
2. to secure knowledge to evaluate whether the offerings will have a high or low level of customer acceptance.

It is a hectic period. What follows are the procedures for a market visit.

The Preparation

The store provides the expenses for the trip. Some stores use one hotel to accommodate buyers, this makes available social and business interactions among visiting personnel. If there are any problems securing hotel reservations, the buying office has personnel assigned to ease this task. The buyer is given money for food and necessary expenses, and provided with transportation expenses.

Sunday is the usual day for departure so that a full week can be spent in the market. The length of the stay depends upon the season, the location of the store, the number of markets to be covered, and the type and quantity of merchandise to be bought. The trip for the fall season is usually the longest trip extending to a period of two weeks.

A. The buyer registers her "arrival" for the new season's purchases.

B. Resident buyer and store buyer discuss the same classification of fashion merchandise.

C. Meeting with market representatives to review samples and discuss fashion themes or merchandising appeals to the new season.

D. The buyer examines the RBO's fabric forecast for the new season.

E. The buyer places an order with the RBO that will meet fashion requirements of her store's customers.

F. The merchandise arriving at the store.

Approximately ten days to two weeks prior to departure, the buyer will write to the resident buyer counterpart so that there is preparation at the market end. In some cases, important resources are similarly advised.

The market will know when the buyer arrives. Trade publications solicit hotels for the arrivals of buyers and publish lists, which are sold to manufacturers. A buyer can avoid being listed by requesting the desk clerk to eliminate his notice of arrival. Manufacturers and their sales staffs scan publications for arrival notices so that they can visit or call on the buyers at the resident offices, or expect them in their showrooms. (See illustration of "Buyers Arrival" from *Women's Wear Daily.*)

The Visit to the Resident Buying Office for the New Season's Purchases

Step One, Monday, about 8:30 A.M., the buyer registers at the resident buying office. Store personnel can contact them there if circumstances warrant.

Step Two, the buyer meets with the resident office buyer responsible for the same classification of fashion merchandise. The meeting will include a full-scale discussion of:

1. general market outlook;
2. trends;
3. resource developments;
4. merchandise information, which a market specialist should know after having "digested" the market.

The meeting will include a review of samples culled by the representative. Market representatives usually maintain a rack of merchandise in the office for this purpose.

A competent market representative makes a list of recommendations for the buyer's reference. The list will include:

1. selected, important resources;
2. style numbers;
3. colors and fabrics for the season.

Step Three can be a discussion with either the resident fashion director or division merchandise manager, or both, to obtain an overview of fashion themes or merchandising approach to the new season. (The fashion director has probably arranged a fashion show for one evening during market week in the office or at a hotel for all visiting store buyers.)

Step Four on the first day varies. The buyer may see resource sales personnel in the office or visit stores, particularly if the market is New York City. (This can be done during the week, sandwiched between manufacturer visits, or during evening openings.)

Step Five, and the last step, is the most important one—to compile a list of manufacturers who must be seen on this trip. This list will be divided into five sections covering every day of the work week. (Sometimes manufacturers will make time available during evenings or on Saturdays.)

Market Coverage Techniques

The buyer's list of manufacturers is arranged in order of importance. The first order of importance to be considered is the fashion trend, which most often is available from the higher priced resources. The first visits are therefore made to the resources who represent the highest priced levels of each classification of merchandise; the next step is to review manufacturers representing the lowest levels within the same classifications; and finally, the medium or moderate levels. This may seem out of context, but the reasoning is sound in a market that is known for speed of imitation. By looking first at the highest and then at the lowest price levels, a comparison of styling, value and knock off state can be easily made. The technique gives more confidence to buying merchandise in which there will be the greatest investment—the middle price ranges.

During the visits to the resources the buyer should acquaint himself with the executives of the important firms. This can lead to advantages such as improved delivery dates or better terms. Part of professionalism is knowing the right people in a relatively small world.

Occasionally, to broaden technical knowledge and to understand the resource's methods of doing business, factories and shipping rooms should be visited. In the specification merchandising area this is a must. The specification buyer must inspect production and shipping facilities firsthand to make sure of a resource's ability to make and ship goods as contracted. In reality the specification buyer is an expert because of the part being played, the jobber role as a producer of the styles. The buyer has "created" the style(s), specified the amount of goods to be put into work, and has assumed the responsibility for back-up merchandise —the usual manufacturer responsibilities.

Selecting Merchandise and Placing Orders

Each resource supplies the buyers with showroom order pads. Most buyers use these pads to make notations of styles, colors, prices, and

During market week, the resident office buyer will arrange fashion shows for all visiting store buyers.

any other necessary details on the merchandise they have seen. The "paper" is retained by the buyer and used later to compare the same or similar merchandise. You may wonder how one can have as many as fifteen or twenty different copies of orders and be able to make selections in the quiet of a hotel room or back at the store. It is amazing how one improvises a system. Techniques might include:

- A good memory.
- A rating system next to each style and/or resource. Systems may use checks (✓ fair, ✓✓ good, ✓✓✓ excellent, ✓✓✓✓ for possible promotion), stars, comments, or any notation with which the buyer feels comfortable.

There are a number of procedures a buyer will follow to visit the market. A sportswear buyer might shop one entire classification before working on the next classification. Some buyers prefer visiting various top houses for different classifications for a general feel of fashion trends of the new season. It is a matter of choice, how one "attacks" the market. During the visit there is a tailoring process—the selection of merchandise for the season ahead.

What is uppermost in the buyer's mind?

- Market trends and their salability
- The specific styles within trends
- The resources that produce these style
- The assurance of delivery for planned stock composition
- The appropriateness of dollars and units planned (before market trip) for each merchandise classification

Of course the buyer knows the important resources that must be covered and these resources are prominently listed. The shopping list will also include recommended new companies for the buyer to visit, if time permits.

After or during the trip, the buyer must allow time for a selection process. It takes different forms: to cull out the wanted resources and styles at the hotel after each day is over; to wait until the last day of the trip; to defer the selection process until returning to the store. In some cases, particularly with preferred resources, an order may be given in the showroom after reviewing a line.

Some stores require that all orders must be countersigned by a merchandise manager. In this instance, there are several alternatives if an order must be given immediately. Give the order in the showroom with a notation "to be confirmed." Another way is to call the merchandise manager. If he is in the market at the same time as his buyers, permission can be obtained easily.

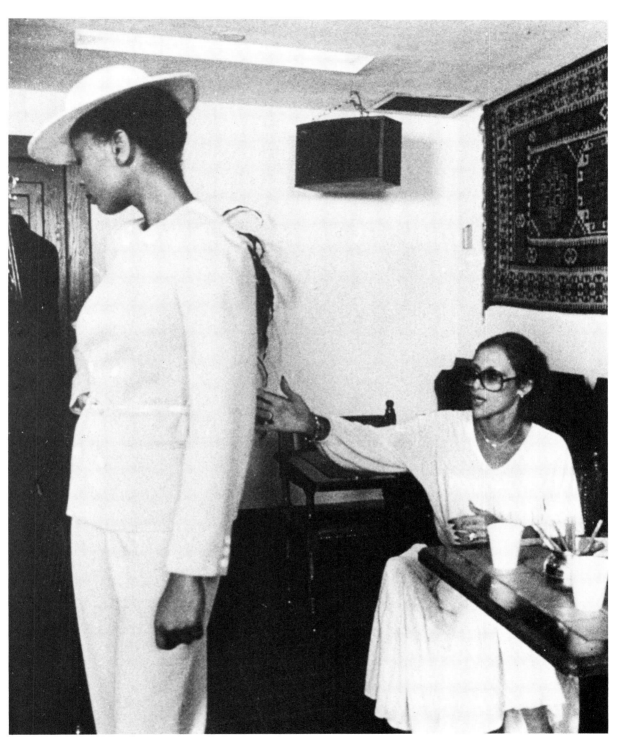

Buying and selling the line.

When all orders are ready to be sent to the selected vendors, they are analyzed against the plan to insure a proper coverage of classifications, price lines, units, dollars, colors, sizes, and other required areas.

THE MARKET VISIT FOR STOCK REQUIREMENTS

In the preceding sections, the market visit was discussed for the purpose of stocking merchandise for a new season. However, the buyer's visits to the market occur as often as there are needs. In such cases the activities can be modified substantially. The resident office will probably not be a "beehive" of activity and the representative will be more relaxed and available to shop the market with the buyer, possibly for a day or two. This interrelationship can include lunch and in depth analyses of the department's activities, comparisons with departments in other member stores, and market news for current and future use.

The nature of this type of market visit can include any specific, or combination of:

1. Stock fill-ins.
2. Promotional merchandise.
3. New market developments.
4. Reusage of money. Manufacturers may not produce styles selected because of minimum store support. The buyer has spent a part of the OTB for goods that will never be received. Therefore cancellation of "dead" styles, allows OTB, or utilization of money thought to be placed for future, or current merchandise. This practice is particularly exercised by better-priced buyers. They often visit the market about one month following an order placement for a new season.
5. Shopping of stores.
6. Museum trips for fashion relevancy.
7. Visits to trade associations—Wool Bureau, Cotton Council, etc.
8. Resources not covered when pressured for time.
9. Committee activity with merchandising groups of the resident office—for development of private label merchandise, order placement for foreign merchandise, and any other group activity.
10. Meeting with manufacturers as sources of promotional money. Large chemical and fiber companies enter into third party arrangements whereby they supply the money for store ads featuring the companies, the manufacturers, and the retailers. (This procedure is not contrary to the Robinson-Patman Act.*)

*Concerned with defining unfair price discrimination and inequitable quantity discounts, brokerage payments, and promotional payments between two parties, buyer and seller. Primary sources (textile or related prime suppliers) are third parties and therefore are not restrained by the Act.

SPECIALIZED BUYING ARRANGEMENTS

The discussions on buying merchandise has been devoted largely to goods that are purchased in the showroom at established prices. However, there are times when negotiations are required to establish a price for merchandise, or when merchandise is taken into stock under special arrangements.

When a manufacturer's inventory consists of styles that sold well or end-of-season broken assortments of best-selling styles (manufacturers never end a season with a "clean stock"), they will be offered to stores at promotional prices (lowered costs). Most retailers, on the other hand, schedule periodic promotional events that feature off-price merchandise at "new" lowered prices—bargains.

The retailer has three alternatives to prepare a promotionally priced stock:

1. markdown merchandise in stock;
2. purchase current merchandise at less than showroom prices (by pressuring manufacturers);
3. purchase manufacturer's slow-moving styles or their remainder stock of best sellers.

The negotiations for merchandise discussed in #2 and #3 include trading, attempting to obtain the lowest price.

Price negotiation is also part of specification merchandising. Naturally, the buyer/seller dialogue relates to the size of the order, when the merchandise is to be produced (lowest prices can be obtained when goods are produced during the manufacturer's slow season), and the manufacturer's cost.

Still another specialized arrangement is initiated by a manufacturer with a selling weakness in an attempt to enhance purchase terms by offering a sales guarantee to the buyer for a given period, ranging from a weekend to a two-week period, to establish a rate of sale. There are three methods used: *sales guaranteed, consignment, memorandum.* Parenthetically, in consignment selling, title (ownership) of goods does not pass to the store, but passes directly from the vendor to the store's customers. In the case of guaranteed sales, title does pass to the store. Memorandum selling is a vague term that has trade-practice rules for interpretation. It is needless to say that a successful manufacturer does not have to resort to this practice, which at best, is dangerous from his point-of-view, especially if it is widely practiced. The buyer who questions the salability of merchandise, or wants to limit risk under certain circumstances, may accept such a deal. But caution must be exercised. Primarily an order is a contract and must be clear enough so that there is no question of what was intended because there is a contingency of loss to someone, a markdown, loss of time, plus transportation charges.

JOB LOTS

The practice of buying job lots requires experience and understanding of what is at stake. The professionals of discount stores and other mass distribution firms have the practice down to a science, all others are wise to be wary.

A job lot is an assortment of goods that a vendor has not been able to sell at regular prices and offers them at reduced prices. Usually the job lot is a package of assorted styles at a given price for all units, regardless of original values.

The buyer should be aware that the merchandise would not be available if someone did not make a mistake. It is easy to become the one who will make the second mistake. The inherent dangers are:

1. Broken sizes and colors—The sizes are often end sizes (abundance of either small or large sizes); the colors are off-shades.
2. The attractive price—Although a considerable reduction, it may be expensive because the real value is customer acceptance. Job lot goods are usually available late in the season when regular stock is to be marked down—possibly below cost—to move the goods. Will the new goods be a bargain?
3. Quality—Job lot merchandise must be compatible with the quality of regular goods, otherwise customers will look askance at future promotions. If the goods are below expectations they are difficult to return unless there is a good relationship with the resource.

If a job lot purchase is a necessity, the buyer should seek resources of known quality and with good store relationships. The buyer should visit the warehouses to inspect the goods. An inventory in the shipping room should be taken as an analysis of stock composition value. Anything less than retail stock should not be purchased, unless it complements goods in the retail stock.

SPECIAL PROMOTION BUYING

There have been several references to the need for buying goods to support departmental and store events. This section is about buying goods at less than original costs in order to obtain customer traffic days in line with store policy.

The best rule used in approaching this problem is, "a buyer's first loyalty is to the department's stock." Before any promotional merchandise is bought a thorough analysis should be made of inventory to learn if there is any merchandise from stock that should be marked down. Present merchandise represents that which the customers have seen, from selected resources, and in known colors, sizes, and silhouettes. Good values can make good customers. Particularly when the customers recognize that the reductions are from stock. A "wash*" procedure will ensure a healthy stock condition.

The best technique to employ is to solicit key and stock resources—the same people from whom merchandise in present stock was purchased. In fact, the best way to purchase promotional goods is to list the best-selling styles of the season, eliminating those that are needed for future selling and attempt to buy them at substantially lowered prices that permit ample markup yet with considerable savings for customers. The advantages are apparent:

1. The acceptance levels of the merchandise is known.
2. The customers will recognize new values.
3. A manufacturer will not jeopardize a good relationship by delivering poor merchandise.
4. The quality level of the department is not lowered, even in the face of clearance days.

PRIVATE LABEL BUYING

Private label buying has been referred to many times as specification buying. It is a practice that has become widespread due to the advantages it offers a store, such as the opportunity:

● To take the merchandise out of a competitive position to attain higher markup and to lower retail prices.
● To offer merchandise as "Made exclusively for . . ." or to upgrade merchandise. Exlusive merchandise, which is of a better quality than market offerings, influences consumer patronage.

In its simplest form, a buyer may request the manufacturer to make slight modifications on a style, such as the color or style detail. In its most complicated form, the buyer will develop a style, select the fabrics, and supply the size proportions.

When private label development plays an important role in a retailer's merchandising strategy, it requires:

1. seasoned buyers working with fashion directors or stylists;
2. specification department;
3. quality control knowledge (a department);
4. large order commitments;
5. reliable manufacturers.

*Marking goods down.

Larger chain and mail-order houses are the leading exponents of private label buying and can control the merchandise on the levels of price, quantity and quality.

Many stores use private labels by simply contacting a key resource and explaining the goals intended. Quantity, colors, order date placements, style details, are worked around the manufacturer's line. Special merchandise is then made available for the department.

The difficulty with private label buying is that the store must act in the guise of a manufacturer. Therefore, the responsibilities usually attributed to the manufacturer such as styling, availability of forward or reorder stock, and advertising, are undertaken by the store through the buyer. *Reorders* are not available from the manufacturer's stock, they are provided for by store commitments.

OBTAINING A HIGHER PROFIT FOR THE DEPARTMENT

Profit margin is one of the criteria for evaluating a successful buyer. When a buyer places an order with a resource, there are three elements to consider that relate to higher profits for the department:

- Quoted price (cost)
- Terms
- Cost of transportation or shipping

Profit is the difference between cost and retail. Therefore the cost must allow retail values to be supportingly high to realize a markup percentage as established by management. The buyer must at all times concentrate on those resources that avail sufficient markup. As an example, a blouse at $5.75 cost with a manufacturer suggested retail price of $8.95, or a markup of 36 percent, would certainly not be suitable for a full-service store. The expense of doing business would not allow the buyer to concentrate on this style. It would bring the profit margin down. The buyer must at all times refrain from buying goods that offer a short markup. When a style is offered with a short markup, the buyer should shop other resources for replacements.

Giant organizations can use their purchasing power to obtain three merchandising advantages:

1. cost;
2. preferential delivery;
3. merchandise exclusivity.

Hence, they are in a position to influence manufacturers to exercise a form of price discrimination. This is tricky because the Robinson-Patman Act seeks to prevent large retailers from using their power to obtain discounts that are not justified by the savings through sizable orders. However, the Act does allow some forms of price discrimination provided that the following is part of the purchase arrangement:

1. products are physically different;
2. buyers are not competitive;
3. competition is not injured;
4. price differences can be justified by differences in costs;
5. market conditions change, viz: manufacturing costs increase or decrease; competitive manufacturers change their prices.

Obviously, the most widely used ploy is to obtain price advantage through specification merchandising—developing styles that are different (in some form) from those offered to other retailers.

Smaller organizations can obtain price advantages by:

1. specification merchandising (joint efforts with non-competing retailers);
2. offering better terms to manufacturers (e.g. early payment and early acceptance of goods);
3. buying as part of a syndicated deal (resident buying offices frequently create group purchase deals for member stores);
4. long-term commitments.

METHODS TO REDUCE COSTS

Following are methods to reduce costs, not in terms of reducing the stated wholesale value, but actually lessening costs for additional profit.

- Cash Discounts
- Anticipation
- Shipping or Transportation Charges

Cash Discounts

All fashion firms offer discounts for the prompt payment of invoices. These are referred to as *trade discounts.* In the area of women's ready-to-wear, usual terms are 8/10 EOM. In effect, a bill paid by the 10th day of the month following delivery is subject to a discount of 8 percent. All bills dated on the 25th of the month, or later, are considered dated as of the 1st day of the following month. Buyers will often ask orders scheduled for shipment on the 20th or thereabouts to be delivered on the 25th of the month. This gives the advantage of capital usage, approximately thirty days more.

Theoretically, late payment does not permit the store to earn the trade discount, but stores take it regardless of late payments. The enforcement of the rule of discount is unusual.

Anticipation

This is a way of securing an additional discount by paying a bill of cooperating resources before a due date. The rate of anticipation was generally calculated at the rate of 6 percent per year. Today, in a time of high-money cost, most retailers take anticipation at the current rate of interest. In a large organization, the accumulated anticipation sum for a department can be a substantial sum. (The rate of anticipation will fluctuate with increases or decreases of the cost of money, bank rate.)

Shipping or Transportation Charges

The cost of goods must take into account the shipping or transportation charges which over the year can be a sizable departmental expense. Considerable reduction of this expense can be important to producing a profit.

One of the general means to affect savings is to request and receive "F.O.B. store" terms. There is no cost of delivery and title of goods does not pass until goods are received by the store. This is particularly true for important New York stores that buy from resources who ship from New York, New Jersey, and Connecticut.

Another way is to have merchandise shipped from regional warehouses. Some large resources maintain warehouses in three or four regions of the United States and use this as a selling point, since cartage costs are held to a minimum. Giant retailers use regional distribution points where they receive bulk shipments of goods, from warehouse to store, another form of cost savings.

A buyer can also decrease costs of large shipments by having orders shipped by specified carriers. Sometimes deliveries are requested at a specific time for the purpose of consolidating shipments. As an example, a West Coast buyer in New York for goods might request that several manufacturers ship on one day to a designated carrier.

Frequently a buyer will ensure a fast reorder by asking a manufacturer to pay for the charges of air freight. If the manufacturer agrees, the buyer will request the store to pay the manufacturer at the rate charged by the regular carrier. The buyer can affect time and cost savings over a season.

PURCHASE ORDER

No.

DEPT. NO.

MFG. NO.

1. Send separate invoice and separate packing slip for each store.
2. Ship this entire order in one package.

NAME

ADDRESS

CITY

DATE   TERMS

EOM

AUTOMATICALLY CANCELLED IF NOT SHIPPED BY _____

STYLE	CLASS	DESCRIPTION	COLOR	LINCOLN			M QTY	BRANCH STORE			SP QTY	BRANCH STORE			L QTY	QTY TOTAL	UNIT COST	TOTAL COST	UNIT RETAIL	TOTAL RETAIL
				S	M	L		S	M	L		S	M	L						
				12 14 16 18 20 22 24				12 14 16 18 20 22 24				12 14 16 18 20 22 24								
				3 5 7 9 11 13 15			M	3 5 7 9 11 13 15			SP	3 5 7 9 11 13 15			L					
				6 8 10 12 14 16 18				6 8 10 12 14 16 18				6 8 10 12 14 16 18								
ROUTING EXCEPTION ON THIS ORDER		NO ORDER VALID UNLESS IN WRITING ON OUR FORM & COUNTERSIGNED		**TOTALS**																
VIA		BUYER APPROVED																		

SHIPPING INSTRUCTIONS

Show order no. and dept. no. on all packages. Combine all pkgs. into one shipment. Unless otherwise stated on this order send all shipments from the Greater New York Area, except furs and jewelry to National New York Packing and Shipping Co., 327 W. 36th St., NYC, N.Y. From points other than the greater New York Area and all jewelry ship via: 0-50 lbs. uncut 200.00 value insured Parcel Post. Over 50 lbs. ship Roadway Express where available or other motor truck.

Furs - U.P.S.

BILLING INSTRUCTIONS

Mail all invoices to Rogers & Smith, Lincoln, Nebraska. 44503, Accounts Payable Dept. Indicate order no. and dept. no. on each invoice. Under EOM Terms, all goods received on or after the 20th of the month are dated as of the 1st of the following month. Invoices must be rendered by size, color, and style. This order is subject to price, terms, delivery and conditions as stated.

In accepting this order, vendor agrees that he will furnish a guarantee rendered in good faith that the textile fiber products specified therein are labeled in accordance with the Federal Textile Fiber Products Identification Act.

This order is subject to the instructions and conditions stated this and on the reverse side which are made a part thereof.

Figure 14–1. Purchase Order.

MANUFACTURER PRACTICES TO INCREASE DEMAND FOR THEIR MERCHANDISE

Manufacturers often offer services or inducements to accelerate the demand for their merchandise, which can also benefit the department and store. Of course the buyer takes advantage of only those services that are acceptable to management, such as:

- A manufacturer fashion show; a trunk showing of the new season's line complete with fashion commentator
- Blowups of fashion magazine ads for interior displays
- P.M.'s (push money) to sales personnel
- Extra dating, already described
- Hangtags to tie in with national advertising

THE ORDER

Figure 14–1 is a contract that binds two parties to an arrangement which both should honor. It should include and be specific about every detail. The following should be observed at all times:

1. The delivery date should have starting and ending dates. "As ready," "as had," "as agreed," can lead to later controversy.
2. Quantity, style number, quantity for each color, prices for each style, should be mandatory. Omissions can lead to substitutions and unbalanced stocks.
3. Carrier should be stated. Transportation costs vary and manufacturers in violation of shipping orders are charged for the mistakes.
4. Insurance, if any, must be indicated. This is a store expense which should be held to a minimum, in accordance with the store's procedures (every buyer should be instructed about the store's procedures).
5. Special terms are part of contractual arrangements and should be spelled out.

The original copy is given to the resource, the duplicate is made available for the receiving department and the third copy is placed in the buyer's file for the department's receipt of goods (including unit control records). These are minimal requirements; stores with more complicated systems need additional copies.

After sending the resource a copy, the buyer details information on the store's copies for receiving and unit control purposes,* such as:

---

*Adding this information is known as "retailing" the invoice.

1. vendor's number;
2. retail price of each style and total value of order;
3. classification code;
4. other details, for control purposes, are secured from the order.

Note that the illustrated order form provides for payment on the first of the month for any merchandise received later than the 20th. (This is an exception to generally accepted practice, which is the 25th of the month.)

RELATIONSHIP OF THE MANUFACTURER & BUYER

It may be a harsh way of referring to the buyer's power "of the pen" in a highly competitive market, but there is an adage that says power corrupts. The unvarnished truth is that a buyer is a special person in this world. A buyer is often catered to and flattered by the manufacturer. This unusual concentration can turn the head and give out of context self-esteem and importance to the vulnerable.

The other side of the coin is that the competition and opportunism of the business can influence the manufacturer to practice out-of-character acts which should not be admired in any circles.

The reality is—the roster of manufacturers belongs to the store, not the buyer. The buyer acts as an agent for the store and should behave in a manner that does credit to both parties—the buyer and the store. The resource in the final analysis is as good as its reputation and performance. After all, one party feeds and lives on the efforts of the other, with all efforts directed to one group—the customers.

However, despite rules, common sense, and good judgments, there are dirty tricks departments for each. The following lists deal with some of the "tricks" the manufacturers and buyers can play on each other.

The Manufacturer
- Failure to deliver goods within time specified.
- Merchandise delivered is not as ordered; (substitution of colors, or sizes, sometimes styles).
- Delivery of damaged or defective goods.
- Delivery of off-price goods to competitors, despite arrangements to the contrary.
- Earlier delivery to competition against later placed orders.
- Changing of garment sizes to accommodate orders.
- Supplying incorrect delivery information to delay cancellation.
- Deliberately shipping against orders requiring confirmation.
- Showing samples of higher priced manufacturers, then shipping merchandise of lesser quality.

- Shipping piecemeal in violation of order terms.

The Buyer

- Returning merchandise to lower inventory.
- Cancelling orders before due date.
- Returning goods damaged in stock.
- Demanding return of slow-moving styles, particularly from those manufacturers who are attempting to gain store importance.
- Threatening to eliminate manufacturers who do not offer mark-down money.
- Eliminating resources by new buyers without considering past records. (Certain resources cannot be dropped by buyers.)
- Giving verbal orders and then claiming not placing them when goods are delivered.
- Making promises with no intention to live up to the agreement.
- Breaking prices to take temporary advantage of competition (despite promise to maintain price levels).
- Returning goods without the manufacturer's permission.

Listing these merchandising "sins" is perhaps out of tune with sound educational principles, which states, "never teach by negation." License is taken because the discussion is about professional ethics.

We can now discuss other acts with ethical overtones. Buying and selling is a social relationship. There are rules that should be followed despite the advantage of position. Sales personnel make their living by using their time to their best advantage. If appointments are made they should be kept, if not, the salesperson should be notified. Salespeople should also be advised under what conditions appointments can be affected. Sample room days should be honored, and it is unfair for someone to make a trip if the buyer or representative does not appear.

Gifts, money and other gratuities are offered in profusion as a pressure for buyer favor. It is doubtful that there is a buyer who has not had an offering of some kind, ranging from free garments to substantial sums, depending on potential buying power. A buyer should know that any monetary rebates are not his property but that of the store's; they are cost reductions. If a buyer does accept money he is in jeopardy of losing his job; no store will condone disloyalty.

One's reputation is a priceless possession and a bad reputation is one that follows the perpetrator, often making him unable to secure another job.

Commercial bribery has many disadvantages which includes the obligation to remain with the briber under all possible conditions. Many market stories can be told about the guilty, how they tried to "bury" money, how they could not sleep, and how it became a distraction too heavy to bear. Honesty pays off in more ways than one, as a policy, it leads to: personal and market esteem and professional growth and objectivity.

Many firms have guidelines for gift giving. A Christmas gift in appreciation of the courtesies extended during the year is satisfactory, but not requested. Some firms do not permit gifts of any kind.

It should be noted by the new buyer, that an offering can be couched in very clever terms, such as, "How would you like to be a consultant for my piece goods purchases at the rate of $ . . . ?"

The buyer must recognize that the position entails responsibility and the ability to stay within the job duties honestly. Relationships should be made on the basis of good business, courtesy, and empathy.

SUMMARY

- When, how much, and from whom merchandise purchased is a matter of relationships: the seasons observed by a store, the rate of sale, the market conditions, the store's distance from markets, the store's goals.
- The store's policies and a buyer's experience are closely related to how buying practices and techniques are followed.
- Merchandise orders vary with purpose, ranging from the need for immediate stock replacement to future need which necessitates extended delivery lead time.
- A visit to a market is a time when a buyer evidences the art of merchandising—to select the "right" manufacturers—"right" style, colors, and fabrics—in "right" quantities and price lines—in the "right" time.
- Obtaining the best purchase terms is expressed in increased profit.
- In order to obtain merchandise, manufacturers are given contracts —orders—that spell out all the terms of performance.
- When a manufacturer violates the terms of a contract there is the contingency of the return of goods or the loss of store patronage.
- A buyer as an agent of a retail organization should perform within the scope of assigned duties and in accordance with the store policy.

chapter 15

APPLICATION OF PLANNING & BUYING

INTRODUCTION

Merchandising requires the mastery of techniques, the understanding and ability to apply fashion principles, and having the know-how to respond to market realities. Classroom training cannot accurately simulate the conditions of: interpersonal relationships, wide merchandise choices, tensions associated with meeting planned figures and deadlines, and other situations that demand decision-making under pressure. Among the advantages of merchandising classroom training, however, is the opportunity to comprehend and apply the techniques of planning. With practice, a student can become proficient in constructing the dollar plan and the format of a balanced stock—fundamental requirements of fashion merchandising.

This chapter is designed with the following objectives:

- To reinforce planning techniques discussed in the preceding chapters
- To expand the material of merchandising by classification
- To exemplify how merchandising budgets are allocated to construct and maintain a balanced stock

This chapter includes a case study for which you can follow the planning steps, verify the figures, and also "solve" the case with your own plan figures, compute an open-to-buy, and allocate it to classifications and sub-classifications according to your judgment.

THE CASE

You are the buyer for teenage sportswear of a department store (Department 285). Early in January, your divisional merchandise manager said, "You will be visiting the New York market from February 10 to 14 to buy spring fill-ins and summer goods. I have to review and approve your six-month plan for February through July. Here is a six-month plan of last year's figures. Please bring your completed plan to next week's regularly scheduled meeting."

"According to management, national and local economic conditions are favorable and a 10 percent storewide increase is planned for the next six months. Since your figures have been running ahead of plans, if market conditions are right, you can plan up to a 12-percent increase."

During the preceding month, all sources of information such as the resident buying office's fashion director and representative, trade publications, fashion magazines, and road representatives reported optimistic market conditions.

Figure 15–1 is the six-month plan you received with last year's results and space for your estimations.

Figure 15–1. Six-Month Plan for Teenage Sportswear, Department #285.

Department Name _Teenage Sports wear_   Department No. _285_

SIX MONTH MERCHANDISING PLAN		PLAN (This Year)	ACTUAL (Last Year)
	Workroom cost		
	Cash discount %		2.3
	Season stock turnover		1.9
	Shortage %		9.0
	Average Stock		156,000
	Markdown %		11.0

SPRING 19-		FEB.	MAR.	APR.	MAY	JUNE	JULY	SEASON TOTAL
FALL 19-		AUG.	SEP.	OCT.	NOV.	DEC.	JAN.	
SALES $	Last Year	15000	45000	75000	60000	60000	45000	300 000
	Plan							
	Percent of Increase							
	Revised							
	Actual							
RETAIL STOCK (BOM) $	Last Year	39000	135000	240 000	216000	180 000	126 000	average 156,000
	Plan							
	Revised							
	Actual							
MARKDOWNS $	Last Year	3960	1980	2640	4620	8250	11550	33,000
	Plan (dollars)							
	Plan (percent)							
	Revised							
	Actual							
RETAIL PURCHASES	Last Year	114960	151980	53640	28620	14250	85550	
	Plan							
	Revised							
	Actual							
PERCENT OF INITIAL MARKON	Last Year							
	Plan							
	Revised							
	Actual							
ENDING STOCK July 31 Jan. 31	Last Year						155000	
	Plan							
	Revised							
	Actual							

Comments

Merchandise Manager_____   Buyer_____

Controller_____

SIX-MONTH PLAN

You studied the figures and then calculated the figures for your plan. The following is a synopsis of your thinking and how you arrived at your estimations and completed the plan.

Sales

On the basis of experience (last year's figures) and anticipation (economic conditions and favorable market conditions), you judged 10 percent as an obtainable and conservative increase. You took into consideration the probable future need to revise estimated sales upward during the period of operation. But you did not want to chance the possibility of being overly optimistic, which could cause dislocations of excessive inventory and high markdowns.

Sales for the six months were set at $330,000 ($300,000 × 10% = $30,000 + $300,000). $30,000 could have been distributed as an increase to last year's figures in any proportion warranted by your judgment. You decided to increase each month's sales by $5,000.

Retail Stock (B.O.M.)

Last year's six-month turnover was 1.9. You planned a 2 time turn for the same period, calculated as follows:

$$\frac{\text{Sales} \quad \$330,000}{\text{Average Inventory}} = \text{Rate of Turnover/2}$$

The average inventory, therefore, is $165,000. Since an average inventory of six months is the product of 6 B.O.M.'s plus the E.O.M. inventory of the last month of the period, you multiplied $165,000 by 7 and arrived at a figure of $1,155,000, total of all B.O.M.'s of the period plus the B.O.M. of the seventh month.

You then estimated the ending July inventory as $150,000. By deducting $150,000 from $1,155,000, you established a total of 6 planned B.O.M.'s, $1,005.

Since a stock turn of 2 for a six-month period equates as an average stock sales ratio of 3 (6 divided by 2 = 3), you decided to use it as the average figure for each month's stock/sales ratio, except for May and June. You reasoned by increasing May's ratio you would increase April's planned purchases to help to insure a timely and well-balanced inventory of summer goods for May and June, the peak selling months of warm weather merchandise. You planned on bringing in some fall goods in July. Hence, May's stock/sales ratio was set at the highest figure and June at the lowest.

You then calculated a B.O.M. stock for each month (stock/sales

$$\text{ratio} = \frac{\text{Retail stock as of a specified date}}{\text{Sales for a given period}}).$$

Stock/Sales

Month	Sales Ratio*		B.O.M. Stock
February	$20,000	× 3	$60,000
March	$50,000	× 3	150,000
April	$80,000	× 3	240,000
May	$65,000	× 3.5	228,000
June	$65,000	× 2.72	177,000
July	$50,000	× 3	150,000
	Total of B.O.M.s		$1,005,000.

Markdowns

Markdowns were planned on the basis of past experience and retail averages. Total markdowns were estimated as 10 percent of total sales, $330,000 × 10% = $33,000. $33,000 was distributed over the months in the pattern of how they were taken in the past.

Retail Purchases

You estimated retail purchases for each month as exemplified by your planning for the month of February:

Planned sales	$ 20,000
+ Planned stock E.O.M.	150,000
+ Planned markdowns	4,000
Total Provision Requirement	$174,000
Less planned stock B.O.M.	60,000
Planned purchases	$114,000**

The Completed Plan

When you met your divisional merchandise manager, you submitted the plan in **Figure 15–2.**

Your D.M.M. approved your plan with these words, "The plan looks good, please follow through with a classification plan which we will review at next week's scheduled meeting."

---

*With known sales and stock/sales ratio, the B.O.M. was calculated by multiplication.
**$114,000 cannot be adjusted until February when there will be an actual B.O.M. and a summary of unfilled orders.

Figure 15–2. Six-Month Plan Submitted for Teenage Sportswear, Department #285.

Department Name: Teenage Sportswear   Department No. 285

SIX MONTH MERCHANDISING PLAN

	PLAN (This Year)	ACTUAL (Last Year)
Workroom cost		
Cash discount %	2.8	2.3
Season stock turnover	2.0	1.9
Shortage %	9.0	9.0
Average Stock	165,000	156,000
Markdown %	10.0	11.0

SPRING 19- / FALL 19-		FEB. / AUG.	MAR. / SEP.	APR. / OCT.	MAY / NOV.	JUNE / DEC.	JULY / JAN.	SEASON TOTAL
SALES $	Last Year	15000	45000	75000	60000	60000	45000	300,000
	Plan	20000	50000	80000	65000	65000	50000	330,000
	Percent of Increase	33	11	6	8	8	11	10
	Revised							
	Actual							
RETAIL STOCK (BOM) $	Last Year	39000	35000	240000	226000	180000	126000	average 156000
	Plan	60000	150000	240000	228000	177000	150000	average 165000
	Revised							
	Actual							
MARKDOWNS $	Last Year	3960	1980	2640	4620	8250	11550	33000
	Plan (dollars)	4000	2000	25000	45000	8000	12000	33000
	Plan (percent)							
	Revised							
	Actual							
RETAIL PURCHASES	Last Year	114960	151980	53640	28620	14250	85550	
	Plan	114000	142000	70500	18500	46000	62000	
	Revised							
	Actual							
PERCENT OF INITIAL MARKON	Last Year							
	Plan							
	Revised							
	Actual							
ENDING STOCK July 31 Jan. 31	Last Year						155000	
	Plan						150000	
	Revised							
	Actual							

Comments

Merchandise Manager_____   Buyer_____

Controller_____

MERCHANDISE CLASSIFICATION PLANNING

Having planned a dollar inventory figure for each month, you were in a position to plan a "paper" stock in terms of units of consumer demand: coverage of classifications and sub-classifications, price lines, colors, sizes, and fabrics. Your "model" stock was plotted to be peaked April 15, the beginning date of summer goods selling.

You knew that when you visited the market, you would buy:

1. within budgeted dollar figures;
2. proportioned amounts of merchandise within classifications and sub-classifications;
3. at wholesale prices that would cover specific price levels;
4. in colors, sizes, and fabrics for a well-rounded stock.

In the final analysis, your plan would effect a balanced inventory—consistent with anticipated consumer demand.

Prepared with past records and current information on trends you start to plan from the broadest aspect, the relative importance of each classification to the total planned inventory.

You rate classification importance as:

Shirts	15%
Sweaters	10%
Blouses	10%
Pants	15%
Skirts	15%
Jackets	10%
T-shirts	15%
Jeans	10%

You are then in a position to plan in more specific or narrowed terms of anticipated demand. For example, $18,000 of the planned stock was allotted to skirts, a figure that had to be distributed among the classification's components, sub-classifications. The following is the way your skirt budget was broken down:

Skirts

Sub-classification	Percentage to stock (classification)	Open-to-buy in dollars
Box pleated	20	$ 3,600
Straight-line	50	9,000
A-Line	30	5,400
		$18,000

The skirt classification (and all other classifications) was then structured to assure adequate coverage of prices, colors, sizes, and fabrics. You planned skirts as follows:

Price Range	Percentage to Stock
$25	20
20	30
15	30
10	20
	100%

Colors	Percentage to Stock
Blue	30
Red	15
Beige	20
White	5
Green	10
Lilac	20
	100%

Sizes	Percentage to Stock
7	10
9	25
11	30
13	25
15	10
	100%

Fabrics	Percentage to Stock
Denim	40
Cotton	20
Cotton/Polyester	20
Knitted	20
	100%

After having planned a balanced "paper" stock consisting of all the merchandise classifications and narrowed demand elements, you are prepared to submit it to your merchandise manager for approval.*

*During the season the open-to-buy is allocated to fill in stock gaps of the model inventory.

TRENDS & INVENTORY STATUS REPORTS

Fashion merchandisers for large retail organizations require up-to-date data on fashion trends in order to be able to select practical alternatives to make an inventory most responsive to consumer demand. Computer summarized information is indispensable for merchandising a multi-unit retail operation. The types of reports and the frequency with which they are available is a management decision, although some organizations program a system to include buyer requested information. Without at least a weekly summary of the results of merchandising events and a breakdown of all merchandising segments (merchandise by classification), merchandisers would "fly blind"—their decisions would be based on impressions or intuitions. Records could be maintained by hand, but this method is too time-consuming and costly.

To support your efforts to plan and maintain a balanced stock, you receive four reports:

1. *Fashion Flash Report*—distributed semi-weekly; summarizing selling results of the day previous to the report date that meets your criteria (the buyer)—sales in all stores or a given quantity sold in one store **(Figure 15–3)**.
2. *Style/Status Report*—distributed weekly; the most comprehensive summary of fashion activity **(Figure 15–4)**.
3. *Color/Size Report*—distributed semi-weekly **(Figure 15–5)**.
4. *Three-Month Sales Survey*—distributed four times a year **(Figure 15–6)**.

THE RELATIONSHIP OF THE BUYER & DIVISIONAL MERCHANDISE MANAGER

Divisional merchandise managers meet buyers separately each week at a meeting usually referred to as the weekly merchandise review, at which time discussions cover the actual events as compared to plans, the revisions of plans, planned purchases, advertising, and other subjects related to the department's operation.

In order to obtain approval from the D.M.M. to purchase merchandise, a buyer must submit objective evidence for specific merchandise needs. The two methods of evidence are:

1. a list of intended commitments that total a sum within an approved dollar plan;
2. a status report, a form of unit control.

Therefore, a buyer attends meetings with details of the status of every classification and sub-classification: the on-hand, on-order, past

CLASS	VENDOR	STYLE	RETAIL	TOTAL	L	M	N	O	P	Q	R	S	T	U
A3	575	0682	32.00	6	3							1		
B1	617	9512	50.00	11	7	1	2		1		1	1		
B1	617	9619	52.00	3	2	1								
B2	017	3209	64.00	4	1		1			1		1		
B2	027	2096	40.00	4			1		2					1
B2	522	3672	38.00	5	5									
C1	017	2773	54.00	3	2									
C1	017	3339	66.00	8	2		1	3					2	1
C1	017	3354	66.00	4	2									-1
C1	027	2174	39.99	4	2	1						1		1
C1	410	1472	80.00	6	4	1		1			1			
C1	522	3725	33.00	3	3									
C1	802	2603	38.00	1	-1		3			-1				
C1	802	2407	38.00	2			2							
C1	802	3116	38.00	6	1	-1	3	1					1	1
C1	802	7146	17.00	2			2							
C1	902	0855	49.00	7	7		-1		1					
C1	902	0856	49.00	13	5	1	3	2					2	
C1	902	0884	49.00	4	4		2	1	1					
C8	003	0599	5.99	4	4									
C8	061	4462	29.99	8	5		1		1				1	1
C8	061	4463	.00	14	6		1		2		3		1	2
C8	061	4745	24.99	7	2		2			1				
C8	061	4948	29.99	7	3	1		1			1		1	
C8	061	4949	29.99	2	2									
C8	617	4109	29.99	5	2		2		1					
I9	617	9500	29.99	6	4							1		
I9	617	9503	29.99	3	3									

Figure 15-3. Fashion Flash Report.

DEPT/DISS/ S/C

CLASS CODES	VEND	STYLE	CURR. RETAIL	ALL STORES WTD SALES	ALL STORES ON HAND	L WTD SLS	L ON HAND	M WTD SLS	M ON HAND	N WTD SLS	N ON HAND	O WTD SLS	O ON HAND	P WTD SLS	P ON HAND	Q WTD SLS	Q ON HAND	R WTD SLS	R ON HAND	S WTD SLS	S ON HAND	T WTD SLS	T ON HAND	U WTD SLS	U ON HAND
A 1 00	215	4503	10.00	4	31	1	-1	3	21				3											1	8
	253	5191	12.00			1		-2	1																
	262	621	11.00	6	220	1	41	1	39		27		30		1		13		1	2	5	2	37		26
	273	8823	17.00	1	169	1	33	1	10		12		45		12				12		12		10		23
	378	600	5.99	26	59	3	24	-1	1	6		10	11												9
		601		9	62	4	15			4	14	17	10												17
		1000		3	43		-3				20	7	7												37
		2000		45	233	10	4	6	1	2	30	17	84			4									19
	390	4000	9.00	7	214	1	2	3	48			2	42	2	23		29	1					28		42
		934	12.00	3	22		-3		6				12		2	4								1
	399	2009	13.00	17	175		2		14		20		32	3	6	2		2	9						42
		2061	14.00	2	40		7	2	7				8		8		19		9	1		3	17		10
		2040	15.00	3	93		20	1	37		5		34		22	2	19	-1	1	1	11				14
		2044		3	66		25	1	-7		22	3	25		13	2			31				6		10
		2049		7	136		57	1	17	4	-5		8		-5		17	1	9			2	35	1	
		2057		10	57	3	-13		6	1					7		18	3				2			12
		2060	17.00	5	33	13	46		14		11		9		16		4		-4			2	18	4	28
		2063	13.00	13	180	1	20	3	32		10		22		22		9	5	29		12	2	14		22
		3305		1	137	1	22		11								12		11				11	1	9
		3318		1	127	1	9				10	1	14				18		10				10		7
	431	6227	16.00	-1	42	1	15		-2		1						2		-4						
		7030			23		6		6	-1	1	1	49		25		6		29			3	7	2	6
		7051		37	413	4	100	5	46		-11		14				43		11	1		1	57	1	70
		2722	11.00	2	40					1	1								10				18		7
	524	100	8.00	16	239	1	22		36	1	35	3	-3	1	36	1	35	2	34	1	8	3	31	5	90
		101		1	56	4	168	12	30	2	34	-7		30					48		36	1	5	1	35
		102	8.99	117	605	22	31			2	46	6	70						48			18	76	19	72
		103		4	116					2	46		70						48				5		72
	525	104	8.00	16	239		22		35	1	47	2	72	2	28	1	28	1	48			1	31	4	72
		305	7.99	1	56	6	2		30	5	14	2	17		78		8	1	31		2		5		13
		850	5.59	117	605		6		40	6	60		11	9			20	11	-1		38	18	76	19	80
	560	16		1	116		5	12											33						53
	1712		14.00	6	116		20		8	5	24	2	10	3	2				16				5		53
	3011		11.00	1	16		11	-4		6			1									5		15
	3013		9.00	24	380		6			1	45	1	53		36		33	5	45		9		34	5	51
	3081		16.00	2	25		1			1	12		4		-1									1	10
	570	4505	12.00	5	154		2		19	1	24	1	13	1	14		33			1		1	16	1	66
		178	10.00	4	16		6		14	2	17	5			16		4		1				3		4
		186	11.00	3	48		5		7	2	5	3			8		12		9						1
	902	254	12.00	10	54	3		2		1	43	5	3						10				3	2	5
		292	10.00	26	148	2	20	4	-6	5	6		17	2	18	1	4	1	12	2	2	2	14		18
		341	11.00	13	64	1	11	1	-4	6			9		12	2	12	1				1	18	2	28
		1308	13.00	3	28		6			3	8		8		12			1							2
		8206	11.00	5	34		1		3	3	1	2	2	2	8				7			1	10		3
		8278		24	150	5	9	-1	16	8	11	2	19	1	14		-1		29	1	47	2	14	2	19
SUBCLASS	1	1		491	6231	72	806	46	647	62	625	92	855	29	538	28	344	21	589	21	145	37	505	62	1137
A 4 00	110	3000	9.00	4	310	2	-5	1	55	1	59													-1
	170	295	13.00	1	28		9				-2	3			11				-1				-2		49
	186	2120	14.00	7	50				1	3	10	3						-5				-1	
		2154	10.00	15	18				5	7	5						47			8	
	265	2337	8.00	12	227	1	95	2	34	5	45	1	95	2	48	4	36	1	47	1	34	1	-8	2	94
		6462	11.00	26	538	1	14		4	2	58	9	91	1	58	5	7	1	3	3	33	8		7
		6489		22	60	1	4		7	5	7	4	10		6	1	7		10			2		9
	243	175	15.00	1	39				12	1	7	1												

Figure 15-4. Style/Status Report.

DATA ENDING WITH E.O.M.   JULY 1982

A1 ****** SHIRTS AND BLOUSES   (BOP STOCK / FEBRUARY: ******)

CL/PR	BOP PLANS	BOP ACTUAL	FEB Month's Sales Act	FEB OTB / Wk1 Sales	FEB Wk2 Sales	FEB Actual Purch / Wk3 Sales	FEB Wk4 Sales	FEB Plan EOM / Wk5 Sales	MAR Month's Sales Act	MAR OTB / Wk1 Sales	MAR Wk2 Sales	MAR Actual Purch / Wk3 Sales	MAR Wk4 Sales	MAR Plan EOM / Wk5 Sales	APR Month's Sales Act	APR OTB / Wk1 Sales	APR Wk2 Sales	APR Actual Purch / Wk3 Sales	APR Wk4 Sales	APR Plan EOM / Wk5 Sales	3 MO THIS PAGE SALES	6 MO TOTAL PLANS
A1 1.99x																						1
A1 2.99x																						11
A1 3.99x															445	0	0	0	445	0	445	610
A1 4.99x																						21
A1 5.99x															16	0	12	2	2	0	16	139
A1 6.99x																						1
A1 7.99x			10	6	1	1	2	0	22	5	8	6	2	1	109	1	54	32	22	0	141	747
A1 8.99x			2	2	0	0	0	0	1	1	0	0	0	0								2
A1 9.99x			9	1	2	0	2	0	13	15	-2	-1	1	0	32	0	24	7	1	0	35	175
A1 10.99x			8	5	0	0	3	0	7	0	0	1	0	6	4	1	0	1	2	0	22	24
A1 12.99x															1	0	1	0	0	0	18	40
A1 19.99x															1	0	0	1	0	0	1	2
A1 .00			54	31	15	2	6	0	6	2	1	3	0	0	1	1	0	0	0	0	61	41
A1 3.99			1	0	0	0	1	0							1	0	0	0	1	0	2	7
A1 5.99			15	1	0	0	14	0	1384	460	380	398	134	12	73	31	7	6	29	0	1472	1473
A1 6.99																						1
A1 7.99			12	0	0	0	12	0	1274	417	380	349	122	6	36	24	11	1	0	0	1322	1331
A1 8.00																					1	4
A1 8.99			11	0	4	0	7	0	14	10	5	-2	0	1	1	0	0	0	1	0	26	29
A1 9.00			2	0	0	2	0	0	30	2	4	14	6	4	12	0	1	1	-1	0	44	75
A1 9.99																						-1
A1 10.00			33	8	2	16	7	0	32	6	8	2	9	7	11	0	1	4	7	0	76	76
A1 10.50									1	0	0	0	0	1		6	5	0	0	0	1	1

Figure 15–5. Color/Size Report.

Y DEPT. 285 REG. REPORT THRU 12/06/82 18-1
DEPT/

CLASS	VEND	STYLE	CURR.	ALL STORES		L		M		N		O		P		Q		R		S		T		U	
	CLR	SZ	RETAIL	WTD SALES	SALES CURR	WTD SLS	SLS CURR	WTD SLS	SLS CURR	WTD SLS	SLS CURR	WTD SLS	SLS CURR	WTD SLS	SLS CURR	WTD SLS	SLS CURR	WTD SLS	SLS CURR	WTD SLS	SLS CURR	WTD SLS	SLS CURR	WTD SLS	SLS CURR
G1 00	4	47	86.00																						
	41	80		1	1	1	1																		
G1 00	99	9	100.00																						
	01	120		1	0									1											
		140		2	2	1	1	1	1																
	20	140		1	1	1	1																		
	24	120		3	3	1	1					1	1			1	1								
		140		1	1															1	1				
		180		2	2	1	1							1	1										
	69	100		1	0									1											
		120		1	0											1									
		140		1	0																				
			TOTAL	13	9	5	4	1	1			1	1	3	1	2	1			1	1				
G1 00	99	97	86.00																						
	24	60		-1	0					-1															
		80		2	0	1								1											
		100		1	1									1	1										
		160		1	1																			1	1
			TOTAL	5	2	1				-1				2	1									1	1
G1 00	99	98	59.99																					1	1
	23	120		1	1																			1	1
		140		1	1																			2	2
			TOTAL	2	2																				
G1 00	99	102	89.99																						
	23	80		1	1																			1	1
	24	80		2	1																			2	1
		100		2	1									1	1									1	
		160		2	2	2	2	-1	-1															1	1
			TOTAL	7	5	2	2	-1	-1					1	1									5	3
H4 00	124	1206	44.99P																						
	00	160		-1	-1				-1	-1	-1														
	01	140		1	1																			1	1
	10	80		3	2					1		2	2												
		100		1	1							1	1												
		120		0	0																	-1		1	
		140		2	2							1	1											1	1
		160		3	3																	3	3		
		180		6	5			1	1			5	4												
	24	80		1	1	-1						1	1											1	
		100		0	1							1	1							-1					
		120		4	1	2						1	1											1	
		140		5	2			1	1			1	1							1		1		1	
		160		0	0	-1																		1	
		160		3	2							2	2											1	
	28	80		1	1																	1	1		
		100		1	1	1	1																		
		140		0	0							1	1											-1	-1
		160		1	1							1	1												
	41	80		1	0							1													
		100		1	0			1	1													1		-1	-1
		120		4	0			1						1										2	

Figure 15–6. Three-Month Sales Survey.

sales, current sales, projected sales and inventory, in units and dollars. With this information a buyer can prove specific inventory needs, and the D.M.M. can understand the reasons for the plan.

The reports in **Figures 15–7** and **15–8** are presented so that you can "solve" the case. It is necessary to develop a report for each sub-classification to complete the Classification Summary Report **(Figure 15–7)**. If you choose to prepare a comprehensive plan, you must construct a "paper stock" of colors, sizes, and fabrics.

Figure 15–7. Classification Summary Report for Teenage Sportswear, Department #285, as of February 1.

Classification Summary Report for Teenage Sportswear, Department #285 as of February 1

Classification	(Units) On-Hand	(Units) On-Order	(Units) Total Commit-ment	(Units) Open-To-Buy	$ Open-To-Buy	(Units) Selling Last Week	(Units) Selling This Month	(Units) Estimated Selling 3 months
Shirts								
Sweaters								
Blouses								
Pants								
Skirts								
T-Shirts								
Blue Jeans								

Figure 15–8. Sub-classification Report—Pleated Skirts for Teenage Sportswear, Department #285, as of February 1.

Sub-classification Report—Pleated Skirts for Teenage Sportswear Department #285 as of February 1

Price	Units On-Hand	Units On-Hand	Total Commit-ment	(Units) Open-To-Buy	$ Open-To-Buy	(Units) Selling Last Week	(Units) Selling This Month	(Units) Estimated Selling 3 months
$25								
$20								
$15								
$10								

SUMMARY

Your planning started with a six-month merchandise plan wholly concerned with dollar budgeting (based on planned standards of performance). With a completed and approved dollar plan, you had a base figure to distribute your estimated budget to classifications according to their anticipated importance. Your planning then took into consideration what a balanced stock requires for coverage of:

1. each sub-classification's dollar need;
2. each classification's need of prices, colors, sizes, and fabrics.

The finished plan was a "paper" stock broken down into units and dollars for each classification and sub-classification.

Your effort to plan for a new season and to maintain a balanced stock was aided in no small degree by management—by furnishing "tools" that recorded and summarized figures resulting from merchandising events. By carefully studying computer printouts you were kept abreast of all current events and how they compared with past records. These figures were used to estimate future developments within the range of probability.

A balanced stock is predicated on well-conceived dollar and unit plans that take into consideration what customers are likely to purchase. Merchandising by classification focuses on units of customer demand and affords merchandisers the opportunity to minimize investment and maximize profit.

part **4**

THE FASHION BUYER'S ROLE IN ADVERTISING & SALES PROMOTION

In Part One, we discussed the definition of fashion, merchandising aspects and the background leading to current merchandising policies. In Parts Two and Three, we examined the planning and

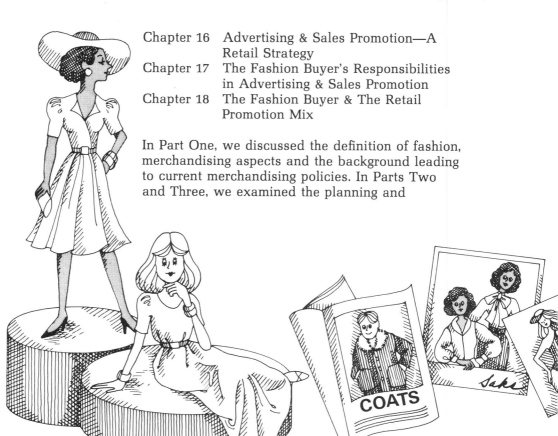

purchasing of merchandise. Now in Part Four, we will take a look at the retail buyer's role in the strategy and tactics of advertising and sales promotion. It should be noted at the outset that our use of the term "sales promotion" (or just plain "promotion"), includes all of the fashion promotional activities—*advertising, display, publicity, special events,* and *fashion shows.* However, since advertising is often the major activity we may refer to the communications mix as "advertising and sales promotion."

The fashion buyer is concerned with using advertising and sales promotion to sell what has been bought. Personal selling, at the point-of-sale, cannot reach out to inform and persuade customers. Advertising and sales promotion, or *nonpersonal selling* is needed to bring customers to the point-of-sale. The results of careful marketing research, planning, and purchasing should be *profitable* selling. This is why merchandise managers and buyers must get involved in the development of an effective promotional program for their store.

The fashion buyer has two general objectives for advertising and sales promotion:

● To produce profitable sales
● To generate customer loyalty and continued patronage

Stores require that their buyers participate in the planning and implementation of promotional events which can attain the product and institutional objectives of retail management. More

than ever, fashion merchandisers and buyers find it productive to use advertising and promotion to solve some of the problems retailers face today. The rapidly shifting consumer markets pose an ever-present challenge to the abilities of the fashion buyers to provide customers with *what* they want—and to be able to tell them *why* they want it and *where* to buy it. The customer who is developing more *selective* buying habits demands more information about merchandise. The alertness of the fashion buyer is therefore constantly challenged by the growing variety of market segments and identifiable target groups—as well as an increasingly aggressive brand of retail competition.

Promotional decisions are an integral part of the overall operations of a store. The strategy and tactics of advertising and promotion as a *team effort* between fashion buyers and the sales promotion departments is an approach which we endorse. This part of the book consists of three chapters which examine fashion sales promotion from the viewpoint of the fashion buyer's role in the store's continuing effort to communicate with customers.

The basic purpose of Part Four is an understanding of the role which a fashion buyer should play in advertising and sales promotion. The bottom line in assessing a buyer's performance is *profitable* sales volume—a result of good *planning*, creative *purchasing*, and effective *promotion.*

When you have finished Part Four, you should be able to:

- Explain how fashion sales promotion is used to accelerate sales and project a store's image.
- Outline the applications of fashion promotion media and how they are used to reach customers with messages which motivate them to buy.
- Explain the role of the buyer in fashion sales promotion in terms of:
    1. appropriate merchandise needed to support a promotional activity;
    2. the planning required for advertising and promotion, and the necessary parts of a well-organized sales promotion plan;
    3. the objectives of a merchandise promotion—product and/or institutional;
    4. the importance of purchasing from resources which can support a promotion;
    5. the budgetary requirements and possibilities;
    6. information and inspiration about merchandise which specialists in the sales promotion division can develop into effective advertising, display, publicity, and special events.
- Analyze fashion sales promotions from case studies, with a critique which states why you think they were effective (or not) in their attainment of retail management's product and institutional objectives.

chapter 16

ADVERTISING & SALES PROMOTION—A RETAIL STRATEGY

INTRODUCTION

If there was ever a business like show business it is the business of promoting fashion. The fashion merchandiser is the producer, director, author, lyricist, composer, set designer, costume designer, and prop man for a fashion show which gives continuous performances. The big difference in this form of show business is that the people in the audience are also the actors—and in this production, a *participating* audience is running the show.

The show business of fashion buying and merchandising is advertising and promotion, which is used here in its broadest sense, to describe all the ways in which a store can communicate with its customers.

Sales promotion in modern merchandising is not limited to newspaper advertising and window display. The promotion of merchandise and the institutional image often employs multi-media advertising; window and interior display; special features and events; fashion shows; publicity and public relations services. The objectives of fashion promotion are to use every medium of communication—including positive employee attitudes to help customers believe in the store's merchandise and in its knowledge of fashion trends. A measure of the success of a store's promotion activities is its ability to accelerate sales as well as its ability to generate a degree of belief and response to the institution.

Most retail stores—regardless of size or location—use one or a combination of promotion activities to inform its customers about products and to persuade them to buy.

The large store which is constantly using promotion to develop its reputation as well as to sell its merchandise must produce a *daily* fashion show which provides more information, more fun and excitement than the other shows in town: An effective way to do this on any scale, large or small, is for fashion buyers and merchandising executives to get into the act of communicating with customers.

Top management of today's retail giants are more actively participating in the making of promotional policy. While the small retailer obviously must confine such decision-making to a small group, the retail giants expect an overall term effort. The long range planning is assigned to an executive committee composed of divisional heads who rely on merchandise managers, fashion buyers, and advertising and promotion practitioners for information and advice.

Therefore, the buyer is part of a sales promotion team which includes the merchandise managers, the fashion office, store service people, and personnel in all of the departments of the sales promotion division **(Figure 18–1)**. It should be understood that the promotion program is planned and themed by merchandise management. Fashion buyers help to initiate and implement promotional planning. The following chapters discuss the buyer's role in the process which relies so heavily on the buyer's special knowledge of how to communicate with customers.

Effective communication implies that the store will get the response from customers which they expected. Thus, the term communication assumes more than just *sending* a message—it includes positive feedback from the store's consumer markets.

THE ACTIVITIES OF FASHION SALES PROMOTION

The fashion retailer initiates the activities of sales promotion: advertising, display, special events, fashion shows, and in an indirect way, publicity. The fashion retailer does not initiate, but is able to influence, word-of-mouth advertising and merchandise packaging. Each of these sales promotion activities has its own structure, approach, and techniques.

They are all *non-personal* methods of mass communication. Non-personal is used in this sense as contrasted to *personal selling,* which involves person-to-person, face-to-face communication. We will distinguish between personal and non-personal selling by the use of the term *promotion* for all forms of non-personal or mass communication.

The various promotion activities have similar communication objectives but differ in methods and media. The retailer uses this variety of methods and media to send messages about merchandise in the form of words and pictures, which can be circulated or broadcast to customer audiences. Products and ideas can also be presented to customers at the point-of-sale in physical form. Sending messages in words and pictures through public information media is done through *advertising* and *publicity.* Presenting merchandise visually (or physically) is done through *display, special events,* and *fashion shows* **(Figure 16–1).**

Figure 16–1. Sales promotion activities and media which are used to "pre-sell," and then to bring the customer to the point of sale in a department store.

Advertising

Advertising is designed to send messages to reach audiences away from the point-of-sale through media such as: newspapers, magazines, radio, television, billboards, or direct mail. The objectives of the message are not always to sell merchandise at a profit. The values of the retail institution, its services, and its personnel can also be conveyed to customers. An advertisement is paid for and "signed" or sponsored by the advertiser—this is the basic difference between advertising and publicity. Inasmuch as the advertiser is identified as the author, customers can either accept or reject the message, often basing this decision on what they already know about the advertiser.

Effective fashion advertising is designed to produce profitable sales. It must deliver store traffic. But its responsibility does not stop here. Fashion advertising must develop a store's personality image, inform customers of important trends, present new store services and special events, and reinforce the fashion authority of its buyers and merchandisers. Simply stated, fashion advertising must sell merchandise and build customer loyalty.

Word-Of-Mouth Advertising

"Word-of-mouth" is not really a promotion activity. The retailer at best has only an indirect control over the occurrence of word-of-mouth advertising. Here the customer serves as the advertising medium, and the messages are the dialogues which occur between customers about stores and their merchandise. A retailer has no direct influence on what a customer might say about his store, its services, and its merchandise. The alert retailer, however, is conscious of this important medium of information and promotion. The prospective customer may make decisions based upon what friends have to report about a store. Poor customer relations can result in gossip about a store which can enlarge and exaggerate the true picture of what the retailer has to offer. On the other hand, good customer relations and genuine value are also subject for discussions among consumers. It is unfortunate—but most vital for the retailer to remember—that "bad news travels faster than good news."

Display

Window and interior (or "department") display can be very effective communications from retailer to customer. A women's fashion store may rely totally on both window and interior display to sell merchandise as well as to emphasize its fashion leadership to its audience. The parade of involved window-shoppers on Fifth Avenue in New York City (even on Sundays), gives testament to the power of attractive, "wish-fulfillment" fashion displays. Retailers use display as a means of projecting current fashion trends and styles which represent what their target group of customers want. Displays can also be a panorama of "best-buys" with prices prominently displayed in windows and in-store. The store's advertising can be reinforced by a window and interior display program which is designed to identify and locate the broad range of products that the store is selling—and help salespeople in the process of personal selling.

Publicity

There are two basic characteristics which differentiate advertising from publicity—payment and sponsorship. The public information media—newspapers, magazines, television or radio may present information in the form of news or opinions about a store, employees, merchandise or special events without payment from the retailer. In this case the retailer has received *publicity*. The retailer, however, is not the author (or *sponsor*) of such messages which appear in the editorial matter (or programming)* part of media. The retailer cannot control the inclusion,

---

*The term *editorial matter* is used here for the non-advertising part of print media. The term *programming* is used for the non-commercial, non-sponsored part of broadcast media.

content or date of publication of such messages. The medium's editors decide whether the message would be of interest or entertainment for its audience.

Special Events

Special events are the innovative devices, features, services, sales inducements, exhibits, demonstrations, and attractions which retailers use to stimulate interest in merchandise and institutional fashion themes. These events supplement advertising, publicity and display and help a store meet its growing competition through interest-generating merchandise and institutional activities.

Fashion Shows

Of all the store's promotion activities, the fashion show may be the most dramatic and compelling. When it comes to presenting the excitement and glamour of fashion, it is hard to outdo a good "in-store" show, which presents merchandise on living and moving forms. Every element of theatre and showmanship can be incorporated in the fashion show. The fashion show, like the other promotion activities can "play to different audiences" for different sales objectives and long-range purposes. It is an activity often presented to audiences of influential customers—who can influence others.

Packaging

Merchandise packaging is usually done by the manufacturer, who designs the package (wrapper or hanger) to protect and to display the merchandise. Packaging can also contain a message which aids in promoting the sale of merchandise. The retail store most of the time has not been involved in the content of the message and information on the package. Consequently, the retailer who is concerned about the quality of his communication to customers should be aware that packaging information, which he did not write, nevertheless becomes part of his message. Some retailers insist on having a say in the content and design of merchandise packaging, especially when they are a large volume buyer of a manufacturer's output.

Public Relations

Public relations for the store affects the atmosphere in which the buyer will have to sell the products which he has selected for customers. Public relations is *not* considered publicity or promotion—but it affects the climate in which a store must also communicate its promotional messages about merchandise. It is like an "umbrella" under which all marketing and merchandising communications (which we call advertising and promotion) operate (see **Figure 16–2**). Every store has public relations whether it wants to or not. In dealing with its customers, it has public relations—good or bad—largely by its own making.

Good public relations does not always need a huge budget. A public-relations program can be started from such beginnings as the salespeople's courtesy to customers, cooperation with vendors, community interest, employee communications, and consistent integrity in all dealings with the public.

In summary, everyone—president, merchandise managers, buyers, salespeople, truck drivers, custodians, telephone operators, stock people, and husbands/wives of employees—every member of the retail team is involved in promotion and public relations. The main thing to remember about a store's public-relations program is that it is really all the little things—like a cheerful greeting, a prompt reply to a letter, or a good word for a customer.

Figure 16–2. The Public Relations Umbrella.

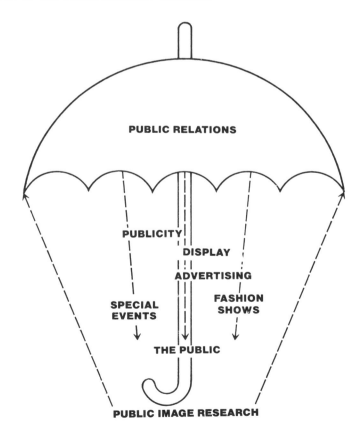

Advertising & Sales Promotion—A Retail Strategy   **295**

ORGANIZING THE PROMOTION EFFORT

Every retailer must carefully plan his total program of promotion so that it will result in the highest number of sales. He must decide how much advertising, publicity, display, and special events will be used. There is a wide variation in promotional activities among the different sizes and types of retail organizations as we will discuss next.

Promotion in Small Stores

The owner or manager, (and possibly an assistant manager), of a small store usually plans the store promotion programs and activities. The small store may do a limited amount of advertising in the local paper during the Christmas and Easter holidays and run end-of-season clearance sales. The store manager or one of his salespeople usually decorates the store windows, or he may employ a free-lance displayperson to change them. Owners of small stores generally depend on their buyers and sales personnel to execute many of the activities of promotion.

Promotion in Chain Stores

Most retailer chains have a sales promotion department with a sales promotion director. He plans promotional activities which will be used throughout the chain and is responsible for carrying them out. He is assisted by a group of merchandising, advertising, display, and sales-training specialists who participate in planning sales campaigns, take responsibility for window and interior displays, and sponsor sales-training programs for all the store units in the chain. These plans are supervised by regional supervisors and carried out by the local store manager. In some situations an advertising agency may handle the advertising.

Promotion in Department Stores

In large department stores responsibility for promotion is centered in the sales promotion director, who is in charge of promotional activities in the parent store and its branches. He confers with merchandise managers to decide how much of the budget will be used for each type of retail promotion. Advertising, publicity, display, and special events directors work under the sales promotion director's supervision.

Promotion in Shopping Centers & Malls

The stores and service establishments in many shopping centers and malls cooperate in promoting the shopping center as a whole. Large centers employ a promotion director who coordinates the overall publicity and advertising activities of the center. The director may also plan special shows and events to gain publicity for the center.

Large shopping centers compete with downtown retailers and retailers' organizations in conducting promotions and attracting customers. Most of the shopping malls throughout the country have an ever-increasing program of promotional customer services, special events, and fashion shows. Many of these provide amusement areas and well-equipped play areas for children, a variety of indoor and outdoor restaurants, an information center, a post office, a theatre, and an auditorium. They hold flower shows, dog shows, boat and automobile shows, fishermen's shows, international fairs, and fairs of individual foreign countries, music contests, recitals, concerts, photography contests, baseball clinics, circuses, exercise classes, dance instruction, a sewing school, civic meetings, style shows, a symphony hall, and on and on.

In large shopping centers the small stores profit because they are able to participate in all center-wide promotions, which are planned by experts. They would not be able to carry out such extended promotion programs themselves. They are also aided in their individual merchandising problems by such publications as a *Shopping Center Reporter,* a helpful guide for customers to the stores in shopping centers.

THE MAJOR PURPOSES OF FASHION PROMOTION

"Why do retailers need advertising and promotion?" Certainly efforts to project store image and to develop good community relations help build reputation and patronage for the store. In addition, all successful retailers know that merchandise does not sell itself. The story about the world beating a path to the door of the person who can build a better mousetrap just does not apply to modern fashion merchandising. With the great variety of complex products entering the market every day, retailers must constantly inform customers as to *what* products they can buy, *why* they should buy them, *where* they can buy them, and *when* are the best times to do so. Hence they must use retail promotion to educate customers about what merchandise will fill their needs and wants and how to use and take care of such merchandise. If a store is lax in performing this function, it is usually replaced by a store that performs the task better.

The story of the "China" promotion produced by Bloomingdales, New York, is a splendid example of a major promotional effort to reinforce their claim that their store is "like no other store in the world." A brief review of this unique six week special event follows at the end of this chapter. It is an excellent model of *a retail strategy.*

By this time, you should be aware of the basic nature and the broad scope of promotional activities. All retailers, regardless of size and type, carry on some degree of promotional effort not only with current and potential customers, but with vendors, competitors (yes, competitors), news media, local government, civic organizations, and employees. You may be able to think of some more individual ways in which a particular retailer makes promotional efforts. You should remember that *you* will be involved in some way in retail promotion regardless of the specific nature of your buying and merchandising responsibility. As a fashion buyer you will be very involved in public relations, advertising and promotion, and selling. You may, however, develop a career with a textile producer or apparel manufacturer which is concerned with *merchandising.* The advertising and promotion effort to sell the ultimate consumer is a partnership between the manufacturer and retailer which supplements buying and merchandising. Many in-store promotions are such joint ventures. **Figure 16–3** shows the *levels of promotion* (nonpersonal selling) between producers, manufacturers, retailers, and consumers.

- National—Promotional activities from *producers* or *manufacturers* to the *consumer*
- Trade—Promotions *between companies* in the fashion industry
- Retail—Promotions from *retailers* to *consumers*

In today's highly competitive retail markets, the merchandisers of fashion may rise or fall based on the effectiveness of their promotional programs. Merchandise managers and buyers manage their promotional effort to attain two general objectives: *profitable sales* and *continued patronage from customers.*

Figure 16–3. Retail promotion (selling) is the final phase of the fashion promotion mix.

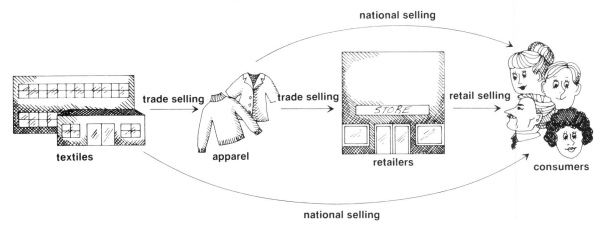

Retail advertising and promotion is different from the efforts of producers of textiles and the manufacturers of apparel. The retailer's objectives, sales appeals and approaches for example, differ greatly from those of the fashion apparel manufacturer. Large fashion manufacturers are concerned primarily with fashion marketing and pre-selling—brand-name recognition and preference. Their advertising may feature and describe specific styles—but their main concern is penetration of designer names and status labels.

On the other hand, the retailer is faced with an even more complex promotional problem. In most cases the products the retailer buys and sells have similar or perfect duplicates which are being promoted by his competitors. In addition, all of the retailer's advertising must assist in building store traffic and in developing customer loyalty. Any single advertisement must not only increase sales in the department running the ad, but help make sales throughout the store. Above all, the cumulative effect of the retailer's promotion must be to develop an image as *the store* for his customers.

PRODUCT & INSTITUTIONAL ADVERTISING OBJECTIVES

The promotional effort includes any activity that is planned to bring customers to the store and influence their decisions to buy at the point-of-sale. A *product promotion* is employed for the *immediate* objectives of providing useful merchandise information and persuasion which can stimulate interest and result in profitable sales. *Long range* objectives are attained by utilizing *institutional promotion* which attempts to build customer loyalty and encourage good public relations for a store. The store must send messages about fashion merchandise, special events, and services, which can compete successfully with the thousands of messages from other retailers. Its advertising and promotion must fight for the customer's attention—arouse interest—activate desire—and stimulate a response to investigate and eventually to buy.

Product and institutional objectives can easily be illustrated through an examination of one of the major activities of sales promotion —advertising. Advertising can be designed to sell either a product or an institution behind a product. It is divided into two broad classifications:

- Product advertising
- Institutional advertising

Product Advertising

Product advertising's objective is the immediate sale of merchandise. These ads will include *identification, description,* and *price* of products so that customers can make discerning judgments before they arrive at the point-of-sale. A product ad can presell merchandise or bring customers to a point-of-sale where personal selling takes over to complete the transaction.

Product ads may be classified by the conditions of sale. Any of the classifications may include the following: regular price, reduced price, special price, off-price, clearance, and mail order.

Mail-order product advertising includes any kind of advertising that will allow a customer to place an order by mail or phone. The media usually used are direct mail and newspapers. Magazines, and even radio and television are possible media for mail order, but are not likely to be employed. Direct mail and newspapers can best visualize and describe products which are offered for mail-order selling.

Institutional Advertising

Institutional advertising attempts to build a reputation for a firm. It promotes the facilities, merchandise, policies, departments, features, services, and/or personnel of a business. Its primary objective is to keep customers sold over a long period of time. Its purpose is to ensure customers' steady patronage by convincing them that the store's name is synonymous with excellence. Perfect case in point: this institutional

ad by Paul Stuart, New York, is a good example of institutional/product mix. The store's main objective is obvious: presenting a fashion lesson in how to create a great sweater wardrobe. Paul Stuart's fashion knowledge and expertise comes through to customers to develop confidence in this store. They are selling merchandise, but also doing much to establish their leadership as a fashion authority. This ad has a *tone* which gives to even a first-time reader a sense of what this store is all about.

The following are basic subject areas that stores promote to attain long-range institutional objectives:

POLICY Purpose is to point out to customers what the store stands for in terms of their needs and preferences (e.g., type of merchandise, conditions of sale, pricing, returns and exchanges, and responsibility).

STORE SERVICES Conveniences to make shopping more pleasant and effective (e.g. delivery, charge accounts, gift wrapping, atmosphere, and coffee shop).

PRESTIGE A store will advertise to establish or maintain its reputation as a fashion authority, its alertness in introducing new fashions and, importantly, its exclusiveness. Another tack is to promote its wide and complete assortments or currently popular fashions. These are long-range efforts to build and sustain customers' confidence.

To some degree all retail advertising and promotion is a mix of product and institutional objectives: The public image of a retail store can be as important to the fashion buyer as the desirability and value of the merchandise she purchased for customers. It is becoming more and more apparent that the perception of a store as a fashion authority—as a bargain center—or as a combination of fashion and value—is often directly related to what customers see in the advertising. A store's image can be projected by the personality of the art, photography, layout and copy in its advertisements. For example, public image research reveals that the response to ads which feature fewer items—with lots of white space, high quality art and photography, and sophisticated graphics—make an impression for the store and its merchandise that is very different from ads which utilize grids of crowded squares of pictures, copy, and budget prices.

The effective use of advertising by the retailer must include a concern for the institutional impact of his product advertisements. In addition to the art, layout, and copy, what is advertised (new fashion trends or peak-of-popularity), how it is advertised (themes or mass assortments), and where it is advertised (rock music AM or classical FM radio) all affect the institutional image. The most successful stores have strong public images which can be described as distinct "personalities" by their customers. These stores never fail to reinforce these personality traits in their advertising and other promotional activities.

THE NATURE OF FASHION PROMOTION

Retailers are always working to make their store the most pleasurable and comfortable convenience for customers. Store buyers are directed to select merchandise with selling points which have the most appeal for customers whose tastes they are supposed to know. The store presents events and offers services which add to the appeal. Merchandise is priced with the purpose of convincing customers of its genuine value. All of the store's communications consist of messages devised to create a belief in the products, prices, events, and services which will result in continued patronage. Stores who send messages that do not create belief may go out of business. Deceptive statements have a way of "coming home to roost." A long-established New York City store (now defunct) used to have an annual birthday sale just about every three months!

It is everybody's job in retailing—store managers, merchandise managers, buyers, and salespeople as well as the promotion director and sales promotion specialists—to create messages which communicate and sell. However, communication is only as good as the meaning it conveys accurately. The retailer must design messages based upon a knowledge of customer motivations and preferences, beliefs about products and their experiences with them.

Messages which are devised to persuade customers to make a decision to act should be a combination of valid information as well as persuasion. Customers demand more and more specific information about fashion trends, styles, sizes, special details, fabrics, colors, construction, and performance to aid them in making buying decisions. They must also be informed about such details as store services, openings and hours, customer consultants, special events, and fashion shows. Customers want a constant commentary on current fashion news and contemporary lifestyles. They want to be "updated." In this sense, customers will rely on a store to continue their education in fashion trends, innovative styling, and personal development. The retailer as communicator must also be a glamorizer, for information which is not attractive and appealing will not persuade.

PROMOTIONAL THEMES & APPROACHES

The retailer need not be inhibited in his attempt to glamourize the products and ideas in his communication to customers. Communication can attempt to persuade with *appeals,* which are reasons to buy based upon rational or emotional motivations or a combination of both. The retailer's *approach* is the way he presents appeals—or reasons to buy. The retailer as seller cannot create basic needs in his customer—but he can stimulate desires and wants which service those needs. Promotion communicates those attributes of products and services which customers need or want. Many retailers feel that their ability to persuade (or motivate) customers to buy those products which contribute to their desired lifestyles and standards of living is the best way to service their customer's needs.

The responsibility of retail advertising and promotion is in the communication of information to create demand and to motivate to buy. Feedback to the retailer from his promotional communication can also reveal how customers see his store, the products, prices and services he is presenting. The degrees of customer belief indicated by responses to a retailer's messages should also be evaluated. If the retailer's practices are not consistent with his words and messages, he will soon discover that customers can recognize the inconsistency and indicate so by their lack of response and loss of patronage. The "image" and personality projected by the store is largely dependent on the quality and effect of these communications for promotion.

The discussions which follow in this chapter continue to examine the "strategic" role of fashion promotion in the business of buying and merchandising. The next chapter (17) looks at the "tactical" role of buyers and merchandisers. It is their responsibility to translate merchandising objectives into consumer appeals, selling points, and approaches based upon their analyses of motivations within target groups in their markets. What the fashion buyer does, from plan to production in a typical newspaper advertisement, is used as a demonstration.

The following chapter (18) reviews the "mix" of promotional activities to provide the fashion buyer with some guidelines for evaluation: analysis and criticism. Involvement in the evaluation of advertising and promotion can result in more effective communication between the buyer and the customer. Every advertisement, every window display, every department display, and every special event speak not only for the store, but for the buyer, the department, and the merchandise. This approach to fashion advertising and promotion makes it an integral part of the total merchandising effort—planning, purchasing, and promotion.

WHAT DOES THE STORE PROMOTE?

The process of determining sales objectives leads to, or may even include, the "what to promote" step. Merchandise managers and their buyers often develop a specific set of standards which help in making such decisions. For example, certain retailers may have a policy to advertise only the most wanted items, or styles which are on their way to becoming best sellers.

It has been proven time after time, as many buyers will verify, that it is a serious mistake to rely on advertising and promotion to correct their buying errors. Experienced advertisers know that you cannot promote customers into buying what they do not want. How does the buyer know what will be a wanted style or trend? Usually this knowledge is a result of a combination of customer-oriented and manufacturer-oriented indicators. It could be called—promoting the promotable.

- The current preferences of customers should be well known to buyers. These have the *most* influence on what will sell the best. Later in this discussion we will review the merchandising-acceptance curve theory from the *promotional* viewpoint.
- The effective merchandiser is conscious of consumer timing for seasonal activities, holidays and traditional events in society, business, education, travel, sports, and leisure.
- The retailer's vendors may be promoting certain styles very heavily. The alert buyer is watchful for such manufacturer-oriented indicators whose activity may predict a best seller.
- Buyers as well as advertising and promotion specialists should be conscious of which products will be easiest to write about and visualize pictorially to their customers. The ability to communicate the value and desirability of merchandise to customers is often a key factor in their acceptance and response. Not every type of merchandise or every style lends itself to the graphics and copy of an advertisement. For example, some items need *visual merchandising* (display).

RETAIL MARKET ANALYSIS & POSITIONING

Before a decision to promote can be made, the retailer should evaluate the nature of his markets and identify the specifics of demand and level of acceptance of various classifications of merchandise. In previous chapters you were presented with an examination of the consumer market in terms of its *demographics*—objective characteristics such as population, education, marital and family status, income—and its *psychographics*—the subjective characteristics which describe motivations to buy. A retail market analysis (or "situational analysis") is a basic study which a retailer must make before he decides on what merchandise to offer, at what price to offer it, and to whom to offer it. This may all sound so simple—yet many retailers who claim they can identify their market, and say they are designing their communication to achieve the maximum response from this market, fall short in the very

Saks Fifth Avenue's advertisements have so much fashion identity that an excitement is created before a word is read. Fashion is clearly spoken here.

Saks Fifth Avenue

Face-to-Face...Design Confrontation By Michaele Vollbracht.

For Sofere, Michaele Vollbracht confronts the challenge of swimwear...and conquers it! For in the pure, simple shape of the maillot he discovers a "canvas" for the excitement and sensation of his designs...his artistry! The result? The face of a temptress beckoning one to slide into a suit that curves, that clings, that defines the power of fashion and the woman that desires it. The fashion of Michaele Vollbracht. In black/red/turn, nylon and spandex for sizes 6 to 14, $50. In Sand and Sea Collk on Seven — where we are all the things you are. Tomorrow, in New York, the sun will dazzle when Michaele Vollbracht joins us to personally present his collection. Informal modeling from 12 to 4.

Photographed at the Galaxs Towers Condominium.

Saks Fifth Avenue is open this Sunday...and every Sunday through December 26th! Join us in New York, White Plains, Garden City and Springfield.
New York: inquiries, 753-4000; phone orders: 940-4790; open Thursday from 10 am to 8:30 pm • White Plains open Monday and Thursday from 10 am to 9 pm • Springfield and Garden City open Monday a
9:30 am to 9 pm • Bergen open Monday thru Friday from 10 am to 9:30 pm • New York, White Plains, Springfield and Garden City open Sunday from 12 noon to 5 pm • Also available in Boston, Bala Cynwy

BERGDORF GOODMAN
PERRY ELLIS 1982

A distinctive layout and brilliant fashion illustration gives this Bergdorf Goodman newspaper ad a style all its own. The entire treatment demonstrates an attention to detail which its customers surely must appreciate.

vital first part of the claim. Strange as it might seem, this apparently obvious consideration is the one which is least considered. Defining the retailer's target market is a process which identifies the types and numbers of customers to whom his merchandise, services, and promotion is being directed. Marketing managers call this "positioning a product." Merchandising managers and fashion buyers are positioning their purchasing and the promotion of their departments to attract a specific group (or groups) of customers.

The store that is mentioned several times in this chapter, Bloomingdales, New York, is a natural choice to illustrate what "positioning a product" is all about. This store has used fashion sales promotion most effectively to reinforce its present slogan—"like no other store in the world." There is no question about who Bloomingdales is and who is their customer. Their advertising, display, special events, publicity and public relations programs, all make contributions to the store's day-to-day personality projection and long-range image. (Their "China" promotion described at the end of this chapter is a splendid case in point.)

A contrast to stores that know their customers is the following example of a store that recently presented a special event for women who wear half-sizes (14½–24½) and full sizes (38–48) in dresses. The buyer wanted a fashion show and special event for these full-size women customers. An advertisement was run featuring the selected merchandise and describing the event that included a formal fashion show, "Advice for the Large-Size Woman"—and a specially prepared "dietary lunch." Nine customers showed up. Apparently this store's customers did not want to be told they had a "large-size" problem. The event was rerun later and this time featured a fashion show and a presentation of a film whose subject was "how the full-sized woman can make the most of the wonderful fashions being made just for her." But the biggest hit of all was an all-you-can-make-do-it-yourself ice cream sundae bar with unlimited creative opportunities for ingenious full-size "ice cream junkies." *This* promotion was a sell-out! The first event approached its customers with a negative statement. The second time around the store was giving its customers positive advice and support.

Now, let's take a look at retailers who develop their image and appeal to their customers by running newspaper ads which feature famous American designers (see previous page). In the Bergdorf Goodman ad the store shares "equal billing" with Perry Ellis. This association and the entire look of the ad say something about the style of the store as well as the style of their customers. In the Saks Fifth Avenue ad, Michaele Vollbracht is presented as a favorite—and as a perfect choice to satisfy the needs of a specific segment of Saks customers. The copy "defines the power of fashion" and identifies "the woman that desires it." The development of these ads should consider the nature and self-image of the customer who typifies this target group. The copy and art in the ads should be designed for the specific behavior of a consumer.

The copy and art should reflect how and when she makes her buying decisions, what she reads or listens to, and what her level of acceptances are for this trend, this look, these styles. In other words, the ads should contain messages which reflect a knowledge of the customer. Are they men and/or women? What are their *demographics* (age, income, education, occupation)? Where do they live in relation to the store? How knowledgeable are they in fashion trends? What are their *psychographics* (attitudes, values, motivations, desires)? How many retail ads can you find in today's newspaper which reveal that the advertiser really knows who should be the interested reader of this ad?

THE FASHION SALES PROMOTION PLAN

A store plans its promotion events in much the same way as buyers plan their buying. The decision to promote merchandise is the initial step in a promotion plan. In order to decide whether to promote, what to promote, and which activity to use to promote store management consider the following factors as a basis for planning any merchandise or institutional sales promotion plan:

1. Sales Objective—What is the objective of the event which will be promoted to customers?
2. Themes—What central themes will be featured in the event? What merchandise will be selected for promotion?
3. Audience—To what segment of the target market should the message be directed?
4. The Activities—What combination of promotion activities will be utilized to appeal most effectively to the segment of the target market?
5. Timing—What will be the schedule and frequency of the activities employed? What kind of a timetable will be utilized?
6. Responsibilities—Who will create and execute the various messages for advertising, publicity, display, and special events?
7. Budget—How much will be budgeted for expenses?
8. Evaluation—How will the results of promotion be evaluated?

These are the considerations which the retailer should include in planning a promotion for a single event, or a program for the next six months, or for a year. Certainly more planning is involved in a long-range promotion program than in a specific promotion event or an individual advertisement. However, the same considerations listed above would apply to both a single event or an entire program. Each of a store's sales promotions are planned at certain times of the year to take advantage of seasonal peaks, traditional buying patterns, and special opportunities to level out periodic dips in sales volume. Stores continue to present traditional events just about every month of the year—January White Sales and inventory clearances, February cruise and Valentine's Day promotions, March Easter promotions, April and May vacation events, June brides, July clearances, August back-to-school, September fall and winter events, October to December Christmas and Holiday gift promotions and many more.

It is the special-interest events which are planned over the long-range between the traditional events that develop a store's personality and image. These special and traditional events, which are done in the store's own style—with the store's identifiable "stamp," make up the sales promotion plan and planning calendar. In the following discussion we start off by examining what is perhaps the most important part of any plan—its *objectives.*

Only after correctly identifying who are the customers for a particular offer of merchandise, can the retailer express his sales objective. This statement of objective is the basis for designing the promotion message, and afterwards it will be used to evaluate the effectiveness of the communication. In defining a promotion objective, the retailer starts by considering the following:

1. What is the present stage of *merchandise-acceptance* by the customer for the product?
2. At what stage is the customer in forming a decision to buy?
3. Is the objective of the message one which could possibly have a result that could be measured?

THE MERCHANDISE-ACCEPTANCE METHOD

Customers are often described as being in a particular stage of acceptance in the making of a decision to buy. The promotion objective is affected by an evaluation of which stage describes the maximum number of customers for the buyer's offer **(Figure 16–4).**

Pioneering Stage

Customers are not aware of the designer, the styles or their desire for such merchandise. In this case the promotion objective might be to introduce and activate primary interest.

Acceptance Stage

Customers are in the process of being exposed to several merchandise offerings of a similar nature. They are becoming aware of appeals and features of the products and interest and desire is being increased. The promotion objective here could be to heighten desire and work on motivations-to-buy.

Popularity Stage

Customers have begun to make decisions to buy and are in the process of shopping for the "right merchandise at the right price." The promotion objective should be to persuade customers that your store's version of merchandise, and that your store, is their right decision—and why it is.

Decline Stage

Customers are no longer buying the merchandise as in the previous stage of popularity. The promotion objective in this stage is to offer opportunities for bargains which may serve to build and retain customer loyalty.

The message of "merchandise-acceptance" is that a clearly identified promotion objective for an event which is to be advertised, (or any promotion activity, program or campaign) is only as accurate as the fashion buyer's ability to understand the wants and needs of customers. In addition, buyers and merchandise managers must know "where their customers are at"—in respect of their present stage of acceptance and decision to buy. There are some cases where buyers who are not innovators, discover that very few of their customers are ever interested in products which are in the pioneering stage. An examination of merchandise-acceptance of certain other products, however, could reveal that many of their customers are interested in these products only when they are in the pioneering stage. The store and its buyers must consider

Figure 16–4. The merchandise-acceptance curve is part of buying decision and advertising appeals.

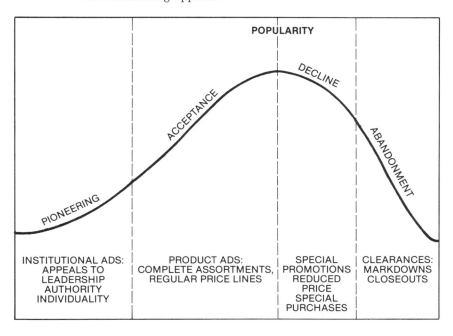

what is selling and to whom, when they define promotional objectives. The following discussion will deal with how merchandisers and buyers translate *promotional objectives* into *merchandising communications.*

THE SALES PROMOTION PLANNING CHART & CALENDAR

The sales promotion planning chart is a part of the promotion plan that is organized around the "when" of advertising and promotion. It also may indicate the what, how, who, and how much cost for promotions. Promotions which are based on traditional seasonal events, Christmas Gifting, January White Sales, August Fur Events, Valentine's Day, Mother's Day, Father's Day, are not difficult to locate on the Calendar. The timing of other promotions is not as obvious, and their timing is extremely important to sales success. For example, the promotion of a sales event should occur in advance of the timing of the event and only during its beginning. Advertising, display and other promotion activities should be planned to break in advance of the maximum sales period in order to stimulate early customer responses for additional sales. Most experienced advertisers and sellers know how useless it is to promote their "dogs and cats" (buyer's mistakes). Merchandise which has been initially rejected by customers, or has passed its peak of merchandise-acceptance should not be featured in advertisements or displays. Merchandise which is most wanted by customers, or new products with great potential appeal should be selected for advertising and promotion. The planning of sales promotion includes the developing of long-range (six months to a year) sales promotion planning charts for each promotion activity, such as this one for *advertising* in **Figure 16–5.** This sales promotion planning chart is a useful tool which aids store managers in month-by-month planning of advertising expense/sales volume ratios for the most effective acceleration of sales. The sales promotion chart reproduced here has space in each month's slot to indicate the activities planned for the current month. The previous year's monthly volume of sales in dollars, and the dollar sales volume anticipated for the current month, can be compared side-by-side, as well as total dollars for advertising; the percentage of this month's advertising dollars to total dollars for the year; the percentage of the month's sales to sales volume last year (and planned for this year); and so on as seen in the chart. This is valuable information for buyers and merchandising management to consider and compare in their sales promotion planning for the next six months to a year.

Retailers have two sources of advertising funds, namely the allocation from their own sales promotion appropriation, and cooperative advertising allowances received from manufacturers. The sales promotion appropriation as an expenditure is quite important to retailers. The

LONG RANGE SALES PROMOTION PLANNING CHART

JANUARY

January 19__ produced 6.5% of average total store sales for the year   January 19__ produced 6.5%

	ACTUAL 1983	PLANNED 1984
Sales	$	$
Total Advertising	%	%
Total Adv. Percentage	%	%
% of year's sales in Jan	%	%
% of year's adv. in Jan	%	%

FEBRUARY

February 19__ produced 5.8% of average total store sales for the year   February 19__ produced 5.8%

	ACTUAL 1983	PLANNED 1984
Sales	$	$
Total Advertising	%	%
Total Adv. Percentage	%	%
% of year's sales in Feb	%	%
% of year's adv. in Feb	%	%

MARCH

March 19__ produced 7.7% of average total store sales for the year   March 19__ produced 8.1%

	ACTUAL 1983	PLANNED 1984
Sales	$	$
Total Advertising	%	%
Total Adv. Percentage	%	%
% of year's sales in March	%	%
% of year's adv. in March	%	%

APRIL

April 19__ produced 7.9% of average total store sales for the year   April 19__ produced 7.0%

	ACTUAL 1983	PLANNED 1984
Sales	$	$
Total Advertising	%	%
Total Adv. Percentage	%	%
% of year's sales in April	%	%
% of year's adv. in April	%	%

MAY

May 19__ produced 8.0% of average total store sales for the year   May 19__ produced 7.9%

	ACTUAL 1983	PLANNED 1984
Sales	$	$
Total Advertising	%	%
Total Adv. Percentage	%	%
% of year's sales in May	%	%
% of year's adv. in May	%	%

JUNE

June 19__ produced 7.5% of average total store sales for the year   June 19__ produced 7.9%

	ACTUAL 1983	PLANNED 1984
Sales	$	$
Total Advertising	%	%
Total Adv. Percentage	%	%
% of year's sales in June	%	%
% of year's adv. in June	%	%

JULY

July 19__ produced 6.4% of average total store sales for the year   July 19__ produced 6.3%

	ACTUAL 1983	PLANNED 1984
Sales	$	$
Total Advertising	%	%
Total Adv. Percentage	%	%
% of year's sales in July	%	%
% of year's adv. in July	%	%

AUGUST

August 19__ produced 7.5% of average total store sales for the year   August 19__ produced 7.7%

	ACTUAL 1983	PLANNED 1984
Sales	$	$
Total Advertising	%	%
Total Adv. Percentage	%	%
% of year's sales in Aug	%	%
% of year's adv. in Aug	%	%

SEPTEMBER

September 19__ produced 7.9% of average total store sales for the year   September 19__ produced 7.9%

	ACTUAL 1983	PLANNED 1984
Sales	$	$
Total Advertising	%	%
Total Adv. Percentage	%	%
% of year's sales in Sept	%	%
% of year's adv. in Sept	%	%

OCTOBER

October 19__ produced 8.7% of average total store sales for the year   October 19__ produced 8.8%

	ACTUAL 1983	PLANNED 1984
Sales	$	$
Total Advertising	%	%
Total Adv. Percentage	%	%
% of year's sales in Oct	%	%
% of year's adv. in Oct	%	%

NOVEMBER

November 19__ produced 10.4% of average total store sales for the year   November 19__ produced 10.5%

	ACTUAL 1983	PLANNED 1984
Sales	$	$
Total Advertising	%	%
Total Adv. Percentage	%	%
% of year's sales in Nov	%	%
% of year's adv. in Nov	%	%

DECEMBER

December 19__ produced 15.7% of average total store sales for the year   December 19__ produced 15.9%

	ACTUAL 1983	PLANNED 1984
Sales	$	$
Total Advertising	%	%
Total Adv. Percentage	%	%
% of year's sales in Dec	%	%
% of year's adv. in Dec	%	%

Figure 16–5. Long-Range Sales Promotion Planning Chart.

average retailer's largest expense items are rent, payroll, and sales promotion. Remember too, that advertising and promotion are largely responsible for generating customer traffic and consumer buying which aid in generating the entire sales income of the store.

HOW MUCH FOR SALES PROMOTION?

Store management must prepare a budget for sales promotion in much the same way as its budget for buying merchandise. The overall amount which the average retailer appropriates for all activities of sales promotion is approximately 4 percent of sales. It is called the appropriation for sales promotion and is usually prepared for a six-month period and adjusted during this term if circumstances require it.

The size of promotional appropriations is dependent upon many factors. It is difficult to describe a typical store when we discuss how much is spent for sales promotion. The decision on how much to spend for advertising and promotion is made only after careful study by top management in the merchandising division *and* the sales promotion division. Each retailer has individual promotional goals and objectives depending upon: how long the store has been established, how well known it is in its trading area, the pattern of its customer traffic, current economic and local conditions, its size, its location, its merchandise philosophy, its fashion authority, the nature of its competition, the quality of its advertising and promotion efforts, and the costs of newspaper space and other media in the store's trading area.

Very few retailers can afford to spend more than 4 percent of their sales for promotion, and many spend only a fraction of 4 percent. Smaller stores may use little or no advertising, relying on window and department display and direct mail as their methods of communicating with customers.

The net result of sales promotion expense over the long range should be to increase profits. Buyers and merchandise managers must be in agreement on exactly what advertising and other promotional activities can produce. Sales promotion cannot sell merchandise that customers do not want. The purpose of a consistent promotional effort is to sell a volume of merchandise at a profit which justifies the promotional expense. The entire management of the store must agree on a planned program which will provide for volume and profit, reinforce its public image and take advantage of special opportunities.

HOW THE STORE BUDGETS FOR PROMOTION

The retailer makes an attempt to accurately predict his anticipated sales volume—upon which the size of his appropriation for promotion will

Figure 16–6. The retailer's sales promotion appropriation with allocations to separate activities and media.

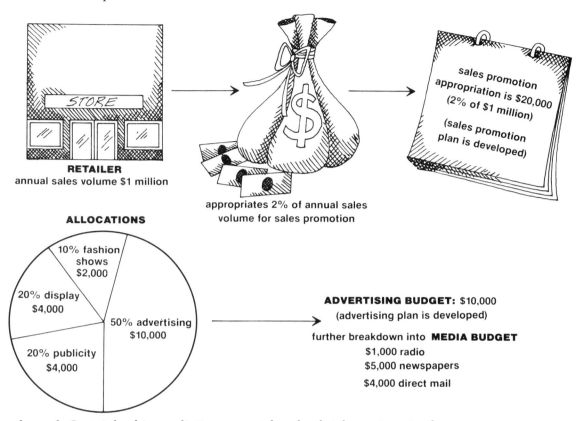

RETAILER
annual sales volume $1 million

appropriates 2% of annual sales volume for sales promotion

sales promotion appropriation is $20,000 (2% of $1 million)

(sales promotion plan is developed)

ALLOCATIONS

10% fashion shows $2,000

20% display $4,000

20% publicity $4,000

50% advertising $10,000

ADVERTISING BUDGET: $10,000
(advertising plan is developed)

further breakdown into **MEDIA BUDGET**
$1,000 radio
$5,000 newspapers
$4,000 direct mail

depend. Certainly this prediction cannot be absolutely on target—the best that the retailer can do is estimate and adjust the promotion expense/sales volume ratio for the six-month period. There are three traditional methods that retailers employ:

- The "top-to-bottom" method (percentage of sales)
- The "bottom-to-top" method (promotion by objectives)
- "All-one-can-afford" method (special problems or opportunities)

Top-to-Bottom Method

The top-to-bottom approach is the method most likely to be used by large retailers. Store management designates goals for sales volume over a six-month or one-year period. The estimates for the various advertising and promotion activities are calculated using the stores pre-determined appropriation percentage (approximately 1 to 4 percent). All of these goals and estimates represent a combination of figures out of the store's past experience, and its anticipation of "beating its past year's figures." The top-to-bottom approach is a natural approach for large, well-established retailers whose sales volume has reflected a steady growth through the years.

Once the total appropriation for all promotion has been determined, the next step is to allocate (or divide) this expense among the various activities of sales promotion. **Figure 16–6** is a graphic example of appropriation and allocation breakdowns by percentages. For example, an advertising allocation is then divided into media budgets—newspaper advertising, radio and television, direct mail. The next step is to allocate portions of these funds to store divisions and their individual departments. The method is similarly applied for display and other promotional activities.

The top-to-bottom method allows management to exercise tight control of promotion expenses, compared to the sales volume produced by promotional activities. The control is exercised by changing the percentage ratio. The most serious flaw of this method is its inability to take advantage of opportunities which additional advertising and promotion could produce in sales volume. The problem with this "percentage of sales" method is that it may allocate more (or less) than is justified by the volume of sales.

Bottom-to-Top Method

Bottom-to-top budgeting attempts to overcome the flaw mentioned above by allowing specific merchandise divisions or departments who are responsible for sales to plan promotion expenditures. The philosophy here is that buyers and merchandisers are closer to consumer buying behavior and merchandise-acceptance than top store management and consequently are better equipped to estimate sales goals.

Bottom-to-top budgeting for promotion is done divisionally or departmentally, producing estimates on a day-to-day, week-to-week basis. For example, merchandise managers and their buyers may calculate the number of lines of newspaper advertising space they will need for a prescribed period. This results in a newspaper advertising schedule and an advertising budget for the period.

It is easy to see why this is not a widely used method. Store management in most large stores is not likely to give up their centralized control of sales promotion expenditures.

"All-One-Can-Afford" Method

The previously discussed approaches (particularly the top-to-bottom) are easily the most likely used by major retailers. The traditional predictability of consumer demand and buyer behavior seem to work well for the use of these methods. The unpredictable, however, seems to be more and more a factor in our uncertain economy, and stores are now more often faced with fluctuating demand and sales volume. Very strong competitive pressures from competitive retail innovators plus the changing practices of the manufacturers of fashion merchandise are now compelling retailers to reevaluate their estimates of sales, periodically.

The established retailer is increasingly confronted by competitors who open new stores or present new services for customers. "Meeting the competition" is the most likely reason for a retailer to depart from his traditional budgeting method and to use the "all-one-can-afford" method of budgeting for promotion.

The ideal method for sales promotion budgeting may be a *combination of all three methods.* The retailer must consider several things at the same time:

1. The percentage return of volume and profit on the promotional expense.
2. The need for advertising and promotion continuity for *institutional* as well as *product* objectives. In other words, the *cumulative* effect of promotion as a long-range investment (institutionally) must be considered as well as promotion's short-range contribution to the profit picture.
3. The need for budget to take advantage of special opportunities for promotional events and special problems in meeting competition.

The most effective budget planning is done on a continuous basis, with the needs of the store subject to *frequent evaluation.* The experience of the *current planning period* is the best information for decisions on the upcoming planning period. Long-range sales promotion planning and budgeting is most productive when it has a built-in option for interim repositioning of objectives and promotional needs.

COOPERATIVE ADVERTISING

A manufacturer of a brand name line of sportswear may say to the retailer: "If you will run an ad featuring my sportswear separates in your local newspaper, I will pay part of the cost." The share paid by the sportswear manufacturer may be 50 percent, or any other portion that is agreed upon. This is fundamentally the procedure used in cooperative advertising. It would seem that this arrangement should be ideal, and mutually advantageous to both the retailer and the manufacturer.

Cooperative advertising has its disadvantages along with its advantages, however. In order to understand these, let us examine a typical case: Suppose a branded-apparel manufacturer makes an agreement

"Come Discover the Glory of Greek Island Eyes by Estée Lauder" is typical of headlines in coop ads. Here, Estée Lauder participates with a major retailer to launch their new collection of colors "inspired by the islands of Greece."

with retailers to pay 50 percent of the advertising space costs of any newspaper ads which the store will run. This agreement can specify the type of art and copy to be used in the ads and, in some cases, the manufacturer supplies newspaper ad prints or newspaper ad mats* containing art and copy, which are complete except for the store's price(s) and name. The retailer runs the ad in his local newspaper. The newspaper bills the store for the space and the store pays it. The retailer then sends his own bill to the manufacturer, with a copy of the ad, showing what the manufacturer's share of the total newspaper cost is. The manufacturer then sends the retailer a check to cover that sum. This is a relatively simple and clear procedure. But there are disadvantages.

Cooperative advertising can be of real value both to store and to manufacturer. The terms should be clearly agreed upon in advance, including the schedule of space, dates, newspapers, and the basis of charging. Total expenditures should be limited in some way, as in terms of a percentage of purchases. There should be agreement whether the advertisement is to be run by itself or a part of a departmentalized store advertisement, and whether supplementary sales promotion is to be offered at the same time without further cost.

Written cooperative advertising agreements avoid many arguments as to what was actually in the arrangement. Most large companies have standard printed agreements ready for the dealer. They specify every possible detail right down to the correct size logo which the manufacturer requires for the advertising to be eligible for cooperative money. The written agreement serves also to prevent legal involvement with reference to preferential treatment of one dealer where others are to be granted the same or similar treatment.

*A treated composition material similar to cardboard or plastic which is a cast impression of the "raised metal" photoengraving of a mechanical of an ad containing copy and art.

Cooperative advertising can be an important part of the advertising plan. It should not be the reason, however, for a buyer to stock an item, unless this merchandise is important to customers.

Disadvantages of Cooperative Advertising to Manufacturers

1. Stores often do not give manufacturers the benefit of their retail contract rate, and often charge a rate as high as the national advertising rate. The national rate is generally two to four times higher than the local rate.
2. Stores often run manufacturers' ads as part of departmentalized advertisements, and divide the total cost of space, include headings, copy, and logotype, among various manufacturers. They also may charge for artwork and production when they create their own ads, rather than use the manufacturer's newspaper ad print or ad mat.
3. There is invariably a great amount of recordkeeping and accounting correspondence.
4. Despite warnings, stores are very slow in sending bills. Friction is the result.
5. Stores that have contracts with papers to use a certain amount of space a month, or a year, may use manufacturers' advertising on poor selling days, reserving good selling days for their own store promotions.
6. It is often difficult to control how a store will advertise the manufacturer's product. Many stores will not use a newspaper ad as supplied, but will revise material that they feel emphasizes the manufacturer rather than the retailer. In making revisions, the store may eliminate elements that identify the manufacturer and complement his national advertising.
7. Much cooperative advertising is not coordinated with the stores' planned promotions. There is a difference in style and content, and little or no supplementation of window and interior display.
8. The competition between manufacturers may cause them to spend more money in cooperative advertising than is warranted.
9. Some retailers consider advertising allowances as discounts. Some will ask for a blanket "3 or 5 percent advertising allowance" for unspecified promotional efforts. The manufacturer can guard against this by paying only upon receipt of tear sheets of ads.

Disadvantages of Cooperative Advertising to Retailers

1. The lure to buy merchandise because of the influence of financial participation by the manufacturer in promotion is great.

2. Frequently the retailer is burdened with the launching of the promotion of comparatively little-known names.
3. At the insistence of the manufacturer, cooperative advertising frequently lacks good identity with the retailer's format. This practice disrupts the continuity of the retailer's advertising.
4. There is a possibility that the merchandise being cooperatively advertised is not in keeping with the store's objectives and personality.
5. If the store buyer handles the cooperative advertising agreement, there is a danger that the advertising director may not be consulted until it is too late to incorporate his thinking.

Advantages of Cooperative Advertising

1. It gives the manufacturer and the retailer additional exposure for their advertising dollar by sharing the advertising cost.
2. It can give a branded line the sponsorship of prominent retailers.
3. It may indicate to a manufacturer the degree of appeal of certain products in his line.
4. Retail advertising usually gets a better position in a newspaper than national advertising and is much lower in cost, because of the difference in rates between retail and national newspaper advertising space. This difference in rates is being eliminated by many newspapers and by some local radio stations.
5. It can give a retailer identification with well known and accepted national brand names.

Other Implications

A section of the Robinson-Patman Act requires that advertising allowances be made available to all stores on a proportionate basis when the stores are located in the same marketing area. A store is considered to be in the same marketing area when it competes for the same consumers' business. If there is doubt as to what constitutes a "marketing area," the U.S. Department of Labor's Bureau of Labor Statistics will provide answers to any questions regarding marketing areas. Still, there is always the danger of some store feeling that it has been discriminated against, even if not legally so. Cooperative advertising can create ill feeling by the retailer who feels he is not getting his fair share.

The pressure on buyers from manufacturers offering to pay for cooperative advertising can get to be too high. The buyer should attempt to make the "best deal" only with those manufacturers whose merchandise is most wanted by customers. If a buyer permits this allowance to sway better judgment and tries to promote anything but the most desirable merchandise—he could be in trouble.

ADVERTISING—TO REACH THE BUYER'S TARGET MARKET

The emergence of a retail "management by objectives" philosophy includes the identifying of specific objectives for sales promotion—with a major role allocated to advertising. The appearance of segmented markets, the ever-changing patterns of customer loyalty and patronage, and the increasing variety of fashion merchandise (especially designer names, status labels) have compelled retail managers to rely more and more on advertising and promotion.

Of all the promotion activities—advertising has the most potential for communicating with large groups of customers. Its role in presenting merchandise for immediate selling is no more important than its cumulative effects in presenting the store's "fashion philosophy," customer services, and involvement in public and community affairs. The store which does not make a serious effort to create productive and believable advertising may be losing much more than sales. Advertising should be used constantly to reach the buyer's target market with advertisements that stimulate the customer's interest, provide useful information, and develop loyalty. Today, market segmentation is the major strategy used to define the retailer's market. This is a process of describing segments of the target market through variables such as *demographics* (age, sex, occupation, education, etc.); *psychographics* (attitudes, values, desires, needs); *geographic location; benefits* (as perceived by customers); *situations* (different roles people play); *usage* (heavy users, light users).

SELECTING THE MEDIUM

The function of media is to provide a means for transmitting advertising messages to the target market. The merchandise offering must be carried in a medium which is appropriate for it, and in this way the nature of the message influences the choice of a medium. It is difficult to develop effective appeals for various classifications of merchandise without understanding the medium which is going to carry the message, and the characteristics or profile of the target markets in the audience which receives the medium.

Store management should also consider the media available in their area which may be used to communicate with their designated market segments in their target markets. The retailer's most important decision may be the defining of his segmented markets. The decision can affect all other merchandising and sales promotion activities. For example, if a retailer in a fashionable Chicago suburb decided to cater to upper-income women with designer-label fashions at better prices, this decision would lead to decision on merchandise planning and purchasing, advertising and the selection of media. In addition, the market segmentation decisions would be the basis for such decisions as: Which group to send a mail-order catalogue? Should local radio be used as well as newspapers?

Newspaper Advertising

For most retailers the most obvious choice of a medium is the newspaper. The fashion buyer's role in advertising is most apparent in the creation of newspaper ads. This will be demonstrated in Chapter 17. Most of the advertising in newspapers throughout the country is retail (or local). It should be noted that retailers earn a local rate from newspapers and pay considerably less than national advertisers (producers and manufacturers) for advertising space. The cost of reaching customers through newspaper advertising (referred to as *cost-per-thousand* or *c.p.m.*) is lower than most other media. The time needed for preparation and publication of newspaper ads is also shorter. It has been estimated that newspapers are read by about 90 percent of our people. The advantages of using this high coverage are obvious for stores that need to communicate with customers on a frequent and consistent basis. Retail advertising budgets for most stores are at a peak in November and December. Promotion expenditures for specific merchandise categories may be higher at other months of the promotion year. For example, linens and domestics are advertised and promoted heavily in January, sportswear in September, and October is traditionally a peak month for fall clearances.

Newspapers are characterized as a *public information* medium. The customer's reliance on the newspaper of his choice for information and advice can be an asset to the buyer who insists that her ads be given the size and position in the paper which will effectively communicate to customers just how creative and on-target their planning and purchasing has been.

Magazine Advertising

Magazines are a medium limited to retailers who have widespread distribution geographically, such as Sears or J.C. Penney, or those such as Saks Fifth Avenue or Neiman-Marcus, who are so prominent that they draw customers from a distance and visitors from "far-and-wide." Except for magazines that have *regional* editions, much of the circulation of a magazine is distributed to readers who have common demographic and/or psychographic descriptions, rather than a common trading area.

The extensive preparation and publication time needed for magazine advertising limits its usefulness for product advertising which has to reflect the most current trends and prices in fashion merchandise.

Magazine advertisements are ideal for the store who wants to send *institutional* messages to an even more selective group in their target market than a newspaper can deliver. The ads (right) illustrate the contrast between a store's newspaper and magazine advertising.

Store managements plan to use other advertising media besides newspapers and magazines. Retailers are using radio and television more now than in previous years—when store managers felt that broadcasting's time and production costs were prohibitive. It was also felt that the time slots offered to retailers were too limited for effective exposure. Recently, however, the retailer has begun to expand his media mix. The rise of retail television is a dramatic example. The number of commercials from 1975 to 1981 has more than quadrupled! The amount of budget in dollars spent by retailers in 1981 has increased similarly.

The two Lord & Taylor ads present their store as the place to find "the perfect gift." The newspaper ad (left) features specific "Christmas Shops" and lists gift suggestions. It is more product-oriented than the magazine ad (right) which presents Lord & Taylor as the institution of perfect gifts and customer services designed to lavish attention on the shopper.

Radio Advertising

The use of radio advertising by major retailers is small compared to the large amounts spent in newspaper advertising. Recent figures for retail advertising reveal that newspapers get approximately half of most retail advertising allocations, whereas radio and television combined get less than 20 percent of the allocation. This is true for most large retailers, discount operations as well as regular-priced department stores.

However, the use of radio if not as large an effort is a relatively universal one among retailers, who use radio as a back-up for their considerably larger newspaper advertising effort. It seems that the potential for retail radio advertising is unlimited. Its cost-effectiveness is excellent and improving—and its overall utilization is rising. Today, radio is second only to newspapers as a retail advertising medium!

The most frequent use of retail radio commercials is necessarily institutional. Because you cannot see the product, radio is used to communicate appealing store services and facilities, special events, sales, clearances, and any type of a fashion or style-trend message which can be dramatized through the use of voices, music, and sound effects. Because of its relatively shorter life, repetition in a radio commercial is effective and it is frequently used to increase the response to the retailer's newspaper messages.

The flexibility of short preparation and programming time is also an advantage, as with newspapers. Opportunities for the retailer to communicate new trends and new offers are obvious. In spite of its limitations, radio may be retail's fastest growing medium—with a cost per thousand that rivals newspapers. Like newspapers, radio advertising is cost-effective for the small retailer as well as for the giants.

Television Advertising

The increase of retail television is partly a result of changes in the retailer's trading area. Large segments of his market now live in suburbs. Some stores must now use a combination of newspapers and radio stations to communicate with their customer audience, which has become more dispersed. For larger stores, television advertising with its ability to reach the largest local audience at any one time is an attractive alternative, if not a replacement for newspaper advertising.

Retailers have also used television to develop a strong store image. This medium has proven amazingly effective in the promotion of fashion. The impact of television in over 90 percent of American homes is well documented. Now, the possibility of creating and reinforcing a store's fashion authority in a relatively short time is a new development in fashion merchandising. This is now being complemented and supplemented by the fashion manufacturer's growing investment in using television as a major medium for marketing brand-name fashion. Many of these campaigns offer the store opportunities for tie-ins.

Most retailers find that newspaper advertising is better adapted to product and price advertising, whereas television with its dramatic visualizations can send a more emphatic institutional message. Color television, however, has the capacity to show styles and fashion in motion with more appeal than a black-and-white newspaper advertisement.

Regardless of the increased use of television by retailers, some still feel that costs of producing commercials, while they are not necessarily prohibitive, are too much for their limited budgets. In addition, they realize that the demands of television writing and filming require the creative talents of an advertising agency or film-making specialist. Several of the leading advertising agencies in the country are now producing commercials for larger retailers. It should be noted that these commercials are basically institutional in nature—even if they feature products. A newspaper ad can present many assortments or related groups of products—but a television commercial would find the limitations of time and attention-span a problem in featuring more than one or two styles. Also to be considered is the greater amount of time needed to prepare a television commercial (three to four weeks) as compared to a newspaper ad (one to two weeks). Certainly for the present, retail newspaper advertising can be more timely. However, as this is being written, several retailers in major market areas have launched a series of 30-second "Fashion Updates" or "Fashion Reports," which are broadcast through peak selling seasons several times a week on morning talk shows. A *Fashion Monthly Report* for consumers on cable television is in the works.

Despite its current limitations, as new technology and lower-cost production techniques develop, the potential of television to sell fashion seems unlimited. The marketing success stories for designer jeans and other designer and status-name fashion products are largely a result of television advertising campaigns. From 1979 to 1980, spending by fashion apparel manufacturers rose 65 percent to over $90 million! The possibilities for fashion merchandisers to promote store image by televising mini-fashion shows, store services, and special events, may be their most dramatic and exciting effort yet.

Sears, Roebuck has produced an experimental "catalog" on laser videodisc. In selected stores, Sears customers are able to watch presentations of newly arrived fashions. One of the cable systems is planning a 24-hour "shopping channel" to include fashions that can be ordered on the spot!

Direct-Mail Advertising

The use of mass media (newspapers, magazines, radio, television), to reach customers may have some disadvantages for the retailer. The most obvious disadvantage of mass media is ineffective or wasted circulation, which reaches areas that for various reasons do not include the store's customers. Direct mail is more flexible and more versatile. The size and format of a personalized letter, flyer, brochure, circular or catalogue is limited only by the cost of postage and post office regulations. The most effective use of this medium is to do mailings to known and charge-account customers, and potential customers for sales and special offers. Manufacturer-produced statement enclosures imprinted with the store's name can be mailed with each charge-account bill. Fashion buyers should be aware of the availability of statement enclosures prepared by their resources. These can produce additional mail-order sales.

The effectiveness of direct mail as a retail medium will largely depend on how good, accurate, and current is the store's mailing list. The resourceful retailer develops a list of known and potential customers. In small stores, managers and buyers should encourage salespeople to solicit names, addresses and phone numbers of their customers to develop the mailing list. The list should be organized so that certain parts of it can be used individually for offers of special interest. Direct mail can be expensive in "cost-per-thousand" (c.p.m.), but it can also be the most productive medium in terms of customer response. For the small fashion store direct mail is usually the first type of advertising utilized.

Direct-mail advertising should not be confused with mail order. Mail order is a method of retailing in which a sale is initiated through advertising and completed by an order through the mail.

A RETAILER'S STRATEGY—BLOOMINGDALE'S "CHINA" PROMOTION

The fashion store's advertising and promotion "mix" is a reflection of its location, size, personality, positioning, and sales volume. Only the largest, most prominent retailers employ the whole mix on a consistent basis. A dramatic example of the full utilization of sales promotion is supplied here by one of the most outstanding special events ever presented by a fashion store—Bloomingdale's "China."

For six weeks in the fall of 1980, Bloomingdale's stores from Boston to Washington overflowed with Chinese fashion, food, arts and crafts, furnishings, and antiques. Bloomingdale's buyers made about 130 trips to China to prepare for this promotion—and they bought over $10 million* of merchandise! The planning started in July of 1979 in commercial agreement with China, which Bloomingdale's hopes will continue the country's importance as a supplier for years to come.

The advertising and promotion theme used in this major event indicates the degree of Bloomingdale's commitment—"China—Heralding the Dawn of a New Era." Another keynote, "Come awaken to a country steeped in forty centuries of ritual and opulence," reveals their

CHINA
HERALDING THE DAWN OF A NEW ERA

FOR IMMEDIATE RELEASE

Contact: Debby Weber
          (212) 223-7205

CHINESE CRAFTSMEN DEMONSTRATE TH[...]
DURING BLOOMINGDALE'S CELEBRATIO[...]

NEW YORK, NEW YORK, SEPTEMBER 24, 1980 [...]
has a long history of importing mercha[...]
well travelled and the exotically unf[...]
world. Now it is importing artists [...]

Tonight, Bloomingdale's beg[...]
of China. There will be merchand[...]
turned into a living theater. S[...]
artists and craftsmen are here [...]
skills throughout the store to[...]
September 29, and October 6 [...]

Double embroidery a[...]
creates two different imag[...]
who comes from Soochow, [...]
this complicated art wh[...]
mother who had learned [...]
embroiders the front [...]
time, creating a dif[...]

All of these artists [...]
children, taught by their parents in the a[...]

10

Lilac Padded Silk Tapestry Informal Robe
Guang Xu Period
1875-1908

This pale purple robe with cotton padding was worn in winter by the Empress and Imperial concubines. It is woven with butterflies and five bats, encircling a central *shou* character medallion in gold filé, blue and yellow. The combination of bats and *shou* character symbolize longevity and happiness, but here the two symbols have a special meaning. In Chinese, the word for "bat" is *fu*, a pun on the Chinese word for happiness, which is also *fu*.

These photographs by Albert Watson were commissioned by Bloomingdale's and photographed in the Palace Museum in The Forbidden City.
© 1980 Bloomingdale's

Bloomingdale's China promotion is part of their "legendary" series of storewide special events. Their comprehensive effort uses every activity of advertising and promotion to communicate drama to customers. Here, press releases for media coverage and a page from a consumer brochure featuring exquisite Chinese ceremonial robes.

40 centuries of ritual and opulence

Never before has
the influence of a
country been so
thoroughly felt,

Sept. 24—Nov. 8

This newspaper ad is an impressive double spread which launched the "CHINA" special event. It invites customers to "incredible exhibits, myriad markets, exotic atmosphere, oriental environments, and shimmering shops." The invitation is hard to resist—it establishes its drama and introduces its recognizable motif.

NMENTS
o gigantic foo dogs flank the entrance to
ranging from a farm house in Canton to a
lack fantasy room in Shanghai to a
980. On 5.
ion. A faithful reproduction of the royal
ina's most beautiful gardens. On 5.

OUR SHIMMERING SHOPS
Three Pools That Mirror the Moon. A trove of opulence inspired by the garden city of Hangzhou and filled with the most elegant accoutrements—handknit cashmeres to antique embroidered robes. On 3.
Warriors of Sian. The startling archaeological finds from Sian form the background for a men's shop unlike any other. Main Floor.
The Children's Palace. Presided over by a giant papier-mâché dragon, a world of enchantment with clothing, toys and accessories for children of all ages. On 2.

OUR APPRECIATION
To Pan Am, for flying us on over 200 trips to the Gateway of China, we wish to express our thanks. It was a Pan Am China Clipper that broke the first trail across the Pacific, sweeping away the barriers of time and space forever.

And sincere thanks to Murjani International, Eastman Kodak, Monarch Importers and Christie's for helping us bring China to Bloomingdale's.

American Express makes travelling a breeze, crosstown or cross-continent. Bloomingdale's is pleased to honor the American Express Card.

e'S

EVENINGS
ESTNUT HILL JENKINTOWN, PA, WHITE FLINT MD, AND TYSONS CORNER, VA

Many manufacturer/retailer "productions" are featured in a special event of the "CHINA" magnitude. Example: Revlon's Ultima II and its "Shanghai Beauty Express."

Take the Shanghai Beauty Express. You may never want to get off.
The Ultima II Shanghai Beauty Express has everything you need to look beautiful everywhere you go. Eyeshadows. Lipsticks. Blushers. Nail enamels. And it even has something to make you feel beautiful: Ciara perfume spray. When it comes to price, the Shanghai Beauty Express shows another pretty side:
It's all yours for just 15.00
The Shanghai Beauty Express only runs at Bloomingdale's. On a limited schedule. Catch it at the Ultima II counter on The Main Course.

Come to
CHINA
at
bloomingdale's

deep admiration for the Chinese people and clearly demonstrates their desire to present the superb fashions, arts and crafts of China to their customers.

The entire promotion, beyond the fabulous series of special events is thought of as a merchandising investment with institutional as well as product objectives. The results? Bloomingdale's slogan—"like no other store in the world" was substantially reinforced, along with a substantial increase of the more than $1 million a year in sales of Chinese merchandise that the store has done since 1972!

The materials featured here are but a few from this extensive campaign. They are a striking example of this store's advertising and promotion mix just through the features and special events they describe. The store assembled vast collections of merchandise, culture, and environment. The opening was launched at a celebrity-filled gala to benefit UNICEF.

The window displays and interior departmental displays were irresistible visual stimuli to dazzle the customer—everything from one-of-a-

*At retail price.

kind antique robes to silk blouses made to Bloomingdale's own specifications; from exquisite porcelains and ceramics to antique, traditional and custom-made furniture designed with the cities of China in mind. Bloomingdale's famous model rooms allowed customers to virtually "walk-through" Chinese homes and palaces!

Merchandise from every part of China could be found in almost every department of the New York City store. Special shops carried exclusive items developed for the event. Some of China's most gifted artisans and craftsman had been flown to New York to demonstrate their skills. Exhibits provided a museum of China's past and present cultures. Photo galleries, art galleries, audio-visual documentary presentations, arts and crafts demonstrations, and food sampling could be found on every floor of the stores involved. The restaurant offered exotic menus of China's delicacies, and an assortment of fifty different kinds of tea! Chefs from New York's finest restaurants had prepared the food. These illustrations are just a small part of the extensive advertising, publicity and special events which brought thousands of customers to see the exhibits, watch the demonstrations, taste the food, and buy the merchandise.

SUMMARY

If strategy can be defined as "artful managing," it is never more apparent than in the "art" of fashion buying and merchandising. The buyer's retail strategy must include an artful management of planning, purchasing, and promotion which can challenge the competition in stimulating the interest and desires of customers. Regardless of size, the retailer can be innovative in the buying and selling of merchandise. It is interesting to note that every major store in the trading area of Bloomingdale's, New York City, was featuring merchandise from China at the time of their promotion. It is also interesting that if you researched it, you would find comparatively little advertising, promotion, and publicity for the merchandise and institutional events featured by these other stores. Bloomingdale's strategy was to make the most of this historic new relationship between the two countries. They spared no effort to make a big impression which would associate their store with "the China marketplace." Their strategy includes tactics that will continue to reinforce that impression.

There may be limitations on how much merchandise a buyer can find in the fashion markets here and abroad which is different and better than the offerings of the competition. There is no limitation, however, on new ideas and better ways to advertise and promote the fashion they have bought. This chapter has attempted to present sales promotion as the strategy of "show and tell" in the "show business of fashion."

17 THE FASHION BUYER'S RESPONSIBILITIES IN ADVERTISING & SALES PROMOTION

INTRODUCTION

It is the fashion buyer who is charged with the major responsibility of knowing the nature of her customers and what customers want in terms of personal fashion preferences.

The buyer must consider the types of merchandise and the levels of customer acceptance for certain trends and styles, in order to identify advertising and promotion objectives. These objectives will help to determine the content of the messages beamed to customers designed to attract attention, to stimulate interest, and to activate purchasing responses.

All levels of the fashion industry use product and institutional advertising. We shall examine next, the newspaper advertising of a department store to indicate the different methods used to attain immediate and long-range sales objectives.

PRODUCT OBJECTIVES

Product objectives involve immediate or short-range results in the form of sales of specific merchandise or actual increases in department and/ or store traffic. Most of the retailer's newspaper advertising, especially the promotionally-priced store, will consist of product advertisements. The copy in these ads will include detailed descriptions of identified styles, brands, and prices. Product advertising could be considered the fashion buyer's effort to "pre-sell" or influence the customer—a supplement to point-of-sale visual merchandising (display) and personal selling. The most frequently used form of newspaper product ads are:

SINGLE-ITEM ADS Feature the most-wanted or most-stimulating examples of the store's current offerings.

ASSORTMENT ADS Designed to show the range or depth of a certain style or classification of merchandise.

THEME ADS Group related or unrelated products (among many others) under a style trend, fabric, color, seasonal, or special occasion theme.

OMNIBUS OR DEPARTMENTALIZED ADS Feature unrelated products from different departments in a single compartmentalized ad.

INSTITUTIONAL OBJECTIVES

Characteristically institutional advertising does not describe merchandise in a way which would motivate a customer to a buying decision. Institutional objectives are a long-range investment in image-building designed to enhance a store's fashion reputation. Many of the store's institutional events are public relations oriented and designed to be an integral part of the store's public relations program. Any medium can be used to present *ideas,* but the presentation of tangible merchandise usually requires detailed information and description which can best be transmitted in words and pictures. The successful merchandiser is also involved in presenting intangible ideas which appeal to the customer's attitudes, values, and lifestyles. The store becomes a headquarters for information, advice, instruction, and entertainment. The successful fashion buyer is involved in catering to psychological as well as material needs of the customer. The current thrust of most fashion advertising and promotion is to integrate some institutional message in every product message. The best retail advertising today is an attempt to present merchandise that is highly desirable and capable of motivating customers to buy. The *way* merchandise is presented in terms of layout, art, photography, and copy approach will also send a message about the store. Inasmuch as many products are basically similar, the fashion ad must sell something more. The store's ambiance, its services, policies, and personnel now become part of the product!

HOW OBJECTIVES ARE DEFINED

One of the ways a fashion buyer develops an advertising or promotion objective is by considering how close the consumer is in making a fashion purchasing decision. We had previously referred to this as the stage of merchandise-acceptance, (Chapter 16).

Sales objectives should be very clearly understood by the buyer. When the performance of the advertising or promotion activity for the buyer's department is evaluated there should be no doubt as to whether objectives have been attained. The fashion buyer can evaluate advertising and promotion effectiveness only if the objective is specifically understood and *stated.* In this way the design of an advertisement will be part of the objective. A fashion product ad is different from one designed to generate sales through the use of a coupon-response: the message and consumer objectives are different.

There is also a difference in objectives between advertisements designed to bring in new customers and those whose objective is to increase the responses of present customers. The objective may be to generate more department traffic, or to introduce a new collection. In each, the copy, art, and layout of the advertisement will be individually designed to attain the specific objective.

HOW THE BUYER IDENTIFIES & STATES AN OBJECTIVE

Let us look at a store that has decided to feature a new American designer's collection of men's sportswear. The men's sportswear buyer's sales promotion objective might be the following: To emphasize to customers that this store has the very latest and largest assortment of this designer's fashions (and in fact has a special department featuring the designer collection). How could the buyer implement such a promotion objective? Since the specific segment of the store's market is not indicated, how is the medium selected that would best carry such a message? Is the buyer assuming that the designer's style is unknown to all or to most of the customers who will receive the message? What manner of measurement will be used to evaluate whether the message has been effective?

Figure 17–1. The selling process presents appeals to the customer's motivations based upon the product's selling points.

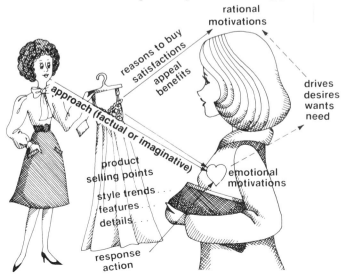

Consider how this objective should have been stated: To develop substantial brand awareness and preference from a market segment who are potential customers for a new designer's styles, but are not as aware of the brand as present customers. This group within the store's segmented market is composed of men, 25 to 35 years old, who are business executives and professional men, earn over $35,000 a year, and live in a metropolitan area. Now that the target market is identified, the selection of media to most effectively reach it can be made. The buyer's intent is incorporated as part of the objective, which makes it easier for the advertising department to research the media coverage for the most effective target group audience and then create a persuasive message. The merchandise manager can now more realistically assess whether such an objective is attainable in terms of the advertising *coverage*, *reach*, and *frequency* necessary to make an impression. What could it mean in additional sales? Is it worth the costs and efforts involved?

THE INNOVATIVE BUYER

The innovative buyer is constantly developing new occasions and special events to stimulate interest in customers which go beyond the traditional (and somewhat worn out Mother's Day, Valentine's Day, Back-to-School) shopping periods. The creative buyer develops merchandise promotions that recognize their customers' new lifestyles and needs to buy. These promotions should feature products and information that can help and inspire customers to enjoy and value what they buy. Retailers should also inform customers, whenever the advertising message permits, why customers should patronize their store. The uniqueness, services, and atmosphere of an exciting store can be incorporated into the advertising copy.

WHAT MOTIVATES CUSTOMERS TO BUY

Any discussions of appeals should be based upon a thorough analysis of what motivates customers to buy. Customers respond in their buying behavior to their own needs, wants, attitudes, or habits. The buyer is interested in why customers act as they do and more so why they buy as they do. In order to present customers with powerful incentives to buy it is necessary to analyze customers' lifestyles and preferences.

No analysis of customer needs or wants can be totally accurate or complete. The behavior of individuals is variable and often unpredictable. Each customer may have different motives from time to time. Reasons to buy must be based upon what merchandisers and buyers feel are the present motivations of their customers. The buyer is involved with the following important considerations involving consumer behavior:

1. There are *rational* as well as *emotional* motives. Rational motives could be economy, dependability, service; while emotional motives could be sexual attraction, status, individuality.
2. More than one motive, sometimes many motives, can be involved in each purchasing decision, with perhaps one or several of more importance than others.
3. Motivation can be classified into three different groups:
   - *Primary Motives* "WHY?"—Why do customers decide to buy a product?
   - *Selective Motives* "WHAT?"—What styles or brand of product is preferred?
   - *Patronage Motives* "WHERE?"—Where or to which store will the customer go to buy?

The consumer's search for identity is one of the basic motivations considered in retail promotion today. Good fashion is no longer limited to the affluent "jet-set." There are customers in every small city and town in the United States who are as much a part of the vast fashion market for retailers as any of the "elegants" portrayed in the pages of the trade and consumer fashion publications.

The retailer does well to think now of a market in terms of individuals, not masses. There are several selective segments within a general market for the store's merchandise and services. The aware retailer realizes that customers more and more have unique motivational systems and buying behavior patterns. There are lucrative markets for products which can be obtained or developed to justify their own special promotional treatment.

AFTER MOTIVES—SELLING POINTS

In devising appeals, the unique attributes and *selling points* of the product, as well as motives, must be considered. The creative buyer analyzes a product before purchasing it for customers.

- What is its present level of acceptance and demand?
- What is its level of quality in terms of materials and workmanship?
- What does it do for the customer?
- How well does it do it?
- How does it compare with the competition?
- What will it sell for?
- Does it have any special identity?

From such an analysis, the buyer should communicate to the customer, those attributes which have the most interest and appeal. These attributes become the important selling points that the copywriter will use to convince customers that this product is different, better, or more desirable. The customer is presented with reasons to buy in terms of satisfaction and benefits derived from the product. The way to develop appeals is to think of customer benefits as well as product features as selling points. "Sell the sizzle—not the steak!" has been a traditional principle in the selling process. Customers buy benefits and satisfactions from products as much as the product itself. A successful appeal is based upon an accurate analysis of which "sizzles" customers most want—and which features of products offer the most promise of "sizzling" satisfaction.

THE BUYER SELECTS APPEALS

Buyers who know their customers, who have stated their specific sales objectives, selected merchandise to advertise, must then select believable reasons to buy—appeals. The appeal is an attempt to link the attributes of merchandise, features of its styles, store services, and special events with the desires and motivations of customers.

The selling process is therefore a "linking" of product selling points to consumer motivations (refer to **Figure 17–1**). The success of this "linking process" is dependent upon the buyer's knowledge of what are the most powerful appeals to the customer. It is the buyer's responsibility to convey these appeals (or "reasons to buy") to a copywriter.

It is the buyer's responsibility to select appeals that reflect benefits known to be desired by their customers. The buyer is the most informed (or should be) of merchandise features and product selling points that will appeal to consumers. The retail copywriter will want the buyer to answer the following questions before starting to write an ad. *Does the merchandise advertised. . .*

- give the customer a feeling of prestige?
- make the customer feel more unique?
- give the customer extra comfort?
- provide the customer with a feeling of security?
- help the customer to be attractive sexually?
- lighten the customer's work load?
- make the customer feel like an expert bargain hunter?
- give the customer an inner concept of being a fashion leader?
- protect the customer's welfare or good health?

Good advertising copy is developed from such accurate information provided by buyers who know their customers' wants and needs—and who understand consumer behavior.

WHO DOES THE BUYER WORK WITH?

The operating divisions of the typical retailer will vary in structure and activity determined by the size and organization of the store. The sales promotion function in a small store is the responsibility of the owner who may do the planning and merchandising of sales promotion with several other key people, such as buyers and senior salespeople. This group may plan sales promotion activities, buy the merchandise, operate the store, and also trim windows and interior displays, with the help of salespeople or stock people. The owner and this "promotion committee" will select merchandise for advertising and display based upon sales objectives and themes which have been previously adopted. The larger retail organization relies on a sales promotion division organized into individual departments of promotion specialists who concentrate on the job of communicating with customers.

The Sales Promotion Director

The executive who supervises the entire sales promotion effort is usually called a *sales promotion director,* and sometimes "publicity director" is used (but this is a misnomer by our definition). The sales promotion director's responsibility is to generate and coordinate all promotional activities of the store, and to supervise the activities of the department managers and the staffs of the advertising department, display departments (window and interior), publicity departments (product and corporate), and special events department. Most of the fashion buyers' sales promotional involvement will be in the advertising activity. The following are job descriptions of the personnel of a typical retail advertising department.

The Advertising Manager

Most large stores are involved in different forms of advertising in a variety of media—newspapers, magazines, radio, television, direct mail. The advertising manager is responsible for the implementation and effectiveness of the coordinated advertising effort, described in the advertising plan, which is derived from the master promotion plan of the store. The advertising department is staffed as follows:

COPYWRITERS These are the advertising writers who are skilled in creating headlines and copy for the store's advertisements, radio and television commercials, and direct mail. Copywriters must know the store and its customers intimately in order to present merchandise in a stimulating and action-compelling style. The copy must reflect the buyer's reasons for buying the product for their customers, as well as the personality and policies of the store itself.

COPY CHIEF When an advertising department is large enough to employ many copywriters, a copy chief supervises and coordinates their work. The copy chief works with the sales promotion director, art director, and advertising manager to develop advertising and promotion formats and styles which express the store's image and philosophies.

ART DIRECTOR The art director coordinates his efforts with the sales promotion director and advertising manager to visualize merchandising and sales objectives in advertising and promotion. The art department is staffed with layout artists, fashion artists, illustrators and photographers—all supervised by the art director. The art director has the responsibility for the advertisement's physical appearance, its design, and its effectiveness in visually interpreting the sales message contained in the copy.

LAYOUT ARTISTS Layout artists design the ad, and arrange its elements of copy and art. They are skilled in graphics who use the techniques of visualization and layout to give the ads eye-appeal and sales appeal.

FASHION ARTISTS, ILLUSTRATORS, AND PHOTOGRAPHERS Artists, illustrators, or photographers confer with layout artists, copywriters, buyers and department managers to determine what are the important product selling points and fashion themes which should be emphasized in their finished drawings, illustrations or photographs. Layout artists, fashion artists, illustrators and photographers in a large store are usually supervised by an art director.

ADVERTISING PRODUCTION DEPARTMENT The advertising production manager and staff are involved in the process by which an advertisement is prepared for printing. The department is involved in the "pasting-up" on art board of copy and art as designated by the layout.

The advertising production department specifies pre-selected typefaces for the headlines and body copy. These are set in typography which is identified with the store. The drawings and/or photographs are sized and prepared for the particular printing process involved. The completed paste-up (or *mechanical*) contains all elements of copy, art, logos, and graphics designated by the layout.

The production department has the responsibility for effective translation of copy and art into print. The copy must be converted into typography (type), and the art into photo engravings, or whatever other vehicle is needed for the particular printing process involved. Advertising production is usually under the supervision of the art director and the direction of the advertising production manager. The art director and the production manager are skilled judges of design, proportion, color, and reproduction.

THE ELEMENTS & STRUCTURE OF
A PRINT ADVERTISEMENT

The fashion buyer's participation in the planning and creation of advertising will depend upon the type of store—its policy and its selection of media. The buyer might have some involvement with magazine, radio, television and direct-mail advertising. But the most likely involvement —and the most significant at the present time—would be in newspaper advertising.

The key elements of a newspaper ad (or any other printed advertising: magazine, direct mail) are described in the discussion which follows: What makes an ad? To some it is "salesmanship in print." The B. Altman ad contains *copy* which sounds like *personal selling.* It is personal—and it demonstrates along with the artwork a knowledge of the customer to whom it is directed.

The key elements in a print ad are: *copy, art* (photographs or illustrations), and *white* space.

B. Altman's copy in this newspaper ad is chatty and personal. It says that B. Altman is prepared to give fashion information and advice to its customers. The layout, art, and typography are uniquely suited to the copy style.

Copy

All print advertisements begin with white space, the size of which is determined by the dimensions of the ad. The first element that is considered for this space is *copy.* Copy is the means by which the advertiser's selling objectives are articulated to the reader. It is what the potential customer reads, and it includes: headline, subheadline (subhead), body copy (or text), the advertiser's signature, logo (logotype), and slogan.

Regardless of the specific objectives of an ad, its ultimate purpose is to stimulate sales. The copywriter's job is to create the right combination of words that will attract the reader's *attention;* arouse his *interest* to read more; create the *desire* for the product; and stimulate *action* to buy. The selling process (*AIDA**) is evident here, as it will be in other sales promotion activities.

Customers are exposed to great variations in copy in newspapers and magazines. Some copy may tempt a customer to take immediate action and other copy may fail—even when the customer is a good prospect for this product. Why does one piece of copy sell—while another does not register at all?

If we could answer this question there would be no need for investigating customer wants and needs through copy research and testing. Writing copy is a unique skill which is developed by those who study fundamental facts about their customers and the product they are selling. It is the buyer's responsibility to provide copywriters with accurate information about customer motivations-to-buy, product appeals, and approaches. The copywriter should be familiar with advertising media characteristics, and the techniques of layout and illustration that make the copy come alive. The copywriter should have a visual concept of his words which will enable him to work with an art director to produce the most emphatic visual/verbal message. Certainly, it is obvious that the buyer's role as a resource for appeals and selling points is vital to the creative connection needed to produce a winning ad.

The keynote for all copy today is believability. The copywriter must have compelling style to be seen and read—but believability sells. Cleverness in fashion advertising is admired by many readers, and generally enjoyed by members of the advertising fraternity, but "it's not creative unless it sells."

Art

In advertising, "one picture is *not* always worth a thousand words." But the inclusion of compelling *art* (photograph and illustration) in an ad

---

*AIDA is a mnemonic used to describe *effective selling procedure.* The steps are: *A* —attracting attention; *I*—arousing interest; *D*—creating desire; *A*—stimulating action. In personal selling we can add *S*—insuring satisfaction.

can be vital in determining its effectiveness. An effective photo or illustration helps to select the audience for an advertisement. It assists the copy to portray how satisfactions are realized and problems solved by using a product. Illustrations are imperative for recognition at the point-of-sale.

As a result of television, movies, tabloid newspapers, photo magazines, and picture books, customers have become picture-conscious. People want to see. Today, the camera goes everywhere to see for us.

However, the visual value of an advertisement ought not be over-rated. Only those ads that are seen and read are truly effective. It is most unusual for anything but the simplest sales message to be carried by a picture alone. Surely the picture can attract attention, but it is the information supplied, based on customer motivation, that sells.

The most effective ads use illustrations and photography which fit the sales objective. A picture that can attract the eye, set a mood and then "bring the message home" is helping to sell.

The experienced art director knows the types of illustration style and subject that will attract specific audiences. It is his job to translate the copy into informative visualization that shows how merchandise is used to satisfy a customer's wants. Importantly, a good illustration can show what a product will do for a reader in his own lifestyle. The two major types of art used in fashion advertising are *illustrations* and *photography*.

FASHION ILLUSTRATION AND FASHION PHOTOGRAPHY There are disadvantages as well as advantages to photography and illustration in fashion advertisements. The printing methods and paper used in newspapers generally are inferior to those in magazines. This is why photographs do not reproduce as well in newspapers as they do in slick magazines. So, some retailers will use fashion illustrations in newspapers, and photographs in magazines. Recently, there have been improvements and changes* in printing production methods used by newspapers which have facilitated an overwhelming increase in the use of fashion photography.

But there is another factor. Photography may not be as "kind" to merchandise as an artist's interpretation. The cost of high quality, dramatic photography—plus model fees—are prohibitive to many smaller retailers. Yet photography has a realism and news interest that are most desirable. And the dramatic true-to-life impact of quality photography is a mainstay in national advertising done by fashion producers and manufacturers.

---

*The changeover to offset lithography from letterpress printing has resulted in a wider use of photography and color in newspapers.

Illustrations are characterized as being either *pictorial* or *symbolic.* *Pictorial,* or descriptive illustration, portrays merchandise in true-to-life form so customers can see how a product looks and may be used. When this is accomplished by clear, persuasive copy, customers can decide to purchase by merely seeing and reading the advertisement. In ads that seek immediate sales, the pictorial illustration is most important.

Symbolic, or decorative illustration, is fundamentally impressionistic. It seeks to create a mood or atmosphere. It may suggest the primary nature of the merchandise, but it leaves the details to the reader's imagination. Symbolic illustration also may be so abstract that it only hints at some feature of the product or its derivation.

White Space

When one decides to run an advertisement, one of the first decisions to make is: how much? What is purchased from an advertising medium for an ad is the blank space which is considered as its basic physical element. The division of this space will be a determining factor in its being noticed and read. The space in the advertisement which is unoccupied by copy or art gives emphasis and contrast to the design. We refer to this as the *white space* in the advertisement. Dividing white space is accomplished by the particular arrangement of copy and art elements within the dimensions of an ad. The working diagram of this arrangement is called *layout.**

Layout

Layout consists of the arrangements of the physical elements of copy, art, and white space within the boundaries of an advertisement. The function of a layout is to provide a blueprint in which the elements are placed and sized. Layout can help the art and copy do their selling job more effectively in the following ways:

DISTINCTIVENESS Through techniques which involve unique uses of white space, visuals, perspective, color, proportion, and balance, the layout can give advertising an identity that is recognized by the customer. The advertisement that pleases the reader by virtue of its attractive design is more likely to be read.

GAZE MOTION The arrangement of elements in an ad can guide the eye by offering a visual path for it to follow. This helps assure that important elements are noticed and read.

---

*In the case of direct-mail advertisements, the layout is usually worked on a blank dummy of the circular, booklet, pages of catalogue, etc.

EMPHASIS Layout can arrange elements so that some are emphasized over others. By attracting added attention to certain parts of copy, it is possible to present a stronger appeal to the customer.

BALANCE An attribute of good design is balanced structure. Good design has a stability which makes it attractive to look at. The layout artist attempts to balance various sizes and shapes of copy and art to achieve clarity, harmony and unity in the design. Balance in a layout means that all the segments of an ad have the same characteristics of power or weight. Elements of art and copy are arranged to attain balance. The power or weight of an element is determined by its size, shape, intensity or color. From an optical viewpoint an ad is divided at a point about five-eighths of the way up the page. It is this optical center which the eye invariably chooses on a printed page. When copy and art elements are symmetrically arranged in equal weight on both sides of the horizontal, vertical and diagonal dividing lines of an ad it is in *formal* balance. When the arrangement is asymmetrical the ad is in *informal* balance. Formal balance, as the term implies, is more static to the eye. Informal balance has more gaze motion and presents a more dynamic visual effect.

THE ADVERTISING PLAN

An advertising plan* is a schedule for a prescribed period of time, from a year to a week, of the advertising that a store intends to employ in order to attract business. Its format is usually that of a planning calendar with months, weeks and days designed to accommodate the necessary information. The advertising plan is formulated after the sales promotion appropriation and the sales promotion plan have been determined. It contains the following information:

1. Dates on which advertisements will run.
2. Divisions, departments, merchandise, services or ideas which will be advertised.
3. In the case of retailers: Estimated sales in dollars of merchandise featured in product ads.
4. Media to be used.
5. Amount of space to be used in each medium.
6. Cost of space in dollars, and as a percentage of sales.

*Refer to previous discussion of *Sales Promotion Planning Chart* in Chapter 16.

The advertising plan should be flexible to permit revision upward or downward if necessary, should sales increase or decrease beyond expectation.

Types of Advertising Plans

The different types of plans used by fashion retailers are as varied as the different types of retail organizations that presently exist. For purposes of clarity and simplicity, we will discuss advertising plans that have common characteristics regardless of the size or type of retail firm. In other words, the following methods of developing advertising plans are generally similar for most retailers. We shall consider two types of advertising plans.

THE WHOLE-STORE PLAN The planning of advertising is designed to consider objectives of the "whole store" as well as the individual divisions or departments of the store. When the objectives of the whole store are being discussed by store management there is no attempt to include individual divisional or departmental breakdowns. The whole-store plan is viewed as a basis for the development of detailed divisional plans later on. The whole-store plan:

1. establishes the objectives for the store for the period being planned;
2. establishes the advertising allocations for this period;
3. outlines the major selling events which may include all or several divisions and their departments.

THE DIVISIONAL/DEPARTMENTAL PLAN After store management has formulated the whole-store plan, they submit to divisional merchandise managers plans which are outlines for advertising in various media (newspapers, direct mail, radio, etc.). Each outline will indicate: 1) the advertising budget for each class of media that the division is granted to aid in reaching its sales goals for the period; 2) the particular selling events planned by the store in which this division is expected to participate. As each merchandise manager receives these budgets he uses the information to plan in detail the events which his departments will undertake for the period. These plans detail specifically:

1. the types of merchandise to be featured;
2. types of promotion;
3. price lines and conditions of sale;
4. preferred medium;
5. timing.

Thus the individual divisional/departmental plans for advertising grow out of the whole-store plan.

The sales promotion director and advertising manager receive the individual plans and coordinate these into a master advertising schedule for the entire store.

THE BUYER'S ROLE IN THE CREATION OF A NEWSPAPER AD

From *advertising plan* to *printing production,* the fashion buyer is (or should be) involved in the initiation and execution of fashion advertising. The newspaper ad, especially, is a vital medium of communication between the buyer, her store, and the customer.

How is a newspaper advertisement born? What are the various stages in its creation? Who decides what is to be advertised, when, where and how much for the advertisement? We will illustrate this entire procedure by tracing the life history of a newspaper ad from advertising plan to production.

Let's illustrate the buyer's role in all of this by examining the procedure that initiates and produces a typical retail newspaper ad (**Figure 17–3**).

Buyer's Plan for Advertising

A store buyer will work with the merchandise manager and the advertising manager to develop several weeks in advance a monthly plan for advertising. We referred to this previously as the divisional or department plan. This plan will include descriptions of ads to be run; items to be featured; prices; estimated dollar sales of the advertised merchandise; the size and cost of the ad, the type of medium to be used, and the day of publication. After the merchandise manager has coordinated the individual department plans, the divisional plan is submitted to the sales promotion director and advertising manager for approval and integration into a store advertising schedule.

Buyer's Information Sheet

The buyer knows of an ad that is coming up by referring to the approved advertising schedule, usually a week to ten days before publication. The buyer then fills out a Buyer's Information Sheet.* It is essential that information for product advertising originate with the buyer—the buyer knows the needs and wants of his customers better than anyone. The

---

*Also known as: Advertising Request Form or Advertising Copy Information.

buyer of fashion merchandise should know the product's selling points and should be best equipped to tell customers what satisfactions they will derive from the purchase of these products. A buyer has the responsibility for selling merchandise quickly, and at a profit. The buyer should be the most concerned with the creation of an effective ad.

The Buyer's Information Sheet, in addition to necessary factual information, should contain all of the aforementioned reasons for offering the merchandise, and most important the customer's reasons for wanting the styles involved. If a buyer neglects to include sufficient information of this nature, copywriters may not bother to "dig," but will use whatever facts are available. This type of copy is often written by "formula" and lacks the customer's point-of-view. It may not accomplish sales objectives. **Figure 17–2** is a typical Buyer's Information Sheet that is used by buyers in a major department store.

The Comparison Office

The Buyer's Information Sheet in many stores is made out in triplicate. The buyer keeps the third copy. He sends the original form to his divisional merchandise manager for authorization. The original and second copy are sent to the comparison shopping office along with samples of the merchandise. This is part of the system to ensure comparative shopping in competitive stores of the to-be-advertised merchandise. The original copy is sent to the advertising department after the comparison office has verified that the merchandise has been, or will be shopped before publication of the ad.

Figure 17–2. Typical Buyer's Information for Advertising Form.

ADVERTISING REQUEST

Dept. # | Ad # (for Adv. use)

Page ____ of ____

ART WORK / PHOTOGRAPHY

Is merchandise in Loan Room — YES / NO

Do not request new art before checking if old art is available.

# of Illust.	# of New	# of Old

Date and medium in which old art last ran. Attach proof.

DATE	MEDIUM

Indicate specific item(s) to be illustrated, style #, model #, etc.:

MEDIA INFORMATION

Medium	Date	Size

If pickup, attach tear sheet.

STORES COVERED BY AD

Store	Full Asst.	Partial Asst.
ALL		
L		
NC		
GI		
C		
B		
CB		

If partial asst. indicate below which items at which stores. If not available at store, mark NA

FOR VENDOR PAID ADS

Other requirements:

If unusual vendor requirements, attach contract or spec. sheet.

COPY INFORMATION: GIVE ALL FACTS CUSTOMER NEEDS TO PURCHASE.

TYPE OF AD (check one) — Z ☐ Sale — VI ☐ Regular Price Volume Response — DI ☐ Regular Price Institutional

Mail Orders Filled ☐ Phone Orders Filled ☐ Use Coupon in Ad ☐ Use Mfgrs. Name ☐

Merchandise Description. Be specific, list each item. Asterisk items to be featured.	Style # (* if to be used in ad)	Colors, sizes, finishes, fiber content, dimensions, other pertinent information.	Quote phrase (if any)	Quote Price	Current Price	Advertised Price

What copy approach should be used?

What emphasis in illustration(s)?

Customer benefits of item(s). Why should customer buy items at R&S? Be concise. Bullet info. when possible.

Delivery or handling charge?

The above merchandise and pricing information conforms to R&S advertising policy and Federal and local regulations.

Buyer	Adm. or VP	Adv. (If. Req.)	Comparative Claims Rep.

Putting the Ad "In Work"

The advertising manager checks the form against the advertising schedule and puts the advertisement into production. The ad manager begins by conferring with the copy chief and art director to determine the most effective manner of presenting the sales message. The discussion revolves around information supplied by the buyer and derived from examination of the merchandise itself, and continues until an exchange of viewpoints and suggestions produces ideas for copy, layout, and art. The merchandise manager and the buyer are often participants in such planning discussions. In many stores, the advertising manager will do rough preliminary layouts to indicate to the layout artists, several ideas for the ad. These layouts may include headline and text copy suggestions from the copy chief. Now the advertising department staff can put the ad "in work."

Copy

The copywriter receives the approved Buyer's Information Sheet plus the rough layouts and copy suggestions. Copy is the "thinking behind the ad" and is largely responsible for the layout design and art that will be used to interpret it. The sales message to the customer is developed from sales objectives and appeals supplied to the copywriter by the buyer in his Information Sheet. The copywriter has the rough layout, copy suggestions, and the buyer's thinking as ammunition in creating copy for a persuasive advertisement which can be dramatically visualized.

Layout

The final copy with all its components—headline, subhead, text, description, prices, slogans and other repeated details—is sent to the buyer for suggestions and approval. After the necessary revisions and approval are obtained, the copy and rough layout are given to a layout artist who does a finished or comprehensive layout. The layout should visualize what the copy is saying—the art should "work with the copy." The layout indicates very clearly what the actual advertisement will look like. In the comprehensive layout, all copy and art elements are exactly in place. The layout art is drawn to carefully simulate the photographs or illustrations that will be used in the actual ad.

Advertising Production

The advertising manager, who is responsible for the overall quality of the advertisement, checks the comprehensive layout and (depending upon store policy) may show it to the buyer. Once approved, an artist

A . The buyer confers with merchandising manager.

B. Advertisement planning meeting between the buyer, merchandising manager and advertising director.

C. Copywriter develops copy appeals and approaches from buyer's information sheet and merchandise sample.

D. Layouts are started by art department based on copy, buyers information and merchandise.

E . The art department creates illustration and/or photography according to the layout.

F. Advertising productions pastes-up all elements into a mechanical for platemaking printing production.

G. Proofs are checked by art department and the buyer.

H. The customer sees the ad in local newspaper.

Figure 17–3. The evolution of an advertisement.

and/or photographer is assigned to execute the illustrations or photographs, as indicated by the layout.

At the same time, the advertising production staff is working with a duplicate of the layout. They will do a typographical layout to indicate the size and style of type (following styles pre-established for the store), logos, slogans, and repeated elements that will be used in the ad.

Printing Production

The finished illustrations or photography are sent to the buyer for approval. If it is approved the art is "sized" or marked for reduction to fit the layout. Additional instructions are sent to photoengravers as to the manner in which the engravings or "cuts" are to be finished. This is delivered with the copy, layout, and typographical layout to the newspaper for reproduction and first proofs. The newspaper completes the advertising promotion process by preparing the elements of the advertisement for printing production. This is done by first making photoengravings of illustrations or photography. Then, typographers set type according to the typographical layout. The engravings and type are then arranged exactly as in the layout. Then the first proofs of the ad are "pulled" on a proof press.

The newspaper completes the advertising production process by sending these proofs to the store's advertising department. The advertising manager dispatches one copy to the buyer and two other copies to the art and production department. Each is responsible for their respective revisions and corrections of reproduction, placement or content. Once these revisions and corrections are made, corrected proofs are sent back to the newspaper. A new set of revised proofs are pulled and submitted to the store for final approval. The advertisement is now ready for its scheduled publication.

The entire process we have just described could possibly be done in five working days. But this would be a teeth-chattering emergency schedule, not conducive to effective quality. Most stores operate within a 10 to 14 day schedule.

SUMMARY

The primary objective of all fashion advertising and promotion is to increase the sale of fashion merchandise to as many customers as possible. The evaluation of the effectiveness of promotion must include an analysis at the point-of-sale. The fashion buyer has planned and purchased with this result in mind—to sell at a profit what has been bought. The results of promotion should also include the long-range objectives of fashion leadership for the department and the store's image. Everything the fashion buyer says in her advertising and promotion of merchandise should also include references to her store's unique services, the intrinsic value and quality of its merchandise selections, the range and depth of assortments, her on-target knowledge of fashion trends, customer lifestyles, and information for customers on how-to get the most out of her purchases.

It is important to remember how each of the promotion activities work separately and together to communicate with customers. Chapter 18 will continue to discuss and describe in detail the other promotion activities that work with advertising in a promotional mix to attain the "sales and image" objectives of the retail store. The communication mix of the retailer and the subsequent promotional responsibilities of the buyer include much more than newspaper advertising. The previous chapter also discussed other retail advertising such as radio, television, and direct mail. The fashion buyer has a part in the other retail promotion activities: display, publicity, special events, and fashion shows. Special attention is directed to window and interior display which usually ranks second to advertising in importance as a promotional asset for the fashion buyer. The role of the buyer varies in these activities— again depending upon the target market positioning of the store and its sales promotion policies.

18
THE FASHION BUYER &
THE RETAIL PROMOTION MIX

INTRODUCTION

Advertising has been described as the spearhead of the promotional mix of the fashion retailer. Together with publicity it uses mass media to bring customers to the point-of-sale. At this point, the mix of promotion can do its job. Window and interior display, special events, fashion shows and finally personal selling should reinforce the messages that customers have already received.

If advertising and publicity have pre-sold the customer on the store's merchandise and its fashion authority, the other promotion activities will supplement the store's short-range objectives to sell at a profit—and its long-range objectives to add to its fashion image. The fashion buyer and the department manager can add to promotional impact by inspiring and encouraging their salespeople to coordinate the department's personal selling with non-personal selling. Salespeople should know what, how, and when merchandise is being promoted. Merchandise should be ready for customers when they are ready to buy—with information and advice at the point-of-sale.

Overall, the advertising and promotion effort should be considered as both a current expense and as an investment which will return dividends in the long run. The sales promotion appropriation becomes more cost-effective as the cumulative benefits of well-conceived advertising and promotion activities achieve consumer's appreciation and, therefore, patronage.

WHO IS RESPONSIBLE FOR DISPLAYS?

The display responsibility in a retail store is divided between the merchandising and display divisions. Buyers are responsible for the selection of merchandise and themes which will satisfy the objectives of the store's Sales Promotion Plan. They must develop ideas which will sell merchandise and the store to the customer.

The display director for window and departmental (interior) displays reports to the sales promotion director. In larger stores there may be a window display director and an interior display director. The window display director confers with division merchandise managers and the store manager to set policy on assigning windows. The display director designs displays based on merchandise and fashion themes for windows and for designated interior display spaces inside the store. The display director must coordinate all of the store's displays to reflect the store's personality as well as attain sales objectives set by store management, merchandise managers and buyers. Display must sell merchandise and project the store's fashion philosophy. The display director has a staff of window and interior display people who are skilled in all aspects of creating prestige and selling displays. They are trained to design and use display backgrounds, props, materials, and mannequins. They are skilled in the creative techniques of color and lighting.

The display division is responsible for all window mannequins, props, fixtures, materials, and signs. Signs are produced in the store sign shop which is capable of preparing hand-lettered or machine signs, counter cards, banners, placards and posters for columns, elevators, walls, and department areas. The display division is not only responsible for the design of window and interior display. The display director must consider the unity and coordination of window display and store-wide interior display. This includes the walls, columns, ledges, door-ways, elevators and other "free areas" which are designed for storewide display.

In many stores, buyers handle their own department display, calling upon the display department for fixtures and signs. In this case a request is filed for whatever props and signs are required, with the copy for the signs written by the buyer and his assistants. Departmental display, since it is concerned mainly with the arrangement and selling of merchandise, is often executed by experienced salespeople in the department, who have been assigned this responsibility by the buyer. In many stores, the buyer may call upon an *interior* (or departmental) display director and the fashion director to assist in this department display responsibility. For very important promotions, buyers will request special department displays which the display department can plan and execute. This is similar to the procedure used for requesting an advertisement or a window display. In cases where merchandise is loaned to the display division for other than department display, loan slips are used as a receipt for such merchandise. Thus merchandise which is outstanding for more than a prescribed period of time can be recorded and recalled.

THE COST OF DISPLAYS

The costs of display are largely internal, but they are substantial, nevertheless. Display costs are especially high in stores which must rely on self-service selling rather than personalized selling.

As vital as space for display is to the modern retailer, there is a growing problem in the lack of available display space in windows and interiors. There is always competition between stock space, selling space and display space. The vast growth of the quantity and diversity of products and brands which the competitive store must carry is primarily the reason for this. The number of items carried has increased tremendously in the last thirty years, whereas the floor space of the average retail store has not increased substantially.

How are Window Display Costs Determined

Display space is more and more at a premium. In estimating space costs, accounting departments must make a determination as to what a specific window in its location is worth to the store. Store windows are among the most valued areas of space in the store. The importance of window display as a salesperson and traffic builder is universally accepted. Windows that face busy thoroughfares are especially prized. Their share of rent charged is usually higher per square foot than other areas in the store.

The general practice among retailers is to prorate the costs of display. These costs include: the specific rent charge for the window space, together with its proportional share of the costs of display props, fixtures and materials, the salaries of the display director and his staff, and the other variable costs such as lighting and maintenance. The "costs" of window display are charged to each selling department on a previously established proportionate basis. The criteria for "giving a buyer a window" is seldom based solely upon anticipated volume, since the windows are not as flexible a supply of sales promotion as advertising. For example, you can buy extra pages of advertising, but adding on several more windows for peak selling periods is not possible.

THE IMPACT OF RETAIL WINDOW DISPLAY (VISUAL MERCHANDISING)

Display is as powerful a communicator for sales response and fashion prestige as advertising and the other promotion activities. It is much less of a problem to evaluate the response of an ad that has brought customers to the point-of-sale, however, than to evaluate the effectiveness of display on sales. It would be very difficult, for example, to determine whether a window display or the consequence of store traffic from other stimuli resulted in a good sales day in a particular department. There are many variables that may affect customers.

If you compare window display and advertising further, you can see several other common denominators. They have the same fundamental purposes, either (1) to sell merchandise immediately *(selling displays)* or (2) to build a reputation over a longer period *(prestige displays)*. In other words, as in advertising, there are *product* and *institutional* type windows. There are two main types of window displays:

- Selling displays
- Prestige displays

SELLING DISPLAYS Selling displays, like product advertisements, are designed to produce immediate sales by featuring the "right merchandise, at the right time, at the right price."

PRESTIGE OR INSTITUTIONAL DISPLAYS Prestige or institutional displays are designed to impress customers with the leadership and originality of the store rather than to stimulate an immediate purchase. The purpose of prestige windows is to convince customers of the desirability of this store as a place to shop. Prestige displays make their appeal through the newness, the fashion-rightness, the exciting assortments, and the timeliness of the merchandise.

Window displays and advertising must both fight for attention and interest yet register their impressions rapidly and emphatically. In the case of printed advertising we are dealing with two dimensions. In the case of window display we are operating in three dimensions. We could say therefore that some of the principles that make an advertisement effective also make a window display effective.

Display is used as a major promotional activity in a great variety of ways by different stores. Exclusive fashion stores such as Neiman Marcus, I. Magnin, Bergdorf Goodman, Lord and Taylor, and Saks Fifth Avenue rely very heavily on both window and department display to convey their fashion authority and to inform their customers about fashion. We could consider such famous "display avenues" as Fifth Avenue in New York City as a veritable street for "wishfulfillment." Almost at any time of the day or night (as long as the window lighting is on) large groups of window shoppers can be seen taking their display walks. They can be observed in front of store windows dreaming their own inner fashion concepts.

Advantages of Using Window Display As A Separate Activity

Some stores regard window display as an activity separate from other forms of sales promotion. Their thinking, as mentioned before, is that window traffic represents a "circulation" similar to that of advertising and could be regarded as apart from other sales promotion media.

1. The selling productivity of each window can be more accurately evaluated.
2. Merchandise can be featured which is specifically suited to window display.
3. Windows can be kept more timely. For example, on rainy days the displays can feature umbrellas, rain boots, and raincoats.

Advantages of Using Windows in Conjunction With Advertisements

1. The window could make it possible to reach customers who missed seeing the newspaper advertisement.
2. The repetition creates a strong impression on the customer that the store considers the merchandise and ideas featured as especially worthwhile.
3. Buyers have an incentive to develop bigger and more original promotions when they are promised the double-action impact of an ad *and* a window.
4. Many practitioners of sales promotion believe that consistent and repetitive emphasis on important merchandise will produce greater sales. They believe that advertisements and window displays used in combination are much more productive than either might be alone.
5. Some stores will try to duplicate the elements and the appearance of the ad in their window display.

How Often Should Windows Be Changed?

Surveys of retail stores in large cities have revealed that most stores change their window displays once a week. Stores in smaller cities will tend to change windows more often. This is because the store in a small city or town, located in a compact business district, is likely to have its customers pass its windows more than once a week. On the other hand, the metropolitan store located in a large, spread-out business area may not have people passing its windows even once a week. The exception would be those customers who are employed in the vicinity of the store.

Regardless of location, however, each store must determine its own policy on frequency of change. The following questions related to the problems of the specific store could be asked:

1. *What is the nature of the neighborhood location? Is it business or residential?* A store in a residential section would have its windows seen more often by any one customer than a store in a business district.

2. *What type of merchandise does the store carry? What is its "personality" and the nature of its service to customers?* For example, is it necessary for a wallpaper and paint store to change its window display as often as a fashion boutique?

3. *How many people will pass the windows each day?* A store located in a high traffic area might have to change its window displays more often.

What are the Advantages of Frequent Change?

1. Displays can be more timely—tie-in with the most current fashion trends.
2. Customers are exposed to a greater variety of merchandise.
3. Merchandise is less likely to be damaged by soil and fading from the sun. Merchandise left in windows too long can result in expensive markdowns, if the merchandise gets soiled or faded.

Objectives of Window Display

1. *To make fashion statements on styles and trends—To project fashion leadership, prestige, and quality.* Store management establishes display policies which change and rotate windows often enough (forty or more times annually) to present the most current and most appealing fashions.

2. *To make a value/price statement.* Store management sets display policy which will feature most-wanted, top-value fashion plainly price-ticketed.

3. *To supplement and reinforce advertising and other promotion activities.* Advertising and display often work together to make "more than twice the impression" on a customer than either activity could make alone.

4. *To bring merchandise out where it can be seen by customers.* Windows can expose hundreds of fashions which might never be discovered in the department. However, in spite of the tremendous power of window display, fewer windows are planned for in new retail department store construction. The reason for this has been the diminishing prominence of the metropolitan or downtown department store—and the increasing appeal of shopping center, mall, and suburban stores. Some of the large branch stores in the fashionable suburbs have very few windows—because their customers are not as prone to window shop. Furthermore, suburban store construction often employs the *open win-*

dow which has no back and allows a customer to see the whole store as a window display. The suburban customer usually drives to the store and enters it from parking areas. Main entrance windows are often never seen in shopping centers and malls. The metropolitan store is more likely to draw customers from public transportation. These are the window shoppers who stroll from one store to another—taking in an entire "string street" of window displays.

As the cities rebuild their "main streets," we may see more department store window display. Specialty stores must use window display to bring customers in to the point-of-sale. Some of the most dramatic "visual merchandising" is done by specialty stores, who find in this activity they can compete with the larger promotion budgets of department stores.

What are the Different Types of Window Display?

The following types of window display are designed to present merchandise in planned patterns and relationships for specific purposes. In each there is a different merchandising objective.

SERIES DISPLAYS Series displays are those in which several adjoining windows are used to display a common merchandise theme. A series display for a storewide French prêt-à-porter theme could feature: a collection of French designer-label dresses in one window, French leather gloves and handbags in the second, French sportswear in the third, boutique accessories in the fourth, and so on.

RELATED DISPLAYS Related displays are those in which related merchandise is placed in one window: thus they tell a complete merchandise story. For the apparel departments, a related display might be designed around fashion information which indicates that black will be a dominant color for fall coordinates and outfits. One window could thus feature black dresses, black coats, black coordinates and appropriate accessories.

SINGLE-CATEGORY DISPLAYS Some retailers have found that related windows, while attention-compelling, often lack the selling impact of windows which concentrate on only one category of merchandise. In the latter, all attention is directed to a single type of merchandise at one price. The main objection to related displays is that they show so many different items that none get the emphasis and attention which concentration could provide.

CAMPAIGN DISPLAYS Campaign window displays are those in which the same type of merchandise is featured week after week in the same windows. The windows may change, but the merchandise category and keynote keep repeating a single sales message. For example, campaign displays can be effective in establishing a reputation for a particular item, brand or price line through repetition. The success of campaign displays demands that they appear in the same windows each week, and the display design-style followed should have recognizable continuity.

SINGLE-PROMOTION DISPLAYS Single-promotion displays are those in which one major selling event is featured in all or most of the store's windows. Most stores have traditional annual promotions which are important enough to assign all or most of its windows. Under the single-promotion display plan, all windows might be devoted to an annual "fall furniture festival," with displays of many different rooms of furniture and home furnishings.

Open & Closed Windows

A current trend in the design of store fronts is the use of *Open* windows instead of *closed* windows. The open window replaces the conventional closed-in compartment which we see in so many stores. The open or "see-through" windows permit customers passing by to get an unobstructed view of the interior of the store. The open window has been most popular with stores in shopping centers which depend largely on automobile traffic rather than passer-by traffic. The boosters of open windows maintain that customers of shopping centers (except those centers with networks of promenades) arrive with specific purchases in

Open Window.

Closed Window.

mind, leave their cars in nearby parking lots, and then go quickly to previously selected stores. There is no necessity or time for window shopping. Under these circumstances open windows are all that are needed.

The open window has the following advantages:

1. Selling areas are closer to the customer on the sidewalk.
2. An immediate impression of the interior of the store is conveyed to the busy passers-by.
3. Customers can see the activity inside and may be impelled to "join in."
4. The initial construction and subsequent maintenance of open windows is less than closed windows

There may be much to say for the open window in shopping centers that do not have public sidewalks. But many retailers still object to the "see through" window. They feel that the open window has the following disadvantages:

1. It is difficult to emphasize a single item or an idea.
2. It does not permit as dramatic a selling display or prestige presentation as the closed window.
3. It creates a "fishbowl" atmosphere in which customers and the interior of the store are "on view." (Especially disliked by men shopping for themselves.)
4. It reveals the interior of the store when it is empty, and may discourage customers from entering.
5. It gives up the stock space offered by the interior walls of closed windows.

The question of closed versus open windows necessitates the study of the advantages and disadvantages of each type. The type of store and its particular location are the main determinants. If a retailer expects a large volume of passer-by traffic, the closed window probably offers more possibilities for dramatic selling windows. Previously in this chapter mention was made of a third window display alternative—*no* windows.

THE ELEMENTS OF WINDOW DISPLAY

In the two-dimensional advertisement we are dealing with elements of art and copy which we arrange or "layout" into the space available. In window display we are using physical rather than graphic elements, arranging them in three-dimensional space for maximum attention and selling effect. These physical elements are:

- Merchandise
- Functional Props
- Decorative Props
- Structural Props
- Backgrounds
- Display Materials
- Color
- Lighting

MERCHANDISE The merchandise itself, apparel and/or accessories.

FUNCTIONAL PROPS Functional props include mannequins and forms which "wear" apparel, or abstract props or fixtures which hold merchandise.

DECORATIVE PROPS Decorative props are used to establish a mood or setting for merchandise.

STRUCTURAL PROPS Structural props support functional and decorative props, fixtures, mannequins, or other units. Structural props are architectural in design and can change the organization and physical contours of the window.

The elements of a window: merchandising, mannequins, props, signs, display materials.

BACKGROUNDS The back and side walls of the window display can provide the merchandise with a framework that will create an appealing mood or realistic setting which will demonstrate the use of the products. The two basic types of background are:

1. decorative;
2. pictorial.

The *decorative* classification includes all fixed backgrounds, such as wood panels and draperies. It also includes movable backgrounds, screens, and panels. Decorative backgrounds are designed to serve as an ornamental framework for the merchandise. Pictorial backgrounds provide the merchandise with a realistic environment similar to the scenery in the theatre. They suggest when, where, and how merchandise can be enjoyed. This is why many display directors prefer it to the less dynamic decorative background.

DISPLAY MATERIALS A great variety of display materials. . . as wide a selection as creative imagination (and budget) will allow. These are used for floors, walls, decoration, pictorial settings, and atmosphere.

COLOR Colors suggest many different things to people. There are certain responses to color that are generally assumed to be universal. For example, red suggests heat and fire—excitement. Yellow suggests gaiety and the sun. Green is cool and relaxing. Blue is soothing, like the sea and sky. White is usually associated with purity and cleanliness. Black and gray are neutral and are therefore well suited for walls and backgrounds. Other colors seem to blend into these neutrals.

LIGHTING Natural daylight is largely composed of cool blue light, while artificial light is largely warm and yellow. In practice, display directors use yellow light for merchandise that is worn at night. Merchandise for daytime use can be shown under daylight blue lighting. Warm lighting acts to neutralize cool colors and intensifies warm colors. Cool light neutralizes warm colors and intensifies cool colors.

In practice, the effective use of these elements in window display is based upon the same criteria that apply in other sales promotion activities. The customer must be attracted, his interest aroused by merchandise (or ideas about it), and he must be given specific reasons to buy suggested by his wants and needs. The display director must use his creative skills to make display dramatic and attractive. His first responsibility, however, is to fulfill the buyer's and store management's sales objectives. The buyer who can discuss design and elements of display as well as sales objectives, is in a position to obtain more effective results.

How is Balance Used in Window Display?

As an advertising layout, balance is an essential quality of a well-designed display. It involves the arranging of merchandise and props around the optical center of interest in such a way that their weights will balance when they are equally distributed. Symmetrical balance is obtained by placing two objects of the same weight at equal distances from the center. *Informal balance* is obtained by placing heavier units toward the center and lighter ones away from the center. *Formal balance* arranges a large unit in the window's center of interest with the lighter units in harmony with it to provide symmetry.

Formal balance is used when it is desirable to have a dominant point of interest in the display with subordinate elements each having equal attention-power.

Informal balance is used when the units to be displayed vary their attention-power but are arranged in a dynamic balance. The difference in attention-power may be caused by shape, color, or arrangement. Informal balance lends itself to dissimilar units.

To achieve attractive balance in window display, one should also consider proportion. By proportion we mean: (1) the shape or size of one display unit as related to another; (2) the shape or size of the unit as related to the window itself. Windows are most interesting to the eye when space relationships and proportions are varied.

When units of different heights are used in window display, the general practice is to arrange larger units towards the rear of the window with smaller units or those which have intricate detail toward the front.

When Should Signs & Prices Be Used?

DESCRIPTIVE SIGNS Most stores believe that descriptive signs are an essential element to all window displays. Many stores have a policy that no merchandise can be displayed without descriptive signs. Signs can mean as much to a window as copy to an advertisement. A sign can present a merchandise theme, introduce a fashion trend, give the background of a product, tell why it is desirable, why it is an excellent value, and so on. Window signs can be printed or hand-lettered. They must follow the "look" of the entire display, much the same as the typography style in an ad. The sign should be legible and easy to read. The copy should be concise and not attempt to go beyond one important keynote. Too many appeals can confuse the onlooker so that no message gets through. Generally, the principles for advertising copy would also apply in the writing of window signs.

PRICES Except for the "low, low price" promoters, most department and better specialty stores follow a policy of not pricing merchandise in their windows. Stores, which do use prices in windows, control the emphasis that they place on price, by varying the lettering, shape, size, and color of price cards.

A Checklist for Effective Window Display

These guidelines, suggested by the experience of many display directors, are also important for the buyer:

PLANNING Good window display is a product of careful planning and scheduling. The components of an effective window need to be planned in advance with enough time for preparation and installation.

THE MERCHANDISE SHOULD BE IN DEMAND Windows, just as much as advertisements, should feature merchandise in which customers have indicated high interest. What will be most-wanted fashion is usually effective in windows. Merchandise with high impulse to buy will make the windows more productive, and customers will be impressed that the store has the right merchandise at the right time.

TIMELINESS Window displays should be in tune with whatever is current. The display director and the buyer should be alert to all that is happening in their area, in order to capitalize on events of public interest. For example, the opening of the opera season could suggest a theme for evening wear and accessories.

THE POLICY AND IMAGE OF THE STORE SHOULD DETERMINE HOW MUCH MERCHANDISE The right amount of merchandise for a window display is very important. There are no concrete rules concerning the number of items that should be featured. This depends upon the "personality image" and character of the store and what store management wants to say to its customers. The important thing is that the merchandise should demonstrate, in assortment and quality, the basic appeal of the store itself.

MERCHANDISE SHOULD BE SUITABLE FOR WINDOW DISPLAY A window display should not include merchandise that is out of proportion to its setting. Large pieces of furniture, for example, should be placed in a window large enough to enable customers to visualize how it might look in a room. Smaller items, such as fashion accessories, should be displayed in smaller settings, to prevent merchandise from looking lost in a disproportionate large space. Generally, bigger items should be placed further back from the glass and small items should be brought close to the glass so that important details can be examined by customers at comfortable eye-range.

SIMPLICITY Simplicity is a good general rule for all categories of design. Window display is no exception. An overworked, over-cluttered display works against its sales objective because it is not readily understood. The customer does not receive a single, emphatic impression.

LIGHTING Lighting can be a key to effective or ineffective window display. Customers must be able to see merchandise clearly in order for it to arouse their interest and desire to buy. Inaccurately directed lighting creates glare and makes it difficult to see any of the units clearly. Improper distribution of light obscures certain units of display and creates unattractive shadows and too much reflection. If the display people wish to emphasize certain units and de-emphasize others, they can direct lighting accordingly.

CLEANLINESS AND ORDER It goes without saying that the window must be neat and clean. It is surprising how many stores fail in this respect. Cleanliness in display involves more than the merchandise. Mannequins, props, fixtures, walls, flooring, glass and signs must be clean and in good order. Customers are repelled by cracked noses, crooked wigs, and dead insects. Windows should be checked regularly (each day) to spot any imperfections in cleanliness and order.

INTERIOR DISPLAY

More and more buyers now regard interior display as a necessary partner of window display and advertising. Effective interior display can supplement those sales promotion activities which contact customers before they come to the point-of-sale. Interior display can act as a kind of insurance for the effort and expense of advertising and window display activities.

Interior display could be further classified by sales objectives.

- *To present assortments.* An assortment display shows the customer a wide range of merchandise, which can include styles, colors, materials, and prices.
- *To introduce ideas.* Displays that present background information, new uses and care of merchandise, the "romance" of the particular item or its designer, and so on.
- *To suggest related merchandise.* Related merchandise is grouped to promote an associate sale and help the customer visualize how certain items of merchandise will look and act with others.

Many retailers consider window and interior display to be of equal importance. The display departments of some large stores maintain separate interior display staffs and will assign a staff member to each floor or to certain departments. No matter what its size, no store can afford to be without display. The exceptions are some of the new "windowless" buildings which are constructed for stores who emphasize other sales promotion activities and attempt to presell their merchandise with extra-heavy advertising and publicity budgets. Such stores do less in interior display, and their "selling from pipe racks" is incorporated as part of their image to customers. The general trend, however, is in the direction of more and better interior display. Many manufacturers of fashion use their selling showrooms to suggest to the buyer ways of displaying their styles in the department. The excitement of fashion apparel involves all of the senses—with sight and touch high on the list. Effective display allows the customer to see and feel and react to this excitement.

Objectives of Interior Display

1. To help customers *locate merchandise* that they have seen in windows and advertisements.
2. To help salespeople sell merchandise by providing *additional information* and selling points to customers.
3. To *suggest related items* to a customer and help salespeople build a larger sale.
4. To give each department an opportunity to *bring its merchandise out* where customers can see it, sometimes providing the only sales promotion activity other than personal selling.
5. To provide the store with a new *personality* for seasonal and storewide events. This can be done throughout the store or in separate departments. The innovative buyer can help develop new looks and personality for the department, which the display director and the carpenter shop can design and build.

What are the Different Types of Interior Display?

Most buyers find that their interior display problems are as individual as the character and physical facilities of their department. Store management should make decisions concerning a coordinated interior store design, and also provide means whereby each department can fit into this design with its own merchandise assortments and personality.

Most interior display can be classified as follows:

- Showcase displays
- Counter displays
- Environment displays
- Wall, column, ledge, aisle and island displays

This interior display featuring Adolfo's designs (left) for men makes use of interesting functional and decorative props. Burdine's adds to its impact with mounted tearsheets featuring the merchandise "as seen in *Gentlemen's Quarterly (GQ)*." Serendipity restaurant/boutique (top), New York, blends unusual merchandise with one-of-a-find objects for ever-present interior displays which are all for sale!

As previously discussed in "Who is Responsible for Display," the buyer can work with the display director to determine which kind of interior display will be most effective for his merchandise and department. The buyer should consider the department's space and traffic patterns and decide what are the sales objectives of the department's display. Interior display should be developed from the qualities of the merchandise itself as well as the look which the buyer wants for the department.

SHOWCASE DISPLAYS There are several kinds of showcase displays, all characterized by their degree of accessibility to the customer.

- *Sides of selling cases*—where merchandise can be seen through the glass.
- *Glassed-in wall cases*—behind the counter where stock is kept, but where merchandise is also visible.
- *Shadow boxes*—above and behind the selling counter in open, recessed areas
- *Interior windows*—usually built into spaces alongside doorways, elevator banks, escalators, and staircases.

COUNTER DISPLAYS A display on a selling counter must be limited because of the danger that it might interfere with personal selling and obscure other merchandise which customers should see. There are other items beneath glass counters in cases that counter displays should not hide. Counter displays are important and can be effective in helping salespeople to illustrate and convince customers of selling points necessary to create the desire to buy.

Interior and department display: (A) Shadow box. (B) Floor fixture. (C) Gondola. (D) Counter display. (E) Case. (F) Floor case. (G) Counter case.

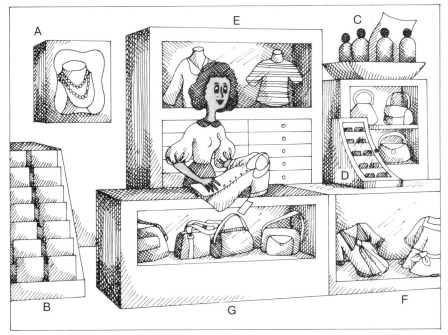

ENVIRONMENT DISPLAYS This type of display is basically different from the typical selling display. Of course, the purpose of both is to sell, but the approach is different. In the environment display, merchandise is placed in a realistic, life-size setting, which helps customers to imagine the satisfactions that they could obtain from owning it. Furniture, appliances, rooms, and even houses are featured in environment displays.

MISCELLANEOUS DISPLAYS There are several other miscellaneous interior display techniques that stores use as their space and facilities allow.

- *Walls, columns,* and *ledge space* can be utilized as display areas. Substantial amounts of unused wall and ledge space can be developed into effective and attractive store and departmental displays.
- *Island displays,* like wall displays, can be used to stir areas of floor space which might otherwise be idle. Every store can find certain areas where traffic is light enough to permit free-standing display units. When these are placed at the end of an aisle, which comes to a dead-end, they are called *aisle displays.*

Who Uses Interior Signs & Price Cards?

The character of the store will largely determine whether interior signs and price cards should be used. Our previous discussion on signs for window display generally applies to interior display. Except for a few exclusive specialty stores, most stores use interior signs and price cards. The variety of signs used by stores include the following:

- Counter signs
- Hanging signs
- Banners and flags
- Elevator cards
- Posters
- Easels

PUBLICITY

Publicity has been defined as an "unsponsored" and non-paid message —verbal or written—in a public information medium, about a company, its products, policies, personnel, activities or services. It is a sales promotion activity.

Any discussion of publicity invariably includes two other activities which are incorrectly used as synonyms for publicity and vice versa. These are public relations and advertising. The retailer and buyer should understand that publicity, retail public relations, and advertising are related, but the differences between them are very fundamental. The following analysis indicates these differences and relationships.

Publicity can result either from special events or fashion shows which are deliberately created by the store, or from an alert coverage of a fashion event which is of interest to the store's customers. The practice of retail publicity should not, however, rely on accidental fashion happenings. The publicity director together with the fashion office, merchandise managers, and buyers should plan fashion events that can result in news and publicity.

Unlike advertising, publicity cannot be purchased or controlled. Where, when, and how the message appears cannot be directed by the publicity director. The director's only "control" is in suggesting and informing fashion and business editors of the happening of store news that would be of interest to the medium's readers. The retail publicity director who uses a professional approach, and submits news of genuine value to a publication's readers, has the best chance to get his message in the editorial matter of a publication or in the programming of radio and television.

Created or planned publicity is used or not used, subject to the judgment of the editor or columnist who receives the material. Where and how it is used—in a column—in a feature story—or as a separate news story—is the decision of publication editors.

For example, the *same* publicity material could be sent to several newspapers and magazines. It might be treated in a very different way in each one. It could be developed as a feature story in a fashion magazine, as a small news article in the fashion section of another, and be omitted from others. The distinction in any publication between editorial matter and advertising (or as in radio or television, programming and commercials) is a most important one. Editorial matter consists of general news, feature pages, special sections, and columns which are written and supervised by news editors, fashion editors, business editors, etc. Advertising is a paid message from any business or individual who cares to purchase the space. As long as an advertiser can pay for his ad, and comply with the acceptability standards of the publication, he can have his advertisement published. If store management knows of, or develops an interesting "news angle" or news story about their store, its products, policies or personnel—it can be sent as a *press release* to editors for their consideration. Editors may include the story in the publication if they feel it is of genuine interest to their readers. An editor's job depends on sustained readership which results in circulation.

Public relations is *not* sales promotion. A retailer may employ a public relations campaign in a long-range program to create favorable public opinion about his store. This would be a sustained effort to serve as a guideline for all communications with the store's customers, vendors, employees and the community. As such, public relations policy helps set certain criteria for publicity, advertising and promotion, and community relations.

A retailer's public relations program is concerned with everything that the store does which will influence public thinking and attitudes. Recall the Bloomingdale's case in the previous chapter.

Publicity, advertising, and other sales promotion activities can be an important part of the retailer's public relations program. Therefore publicity is a communications element of public relations.

Advertising can also be a contributor to a public relations program. In many firms where advertising is employed as the major contact with the customer public, it may constitute most of the public relations program. Advertising involves the sending of sales messages through various media. The space for these messages is purchased from various publications such as newspapers and magazines; time is purchased from radio and television stations; postage is purchased for direct mail. Advertising is generally designed to produce sales and develop images. It is characterized mainly by the fact that it is paid for (sponsored), and therefore directly controlled by the advertiser. The advertiser selects the medium and decides when his message will appear. He writes the copy and determines the art and layout. What the advertisement says, and how it looks, is his responsibility and under his direction.

Why is Publicity so Important?

One of the most popular misconceptions in sales promotion practice is that publicity is "free advertising." This is a serious error since the ultimate use of publicity material is not under the control of the interested party. Advertising and publicity are basically different in that advertising is a message from the interested party, and publicity is a message from an information medium about an interested party. Retail publicity and public relations can work to create a receptivity for a store's advertising.

Publicity is a unique form of sales promotion because it involves the planning of a program to get influential columnists, commentators, publications and personalities to say interesting and complimentary things about a store, its personnel, and its activities. It is one thing for customers to read and hear from the store itself just how good it is. But it is very impressive to customers to hear such things from fashion editors and read it in their fashion pages.

Who is Responsible for Publicity?

The responsibility for writing and releasing news for the purposes of fashion publicity is usually left to the store's publicity department. Even the smaller retail organizations have begun to recognize the value of a publicity and special events program in their sales promotion efforts. Larger stores have a special events department and a director of special events. In some stores publicity and special events are combined into one department. The fashion office with its director is usually responsible to the merchandising division, and in some stores to both merchandising and sales promotion. The fashion office does the researching and development of fashion trends, fashion clinics, and fashion shows for both the merchandising and sales promotion divisions. **Figure 18–1** shows the interrelationships of the merchandising, sales promotion, and fashion offices.

Although publicity programming and execution are the responsibility of the publicity department, no retailer could expect to do an effective job without additional help from buyers and merchandise managers. Certain information can only be obtained from those who know the merchandise and their customers most intimately. Buyers, their salespeople and fashion coordinators can contribute to the information and exposure needed by the store's publicity director. For example, buyers help obtain photographs from apparel manufacturers for the publicity department. Buyers may also arrange editorial credits (called "store credits"), for their store, in magazines featuring the fashions which they have bought for their customers.

Fashion directors are very publicity-conscious. They will work with the store publicity department to develop publicity for their own fashion clinics and fashion shows—and also to stimulate publicity for fashion trends which they consider important for their customers.

Figure 18–1. Retail organizational structure showing relationship of sales promotion division and fashion office to merchandising divisions.

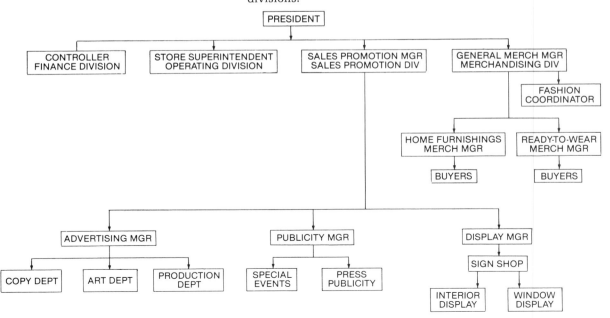

How Do You Get Publicity?

An understanding of what is fashion news and how editors evaluate news for their own publications is most important for the retail publicity director. The trite and obvious "you gotta know the right people" is indeed a misconception on how retail publicity is obtained. Knowing who are the right people to send publicity material to, and maintaining continuous and friendly contact with them, is important. It is essential that the publicity director has a knowledge of the layout and content of the fashion and business pages of newspapers and magazines which reach the store's customers. An analysis of the average newspaper reveals that everything in it is not "news." The newspaper tries to give all of its readers good reasons to read its various sections and departments. Thus, each publication presents a varied menu of news, columns, editorial comment, special features, departments, feature pages, and supplement sections. The publicity director's responsibility is to write for some part of the newspaper's editorial matter. The better acquainted he is with the requirements of the newspaper, or any other medium, the better he can develop his material for the medium's specific use.

What Kind of Fashion Story Gets Into the Media?

Special events in stores which involve customers are particularly good possibilities for publicity. The store's publicity department sends out releases on such events, articles on new fashions, designers, collections, fashion shows and showings, store services, new facilities, personnel developments, contests and other institutional happenings. The store which plans a constant round of promotional events will direct its publicity department to develop and coordinate these activities. The publicity director and special events director may cooperate in elaborate publicity campaigns which can involve specific departments or the entire store. Refer to the whole-store schedule of events for the Bloomingdale's "China" promotion in Chapter 16.

Types of Special Event Publicity

The nature of special event publicity varies with the size and type of the retail organization. Many special events are designed solely for their publicity value, yet still manage to sell merchandise as well. Certain events prove to be so well received that they become traditional on the sales promotion calendar.

SPECIAL MERCHANDISE EVENTS Merchandise events are often developed around imported merchandise or "ethnic fashions." Imports from Europe, Scandinavia, South America, the Middle East, and the Far East have all been central fashion themes for storewide events and

macy's
thanksgiving day parade
Thursday, November 25, 1982

The Macy's Thanksgiving Day Parade is as much of a tradition as it is a special special event. It gets special attention from the media (especially TV) for institutional benefits that far exceed its substantial production costs.

What's 56 years old, 43 blocks long and just a few days a Macy's Thanksgiving Day Parade! Don't miss a minute. From 77th and Central Park West all the way down to Square, our 56th Parade marks the official start of Christmas in New York. The stars! The clowns! The fl and balloons! And of course, Santa's long awaited arrival in New York. Parade hotline: 560-4495. **Come join us on the streets, or watch on NBC-TV, 9 am to noon, Thanksgiving Day.**

Fashion shows are a mix of merchandising and theatre. In this production of men's outerwear by the Men's Fashion Association, New York, the model is playing an important role in dramatizing the product to generate audience response.

merchandise promotions. Other events can feature patriotic, seasonal themes, the fine and performing arts, social and cultural historical eras, and so on.

Merchandise promotions may also include the traditional annual "White Sales" of linens, domestics and bedding which customers have learned to look for every January. Holiday season events—Easter, Thanksgiving and Christmas can be themes for departmental and store-wide promotions (as illustrated by this Macy's Thanksgiving Day Parade ad).

FASHION SHOWS Fashion shows are presented for customer audiences primarily—but they are often used by larger stores to orient, train, and stimulate store personnel. Fashion shows have a fashion mystique all their own. Customers respond strongly to the excitement and drama of a fashion show. The formal or highly structured fashion show is made even more entertaining by integrating real show business—plots, scripts, talent, music, scenery, professional staging, direction and production. Professional fashion models are usually used—but some stores have used employees and customers. A formal fashion show should be presented only where there is a theatre, cafeteria or auditorium with a runway for models and seating capacity for a substantial audience. Some stores do shows in conjunction with leading women's clubs and organizations who use their own members to model. A competent fashion commentator who has speech skills and dramatic ability is an important must for a show. The special features of each exciting fashion should be spotlighted and projected to the audience. A good fashion show can produce good sales, beneficial publicity and long-range favorable public relations.

DEMONSTRATIONS AND EDUCATIONAL EVENTS Stores can promote merchandise as well as develop good public relations through various demonstrations and educational events. For example, gourmet cooking utensils can be sold through a gourmet cooking seminar where customers are taught to "do it the French way." Gourmet cooking utensils, gadgets, knives, and cooking equipment are featured. Education events can stimulate sales of all types of arts and crafts, and various do-it-yourself projects. Educational events such as "New Careers for Women" and "How to Manage Your Money" are an ever increasing part of the store's attempt to develop a "lifestyle" involvement with their customers. Consequently, these demonstrations and educational events do more than sell merchandise—they make new fans for the store.

Many of the demonstrations currently used by stores are presented by manufacturer-trained demonstrators who know how to dramatize the product and its uses. Cosmetics are the most typical department to illustrate such effective retail demonstration. Frequently small trial samples are given to customers which help them decide on a present or future purchase.

The Buyer & The Retail Promotional Mix   **373**

COMMUNITY PROMOTIONS Some of the major retailers have done a substantial promotion job through community events and facilities. Many of these large stores draw customers from outside of their own trading area. As previously discussed, one of the most famous of these traditional community events which gets national attention is the Macy's New York Annual Thanksgiving Day Parade, which is seen in person by hundreds of thousands of New Yorkers and holiday visitors as well as an audience of millions on network television.

Small retailers who have no need for such national exposure have other ways to get involved in the community and generate customer goodwill. They often donate merchandise for raffles and contests which are run by community clubs and religious organizations. They can also contribute a space in their windows and booths in the stores to promote worthwhile community projects.

THE COMMUNITY ROOM Most of the large retailers now have community rooms—especially the full branch stores. The rooms are used for community groups for various meetings and activities. The store in this way can become a center for community action and activity.

CUSTOMER ADVISORY PANELS The many different public relations which stores utilize to get customer feedback says quite a bit about today's retail philosophy, communication, and promotion. Retailers try to *tell* their customers that they "can help us tune in to your needs and desires. You, in turn, will get the very best that America's finest store has to offer." Some stores use a formal system for obtaining customer feedback. They organize customer groups (who are sometimes compensated for their time) into customer advisory panels. These panels are superior to questionnaires inasmuch as they generate a more spontaneous feedback. Customer panels are most costly than questionnaires, but they are generally more informative.

Today's buyer is a purchasing agent for customers who need fashions for very active lives, and individual lifestyles. Today's retail store is a physical facility for many of those activities as well as a center of merchandise distribution. Retail promotion has to tell this story. The customer advisory panel is one method of learning how customers feel about their wants and needs in products and services stores offer.

A FASHION BUYER'S GUIDE FOR PROMOTIONAL PURCHASING

The fashion buyer's role in the third part of the merchandising process (planning, purchasing, and promotion) is to support the promotional objectives of the store with merchandise. Obviously, the planning and purchasing of merchandise is the buyer's major responsibility. The follow-through to *initiate, approve,* and *evaluate* the advertising and promotion of her merchandise and her department is also the buyer's responsibility. The entire process of purchasing with promotion-in-mind involves a series of considerations which we can use to summarize most of what you've read in Part Four of this book.

1. Merchandise and resources should be consistent with the store image.
2. Conditions of sale should be carefully stated in ads. The use of "regular price," "reduced price," "off-price," "special price," "formerly," etc., should be accurately applied. Customers quickly learn which stores are being honest in their advertising.
3. Promotional events should be backed-up with an adequate stock of merchandise. "Delayed delivery" letters to customers are poor public relations.
4. Specification buyers who buy for catalogues and special events should practice the following:
   A. Research the resource—perhaps with a visit to production facilities.
   B. Develop and submit to the resource a thorough list of specifications.
   C. Double-check samples for adherence to specifications and quality control.
5. The buyer should understand the objective of the ad and follow-through to ensure that it is being designed to attain the objective.
6. The buyer should insist on realistic visualization of merchandise. Exaggerated flattery which may be deceptive can produce returns through mail and phone orders.
7. Newspaper ads can be reinforced by window and departmental displays, featuring the advertised items. It is also important to thoroughly brief salespeople on the objectives of the promotion and the selling points of the merchandise.
8. Merchandise which is not selling should not be selected for advertising. Unsuccessful ads should never be repeated (there are no "second chances").
9. New resources should not be used for advertising if comparable merchandise is available from resources with an established quality level and selling rate.
10. Cooperative advertising allowances should be considered as an added incentive to purchasing, but not the primary reason for it.
11. Advertising regular merchandise which is being marked down can reinforce patronage motives. It is good business to give your customers a bargain every so often.
12. Lower prices should not be promoted at the beginning of a season. Customers expect this later on in the season.
13. Off-price promotions should be considered only after examina-

tion of the manufacturer's inventory showing styles, colors, sizes, and quantities.

14. Retail advertising and promotion can be a partnership between a store and the manufacturer. The manufacturer should be made aware that the store's communications affect his relationships with his other dealers as well as the consumer.

15. All promotional orders should specify:
    A. that the order is for an ad, display, etc.;
    B. the date of delivery in no uncertain terms; special conditions and agreed terms.

SUMMARY

Advertising and promotion is a major part of retailing. Effective merchandising requires effective promotional activities. The sales promotion effort must be honest, consistent, and representative of what the store is in terms of its merchandise and services. Every store, naturally, has individual objectives for its promotional activities and what results are expected.

Any evaluation of buyer efficiency would include an analysis of his selling record. Good planning leads to a well-balanced stock. Effective promotions of well-purchased merchandise adds up to *profit* as planned —the "bottom line" of retail operations.

The results of every promotional event are recorded and used as the experience factor for future events. Buyers usually maintain a diary in which the following information is entered:

- Sales volume for each day
- Weather for each day
- Promotional activities (all details such as media, space and time, merchandise featured)
- Any other factors that influenced the merchandising results of that day.

A large part of the buyer's responsibility also includes the important considerations of promotion budgets and promotion costs, which are as important for buyers to know as it is for store management. Merchandising has been thought of as the science (or art?) of buying and selling. If "what is bought must be sold," then the buyer as seller is a *leading* role for all buyers to play.

GLOSSARY

A

ACCESSORIES Fashion apparel that "goes with" or is coordinated with dresses, coats, suits, etc.; includes fine and costume jewelry, neckwear, scarfs, handbags, and small leather goods, millinery, gloves, hosiery, shoes, handkerchiefs, watches, artificial flowers, ribbons.

ACCOMMODATION DESK A centrally located fixture where calls, gift wrapping, and other services are performed for customer convenience.

ACTUAL VALUE OF AN ITEM In event of loss of an insured package, the Post Office will pay only the *actual value* of an item—not the *declared value.*

ADVERTISING Any paid, nonpersonal message by an identified sponsor; appears in media and used to influence sales, services, or the acceptance of ideas by potential buyers.

ADVERTISING AGENCY An organization that renders advertising (and marketing) services to clients.

ADVERTISING BUDGET A plan of advertising expenditures for a specified period: weekly, monthly, seasonally or annually. Generally details by media and by departments or divisions.

ADVERTISING MATRIX (AD MAT) Mold of paper pulp or similar material made by pressing sheet of the substance into metal type or engraving plate. Forms a replica of the original plate (stereotype) for printing process.

AGATE LINE Newspaper advertising unit of measurement—an agate line is one column wide by 1/14th of an inch deep.

ANTICIPATION Paying a bill before it is due, with benefit of extra discount.

APPEAL Motive to which advertising is directed, designed to stimulate action by the audience. Points made in copy to meet customers' needs and objectives, and provide reasons to buy.

AREA Size of store; usually requires additional detailed definition. For example, *total area* would mean gross floor space, including stockroom and non-selling areas, plus sales area; *selling area,* only floor space devoted to selling.

ASSOCIATION OF BUYING OFFICES Organization of New York buying office executives to standardize and unify services available to stores; traditionally the manager of the NRMA merchandise division is ABO executive secretary.

ASSORTMENT PLAN Complete range of merchandise in a category planned to various depths of inventory to meet customer demand.

AUTHORIZING Approval of a charge transaction by credit personnel when the amount of the sale exceeds floor limits or when identification of the customer and account is required.

AUTOMATIC REORDER Reordering staple merchandise on the basis of predetermined minimum quantity; when this minimum is reached, the quantity of the initial order is again purchased.

AVERAGE GROSS SALE Dollar amount of gross sales divided by number of sales transactions or sales-checks which produced the gross sales.

B

BACKUP STOCK Additional merchandise available in warehouse or in forward (in-store) stockroom. Particularly important for runners or best-selling staples.

BALANCE-AND-MIX A complete assortment, in rugs includes accent rugs, broadloom rugs, scatter rugs, Orientals, remnants to satisfy wants, needs, pocketbooks or majority of customers.

BALANCED STOCK Balanced stock and/or assortment makes available what the customers want throughout all price zones or price ranges in proportion to that demand.

BARGAIN BASEMENT Basement or section of a flagship store or branch store that specializes in price lines the "upstairs store" does not carry or of which the "upstairs store" duplicates only the top price lines; the downstairs or basement store emphasizes special values. Also referred to as *budget store* or *downstairs store.*

BASIC STOCKS Items, numbers, or models that must be included in a line of classification. Basic stock is usually staples but non-staple items become basic when, for fashion or fad reasons, they enjoy temporarily increased customer demand. The best rule for basic stock is having what the customers want when they want it.

BEAT LAST YEAR'S FIGURES The unending battle to sell more every day than was sold on the same day a year ago or at least to meet last year's figures and not fall behind.

BEST-SELLER (BEST-RUNNER) Seasonal or year-round or number in a line that sells fast throughout season or year at full markon, that merits continuous promotion in displays, advertising, suggestive selling.

BETTER BUSINESS BUREAU Financed by local media and business interests for purpose of promoting accuracy and honesty in advertising and selling.

BIG TICKET Usually big in physical size and size of price: major appliances, furniture, and other hard goods. Tick-tack-toe system of crossing through squares when item is sold, for read-and-run stock inventory.

B L (BILL OF LADING) Form used by the carrier denoting the consignor, consignee, number and weight of packages, description, shipping charges (sometimes, not always), date, and other information necessary for shipment and receipt of goods into the store.

BLANKET ORDER Pre-season order to meet anticipated needs, placed before production has started; buyer orders against blanket order to meet needs as season arrives and progresses.

BLENDING Two companies consolidate ownership but operate independently. Example: Dayton's and J.L. Hudson's; Carter Hawley-Hale and Neiman-Marcus.

BLIND PRODUCTS Unusual, interesting, intriguing items producing a higher-than-normal markon because of special appeal to customers.

BONUS Additional bonus paid to salespeople for selling slow-moving, pre-season, or higher-priced merchandise, or for a special promotion; sometimes paid by vendor upon approval by store. Also referred to as *P.M.* or *premium money.*

BOOK INVENTORY Amount of retail stock shown to be on hand by a perpetual inventory system wherein sales, markdowns, and discounts are statistically deducted from total purchases to date.

BOUTIQUE An area within a store or an individual shop selling unique merchandise in a unique setting.

BRANCH STORE Owned and operated by the parent or flagship store; generally located in a suburban area under the name of the flagship store.

BRAND A name, term, symbol, design, or a combination of these which is intended to identify the goods or services of the seller and to differentiate them from those of competition.

BUDGET STORE See *bargain basement.*

BUYING SPECIFICATIONS Where store submits definite specifications to manufacturer, rather than selecting from goods already on the market. Private or controlled brands are normally purchased by an individual store or through a RBO on specifications.

BUYING GROUP/BUYING OFFICE/RESIDENT BUYING OFFICE Organization representing group of non-competing stores, formed primarily for servicing stores may be independent, store-owned, or own the stores.

C

CALL SYSTEM Arrangement in some selling departments to give each salesperson, by numerical rotation, an equal opportunity to wait on customers; commonly used in men's clothing departments, major appliances, and furniture.

CALL TAG Tag or form used by delivery driver to call for, and attach to, an article or package to be picked up at customer's address and returned to store.

CARRIER A railroad, trucking firm, airline, express company, bus line, steamship, or river barge company that transports merchandise from vendor to store.

CARRIER (MECHANICAL) Cylinder used to contain saleschecks or media dispatched through pneumatic tube system; carriers are identified by color bands and numbers for type of media and dispatching station.

CARRY OUTS Merchandise carried from store by customer, expediting delivery and saving delivery expense, particularly significant in branch stores. Also called "Take-Withs." Must be forward stock, immediately available.

CASH DISCOUNT Percentage off billed price; concession for paying bills, within time period indicated on invoice. (Example: 2/10 means 2% deductible from bill, if paid within ten days of invoice.) Cash discounts include anticipation; cash discounts are merchandising gains, included in computing gross margin.

CASH RECEIPTS REPORT Form used by salespeople to list cash received from sales of merchandise at end of each day's business; the change fund is first deducted and placed in change fund bag; balance of cash is counted and listed and placed in receipts bag together with the report.

CASH REGISTER BANK FUND Monies given to each salesperson for the purpose of making change (if it is prepared at close of business each day by salesperson; it is a Single-Bank system; if prepared by cashiers, it is a Two-Bank system).

CASHIER METHOD Where customer makes own selection, then takes purchase to cashier for payment and wrapping.

CAVEAT EMPTOR The principle that the seller (manufacturer and/or retailer) cannot be held responsible for the quality of his product unless guaranteed in a warranty. Literally, let the buyer beware.

CENTER CITY The older city located within the original legal geographical area exclusive of suburbs.

CENTRAL BUYING Buying activities of a group of centrally controlled or associated stores; generally for merchandise uniformly carried, where bulk purchases can influence the purchase price.

CENTRAL CONTROL OFFICE Office charged with responsibility for merchandise control system and accurate accumulation of pertinent statistics.

CENTRAL INFORMATION FILE Main data-storage memory in a computer system.

CENTRAL WRAP Area for centralization of excess transactions that cannot be wrapped at floor desks.

CENTRALIZED BUYING All buying done by merchandise staff located in flagship store or buying center, perhaps located in corporate headquarters or warehouse. Central buying increasingly influenced by requests, suggestions, opinions of branch store managers, and their merchandise staffs.

C & F (COST AND FREIGHT) Shipping term indicating seller will pay only freight charges to a destination, not insurance.

CHAIN STORES Two or more stores stocking identical merchandise, owned and merchandised by one individual or one company.

CHECK-OUTS Stations where customers carry self-selected merchandise, pay cashier, and have merchandise wrapped.

CHERRY PICKING Buyer selection of only a few numbers from one vendor's line, other numbers from another line, failing to purchase a complete line or classification of merchandise from one resource (with rapid development of multi-unit stores, cherry picking from large number of resources becomes economically unsound).

CHINESE WALLS Invisible walls separating allied or related departments where salespeople cannot accompany customer to two or more departments to purchase go-with or coordinated merchandise. Example: intimate apparel including foundations, brassieres, lingerie, negligees, and sleepwear.

CHOPPED TICKET Part of price ticket removed from sold merchandise and forwarded to vendor nightly as step in vendor's computerized stock-control for reorders.

C.I.F. (COST, INSURANCE, AND FREIGHT) Shipping term signifying seller will pay all freight charges to destination.

CLASSIC Any style that remains in fashion for a considerable length of time.

CLASSIFICATION All merchandise of given type or use, regardless of style, size, color, model or price (e.g., men's dress shirts).

CLERK WRAP System in which salesperson disposes of entire transaction, including wrappings of "send" merchandise (a semi-clerk wrap is confined to "take-with" transactions).

CLUSTER OF STORES Stores that will produce enough sales volume in a geographical area to bear cost of advertising, central warehousing, and distribution and provide a profitable operation.

C.O.D. (CASH ON DELIVERY) Transaction whereby customer agrees to pay when goods are delivered.

COLLECTION A designer's or manufacturer's group of fashions for a specific season.

COLUMN INCH A print advertising term—one column wide by one column deep.

COMMISSION Percentage of sales paid sales-people as all or part of their remuneration.

COMMUNICATION EFFICIENCY Selection of fast-moving merchandise in immediate customer demand which will immediately bring customers into flagship or branch store.

COMPARISON DEPARTMENT Store department whose function is to compare prices, styles, quality, service, etc., with those of competitors.

COMPETING AGAINST ALL COMERS Policy of a store to meet all competition on quality, quantity, price line, payment terms, selling services, delivery.

CONSIGNEE Shipping term applied to ultimate receiver of goods.

CONSIGNMENT PURCHASE AND DATING Purchase wherein title to merchandise does not pass at time of shipment but at expiration of specified period, when buyer is privileged to return to vendor any unsold goods.

CONSIGNOR Shipping term applied to originator of shipment.

CONSOLIDATED DELIVERY Delivery service of an independent organization which accumulates and delivers packages from various stores.

CONSUMER COOPERATION A retail store owned and directed by its own associated consumer membership.

CONSUMERISM Interest in the consumer's welfare, how honestly and how well the customer is served and informed, how accurate and how adequate that information is, how easily it can be understood.

CONTINGENT Regular on-the-payroll member of sales or sales-supporting personnel or employee called in when needed to work part-time or full-time in whatever department assigned to.

CONTRACT ACCOUNT Customer account with stipulated periodic percent payments.

COOPERATIVE ADVERTISING/DISPLAY Manufacturer, importer, or distributor cooperates (with money) with retailer.

COSTUME JEWELRY Relatively inexpensive jewelry

(versus jewelry of gold, silver, or platinum, generally set with precious stones).

CREDIT CRUNCH A severe tightening of credit influencing both vendors and retailers, due to government efforts to curb spiraling economy.

CREDIT HISTORY CARD Record of customer's account indicating home address, employer, account activity, credit limit, delinquencies, past or present, other miscellaneous credit data.

CROQUI Small, rough sketch from which an illustrative idea or ready-to-wear or home-furnishings number is designed or model developed.

CROSS-SELLING Term applied to salesperson's selling in more than one department.

CUMULATIVE MARKON Percent in dollars, the difference between the delivered cost of merchandise including transportation costs and the cumulative selling prices originally set.

CUSTOMER DEMAND How much merchandise (how many items or how much in dollars at cost or retail prices) customers buy in a stated period of time.

CUT-THROAT COMPETITION Used when low prices on nationally known or nationally advertised products are used as "bait" to draw customers into a store and efforts are made to switch customer to higher-priced full-profit merchandise. (As a rule, assortments of sizes, colors, models, and quantities of bait merchandise are very limited and quantity customer is permitted to purchase is limited.)

CYCLE BILLING Correlation of alphabetical break-downs to specific days of month to facilitate billing of customer's accounts, each breakdown is a cycle and billing for cycle occurs on same day each month.

D

DATING "Deadline" for paying for goods, to allow reasonable grace period for resale.

DEEP-STOCKS OF KEY ITEMS Popular merchandise carried in large quantities, in many sizes and colors: but variety of styles, patterns, types carried strictly limited to best-sellers.

DELIVERY EXPENSES Percent of sales for cost of delivery, including expenses of packing, wrapping, delivering of merchandise to customer, picking up customer returns, postage, parcel post, and express charges.

DEMOGRAPHICS Vital statistics of population (income, age, education, etc.).

DEMONSTRATION SALE Presented by vendor's representatives—territorial sales representatives, demonstrators, or staff sales trainer, or by member of department's sales personnel, to arm departmental staff with facts, selling points and show better methods of presenting advantages, use, and care of a product.

DEMURRAGE Detention of freight car or vessel beyond time allowed for loading or unloading, and subsequent charges for detention.

DEPARTMENTALIZING Organization of related merchandise and subsequent identification as a department.

DEPARTMENT STORE BASE Where resource works closely with a department store not only in production volume sales in the flagship and branch stores but also to influence other stores in metropolitan area in purchasing and promoting the resources item, line, or brand.

DEPARTMENT STORE GROUP Individual stores that work cooperatively with members of Associated Merchandising Corporation, Allied Store Corporation, or May Department Stores, as examples.

DIRECT AUTHORIZATION Salesperson obtains credit authorization before releasing "send" merchandise to delivery (in contrast to draw back system of authorization).

DIRECT MAIL Use of the mails to make announcements, sell merchandise, sell services, sell the store, its divisions, its departments, its character, and its ways of doing business. Personal approach to selective audiences.

DIRECT SELLING Vendor selling direct to ultimate consumer, by-passing wholesalers and retailers.

DISCOUNT MERCHANDISING Low-margin retailing, generally self service, selling goods with less than normal mark up (at less than prices usually offered by conventional retailers).

DISCOUNT STORE Store operating on lower overall margin than conventional store selling same type of merchandise; generally offers less service.

DISPLAY (Visual Merchandising) Nonpersonal physical presentation of merchandise or ideas. Can be window, exterior, interior, or remote.

DISPLAY MANAGER Supervises all window and interior displays, signs, and props.

DISPLAY MATERIAL Free display material, including window and counter exhibits, supplied to store by vendor, now considered a form of advertising allowance.

DISSECTION A specific group of merchandise within a department for purposes of control by dollar volume.

DISTRESS MERCHANDISE Merchandise which, for any reason, must be sold at a sacrifice (at either wholesale or retail level).

DOCK AREA Location for unloading incoming merchandise; generally adjacent to receiving and marking area.

DOLLAR CONTROL Control of stock markdowns, markons, markups, and sales in terms of dollars rather than by units of percentage.

DOLLAR SALES PER SQUARE FOOT Departmental results are derived by dividing each department's net sales by the average number of square feet of selling space occupied by the department. Increasing sales per square feet important objective.

DOMESTICS Term originally applied to yard goods from which sheets, pillow cases, towels, etc., were cut; now broadly encompasses finished products in these classifications.

DOOR-TO-DOOR Shipping term denoting consignment of goods to be picked up at vendor's place of business and delivered directly to store's place of business.

D.O.S. (DEPARTMENT OPERATING STATEMENT) Monthly report of departments operation, including sales, stock on hand, markdown gross margin, expenses all other pertinent factors.

DOUBLE TRUCK Two-page advertisement utilizing "gutter" space to make advertisement appear as a unit, as opposed to two facing pages.

DOWNTOWN OPERATION Flagship or parent store's sales volume and profit contribution.

DROP SHIP When buyer orders, merchandise shipped directly to specific branch store, it is noted on order to "drop ship to _____ store." This procedure saves time and expense of vendor's shipping to central warehouse, store's trans-shipping to designated branch; it also means branch store will not be "out" for a long period; sometimes it is more expensive in terms of freight cost.

E

E.D.P./ELECTRONIC DATA PROCESSING Work done or expected to be done by a computer.

EMPLOYEE DISCOUNT Discount given employees on purchase of merchandise for their own use.

ENCLOSED MALL Shopping center where all stores face enclosed central mall with year-round air conditioning.

END-OF-AISLE Spaces fronting on main traffic aisles, particularly important location for 4½-second stopper displays to develop impulse sales.

END SIZES Extreme sizes of an assortment, smallest and largest (which store seldom carries in depth).

ENSEMBLES Only goods that will harmonize with other goods are bought.

ENTREPRENEUR Person who arranges and manages any enterprise, especially a new or untried business.

ENVIRONMENTAL SELLING Displaying merchandise under conditions and settings similar to those of a customer's own home.

E.O.M. (END-OF-MONTH) TERMS Indicates time allowance for discount is reckoned from end of month during which goods were bought, not from date of invoice.

EQUAL STORE OPERATION Company in which branch stores are operated on same (equal) basis as flagship or downtown store. (Buyer is not responsible for selling operation.)

EVEN EXCHANGE Exchange of article of merchandise for one of same price within same department.

EXCHANGE DESK Station on selling floor for servicing exchanges or refunds.

EXCLUSIVE MERCHANDISE Merchandise not available at other stores.

EXURBIA Areas beyond the suburbs but still accessible to major city facilities into which increasing numbers of corporations and their employees' families are moving.

F

FAD A short-lived fashion.

FEDERAL TRADE COMMISSION (FTC) Federal agency empowered to prevent unfair competition, fraudulent or misleading advertising or deception in advertising among interstate trading companies.

FINANCING CONSUMER PURCHASES Stores provide merchandise for their customers whether the customer pays cash, uses a 30-day charge account, a time payment plan, or revolving credit plan.

FIXTURING Layout and selection of fixtures to arrange merchandise for customer convenience; particularly important for self-selection.

FLAGSHIP DIVISION Downtown or central location where executive, merchandising, and promotional staffs are concentrated. Examples: Broadway Department stores, L.A., located next to central warehouse; May Co., L.A., located in flagship store.

FLASH REPORT Total of daily gross sales by departments prepared at close of each business day.

FLOATING DISPLAYS Moved from location to location within flagship store to branch store.

FLOOR AUDIT (REGISTER AUDIT) Accounting for sales transactions, in a department or section, by using local cash register.

FLOOR LIMIT Arbitrary amount established for floor approval of charge purchases without credit authorization when customer presents proper identification.

FLYING SQUAD Group of salespeople, regular or contingent, with exceptional selling ability and flexibility, who can be added to any regular departmental sales staff when needed; also used in sales-supporting and non-selling areas, such as tel-mail, complaints departments, during peak load periods.

F.O.B. (FREE ON BOARD) Shipping term signifying vendor or shipper retains title and pays all charges to F.O.B. point.

FORWARD STOCK Stock carried in the selling department.

4½-SECOND STOP AVERAGE Length of time customer inspects visual merchandising display in selling department, outpost display, or in window.

FULL LINE Stock of any given classification of goods which includes every variety of style, in every color, in every size, and in every material that a customer can reasonably expect to obtain at given price. A full line consists of four definite categories: 1) staples, 2) style merchandise, 3) novelties, 4) outsizes (for stock that have a size element).

G

GAMBLE ITEMS New products that the store wants to test for customers' acceptance or reactions.

GAZEBO A display fixture, frequently freestanding, upon which various types of fashion accessories are ensembled.

GENERAL MERCHANDISE STORES Includes department stores, dry goods stores, most mail-order houses, and variety stores.

GIFT CERTIFICATE Certificate, suitably engraved, denoting value for which it may be used in lieu of cash throughout the store.

GIFT ITEMS Merchandise particularly suitable for gift giving; unusual, attractive, appreciated by recipient.

GLOSSIES Prints of merchandise photographs supplied to store's advertising of display department for reproduction.

GRAPHICS Illustration, descriptive techniques including sketches, wash drawings, paintings, watercolors, engravings, photographs.

GROSS MARGIN Difference between net sales and cost of goods sold, the "room to move around in" that determines net operating profit after subtracting operating expense. Shrinkage avoided by careful handling of initial markon, markdowns, discounts.

GROUP MANAGER Supervisor in branch store responsible for appearance, the stocks, signing and salespeople selling merchandise that comes from several flagship or main-store departments; usually does no buying, unless re-ordering staples; keeps "parent" department informed concerning what is selling, what is needed, what is not selling.

GUARANTEE A promise or assurance, especially one in writing, that something is of specified quantity, quality, content, benefit, or that it will perform satisfactorily for a given length of time; a money-back guarantee.

H

HALF SIZE Sizing in coats, suits, and dresses for women who are not as tall as the average size.

HARD GOODS Major appliances, including refrigerators, deep freezers, electric and gas ranges, washing machines, dryers, hot water heaters, air conditioners.

HAUTE COUTURE French term for high fashion.

HIGH END Most expensive merchandise in a classification.

HOLD SLIP Form used to identify merchandise that customer desires to purchase later.

HOUSE CHARGE Charge transaction by an employee.

HOUSE ORGAN Publication for store's employees. Increasingly important with establishment of more branch stores in disseminating news from top management whom branch store employees seldom or ever see or hear from.

I

IMPORTS Merchandise manufactured or hand crafted in a foreign country and imported for sale in a U.S. store. Generally provides a higher than normal markon.

IMPULSE MERCHANDISE Articles of merchandise purchased on spur of moment by customer without predetermined consideration.

IN BOND Merchandise shipped by manufacturer several months ahead of store's normal selling season is "held in bond" in store's warehouse until selling season; not charged against department's OTB until removed from warehouse to stock or selling floor.

INFORMATIVE LABELLING Marking merchandise or its packages with specifications (including illustrations) of the merchandise and/or with those facts about usefulness and care that will aid customer in making an intelligent choice, and properly using goods.

IN-HOME SELLING Selling in the home either from "cold canvas" or by appointment made by store earlier. Particularly applicable for major appliances, furniture, floor coverings, curtains, draperies and decorator upholstery fabrics, sewing machines, vacuum cleaners, television sets, wallpaper, paint.

INITIAL MARKON Initial and/or first markon used when merchandise is originally offered for sale.

INITIAL UNITS Initial selection of items, a line, or classification of merchandise, as at beginning of a year or season (any reorders based on customers acceptance).

INSTALLMENT ACCOUNT Credit account in which customer contracts to pay specific amount by week or month.

IN TRANSIT Merchandise that has left consignor's premises and is en route to its destination.

INSTITUTIONAL ADVERTISEMENT Advertisement to improve image of store or tell customers of a store service, policy or objective. (In one sense, all advertising is institutional because it creates a favorable or unfavorable impression of the store.)

INTER-SELLING System by which salespeople can consummate sales in various departments and which provides method for crediting each department with sale of its merchandise.

INTERSTORE TRANSFER FORMS Merchandise is listed to be shipped from central warehouse or flagship store to branch store or from one branch store to another branch.

INTERNAL AUDIT Plan of verification and control for checking store systems for accuracy, validity, and conformity to plan.

INTIMATE APPAREL Women's, misses', juniors' corsets, brassieres, underwear, slips, negligees, robes, lounging apparel.

INTRA-STORE TRANSFER Buying goods from one selling department for another selling department within a store.

INVENTORY, PHYSICAL Determining by actual inspection the merchandise on hand in store, stockrooms, and warehouses; also recording of this information.

INVENTORY RECOVERY Concept based on a reserve created in expectancy of losses through theft and other causes.

INVENTORY SHRINKAGE Takes form of theft, internal or external fraud, record distortion, waste, sabotage, generally laxity, or careless operation.

INVOICE Itemized statement showing merchandise sent to store by a supplier.

ITEM A specific style, color, size, or price of merchandise.

ITEM HISTORY Record of the movement (sale) of a specific item, line, or assortment of merchandise.

ITEMS HARD TO COME BY Merchandise in short supply from vendors, generally due to lack of adequate production facilities or trained personnel.

ITEMS WENT BEGGING Merchandise in over-supply for which there is not longer customer acceptance.

J

JOB LOT Miscellaneous group of assortment of style, sizes, colors, etc., purchased by store as a "lot" at a reduced price.

K

KIMBALL TAGS Pre-punched tags attached to merchandise and containing size and style information, provided for high-speed processing and counting; used in inventory control reports recording, and restocking.

KNOCKOFF Close reproduction of design of a textile or apparel product. Differences in the copy may be shadings in color (not easily apparent to public), smaller size, less weight, often refers to "knock-offs," which sell for lower price than original.

L

LANDED COST Total cost and charges for merchandise on dock after conveyance from foreign port, also term for total cost to buy and bring to (land in) store.

LAYAWAY Method of deferred payments in which merchandise is held by store for customer until completely paid for.

LEASED DEPARTMENT Department operated by outside organization, generally on percentage-of-sales basis. A lessor must abide by rules, regulations, operations, and objectives of lessee.

LEDGER CARD Record of customer's charge-account activity and bill payments, kept in accounts receivable files.

LINAGE Measurement of number of lines to a column or full page of advertising in a newspaper or magazine advertisement.

LINE *1.* An agate line; a vertical measurement of a column of type; 14 lines to an inch. *2.* An assortment of designs presented by a designer or manufacturer.

LOADING/LOADING OF CASH DISCOUNTS Building up gross invoice price of merchandise and crediting cash discounts with the amount of the load. It may be done by the resource through an adjustment of the invoice or, more often, by the store through a bookkeeping entry.

LOAD-UP Making numerous purchases on charge account with no intent to pay.

LOBBY WINDOW Generally a small display window directly inside a door leading into store from street.

LONG PULL Planning future growth for a store, a department, a classification, or a service based on a study and analysis of potential factors.

LOOK A particular design, silhouette or style of clothing.

LOSS LEADER Merchandise advertised and sold at, near or even below cost by store to bring customers into store.

LOW END Least expensive merchandise in a classification.

LOW-MARGIN RETAILING Discount or mass merchandising.

M

MADE-TO-MEASURE Men's suits and overcoats, draperies, slipcovers, and floor coverings are cut and sewn to fit. Generally results in larger sales book.

MAIL-ORDER DEPARTMENT Department charged with proper distribution of requests, received through mails from customers, for specific merchandise; department must account for all cash remittances with requests and properly credit each department for such remittances.

MAINTAINED MARKON Difference between net sales and gross cost of sold goods.

MAKING WAVES The ability to project importance of an event to attract customers and influence them to make a buying decision.

MAN-MADE FIBERS Fibers produced by chemical or mechanical processes versus natural fibers from animals, insects, or plants.

MANAGEMENT BY OBJECTIVES Program of professional management techniques and merchandise as well as economic trend indicators to keep ahead of competition, strengthening management at store and corporate levels. These are geared to the goal of increasing sales per square foot—one of the key factors that measures earnings in retail business.

MANAGING AN INVENTORY Meeting monthly peaks and valleys, in any line of merchandise by increasing inventory prior to peak selling periods, reducing it as peak wanes.

MANIFEST Shipping form used by carriers for consolidation purposes, listing all pertinent information (consignor, consignee, commodity classification, number and weight of packages, and sometimes cost); used by carriers internally to list contents of a particular vehicle, listing same information; also used by stores in transfer operations from central warehouse to branches.

MANNEQUIN A clothes model; a styled and three-dimensional representation of the human form used in display windows and on ready-to-wear selling floors to display apparel.

MANUFACTURER'S REPRESENTATIVE Selling agent, preferably, retail-minded, capable of giving informative talks to selling personnel.

MARKDOWN Reduction in retail price of merchandise, primarily for clearance of broken assortments, end sizes, prior stock, for special sales events, and to meet competition.

MARKET Where retailers buy merchandise.

MARKETING Total research, development, planning, pricing, distribution, promotional activities involved in moving goods and services from producer to seller to consumer. Total marketing requires integration of all these activities.

MARKET PENETRATIONS A store's share of a metromarket in a specific department or classification of merchandise. Within reason there is no limit on how deep a penetration successfully operated departments can make.

MARKET REPRESENTATIVE Member of resident buying office staff whose major responsibilities are to act as market shopper, analyst, merchandise counselor to merchandise managers and buyers of office's member store; also expedites shipment of initial orders and reorders placed by member stores.

MARKING Putting the correct price tag on new merchandise.

MARKUP Difference between cost price as billed (before deductions for cash discount) and retail price at which merchandise is offered. Sometimes referred to as *markon*.

MARRIED TO FLAGSHIP STORE Where buyers devote all "on floor" time to downtown or parent store, operating departments in branch stores by remote control.

MASKING PIECE A flat curtain blocking part of a store window; concentrates shoppers' attention or hides work in progress.

MASS MERCHANDISING Self-service store displaying and selling all kinds of merchandise; displays tend to be massive; customers usually push wire carts to collect and carry their own selection of merchandise to cashier checkout counters.

MASS MEDIUM A channel for advertising that appeals to great numbers of diverse groups of people. Not beamed to a selected audience or class medium.

MEDIA 1. Evidence of transactions with customers

(saleschecks, vouchers, return slips, etc.). 2. In advertising; periodical (newspaper, magazine, shopper publications); direct (direct mail, catalogue, circular novelties, premiums); sign (outdoor or indoor poster, bulletin, sign, point-of-purchase, car card, transit sign); sky-writing; motion pictures; program (theatre, menus, guides); broadcast (radio, television, public address, loud speaker systems).

MEDIA MIX Planning use and coordination of advertising and promotional media, such as interior and exterior display, and newspaper, direct mail, radio, TV, magazine, transit, and outdoor advertising.

MEMORANDUM AND CONSIGNMENT SELLING Vendor agrees to take back goods if they are not sold in a specific period of time. Since the markdowns risk is borne by the vendor, the buyer's maintenance is equal to his initial markon. Under the memorandum arrangement, title passes to the buyer, ordinarily, when goods are shipped, but vendor assumes contracted obligation of taking back unsold portion of goods at a specific time. On consignment purchase, title does not pass to store but instead passes directly from vendor to store's customers—store acts simply as an agent for vendor. Vendor can control retail price.

MERCHANDISE CLASSIFICATION A group of merchandise reasonably interchangeable from the consumer's point of view.

MERCHANDISE CONTROL Department that maintains accurate figures on purchases and sales merchandise, either by dollar, by units, or both.

MERCHANDISE DISSECTION CONTROL Method of controlling sales and purchases of a dissection of merchandise, i.e., by style, by price, by color, by type.

MERCHANDISE MARTS Buildings housing show-rooms for manufacturers and importers where, under one roof, store buyers and merchandise managers can inspect lines from resources in minimum time.

MERCHANDISE SPECIFICATION Buyer sets up or obtains specifications for qualities expressed in necessary technical terms. Proper specifications cannot always be determined until needs and expectations of customers have been carefully analyzed and until some experimental work has been done. Development of private brands or controlled brands has increased need for rigid specifications prepared for or by the store's merchandise divisions.

METROMARKET Center city plus suburban areas from which a retail store draws major portion of customers.

MINIMUM STOCK CONTROL Method of reordering staple merchandise on basis of predetermined minimum quantity; when minimum is reached, quantity of initial order is again purchased.

MODEL STOCK "How much of what" to have, a stock which has the right goods at right time in right quantities at right price.

MOM AND POP OUTLETS Small stores generally operated by husband and wife, with limited capital, in a restricted selling area. Very dependent on wholesaler and/or distributor for financial support.

MULTI-MINI STORE CHAIN A series of centrally owned and operated smaller department or specialty stores, particularly those located in suburban areas or medium-sized communities where larger units cannot be operated profitably.

MULTIPLE SALES Customers to buy multiple rather than single items.

MULTIPLE STORE DATA Total company data is based upon results of both single and multiple-unit operations

N

NEIGHBORHOOD SHOPPING CENTER Ten to fifteen stores, including food, drug, sundry, and personal service stores; 5 to 10 acres; needs at least 1,000 families trading area for support; usually under 100,000 square feet. Sometimes referred to as *strip center.*

NEUSTADT FIGURES George Neustadt, Inc., measures newspaper advertising linage of wide variety of commodities promoted by leading department and specialty stores in the U.S., by week and month, by newspaper, by price line; compares and summarizes.

NON-SALABLE Merchandise soiled or damaged beyond reclamation or saleability, generally disposed of to charitable organizations.

NRMA (NATIONAL RETAIL MERCHANTS ASSOCIATION) The only national retail trade group specifically functioning in the interests of nation's department, chain, and specialty stores; a non-profit voluntary membership organization with administrative headquarters in its own N.Y.C. office building and branch offices in Washington, D.C., San Francisco, and Paris.

NUMBER OF STOCK TURNS Stock turnover is calculated by dividing average inventory at retail into the net sales for the year. Average inventory is the sum of the retail inventories at the end of each month added to the initial opening inventory and divided by thirteen, the number of inventories used.

O

ONE-SHOT PROMOTIONS Merchandise manufactured for specific event; imports that cannot be reordered.

ONE-STOP-SHOPPING Everything a customer would need for self, family, home; located under one roof.

ON ORDER Merchandise purchased but not yet received.

ON THE FLOOR Time spent by buyer on the selling floor, to get the "personal touch" with customers; supervise sales personnel; be involved in selling function; devise new floor visual selling ideas. Unfortunately too many buyers are "married to the flagship store"; devoting little, if any time, to branch store floor supervision.

OPEN ORDER Order placed without price or delivery stipulation; order sent to market representative in resident buying office without specifying vendor.

ORDER FORM Provided for buyers by larger and medium-sized stores and chain stores; provides all necessary protection for buyers; generally made out in triplicate.

OTB/OPEN-TO-BUY A buyer's budget for the purchase of merchandise for delivery within a given period; a resultant figure of dollar planning.

OUTPOST DISPLAYS Merchandise displayed with informative signs, at traffic points away from its regular selling department.

OVER OR SHORT Difference between established sales figure and actual audited figure, often caused by errors in change or missing saleschecks.

P

PARCEL POST Division of postal service that delivers packages and fourth-class literature. There are strict limitations on size, weight, and method of wrapping packages.

P.B.A./PERPETUAL BUDGET ACCOUNT Account established for installment remittances to which cost of additional purchases may be added to extent previous purchases are paid for; a system of revolving credit.

PEAK SEASON Months or season in which an item or line of merchandise is in greatest customer demand. For example, skis during major snow months.

PERPETUAL INVENTORY Retail method of accounting whereby daily sales discounts and markdowns are deducted from book inventory, which also includes purchases and merchandise returns "today" and "to date."

PERSONAL CARE ITEMS Hair dryers, electric shavers, saunas, electric hair curlers, hair setters, electric manicure and pedicure sets; merchandise to help improve customer's appearance.

PICA In print, a 12-point type of a size between small pica and English; one-sixth of an inch.

PICK-UPS Merchandise picked up from customer's home and returned to store by delivery department upon customer's request.

PIECE GOODS Fabrics for home sewing.

PLUS BUSINESS Selling merchandise or services over and above that normally expected.

P.O.N. (PLUS OVER NORMAL) Plus percentage increase department manager "guarantees" on a promotion; device to get an ad, coax a window, encourage ulcers.

P.O.P. Point-of-purchase display and signs.

POST AUDIT Auditing daily net sales the following day; some smaller stores audit simultaneously with present day's sales. A logical impossibility.

PRE-AUTHORIZING Obtaining credit authorization for charge-send transactions prior to packages or merchandise leaving department.

PRE-PACKAGING Merchandise packaged by vendor for display, for "take-with" by customer or delivery by store. (Vendor can pre-package more economically via assembly line method than store.)

PREFERRED RESOURCE Manufacturer, whole-saler, or importer from which important portion of a line or classification of merchandise is bought and to whom store gives preferred treatment.

PRE-MARKETING/PRE-TICKETING Marking of merchandise by manufacturer.

PREPAY Payment of all shipping charges for merchandise by vendor, who rebills charges to purchaser on invoice for the merchandise.

PREPRINT Copy of an advertisement distributed to a store's customers and/or resources prior to publication in a general medium.

PRE-RETAILING System in which all merchandise is purchased to or carried at a pre-determined price, which is on record in the receiving and marking room. (Ready-to-wear is generally an exception due to a desire to re-appraise value upon receipt in store.)

PRE-SOLD MERCHANDISE Vendor's national advertising in magazines, newspapers, and via TV and radio create customer acceptance and in-store demand.

PRESS KIT Organized folder which usually contains press release(s), photographs, fact sheet(s) for distribution to the press for publicity purposes.

PRESS RELEASE In publicity, typewritten story ready for an editor, complete in details, facts, and in a format which makes acceptance by the editor easy to get into print.

PRE-TICKETED Merchandise priced by vendor either on package or on price tickets or tags (often supplied by store to vendor with season letter, price, other necessary information) prior to packing for shipment to store. This saves store time, effort, and money in getting merchandise through receiving and marking room and onto selling floor.

PRE-WRAP Wrapping of merchandise before putting on sale (finding extensive use for types of merchandise of standard quality); also, merchandise wrapped or packaged by manufacturer for store "send" or customer "take-with."

PRICE BRACKETS Definite price zones or price levels.

PRICE CUTTING *1.* Cutting prices below a minimum resale price fixed (or suggested) by the vendor. *2.* Selling below cost or below cost plus expenses of doing business; many discounters have developed a customer following by price cutting, particularly on nationally known brands.

PRICE LEVEL See *price brackets.*

PRICE ZONE Price(s) at which greatest sales volume can be produced.

PRIMARY MARKET LEVEL The basic group in the production cycle and marketing process, manufacturers of fabrics and producers of raw materials.

PRIVATE BRAND Controlled or private-label merchandise developed under store's own brand or developed under RBO's label exclusively for member stores.

PRODUCT DUPLICATION Similar or actual duplication of exact products from two or more resources, frequently increases store's inventory unnecessarily and confuses customer's selection.

PROMOTIONAL KIT Ideas, suggestions, materials supplied to store by vendor, whether manufacturer, importer, or wholesaler.

PROPORTIONALLY EQUAL TERMS Vendor's dealings with all customers on uniform basis regardless of size.

R

RAIDING A COMPANY When one organization purchases another company against the wishes of the management and stockholders of the raided company.

REACTIVATING OF INACTIVE CHARGE CUSTOMERS A promotional program developed to induce former charge customers to make use of their charge accounts.

READY-TO-WEAR Clothing made in standard sizes by manufacturers; mass produced apparel for mass acceptance.

RECEIVING Process of accepting new merchandise at store or warehouse; includes initiating paper work to get merchandise "on the books" and processing incoming transportation bills.

RECEIVING APRON Form attached to store's purchase order contains information concerning status of vendor's shipment; forwarded by receiving department to invoice office, which audits all invoices before bills are paid.

REGIONAL CENTER FOR CHAIN Where a retail organization establishes several stores in a metromarket in order to justify local warehousing, merchandising and advertising expenses.

REGIONAL SHOPPING CENTER 50 to 100 stores, including at least one major department store branch; 35 or more acres; requiring trading area of 100,000 people to support it, usually over 200,000 square feet in store area.

REGIONAL STORE Branch store generally situated at considerable distance from central downtown or flagship store, operating under name of parent store (its merchandise is frequently purchased by regional store's own merchandising staff), frequently operated on autonomous basis.

REGULAR ACCOUNT Conventional charge account, billed each month and to be paid during ensuing 30 days.

REPLACEMENT BRANCH Initially many branch stores were small, mere twigs with space only for a few departments, primarily women's and children's apparel and accessories; frequently located on the main street of a small town or village with inadequate parking facilities or a solo location along a highway. As suburban population increased, the branch store's sales skyrocketed, necessitating building a new, larger branch, generally located in a regional shopping center, and closing of the original branch.

REPLENISHMENT ORDERS To fill-in (complete) assortments in a specific classification; usually referred to as a reorder.

REPRINT Copy of an advertisement distributed to a store's customers and/or resources following publication in a general media.

REPS Individuals or wholesale companies representing a manufacturer or other vendors in specified sales territory, who solicit and accept orders that are shipped from vendor's factory or distributing point, but who do not actually own or stock merchandise.

RESERVE STOCK CONTROL Method of earmarking sufficient amount of stock to maintain business while additional stock is purchased.

RESOURCE A manufacturer, importer, wholesaler, distributor, selling agent, rack jobber from whom a store buys or accepts merchandise as owner or on selling consignment.

RETAIL FRANCHISE Exclusive ownership by store in a trading area of prestige manufacturer's line; frequently a line selectively distributed.

RETAIL HUB A concentration of stores in an area. Example: flagship stores of Macy's, Gimbels, Woolworth's, Ohrbach's, in Herald Square area, New York City.

RETAIL METHOD ACCOUNTING Accounting method in which all percentages are relative to retail price instead of cost price. In cost method of accounting all percentages are relative to the cost. Example: retail method— article purchased for $1 sells for $2, margin is $1 but only 50% of retail price. Cost method—article purchased for $1 sells for $2, margin is $1 but is 100% of cost price.

RETAILING Basically, the business of buying for resale to the ultimate customer; also known as "acting as the customer's agent."

RETURN POLICY Rules and regulations formulated by store's management covering merchandise returns by customers including exchange, credit, cash refunds, adjustments.

RETURNS TO VENDOR Shipments of merchandise returned by store to vendor because of errors in filling store's purchase order, substitutions in shipment, late delivery, defective materials or workmanship or fit, or other breaches of contract.

R.O.G. (RECEIPT OF GOODS) TERMS Cash discount terms that begin when merchandise reaches store (designed to benefit retailers far from resource: also permits check of goods prior to due date for discount).

ROUTING Section of delivery department through which all packages must pass to have their route number indicated. Traffic department specifies routing and type of transportation for incoming shipments from vendor.

ROUTING INSTRUCTIONS Provided by store, to be attached by buyer to purchase order, informing vendor of routing and shipping instructions, specifying type of transportation for incoming shipments from vendor.

RUB OFF Secondary benefit attained by a department from a promotion in another department. Example: opportunities for sales of oversize bed sheets, blankets, comforters, bedspreads because of sale of king or queen size mattresses and box springs.

RUNNER Item that sells and sells and sells.

S

SALES ANALYSIS Sales audit which provides totals of sales by salespeople, departments, classifications, etc.

SALES AUDIT Work of checking media from selling floor for purpose of control, reporting, accounting.

SALESCHECK Form in triplicate listing customer's purchases, including price.

SALES PLAN Department's promotional program for 6-month period, subject to monthly revision to take advantage of opportunistic purchases and other unpredictable merchandising opportunities.

SALES SLIP Slip of paper from a roll on cash register showing only dollar and cents amount of purchase.

SALES SYSTEM Method by which transaction with customer is recorded.

SALVAGE DEPARTMENT Damaged merchandise which is sold to store employees at a fraction of its original price.

SAMPLE ROOM Areas in store or in RBO where vendor sales representatives display merchandise samples to buyers or market representatives.

SEASONAL EMPLOYEES Personnel employed during peak selling periods such as pre-Christmas, Easter, and for storewide sales events.

SEASONAL MERCHANDISE Merchandise purchased to meet demands of specific seasons (extreme instances: purchases for summer and winter clothing, outdoor furniture).

SEASON LETTER Code assigned to merchandise received during 6-month spring or fall season that indicates age of stock.

SECOND SHIFTS Employees reporting for late afternoon or night shifts, replacing daytime sales and sales-supporting staffs.

SEGMENTED MERCHANDISING Merchandising for and appealing to specific age groups or other groups with common interests.

SELLING AREA Part of sales floor devoted exclusively to selling. (Shoe and ready-to-wear stockrooms, fitting rooms and wrapping stations are considered part of selling area when sales could not be consummated without them.)

SELLING DAYS Number of days per month or week that store is open; often refers to period between Thanksgiving Day and Christmas Day.

"SEND" TRANSACTIONS Customer purchases to be delivered by store versus "take-withs" where customer personally carries merchandise from store. "Sends" are greater from flagship stores than from branch stores.

SEPARATE IDENTITIES Where a company owns and operates two or more types of stores, such as Gimbels, New York, a general department store; and Saks Fifth Avenue, a chain of specialty stores.

SERVICE AREA Part of sales floor devoted to servicing the selling area, such as escalators, elevators, stairways, freight landings, rest rooms, show windows.

SERVICE BUILDING Building remote from downtown store used for delivery purposes, repair facilities, workrooms for larger merchandise, warehousing.

SERVICE CENTER An area, frequently near small electrics department, however, may be located in warehouse where repairs or alterations are made.

SERVICE SHOPPER Special salesperson designated to accompany customers who plan purchases in a number of departments.

SERVICE SUPERINTENDENT Senior management executive in complete charge of all customer services.

SHOPLIFTING Stealing of store's merchandise by customers. Of growing concern to all types of retailers.

SHOPPING CENTER Usually defined in size as 20 to 40 stores, including one department store; on 20 to 25 acres; needing 5,000-family trading area; 100,000 to 200,000 square feet in store area.

SHORT MERCHANDISE Merchandise purchased in limited quantities; generally in extreme sizes, to fill an assortment; also, items of purchase that through error were not included in customer's package or were missing in shipment from vendor.

SHORT SKU System which permits full identification of an *item*, making possible the use of source-marked tickets either for backroom processing or cash register input, so that ultimately a store will be able to count sales, not stocks.

SHORT SUPPLY SITUATION Merchandise where buyer has difficulty in maintaining adequate supply.

SHOW (FASHION SHOW) Formal display of merchandise with a theme, program, music, commentator, script, etc., on living and moving models.

SHOWING (OF FASHIONS) Informal display on living and moving models. No particular theme, script, commentator or program; no planned continuity. Usually held in showrooms of manufacturers or in a store's fashion department to show merchandise in use.

SHOWROOMS Spaces maintained in various cities by vendors-manufacturers, importers, wholesalers, and distributors where merchandise is displayed for store buyers and merchandise managers to select styles and place orders.

SHRINKAGE Difference (on minus side) between merchandise on hand shown by physical inventory and that shown as "book value."

SIGNING Writing signs for use at retail point-of-sale (manufacturers make character by obliging with factual information and consumer benefits that make signing easy).

SILHOUETTE The outline, shape or form of fashion.

SISTER STORES Member stores of a resident buying office (The Dayton Company; the J.L. Hudson Company). Stores owned by a corporation (Jordan Marsh, Boston; Jordan Marsh, Florida).

60-SECOND SELLING Sales presentation delivered in one minute to stop customer and develop interest. 80% of items in department store lend themselves to quick initial presentation.

SIZE LINING Method of organizing or grouping merchandise for selling by size. Example: dress department set up with dresses of all colors, types, prices, and identified as "size 10 to 20, "size 38 to 44."

SMALL STORE MEN Familiar with operation, problems, and objectives of smaller retail stores; accustomed to performing all responsibilities and duties assigned to various executives in larger organizations.

SMALL WARES General articles of merchandise usually found on main floor of department stores.

SOFT GOODS Ready-to-wear for women, children, men; fashion accessories, piece goods, domestics.

SOFTWARE General purpose programs, normally furnished by EDP equipment manufacturers, for use in extending the capabilities and functions of the basic computer.

SORTER Personnel in audit department who sorts saleschecks, collates by type of sale, inspects for missing saleschecks; also applied to collector of customers' names in cycle billing; also, sorter of packages for delivery routes.

SOURCE MARKING Pre-ticketing by resource before shipment. Very important in expediting arrival of merchandise on selling floor because not held up in receiving for price ticketing by store and also, less expensive because merchandise does not have to be opened in receiving, ticketed, then repackaged.

SPECIAL ORDERS Readiness to procure for the customer anything not stocked.

SPECIALTY STORES Stores concentrating on specific classifications of merchandise. Examples: jewelry, furniture, books, men's clothing and furnishings, women's apparel and accessories, shoes, intimate apparel, sporting goods.

SPLIT TICKET Price ticket perforated so portion can be removed for unit control purposes.

SPOT CHECK Inspection and count of small, random amount of goods in large shipments.

SPOTLIGHT Light that concentrates rays on a specific area or object.

SPOT SHIPMENTS Freight-car shipment with instructions to spot car at certain siding or at warehouse.

STAPLE STOCK There is always the problem of overlap, in defining basic stock vs. staple stock. Essentially, the difference between basic and staple is assortments vs. single items. Staple stock is made up of items that are practically continuous demand. Basic stock is an assortment of items that are in current demand. Basic stock includes staple stock items.

STATE STUFFER National advertising with "where to buy it" identifications, created for retail use, sized and weighted to fit customer bill envelopes and coincide with postage budget (not to be confused with direct mail).

STOCK BOOK Record of purchases from orders and of sales from stubs of price tickets, usually maintained by buyer.

STOCK CONTROL Broad term for various systems and methods of control stock, i.e., keep it in line with customer demand, one step ahead when demand goes up; slowed up when demand falters.

STOCKKEEPING UNIT (SKU) Item of merchandise which is in stock.

STORE NETWORK Where flagship store with branches develops as a regional retail system beyond immediate metromarket.

STORE'S OWN BRAND (S.O.B.) Store's private brand, presumably offers same quality and quantity for less money (than national brands) or greater quantity and equal quality for same money.

"STORE'S STORE" A retail operation that executives in other stores throughout the United States and Canada visit and watch because of superior operations that can be adapted by their store.

STUB *1.* In merchandise control, second part of price ticket, removed by salesperson at time of sale for unit merchandise-control. *2.* Extra copy of address label of salescheck which accompanies package to delivery depot, where it is removed and filed for use in adjustment of non-delivery complaints. Also referred to as *stubbing.*

STYLE Certain characteristics that distinguish a garment from other garments; a subdivision with a fashion.

STYLE PIRACY Close copy, and sale at a lower price, of a manufacturer's original design by another manufacturer. It can be disastrous for a store when a competitor offers copy at a lower price.

SUBTEENS (GIRLS) DEPARTMENT Separate RTW and accessories department appealing to girls from approximately 9–13 years old.

SUPPLIERS Manufacturers, importers, wholesalers, other resources from whom stores buy merchandise for resale.

SWITCHING CUSTOMERS When a salesperson cannot close a sale, he calls the buyer or department manager or even another salesperson whom he introduces as a departmental supervisor, to take over the sale, more prevalent in men's clothing, furniture, or major appliance departments.

T

TABLOID Newspaper about half the size of a standard size paper, e.g. New York *Daily News, Women's Wear Daily (WWD).*

"TAKE-WITHS" Merchandise carried from store by customer, expediting delivery and saving delivery expense, particulary significant in branch stores.

TALLY (CARD OR ENVELOPE) Form on which each salesperson records amount of each transaction; form is sometimes ruled for cash, C.O.D., and charge columns, has column for classification number.

TAPE, PUNCHED Used in sophisticated cash registers to capture price and classification data at point-of-sale; information is automatically recorded in coded punched paper tape which, in turn, can be processed in computer center.

TARGET AUDIENCE Special group within an audience to which advertising is specifically aimed. Example would be an advertisement in a college publication, addressed to skiers among the student readers.

TARGET MARKET The defined segment of a whole market to which an advertiser directs merchandising, merchandise, and promotion. Can be identified by demographics.

TEST PROMOTIONS Conducted by store for vendor, presenting new products, improved products, or selling idea to ascertain reaction of store's customers.

13th MONTH Five selling days between Christmas and New Year's.

TO PULL In advertising, e.g., "the ad pulled (produced sales) yesterday" or "that type of format doesn't pull."

TOTAL AUTOMATIC BILLING Exclusive use of machine in preparation and mailing store's customer bills.

TOTAL LOOK/TOTAL CONCEPT Instead of large departments of all types of coats, suits, and dresses development of selling areas—commonly called boutiques—appealing to groups of customers, grouped by age, taste, income. Customer no longer has to wander all over store to find things to go-with-the-concept, she can find everything in one place.

TOTAL STORE An individual location only.

TRADING AREA Surrounding areas from which most of store's trade is drawn, varies by individual store location. Each store, main or branch, needs to know to what extent and from what directions it draws customers; checking automobile license plates in shopping-center parking lots, questioning customers who visit store, analyzing charge accounts, etc., will develop this information.

TRAFFIC Number of persons, both prospective and actual customers, who enter store or department.

TRANSACTIONS PER SQUARE FOOT Number of

transactions per square foot of selling space area obtained by dividing the number of gross transactions of saleschecks of a department by the average number of square feet the department occupies for selling space.

TRANSIT TIME Computed from time merchandise leaves vendor, factory, or warehouse until it arrives at store's receiving docks.

TREND The direction in which fashion is moving.

TSD (TELEPHONE SELLING DEPARTMENT) A separate selling department, generally with separate telephone number, to care for sales telephoned to store. A well-organized TSD program can, in effect, provide store with a brand new department that will outsell any existing department in store with no increase in inventory and very little capital investment.

TURNOVER Total number of times, within given period, that stock of goods is sold and replaced.

TWIG Small branch store located in community or neighborhood shopping center, generally carrying only women's and children's ready-to-wear and accessories.

U

UNEVEN EXCHANGE Merchandise returned by customer for exchange for another article at price different from that of original purchase. Exchange can be in favor of customer (she receives new article plus refund) or of store (customer pays additional amount for new article purchased).

UNISEX MERCHANDISE Ready-to-wear and accessories designed for both men and women; frequently sold in the same department.

UNIT BILLING Customer received single statement, list of articles purchased is posted on detachable strip which store retains for adjustment purposes.

UNIT CONTROL System of recording vital statistics of stock on hand, on order, and sold for a given period; "control" is interpretation of statistics as barometer showing change in customer buying habits; works best when barometer readings are taken frequently and seriously.

UNIT OPERATOR Personnel in accounts receivable who sort and file sales and credit media in customer's file and are also available for authorizing. Each individual is generally confined to a unit or breakdown of alphabet in cycle billing.

V

VALUE-ADDED TAX A pyramiding form of assessment. At each level of manufacturing and distribution,

from the raw material until the finished product is offered to the consumer, a tax on the increased value of the product is added.

VENDOR Manufacturer, wholesaler (jobber), importer, or commission merchant from whom merchandise is purchased.

VENDOR CHARGEBACKS Where merchandise is returned to vendor, store submits bill to vendor, frequently accompanied by proof of delivery to vendor.

VIGNETTE 1. Process of deleting background in a photograph used in advertisement. 2. In display, small suggestion of a room setting using complete furnishings but not setting up a room.

VISUAL MERCHANDISING Presentation of merchandise to best selling advantage and for maximum traffic exposure, plus projection of customer "ready-to-buy." Not a display technique but merchandising strategy.

VISUAL SYSTEM STOCK CONTROL Method of arranging stock on shelves in piles of equal quantity for quick visual count.

VOLUNTARY SELF-REGULATION Where an association of manufacturers or other vendors voluntarily develop and police standards of quality and safety prior to regulations voted by national, state, or local city governmental legislations.

W

WALK-OUTS Customers who enter store with acquisitive gleam in eye, walk out dull-eyed and emptyhanded. Example: absence of merchandise information at point-of-sale, lack of informative labeling, items out of stock due to non-existing basic stock plans.

WANT-SLIPS A system where salesperson reorders customers request for merchandise not in stock and tells whether or not a substitute article is sold. The items added to stock on a basis of want-slips may make the difference between profit and loss and play an important part in establishing a reputation for leadership and service. Sometimes store makes the form available to customers to fill out and deposit in a box.

WARRANTY The act or an instance of warranting; assurance; guarantee authorization; an express warranty of the quality of goods made by the manufacturer.

WAYBILL Shipping form similar to manifest or bill of lading, stipulates names of vendor and consignee, shipping instructions, costs, etc.

WHITE GOODS Refrigerators, deep freezers, automatic dryers, washing machines, stoves, dishwashers; all comparatively big ticket items.

WHOLESALER SPONSORED Voluntary retail chains sponsored by wholesalers.

WILL CALL Another term applied to lay-away; also applies to purchases which have been paid for in full but which customer will return and pick up.

WINDOW DISPLAY At retail stores, areas facing the outside of stores used for selling by showing merchandise or ideas to attract pedestrian traffic. Generally glass enclosed. (Glass enclosed displays inside store are not called "window display.") Often called the "face" of the store. Prestige windows are institutional; selling windows are used for immediate sales results.

Y

YOUTH MARKET Women, men under 25 years of age, including babies, children, subteens, teens, young men and women primarily interested in the new, different, unusual.

BIBLIOGRAPHY

Barker, Clare W., Ira B. Anderson and S. Donald Butterworth. **Principles of Retailing.** New York: McGraw-Hill, 1974.

Beaton, Cecil W.H. **The Glass of Fashion.** Garden City, N.Y.: Doubleday & Company, Inc., 1954.

Berman, Barry and Joel R. Evans. **Retail Management—A Strategic Approach,** 2nd edition. New York: Macmillan, Inc., 1983.

Bolen, William H. **Contemporary Retailing.** Englewood Cliffs, N.J.: Prentice-Hall, Inc., 1982.

Boucher, Francois. **20,000 Years of Fashion.** New York: Harry N. Abrams, Inc., 1967.

Burton, Philip Ward. **Retail Advertising for the Small Store.** Englewood Cliffs, N.J.: Prentice-Hall, Inc., 1959.

Buyer's Manual, The, revised ed. New York: National Retail Merchants Association, Merchandising Division, 1979.

Department Merchandising and Operating Results of Department and Specialty Stores. New York: National Retail Merchants Association, published annually.

Dunn, Watson S. and Arnold M. Barban. **Advertising: Its Role in Modern Marketing.** Hinsdale, Illinois: The Dryden Press, 1974.

Edwards, Charles M. and Russell A. Brown. **Retail Advertising and Sales Promotion.** Englewood Cliffs, N.J.: Prentice-Hall, Inc., 1964.

Ferry, J.W. **History of the Department Store.** New York: Macmillan, Inc., 1960.

Gist, Ronald R. **Basic Retailing—Text and Cases.** New York: John Wiley & Sons, Inc., 1971.

Gold, Annalee. **How to Sell Fashion,** 2nd edition. New York: Fairchild Publications, 1978.

_____. **75 Years of Fashion.** New York: Fairchild Publications, 1975.

Gore, Bud. **How to Sell the Whole Store as Fashion.** New York: National Retail Merchants Association, 1970.

Guide for Retail Advertising and Selling, A. New York: Association of Better Business Bureau, Inc., 1963.

Hamburger, Estelle. **Fashion Business: It's All Yours.** Canfield Press, 1976.

Hill, Margot H. and Peter Bucknell. **The Evolution of Fashion.** New York: Holt, Rinehart & Winston, Inc., 1968.

How to Write Better Retail Advertising Copy. New York: National Retail Merchants Association, Sales Promotion Division, 1962.

Jabenis, Elaine. **The Fashion Director—What She Does, How to be One.** New York: John Wiley & Sons, Inc., 1972.

Judelle, Beatrice. **The Fashion Buyer's Job.** New York: National Retail Merchants Association, 1971.

Kleppner, Otto. **Advertising Procedure.** Englewood Cliffs, N.J.: Prentice-Hall, Inc., 1979.

Kneider, Albert P. **Mathematics of Merchandising.** Englewood Cliffs, N.J.: Prentice-Hall, Inc., 1974.

Larson, Carl and others. **Basic Retailing.** Englewood Cliffs, N.J.: Prentice-Hall, Inc., 1976.

Markin, Ron J. **Retailing Management—A Systems Approach.** New York: Macmillan, Inc., 1971.

Mazur, Paul M. **Principles of Organizations Applied to Modern Retailing.** New York: Harper & Bros., 1927.

McClelland, W. G. **Studies in Retailing.** Oxford: Basil Blackwell, 1963

McNair, Malcolm P. and Eleanor G. May. **The American Department Store, 1920–1960.** Boston: Harvard University Graduate School of Business Administration, Division of Research, 1963.

Milton, Shirley F. **Advertising for Modern Retailers.** New York: Fairchild Publications, 1974.

Packard, Sydney. **The Fashion Business—Dynamics and Careers.** New York: Holt, Rinehart and Winston, Inc., 1983.

_____. **Strategies and Tactics in Fashion Marketing—Selected Readings.** New York: Fairchild Publications, 1982.

Packard, Sidney and Miriam Guerreiro. **The Buying Game: Fashion Buying and Merchandising.** New York: Fairchild Publications, 1979.

Packard, Sidney and Nathan Axelrod. **Concepts and Cases in Fashion Buying and Merchandising.** New York: Fairchild Publications, 1977.

Packard, Sidney and Abraham Raine. **Consumer Behavior and Fashion Marketing.** Dubuque, Iowa: Wm C. Brown, 1979.

Packard, Sidney and Alan J. Carron. **Start Your Own Store.** Englewood Cliffs, N.J.: Prentice-Hall, Inc., 1982.

Phelon, J.S., et. al. **Phelon's Resident Buying Book.** New York: The Company, 1982.

Pintel, Gerald and Jay Diamond. **Retailing.** Englewood Cliffs, N.J.: Prentice-Hall, Inc., 1971.

Rachman, David J. **Retail Strategy and Structure.** Englewood Cliffs, N.J.: Prentice-Hall, Inc., 1969.

Rosenbloom, Bert. **Retail Marketing.** New York: Random

House, 1981.

Samson, Harland E. **Advertising and Displaying Merchandise.** Cincinnati, Ohio: South-Western Publishing Co., 1967.

Shipp, Ralph D. **Retail Merchandising—Principles and Applications.** Boston, Mass: Houghton Mifflin Co., 1976.

Stanton, William J. **Fundamentals of Marketing.** New York: McGraw-Hill, 1971.

Sturdivant, Frederick D. **The Ghetto Marketplace.** New York: The Free Press, 1969.

Taylor, Charles G. **Merchandising Assortment Planning.** New York: National Retail Merchants Association, 1970.

Tepper, Bette K. and Newton E. Godnick. **Mathematics for Retail Buying,** 2nd edition. New York: Fairchild Publications, 1979.

Tolman, Ruth. **Selling Men's Fashion.** New York: Fairchild Publications, 1982.

Winters, Arthur A. and Stanley Goodman. **Fashion Advertising and Promotion.** New York: Fairchild Publications, 1978.

Winters, Arthur A. and Shirley F. Milton. **The Creative Connection: Advertising Copywriting & Idea Visualization.** New York: Fairchild Publications, 1982.

SELECTED TRADE ASSOCIATIONS

Amalgamated Clothing Workers of America (ACWA)
15 Union Square, New York, N.Y. 10013

American Footwear Industries Association
1611 N. Kent Street, Arlington, Va. 22209

American Textile Manufacturers' Institute, Inc. (ATMI)
1501 Johnston Building, Charlotte, N.C. 28202

American Printed Fabrics Council, Inc.
1040 Avenue of the Americas, New York, N.Y. 10018

Association of Buying Offices (ABO)
100 West 31st Street, New York, N.Y. 10001

Belgian Linen Association
280 Madison Avenue, New York, N.Y. 10016

California Fashion Creators (CFC)
110 East Ninth Street, Los Angeles, Ca. 90015

Costume Society of America
c/o Costume Institute, Metropolitan Museum of
Art Fifth Avenue & 82nd Street, New York, N.Y.
10028

Cotton, Incorporated
1370 Avenue of the Americas, New York, N.Y. 10019

Council of Fashion Designers of America
32 East 57th Street, New York, N.Y. 10022

Emba Mink Breeders Association
151 West 30th Street, New York, N.Y. 10001

The Fashion Group, Inc.
9 Rockefeller Plaza, New York, N.Y. 10020

Fur Information and Fashion Council
101 West 30th Street, New York, N.Y. 10001

International Council of Shopping Centers, Inc.
665 Fifth Avenue, New York, N.Y. 10022

International Ladies Garment Workers Union (ILGWU)
1710 Broadway, New York, N.Y. 10019

International Silk Association (ISA), USA
299 Madison Avenue, New York, N.Y. 10017

Man-made Fiber Producers' Association, Inc. (MMFPAI)
1000 Connecticut Avenue, Washington, D.C. 20036

Men's Fashion Association of America (MFA)
1290 Avenue of the Americas, New York, N.Y. 10019

Men's Retailers Association
2011 Eye Street, N.W., Washington, D.C. 20006

Millinery Institute of America
10 East 49th Street, New York, N.Y. 10016

National Association of Glove Manufacturers
Gloversville, N.Y. 12078

National Association of Manufacturers (NAM)
1719 State Highway 10, Parsippany, N.J. 07054

National Association of Women's & Children's
Apparel Salesmen Inc. (NAWCAS)
401 Seventh Avenue, Statler Hotel,
New York, N.Y. 10001

National Cotton Council of America
1918 N. Parkway, Box 12285, Memphis, Tenn. 38112

National Knitted Outerwear Association
51 Madison Avenue, New York, N.Y. 10010

National Retail Merchants' Association (NRMA)
100 West 31st Street, New York, N.Y. 10001

New York Couture Business Council, Inc.
141 West 41st Street, New York, N.Y. 10036

United Garment Workers of America (UGW)
31 Union Square, New York, N.Y. 10003

The Wool Bureau, Inc.
360 Lexington Avenue, New York, N.Y. 10017

INDEX